YALE STUDIES IN RELIGIOUS EDUCATION

XV.
MILLHANDS AND PREACHERS

MILLHANDS
&
PREACHERS

A STUDY OF GASTONIA

BY

LISTON POPE

Dean of the Divinity School and
Gilbert L. Stark Professor of Social Ethics
Yale University

85462

HD6338
.P82

New Haven : Yale University Press

First published, April 1942
Second printing, July 1946
Third printing, April 1953
Fourth printing, April 1958

TO

MY WIFE BENNIE

WHO EXEMPLIFIES THE BEST FEATURES OF
BOTH THE OLD SOUTH AND THE NEW, AND

MY DAUGHTER MARY ANNA

WHO MISSED MANY BEDTIME STORIES FOR
THE SAKE OF THE STORY TOLD HEREIN

PREFACE

NEARLY everybody has notions about the proper role of the church in economic affairs. Businessmen and labor leaders, laymen and ministers disagree emphatically, and frequently accuse each other of apostasy. On the one hand, the church is admonished to confine its attention to the spiritual needs of its parishioners lest its inclusive fellowship be broken or its gospel compromised. On the other, ministers are summoned to fearless proclamation of the Kingdom of God in social terms, with less retreat into surplices and cloisters and more attention to practices of factory and market place. The church is blamed for its indifference and praised for minding its own business, commended as an agent of social salvation and denounced as a haven for meddlers, acclaimed as a guarantor of social stability and cursed as an insidious peddler of dope.

Despite the controversy, which is of long standing, very little study of the actual role of the church in economic society has been undertaken. Social philosophers have advanced various hypotheses, among which the theories of Marx and Max Weber are best known. Historians have treated the question occasionally, and have been especially interested in the rough coincidence of the rise of Protestantism and capitalism. Social scientists have described painstakingly the functions of religion in preliterate economies, but have devoted a surprisingly small amount of attention to contemporary modes of the problem. No coherent, refined body of knowledge about the function of the church in Western economic systems is available and argument proceeds without benefit of adequate data.

The multiplicity of popular notions and sociological theories can be reduced to six types of possible relation between religious and economic institutions. Religious institutions, in relation to economic institutions, might be:

in dynamic terms,
    a source of economic changes
    a product of prior economic changes
in static terms,
    a sanction on the prevailing economic organization and
       economic culture

an antagonist to the prevailing economic organization and
economic culture

in purposive-functional terms,

indifferent to the economic sphere as such

irrelevant to economic results, in the sense that no effective
contact is established with economic realities.

Gaston County, North Carolina, affords an advantageous social context in which to test at first hand the relative importance of these diverse modes of relationship. Within the memory of its oldest inhabitants, an agricultural economy has been
superseded by phenomenal industrial development. As in England and New England decades earlier, the textile industry has
been a harbinger of industrial revolution, and many of the economic and social patterns attending its previous cycles have
been recapitulated at accelerated speed. Two decades after the
Civil War, cotton mills began to appear in unprecedented number throughout the Southern Piedmont area from Danville to
Birmingham, and Gaston County, lying nearly at the geographical center of the area, became a center and symbol of industrial transformation. A survey in 1927 revealed that Gastonia, the principal town in the county, had come to have more
looms and spindles within a radius of 100 miles than any other
Southern city, with a total of 570 textile plants and nearly 10
million spindles in this range of proximity. Though it had been
devoted almost exclusively to agricultural pursuits in 1880, the
county was able in 1939 to claim a larger number of textile
plants than any other county in the world, and was manufacturing 80 per cent of the fine combed cotton yarn produced in
the United States. Only seventeen by twenty miles in extent, its
landscape teems now with cotton mills and industrial villages.
Here, then, is a compact, manageable situation in which economic institutions have undergone drastic change recently
enough to allow direct observation of the part played by religious institutions in the process.

As compared with other counties in which comparable transformations have occurred, Gaston County offers several distinct
advantages to the student of social patterns. It is not necessarily "typical" or "average"—whatever those terms may mean
—of other counties in the vicinity or the nation. Things have
happened in Gaston County, such as a violent Communist chal-

lenge to its economic organization, which are fairly unique, but
by the same token are highly illuminating for other regions
where deep-laid social textures have not been similarly laid
open for examination. In respect to economic institutions the
county is more developed and less diversified than many others.
Its religious institutions, on the other hand, are more highly
diversified; Presbyterian and Lutheran settlers have been outnumbered by Methodist and Baptist newcomers and there is a
generous representation of other Protestants and of Roman
Catholics. In the simplicity of its economic forms and the diversity of its religious forms, the county provides a significant
and governable context in which to observe interrelations of the
two spheres.

The interaction of churches and cotton mills in Gaston
County since 1880 has proceeded in three modes of institutional
life. First of all, there have been reciprocal relations in growth,
i.e., expansion, quantitative increase in salient respects, qualitative differentiation and proliferation within each type of institution as compared with the other. Secondly, restraining and
regulatory procedures have been worked out between the two
types of institution, illustrative of the perennial problem of social integration and control. Last of all, the mills and churches
have gone through a severe crisis together, and in so doing revealed fundamental relationships to each other which are normally obscured. A fourth conceivable mode, institutional deterioration, is not yet clearly observable in this particular
county.

In the pages that follow, the focus of interest lies in institutions rather than in individuals or in such imponderables as
"religion" or "economic welfare." Particular, observable cotton
mills and churches are the characters in the story to be un-
folded. Most often they speak through their chief executives,
the mill managers and ministers, but these spokesmen are
hedged about at every turn by the traditions and necessities of
the institutions they represent. Occasionally it is of value to
speculate on the hidden purposes and motives of these executives; though such procedure is always hazardous, it is sometimes necessary for interpretation of the lines that are spoken.
Individuals are represented as significant, however, only insofar
as they represent institutions.

The cast of characters is limited in other respects. Two institutions carry on a dialogue, rather than conduct a forum in which all aspects of community life may be represented. In more technical parlance, analysis in this volume is vertical rather than horizontal in scope; it probes into the roles of two institutions over a period of sixty years and explores the relations between them, rather than undertakes exposition of all social phenomena in the locale. Politics, leisure activities, family relations, education—these and many other fellow townsmen beckon frequently to the main characters, and occasionally it is necessary to pause for a brief word with them, but hurriedly, lest the thread of the ongoing conversation be lost.

Even the most interesting characters of all, the Negro population and Negro churches, must be largely excluded. They are not directly relevant to the immediate problem involved, and adequate interpretation of them presents methodological difficulties well-nigh insuperable. Of 12,392 Negroes in the county in 1930, less than 400 were employed in cotton mills, and even these were marginal workers. Nor does the presence of a Negro population, lacking direct participation in the economic or religious life of the larger community, constitute in any significant sense a control group, because the race line cuts across all other factors. Furthermore, methods of research entirely different from those entailed for white churches are necessary for colored churches; it is virtually impossible to secure information about the latter for the years prior to 1920 because written records are scarce and memories are extremely fallible and contradictory. Almost without exception, therefore, generalizations and statistics in subsequent pages do not include the Negro, though attempts to clarify his status are introduced occasionally.

A combination of observational and historical methods has been used in gathering material. For several months in 1938 and 1939 the author lived in Gaston County, making detailed studies and having interviews with hundreds of residents of all types. Field work ended on the day the second World War began, but two subsequent visits have not revealed any significant changes in pattern. Pertinent literary sources were discovered through research in more than a dozen libraries in various parts of the country and through the examination of manuscripts, letters, clippings, and pamphlets collected by several individuals. About forty unpublished manuscripts and approximately twenty theses written by graduate students have been especially helpful. Compilation of statistics for each decennial year from 1880 to the present involved research in the minutes of ecclesiastical bodies, in textile journals, and in the respective Federal censuses, including those reports of the 1940 Census which are available to date.

In a somewhat different and more extensive form, the material on which this volume is based was presented as a dissertation in partial fulfillment of the requirements for the degree of Doctor of Philosophy at Yale University, and in that connection was awarded the John Addison Porter Prize for the year 1940. A copy of the original manuscript, containing a number of tables, graphs, documentary proofs, and similar paraphernalia which have been omitted from the published volume, is on file in the Sterling Memorial Library of Yale University and is available to anyone having legitimate need of it.

Gratitude for assistance is due to more persons than it is possible to mention. Innumerable residents of Gaston County have provided valuable help, but their names, except where public property, must be omitted here and throughout this volume for reasons which they will doubtless appreciate. This necessity has weakened the direct validation of many assertions and conclusions, but seems inescapable. Professors E. Wight Bakke, Charles A. Ellwood, James Leyburn, Broadus Mitchell, H. Richard Niebuhr, and Howard W. Odum have contributed immeasurably to background, criticism, and encouragement, directly and indirectly. Sources and files of information which would have been lost, except for their diligence, were made available by Dr. James Myers, Dr. James Dombrowski, Miss Harriet Herring, Mr. Ewing C. Baskette, and Mr. Willis Weatherford. Special help in library research was given by the late Dr. S. M. Tenney of the Montreat Historical Foundation, Dr. G. W. Paschal of Wake Forest College, Miss Charlotte Blake of the Gastonia Public Library, Miss Janet Welton of the Presbyterian Committee on Publication in Richmond, and officials of the Ruthenberg Library in New York. Editors Douglas G. Woolf and William B. Dall of the *Textile World* opened a rare file of statistics on the textile industry, and Mrs.

Mildred Gwin Barnwell, executive secretary of the Southern Combed Yarn Spinners Association, helped to interpret more recent developments in the industry. Mr. Henry I. Adams and Miss Lucy Randolph Mason of the Textile Workers Union of America gave insight into the peculiar problems of the labor movement in mill villages. Former Governor Clyde R. Hoey of North Carolina and strike leader Fred E. Beal told of their respective roles in the Gastonia strike of 1929 and were equally gracious, the one in his office in the state capitol, the other in a state prison. To each and all of these persons sincere gratitude is extended. None of them is to be held responsible for the interpretations and conclusions presented here; many of them would doubtless disagree heartily at various points.

For reading the manuscript and making useful suggestions, especial thanks are due to Dean Luther A. Weigle, Miss Harriet Herring, Dr. James Myers, Professor Raymond Morris, and Mr. Jonathan Daniels. Dean Weigle and several officials of the Yale University Press have been considerate and helpful in bringing the material to publication. Mr. Claude Whitehead gave able assistance in compilation of statistics. Mrs. Esther Davison manifested extraordinary patience, skill, and perseverance in transcribing a difficult manuscript into legibility. My parents in North Carolina have greatly facilitated the process of research, and my wife has helped in innumerable ways with patience and enthusiasm.

L. P.

New Haven, Connecticut,
December 5, 1941.

CONTENTS

CONTENTS

LIST OF TABLES

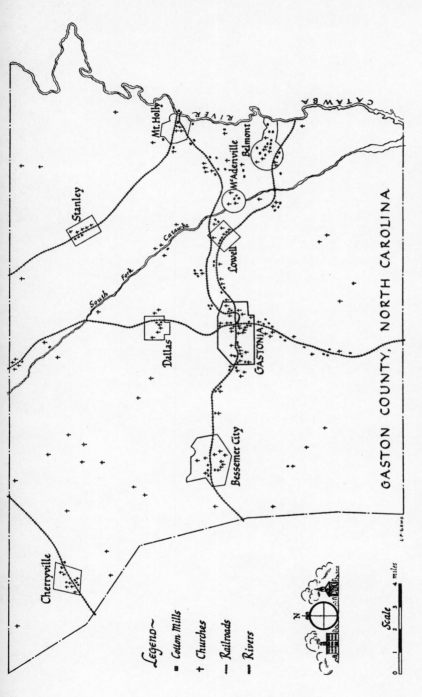

GASTON COUNTY, NORTH CAROLINA

CHURCHES AND COTTON MILLS IN GASTON COUNTY
1939

Legend~
■ Cotton Mills
+ Churches
—— Railroads
━ Rivers

Scale

0   1   2   3   4 miles

PART I

PATTERNS OF GROWTH

MILLHANDS AND PREACHERS

CHAPTER I

THE RISE OF THE COTTON MILLS

EARLY in 1929 the name of Gastonia was catapulted from obscurity into headlines around the world. In rapid succession metropolitan newspapers told their readers of a Communist uprising in the little textile town, of mass parades and the use of troops, of mob scenes and the destruction of life and property. Outbreaks of violence flared for several weeks, culminating in the death of the chief of police and the wounding of several of his officers in an armed skirmish with Communists and strikers. Scores of arrests followed, and two dramatic trials focused the spotlight of publicity on a tense courtroom for additional weeks. At last seven men were convicted of murder and sentenced to prison, only to escape their sentences by flight to Russia.

Readers across America were confirmed in many of their previous notions about the South, gleaned largely from novels and Hollywood, and were supplied with new items of information. Uneasy ghosts of the past were resurrected and stalked again through the public mind: young rowdies and enraged citizens riding the night in disguise; mobs bent on lynching; soft-spoken gentlemen ready to sudden violence; feudal barons who owned people body and soul and ruled in benevolent despotism. New specters of a New South were brought from concealment and placed on display before a national audience. It was revealed that many Southern children were nursed by spindles rather than corpulent Negro mammies; that "delicious Southern cooking" was not enough to forestall pellagra when there were only "fat back" and "corn pone" to cook; that the gentle mistress of the old plantation had a granddaughter who could be a hellcat on the picket line. Wages in Southern mills were depicted as low, hours long. Public officials were portrayed as hirelings of industry. Preachers were indicted as "moral police for the mill owners," and religious fundamentalism was denounced as prejudicial to legal justice. The traditional picture of a columned mansion with magnolias in front and slave quarters behind was replaced by that of a low, oblong cotton mill with a picket line in front and the identical houses of a mill village all about it. Gastonia became a symbol of the New South, and the connotations it carried have been remembered by many who have forgotten its name.

Most Southerners resented the unfavorable publicity attendant on the Gastonia episode and sought to dismiss it as another effort on the part of Northerners to disparage the South. They suspected that a disproportionate amount of attention was being given the affair: Communists had led strikes in other sections of the country, often with comparable violence, without bringing such notoriety to the scene of their operations. Proud of the phenomenal development of industry in their region within a few decades, the natives believed that the industrial strife and the deplorable conditions it revealed were merely temporary aberrations, and that a distorted picture was being presented to the nation as typical. A few Southerners were inclined to announce the end of an economic era, but most of their fellow citizens saw no portent in Gastonia and explained their own excitement (many newspapers called it "hysteria") as due only to the disruption of their usual peace.

The wider American audience was correct in assuming that Gastonia and all it symbolized posed problems of national interest and concern. Southerners were correct in believing that their New South could be understood only by careful appraisal of events more far-reaching than those which transpired in Gastonia in 1929. Back of the violence and headlines lay a series of developments extending over several decades, and some of them had been almost as revolutionary in character as the eruption which focused national attention on their results. For the understanding of those developments and for some insight into the operation of religious institutions in a changing society, the county in which Gastonia is located is a prize laboratory.

THE BACKGROUND OF THE RISE OF THE MILLS

The story of the rise of the cotton mills in the South has been often told. Sometimes it has been told in the mood of a romance, portraying the Herculean efforts of a region, defeated and impoverished in war, to lift itself again from poverty and to regain a respectable place in the national economy through taking upon itself an industrial character formerly despised. Again, the industrial revolution ushered in by the rise of the mills has been depicted as the great betrayal of a culture which, though temporarily broken by war, might have been revived, preserving greater beauty and humanity than its betrayer has been able to bring. Still again, the rise of young industrial giants, unshackled and insolent in power, has been denounced as a farce, a burlesque of a development which, under other conditions or leadership, might have been genuinely beneficial. One mood or other—romance, tragedy, or farce—has generally prevailed in the telling of the tale.

Numerous attempts have also been made to study dispassionately the rise of the mills, and have succeeded in the isolation of a number of factors underlying their emergence. The part played by religious institutions has been largely ignored, despite the fact that it was of considerable importance. In order to see it in proper perspective, however, it is necessary briefly to mention the associated factors, more secular in character, which figured in the complex background of industrial transformation. Gaston County affords an excellent context in which to study the relative importance of the various transforming forces—forces which, in a period of only three or four decades, brought profound changes in the economic life of the entire South and of the Piedmont section in particular. New impulses stirring in the region were less restrained in this county than in most areas, and are therefore more easily studied. The further fact that economic transformation was effected there almost entirely by local leadership and local capital renders close analysis doubly instructive, as contrasted with counties where industrialism was imported.

Prior to 1880 Gaston County was mainly agricultural in economic character. Its agriculture differed in crucial respects, however, from that typical of the Southern plantation economy. Lying at the edge of a mountainous region, its topography was better suited to small farms than to extensive plantations, and that type of economic organization had prevailed from the time of its settlement. Few residents before the Civil War had owned more than three or four slaves; the percentage of slaves in the total population of Lincoln County (including Gaston) in 1810 was 15.2 as compared with an average of over

45 per cent in several eastern counties of North Carolina in which the plantation system ruled.[1] Farms in the county in 1880 averaged about 130 acres in size, with a very small minority being larger than a thousand acres.[2] Cotton culture accounted for only 18.38 per cent of all the acres under cultivation in that year; more than twice as much acreage was devoted to corn.[3] The agricultural life of the county differed greatly, therefore, from the cotton-slavery-plantation system which constituted the basic economic structure of the South. A similar economic pattern extended over many other counties in the Piedmont region and comprised a sort of marginal economy in the Southern scene.

Professor Broadus Mitchell has pointed out that manufacturing had little opportunity to rise in the Southern states during the decades immediately preceding the Civil War.[4] Occasional prophets of industrialism appeared, but they were voices crying in vain against the slavery-cotton-plantation system. Only in counties in which this system was largely absent did independent manufacturing enterprises, as contrasted with small domestic crafts on the plantations, appear to any extent. Gaston County was one of these. At the beginning of the nineteenth century the iron industry reached considerable development there.[5] The tradition of cotton manufacturing was also established in the vicinity before the Civil War. The first cotton mill south of the Potomac was erected, about 1816, on the South Fork River just north of the present boundary line of Gaston County, part of the machinery being made by skilled ironwork-

1. W. B. Goebel, "A History of Manufactures in North Carolina before 1860" (A.M. thesis, Duke University, 1926), p. 77, quoting material gathered up by Tench Cox from the Federal census of that year.
2. Rev. Levi Branson, ed., *North Carolina Business Directory, 1872* (Raleigh, 1872), pp. 99–101. W. E. Hearn *et alii, Soil Survey of Gaston County, North Carolina* (Washington, 1911), pp. 11–12.
3. *Tenth Census of the United States:* "Report of the Cotton Production of the State of North Carolina" (Washington, 1880), p. 58. Of 59,569 tilled acres in the county in 1880, 10,949 were in cotton and 24,679 acres in corn. Cotton was gaining, however, its production having increased sixfold during the preceding ten years.
4. Broadus Mitchell, *The Rise of Cotton Mills in the South* (Baltimore, 1921), chap. i.
5. Hugh T. Lefler, ed., *North Carolina History Told by Contemporaries* (Chapel Hill, 1934), pp. 26, 102–103, 118–122, 226, containing reprints of documents of the period which described the iron industry in the county.

ers in the community and the remainder imported from New England.[6] A second branch of this mill was erected in 1819 and was operated very profitably for several decades. The first mills located within the present boundaries of the county appeared about 1850 when a mill was moved there from another county in order to obtain water power and two mills were built by local promoters. Further development was impeded by the depletion of capital during the Civil War. Three cotton factories continued to operate, however, and the rapid emergence of new mills after 1880 represented a continuation of a previous tendency rather than a completely new departure.[7] Several men who subsequently became pioneers in the erection of mills in the county received industrial training in these ante bellum mills.

The rapid extension of the textile industry in the county after 1880 was facilitated by numerous factors, often analyzed.[8] Natural advantages included an ample supply of water

6. "Articles of Agreement made and Entered into this 27th day of April 1816 between Michael Shenk & Absolom Warlick of the County of Lincoln & State of North Carolina of the one part, and Michael Beam of the County and State aforesaid of the other part. . . ." (MS. in archives of the North Carolina Historical Commission, Raleigh), a contract whereby Shenk and Warlick agreed to pay Beam $1,300 for making a spinning machine, a carding machine, and a roving machine.

7. A sharp debate has occurred as to whether the Southern industrialism beginning about 1880 was a new development or an outgrowth and extension of a trend established before the Civil War and merely interrupted temporarily by that war. Professor Broadus Mitchell, *op. cit.*, has been the chief exponent of the former view. The latter view has been presented by Edgar Gardner Murphy, *Problems of the Present South* (New York, 1905); Richard H. Edmonds, *Facts about the South* (Baltimore, 1894); Goebel, *op. cit.*, chap. iv; and many others. Gaston County contributes evidence in favor of the latter view. Professor Mitchell's thesis draws too sharply the line between the Old and New South. His argument that the plantation system was antithetical to independent industrialism is virtually unchallenged, but it is not to be assumed that the plantation system, however dominant, was the sole type of Southern economic enterprise or that its exclusive sway in certain regions prevented an almost unbroken line of industrial development in other sections, and notably in those in which postwar industrialism flourished. Industrial enterprise is relatively insignificant to this day in counties in which the plantation system was characteristic; it was of some importance, even before the Civil War, in other counties, especially in the Piedmont region. In these latter counties, including Gaston, the war brought an interlude, not a break.

8. Ben F. Lemert, *The Cotton Textile Industry of the Southern Appalachian Piedmont* (Chapel Hill, 1933), chaps. i–iii; C. K. Brown, "Industrial Development in North Carolina," *The Annals of the American Academy of Political and Social Science,* CLIII, 133–140 (January, 1931); Jefferson Bynum, "Pied-

power, available from the Catawba River at the eastern boundary of the county, the South Fork River traversing the county
diagonally, and a number of smaller streams. All the earlier
mills were erected along the banks of these rivers, and subsequent development of cheap hydroelectric power from these
streams made further industrial expansion especially easy.
Natural advantages included also a climate suitable for cotton
spinning, though in some respects not so favorable as that of
New England.

Several economic factors were conducive to further development of industry. As already indicated, organization of the economic life of the county by small, atomistic units rendered transition to an industrial economy much easier than in counties in
which traditions of a plantation economy lingered. Postwar
economic developments stimulated the transition. In the 1870's
the price of cotton dropped severely, and for nearly forty years
thereafter seldom rose above 10 cents a pound.[9] The ante bellum advantage in producing cotton rather than in processing
it was thereby reversed, and cotton mills sprang up in the cotton fields to share with Northern mills the profits accruing from
fabrication.[10]

The construction of railroads hastened industrialization. Before the Civil War, the rise of manufacturing had been severely
hampered by lack of efficient transportation facilities. One railroad touched Gaston County, but it had only one station there.
In 1872 the Southern Railway came through; another railroad
crossed it in 1875, with the present site of the city of Gastonia,
then open country, as the point of intersection.[11] New markets

mont North Carolina and Textile Production," *Economic Geography,* IV
(1929), 222–240; Dan Mabry Lacy, "The Beginnings of Industrialism in North
Carolina, 1865–1900" (M.A. thesis, University of North Carolina, 1935); innumerable brochures of the Gastonia Chamber of Commerce, etc.

9. Lemert, *op. cit.,* p. 31.

10. The advantage gained by the Southern manufacturer in being close to the
sources of raw material must not be overestimated. Cotton loses little weight in
fabrication, and proximity of New England mills to the nation's markets probably offsets their distance from the cotton fields.

11. The little town of Dallas, then the county seat, would not allow the railroads to come through it; residents protested that the trains would keep them
awake and disturb their livestock. Cf. the reaction of English landed gentry to
the first railroads. The roads went through a cow pasture to the south of Dallas, and Gastonia grew up, eventually replacing Dallas as county seat and
principal town.

and supplies were thereby brought within easy reach. Electric
power lines soon followed the courses of the railroads, and mills
subsequently were erected beside railroads rather than rivers.

Human resources were also of crucial importance. The original colonizers of the county were chiefly Scotch Irish and Ger-
mans, moving into the Piedmont and western sections of North
Carolina about the middle of the eighteenth century because of
increasing land rents and other economic difficulties in Pennsyl-
vania; and Scotch Highlanders, moving westward from the
eastern counties of North Carolina as the development of plantations increasingly forced the yeoman farmer off the more fer-
tile land.[12] All three of these groups of settlers had traditions
of craftsmanship, and the attention of their descendants was
easily directed to industry when the prospect of economic advantage appeared. The economic condition of the population
after the Civil War was of more importance, however, than its
ethnic backgrounds. The poverty of small farmers and tenant
farmers provided a great reservoir of cheap labor for any enterprise that promised a decent livelihood. As the price of cotton declined, opportunity for employment at cash wages became increasingly attractive. Thousands of unsuccessful farmers, able to eke out only a mean livelihood in agriculture,[13] stood
ready to furnish man power for new industrial enterprises.[14]
Between 1880 and 1905 several thousand of them came to the
new mills in Gaston County from contiguous rural counties. A
survey of 100 families of mill workers in the county in 1914 revealed that 73 had come from counties immediately bordering
Gaston; 66 had been tenants, not owning land.[15] Beginning

12. See Rupert B. Vance, *Human Geography of the South* (Chapel Hill,
1932), pp. 42–43, 45–46.

13. As late as 1911 farm labor in the county was receiving only 75 c. to $1.25
a day, $15–$18 a month (Hearn, *op. cit.,* pp. 11–12).

14. About 1870 the widespread introduction of the ring spindle, largely automatic in operation, rendered lack of industrial training fairly inconsequential,
and facilitated the transition of workers from farms to cotton mills. Most of
the Southern mills, and especially those in Gaston County, specialized at the
outset in the production of coarser yarns, mostly 4's to 12's, which required
less skill on the part of labor than other textile processes. Finer goods continued to be produced almost exclusively by New England mills.

15. Edgar Ralph Rankin, "A Social Study of One Hundred Families at Cotton Mills in Gastonia, North Carolina" (M.A. thesis, University of North Carolina, 1914), pp. 4–7, 10–11. Only four of the seventy-three families had lived at
the mills all their lives; the median time of residence in a mill village was

about 1905, recruits were drawn increasingly from the mountainous regions farther to the west in North Carolina, Georgia, and Tennessee; the growth of towns in Gaston County had increased the prices of agricultural products sufficiently to allow profitable operation of small farms, and most of the surplus agricultural labor in the immediate vicinity had been already absorbed. Labor agents were sent by manufacturers to distant counties and even into adjoining states; the number of mills was growing so rapidly that an adequate supply of labor was beginning to constitute a problem, and the practice of "stealing labor" had become so prevalent that employers were forced to declare a truce and to seek new recruits. Additional thousands of dispirited farmers and mountaineers accepted the offer of the mill companies to move them and their possessions to the new mill villages.[16]

This labor supply was not drawn, as often supposed, from the class usually called "poor whites." Specifically, "poor whites" in ante bellum Southern society were to be found principally in plantation regions—that is, in the eastern coastal counties—where they comprised a marginal, pauperized, and often diseased group.[17] The mill workers in Gaston County were drawn chiefly from the descendants of small independent farmers in the Piedmont and mountainous areas who had fallen on evil days and lost their land.

The impoverished whites represented, in many respects, an ideal labor supply for the development of industry in the region. They were almost completely homogeneous in race and

twelve years. Rankin estimated that up to 1914 between 15,000 and 20,000 people had come from rural districts to operate Gaston County's mills.

Cf., for occupational and geographical backgrounds of mill workers in other Southern villages, Holland Thompson, *From the Cotton Field to the Cotton Mill: A Study of the Industrial Transition in North Carolina* (New York, 1906); Benjamin Harper Smith, "The Social Significance of the Southern Cotton Mill Community" (M.A. thesis, Emory University, 1925); Lois MacDonald, *Southern Mill Hills* (New York, 1928).

16. As a mill worker explained in 1939, a man had come to his mountain home thirty years ago and painted the mills "all rosy," with the result that "ignorant-like, we come down to the cotton mills." Similar testimony was given innumerable times.

17. B. B. Kendrick and A. M. Arnett, *The South Looks at Its Past* (Chapel Hill, 1935), pp. 47–50, 127. "Po' white trash" supplied labor for occasional mills in the eastern counties of North Carolina (E. R. Hartz, "Social Problems in a North Carolina Parish" [A.M. thesis, Duke University, 1938], pp. 16–18, 144).

language,[18] and no special problems were involved in housing them in the mill villages or in the management of them by the mill executives. The latter, indeed, were of precisely the same racial and cultural background and knew how to handle their employees with a deftness bred of long association. The workers brought with them to the mill villages an individualism nurtured by solitary life on small farms and sparsely populated mountainsides; this individualism resulted, in the sphere of industrial relations, in personal dealing as individuals with the employer, with collective labor action appearing only sporadically and always being short-lived. The early manufacturers, lacking capital and depending heavily on uninterrupted production in order to remain solvent, had available a labor supply largely unamenable to outside influences interested in the organization of labor.

The labor supply was notable also for its docility. This trait has been overemphasized by chambers of commerce and power companies seeking to attract Northern capital to Southern communities, and has faded into the background of promotional literature since the wave of Southern strikes in 1929. The first generation of workers appears to have been, nevertheless, patient and long-suffering in spirit. Its members came to the mill villages as refugees; for the most part, they had been unsuccessful in previous economic pursuits, and acceptance of industrial employment represented a last stand against pauperism. They had been accustomed to working from sunrise to sunset without murmuring, and to expect little in return. They took it for granted that all members of the family would work as early as possible, and offered practically no opposition to child labor in the cotton mills. They begat notoriously large families, even surpassing the immigrants who populated the East with a plentiful supply of workers.[19]

Of the factors favoring the rise of industry in the South,

18. In 1930 only 212 foreign-born whites lived in Gaston County as compared with 65,489 native-born.

19. It is a commonplace that the birth rate in the South exceeds that of any other region in the nation. North Carolina has generally had a higher birth rate than any other state (G. T. Schwenning, "Prospects of Southern Textile Unionism," *The Journal of Political Economy*, XXXIX, 789–790 [December, 1931]). According to the 1940 Census, North Carolina led the nation in the size of its families, with an average of 4.5 persons per family; the average for the South Atlantic states was 4.2 and for the nation 3.8.

perhaps the availability of an almost inexhaustible supply of cheap, tractable labor was the most important. Competition for jobs was so severe that wages were minimal, with the manufacturer furnishing housing and many other facilities for the maintenance of life. Additional thousands of tenant farmers and mountaineers stood ready to take the jobs of mill workers who, through strikes or other forms of noncoöperation, might seem to the employers and to Southern communities to have forfeited their right to employment. Under such conditions employers had a high competitive advantage over Northern mills at a time when lack of capital and experience made an advantage especially necessary. The same factors have preserved traditional industrial relations almost unchanged down to the present, though the argument from necessity has become increasingly less convincing.

Negroes, comprising a relatively small percentage of the population of the county and its surrounding territory,[20] were excluded from the mills almost entirely. The argument that this was because they were less efficient than whites is of dubious validity; several ante bellum Southern mills, including two in Gaston County, had been operated solely by slaves, with satisfactory results.[21] After emancipation, however, the status of the Negro was changed from that of a valuable economic asset to that of the poor white man's last outpost against oblivion— an oblivion to which he had previously been consigned because of his inability to compete with slave labor. Negroes were excluded, therefore, from the cotton mills, or, in the case of the few who were admitted, given the most disagreeable jobs. Their extensive employment would have endangered the availability of an adequate supply of white labor, after the bitterness generated by reconstruction tactics. The rise of the mills represented to considerable degree the economic triumph of the poor

20. Twenty-eight per cent in Gaston County in 1880, and an even smaller percentage in many of the counties lying west of Gaston. The county contained 12,392 Negroes in 1930 as compared with 65,701 whites.

21. Goebel, *op. cit.*, pp. 150–151; Sterling D. Spero and Abram L. Harris, *The Black Worker: The Negro and the Labor Movement* (New York, 1931), pp. 348–349; Robert F. Cope, "History of Early Cotton Mills in Gaston County," *Gastonia Gazette*, November 20, 1934. Whites and blacks were employed alongside each other in a few of the ante bellum Southern mills, without difficulty.

white man over the emancipated black.[22] As the whites moved
into the cotton mills, the Negroes drifted rapidly into farm tenancy and to Northern cities.

Cultural changes, less tangible but no less significant than
the factors enumerated above, also influenced the appearance of
cotton mills in the southern Piedmont region. In many communities, and especially in counties where the plantation system
had not prevailed, a sweeping change in ethicways[23] occurred
during the two decades immediately after the Civil War. In
economic philosophy, agrarianism was modified by a new emphasis on industrialism; in political affairs sectionalism was increasingly qualified by a spirit of nationalism. An earlier Southern liberalism, associated especially with tobacco planters of
the eighteenth century, had been vanquished by provincial
ideas as the interests of the South became identified with the
perpetuation of slavery and reliance upon cotton.[24] The provincial creeds failed to vindicate themselves on the battlefield,
however, and the way was paved for a reëmergence of cosmopolitan viewpoints. In the 1880's, "nationalism and industrialism" had become the creed of liberal spirits in the South.[25]
Many communities set out to compete with the North in industrial enterprise, and thereby to wrest victory from defeat.

The fact that Southern communities deliberately determined
to build cotton mills is of major importance both in tracing the
rise of the mills themselves and in studying subsequent industrial relations in the industry. Towns were willing to make almost any concession in order to obtain mills: taxes were kept
low[26] and often rebated, restrictive legislation was carefully

22. Broadus Mitchell and George Sinclair Mitchell, *The Industrial Revolution in the South* (Baltimore, 1930), p. 32.

23. This term is intended to indicate common social judgments as to what
ought to prevail in society, whether it does or not, in contradistinction to
"mores," which pertains especially to judgments that the folkways actually
followed are the ones that ought to be followed for the welfare of society.

24. A penetrating analysis of this shift in political and economic philosophy
is contained in Clement Eaton, *Freedom of Thought in the Old South* (Durham, N.C., 1940).

25. Dr. S. C. Mitchell, Interview, Blue Ridge, N.C., June 27, 1939. Cf. Holland Thompson, *The New South: A Chronicle of Social and Industrial Revolution* (Allen Johnson, ed., "The Chronicles of America," Vol. XLII, New Haven, 1919).

26. The tax rate in Gastonia has always been low: 20 c. per $100 in 1887,

avoided, natural and human resources of the communities were
offered at nominal prices, and industrialists were accepted as
pioneers and unchallenged arbiters of social and moral welfare.
Villages vied with each other in efforts at industrialization; the
number of cotton mills in the vicinity became an infallible index
to the "progressive spirit" of any "thriving, growing city."
Gastonia boasted in 1906: "There are more cotton factories in
Gaston County than in any other county in the South, and
there are more of these factories in Gastonia than in any other
town in the County."[27] Brochures depicting tiny Southern villages as industrial Edens were prepared and distributed
widely.[28] A contagion for building cotton mills swept over the
entire Piedmont region—one observer remarked that it was
"like the measles."[29]

Without community enthusiasm of this sort it is probable
that the establishment of mills in the South would have been de-
ferred for a few decades, or that their erection would have occurred under different auspices. Despite a prevalent notion to
the contrary, most of the Southern mills were not built by
Northern capital; a major portion of them were indigenous
projects, financed by a great number of local citizens. In the
1880's, an adequate supply of capital could be obtained locally
only through widespread community participation. The richest
man in Gaston County prior to the Civil War had about a thousand dollars available for investment. The Gastonia Town Tax
Book for 1887 listed the property of no citizen at more than
$10,000.[30] It was necessary, therefore, that capital should be
supplied by numerous small investors. Small merchants became,
in several instances, focal points around which capital might be
organized. When a stock-subscription campaign for a new mill

75⅓ c. in 1916, $1.40 in 1927, $1.15 in 1938. The rate for the county in 1938
was 85 c.

27. Joseph H. Separk, ed., *Illustrated Handbook of Gastonia* (Gastonia,
1906), p. 13.

28. For example, an illustrated booklet, *High Shoals, Gaston County, North
Carolina*, published in 1908, contains an effusive picture of the opportunities
awaiting industry there, including pleasures that tired industrialists might have
from fishing in the river. "The wheels of the factory," says the booklet, "have
been so choked with eels that it was necessary to stop and chop them out of
the buckets." The village had only a few hundred inhabitants.

29. W. P. Jacobs, *The Pioneer* (Clinton, S.C., 1935), pp. 66–67.
30. *Gastonia Gazette*, July 15, 1921.

was announced, dozens of would-be stockholders responded, often calling on banks for funds, with small items of real property as surety. Shares frequently were sold on the installment plan, with payments as low as one dollar a month. The services of investment bankers were seldom solicited; an advertisement in the local newspaper was generally a successful substitute. Textile machinery dealers and building contractors coöperated, sometimes accepting stock in lieu of cash payment for machinery and construction costs. Nearly all the managers of the mills were natives of the county,[31] chosen because of their ability at promotion or experience in textile operation rather than because of majority stock ownership.

Up to 1910 the mills in Gaston County were owned, to large degree, by small investors—farmers, merchants, clerks, wage earners, ministers. Subsequently, the relative number of stockholders declined as successful manufacturers gathered stock increasingly into their own hands and furnished most of the capital for new mills. Few public stock issues have been announced since 1921.[32] But traditions of local ownership and community sponsorship of the mills have continued. Citizens still aver that their industry is owned and operated almost entirely by natives. As a matter of fact, this conception is only partly true; of 114 persons holding major offices in the mill corporations of the county in 1935, 52 were not natives of the county and 16 were nonresidents.[33] Notions of community interest in the mills and community responsibility for their success have survived, however, and have affected most efforts to regulate industrial practices. The county has not recognized that it has increasingly been sheltering absentee enterprise; it has continued to think of its mills in affectionate, paternal terms.

31. The writer secured information on this point with respect to all incorporators and officers of Gaston County mills prior to 1900; of a total of 93, only 13 were nonresidents of the county and only 2 were nonresidents of North Carolina.

32. The most recent occurred in 1938, when 205 stockholders responded to an appeal, sponsored by the Gastonia Chamber of Commerce, for the building of a hosiery mill as a community project. Even here, however, one hosiery manufacturer in the county bought a very large block of the stock.

33. A study was made of all presidents, vice-presidents, and secretary-treasurers of mill corporations, as of October 1, 1935, from lists of officers contained in Joseph H. Separk, *Gastonia and Gaston County* (Gastonia, 1936), pp. 114–119.

MOTIVATION OF TEXTILE ENTREPRENEURS

Another significant factor in the industrial transformation of Gaston County and of the Piedmont region lay in the initiative of individual entrepreneurs. Consideration of their motives is hazardous but important, as it provides a nexus between economic and religious aspects of that transformation, insofar as religious institutions may have influenced their action.[34] The question has been a subject of considerable debate. The popular interpretation of the rise of the mills has argued that many of the early capitalists were sincere altruists, promoting industrial enterprise originally in order to provide employment for the impoverished whites and to further the development of their communities and of the South.[35] There was much less cupidity at the beginning than might be suspected, according to this view, but rather a sincere desire to help in the economic reconstruction of the region; from the depression of 1873 until about 1890 there was in the South a new type of philanthropic capitalist, in whom sincere religious attitudes were dominant. This thesis, which largely reflects the interpretation prevailing in Southern mill circles, has been widely accepted.

There is no doubt that Southern mill builders commonly thought themselves to be agents of community welfare, and that they impressed their associates and communities as men of social vision and ethical idealism. In reply to an interviewer who asked him what he did at his mill, one of the industrial pioneers answered, "We make American citizens, and run cotton mills to pay the expenses." An acquaintance of another entrepreneur ascribes to him, in his passion to industrialize the South, "a spiritual impulse as undeniable as that of the Apostle Paul." A historian describes the motives of an early manufacturer in a county adjoining Gaston as being "not merely to build another mill . . . but to gather about it an orderly community of happy, God-fearing, working people, enjoying all the conveniences and comforts of improved social conditions. . . . He carried his religion into his business. He felt that this was the

34. This sort of analysis risks subjectivity, of course, because the relation between the institutional stimulus, the internal motive, and the overt action is not subject to precise demonstration.

35. Cf. Broadus Mitchell, *The Rise of Cotton Mills in the South,* pp. 131–137. But see also pp. 147–148.

way to serve his generation."[36] Similar motives have been ascribed to a large majority of early Southern industrialists.

It has been asserted on the basis of such evidence that the industrial awakening in the South was in a sense a religious movement. Superficial evidence from Gaston County would support this contention. Every early mill builder in the county, with one or two exceptions, was a churchman before he built mills. A study was made by the writer, with the coöperation of one of the few industrial pioneers still surviving, of religious affiliations of all persons who were incorporators or officials of mills in the county up to 1900. Of a total of 93, only 2 were definitely nonchurchmen; 16 were "active" in their churches, 20 were "very active," and at least 29 were church officials.[37] Several of them are described as having been intensely religious, and all evidence indicates that most of them were leaders in the churches as well as in economic aspects of community life. An editorial obituary in the *Gastonia Gazette* described one of them in terms that might be applied to most of the others: "He served his church and pastor well, and was considered a bulwark of safe conservatism and orthodox religion in all the church courts."[38] The preëminent textile pioneer of the county once said to his pastor, "Our record as a textile center has no parallel in the South, but I want to tell you that Gastonia owes more to the Christian religion than we owe to any other cause."[39]

36. Clarence W. Griffin, *The History of Old Tryon and Rutherford Counties, 1730–1936* (Asheville, 1937), pp. 597, 598. Cf. Jacobs, *op. cit.*, pp. 50–51, 65.

37. Distribution among the various denominations fell as follows:

Lutheran	30
Presbyterian	28
Methodist	15
Baptist	3
Associate Reformed Presbyterian	2
Episcopal	1
No information available	12
Definitely nonchurchmen	2

The preponderance of Lutherans and Presbyterians is to be explained partly by the fact that the original German and Scotch settlers of the county were chiefly members of these two denominations. By 1880 Baptists and Methodists approximately equaled the two older denominations in number of members resident there, but were somewhat less well established in their communities than the descendants of the original families.

38. *Gastonia Gazette*, October 15, 1936.

39. *Ibid.*, March 13, 1926. A common statement in the community has held that "the religious influences have kept step with industry and commerce"; for example, see *ibid.*, August 15, 1937.

A resident of Gastonia, who was associated closely with the textile leaders, generalized in 1906:

The moral and religious life of the town has ever been of chief importance. With but few exceptions the chief men in the industrial and commercial development of the community have been staunch churchmen, which fact has made it easily possible for the church life to keep even pace with the rapid growth of other interests.[40]

Despite all eulogies of pioneer manufacturers as Christian philanthropists, examination of early industrial practices seriously modifies the ascription of pure altruism to the textile entrepreneurs. They employed hundreds of children in their factories, and continued to do so after the public conscience had been severely challenged on the question of child labor.[41] They frequently paid wages as low as ten cents a day, and dismissed the disparity between such wages and their own income by pointing out that the wages represented an increase over the former agricultural earnings of the workers. Stating that they were building factories "in order to give employment to fellow citizens," they imported strangers from distant counties to operate their mills, and from the beginning deprecated the civic, political, and social qualifications of the mill worker. They guarded and sought to extend their personal control over mill corporations, gathering stock into their own hands as rapidly as possible rather than promoting widespread distribution of profits and subordinating themselves to social controls. Whatever their motives in proposing the mills, the mill builders quickly became individual entrepreneurs rather than agents primarily responsible to their communities. They may have calculated that they could best serve their communities by reaping large personal profits for investment in additional mills, but their own personal fortunes and power grew immensely in the process and rendered them largely unamenable to community guidance or control.

Introspective recollections of surviving textile pioneers in Gaston County often support the impression gained from observing overt industrial practices, though analysis of interior

40. J. H. Separk, ed., *Illustrated Handbook of Gastonia*, p. 47.
41. See chap. x.

motives is always difficult. One of the principal figures in the industrial development of the county, when asked about philanthropic motives of his colleagues, answered:

It is an insult to my common sense to ask me whether early mill builders built mills to make money or to secure social betterment. Every man wants first of all to make a living—food, shelter, clothing—and then, if he is any account, to make money. Ninety-nine per cent of the motives of early mill men lay in a desire for economic return.

I remember when the first screen was put in a mill house in this town. I went with the president of several mills to a mill house where there were three cases of typhoid. The doctor told us he believed we could keep it from spreading if we put in screens. Soon nearly all the mill houses in town had screens. If you have a store next door to a man whose store front is freshly painted and whose windows are clean, will you let your store front be dingy and your windows fly-specked?

With the metaphor translated into direct speech, the story of the window screens means that the desire for efficient and uninterrupted production prompted most of the village improvements and welfare services generally attributed to the altruistic benevolence of the mill owners. By 1900 competition for labor had become rife among the mills and employers who provided superior living conditions had an advantage in the labor market. The explanation of the window screens would be valid also for water closets, electric lights, welfare staffs, and many other types of village and community improvement. The provision of improved conditions was publicly interpreted, however, in philanthropic terms, and the mill owners were widely accepted as benevolent altruists.

Imputation of motives is always a hazardous business. From the lines of evidence available, in overt industrial practices and in introspective recollections, the popular interpretation of the motivation of textile pioneers must be seriously modified, if not discarded. The basic motive, worthy or not, appears to have been economic rather than philanthropic, though strong religious and moral factors were undoubtedly among the activating forces. An altruistic semireligious impulse was associated with the rise of the cotton mills in Gaston County, but was more largely normative for interpretation of the development than for motivation. Almost without question, the desire for profits was fundamental,[42] and religion appears to have been partly a mask for economic advantage from the very beginning, whether or not it was consciously so used. It is probable that the early manufacturers did not analyze their own motives closely, and it is certain that their pastors, approving industrial expansion, did not protest against the appropriation of Christian justifications by their leading parishioners. It was a time for boosters, not cynics.

42. Greed as cynical and ruthless as that depicted in Lillian Hellman's play, *The Little Foxes*, appears to have been relatively rare.

CHAPTER II

THE ROLE OF THE CHURCHES
IN THE RISE OF THE MILLS

CHURCHES in Gaston County and larger religious bodies with which they were affiliated promoted the rise of the textile industry directly in a number of ways. First of all they helped to create and express public approval of textile entrepreneurs. From the outset, ministers and religious publications praised the new industrialists as redeemers of a people and a region. Ministers were proud to recognize them as "leading members" of the churches, as evidenced in the following passages written by ministers in the county:

The first cotton mill was built on the Catawba in 1846 by Messrs. Neel and Williams (Presbyterians) and the second on the Fork by Messrs. J. and E. B. Stowe (Presbyterians) and spun its first thread on the 1st day of January, 1848. . . . Now is heard the music of the McAdenville mills, the product of the money and the brain and the energy of that most progressive, sagacious and successful man, recently deceased, Rufus Y. McAden.[1]

The following manufacturers were either raised in Goshen [parish] or were members of Goshen: R. C. G. Love (Elder), J. F. Love, Edgar Love, W. T. Love, R. L. Stowe, S. P. Stowe, E. C. Hutchinson, and J. A. Abernathy (Elder). What church can furnish a more imposing list than this?[2]

Sometimes the early industrialists were praised primarily for their contributions to religious life. Thus when George A. Gray, the most enterprising and successful leader in the building of Gaston County mills, died in 1912, the *North Carolina Christian Advocate* wrote of him:

1. Rev. R. Z. Johnston, *Historical Sketch of Goshen Presbyterian Church, Gaston County, N. C.* (Shelby, 1889), p. 4. At Montreat Historical Foundation, a manuscript library of the Presbyterian Church in the U. S., at Montreat, N.C.
2. Rev. J. K. Hall, "History of Goshen Church," p. 8. MS. at Montreat Historical Foundation.

One of the most beautiful traits in the character of Mr. Gray was the simplicity and unassumingness of his life. With all the accumulation of wealth he never grew vain, nor did he ever assume a manner or style of living that put him out of touch with the common people. As nearly as it ever could be said of any man, it may be said of Brother Gray that, like his Master, he was "the same yesterday, today, and forever." He lived close to his church and was always ready to respond cheerfully to any call for help. He was the constant and loyal supporter of his pastor, not only giving liberally to his material support, but, what is vastly more important, giving him unwavering moral support. Central Church, of which he had been a member for many years, will greatly miss him.[3]

At other times Southern entrepreneurs were acclaimed for their contributions to economic and social development, as well as for their generosity toward religious institutions. At the funeral of Mr. Gray, one of his former ministers eulogized him in words which subsequently were placed on his tombstone:

A CAPTAIN OF INDUSTRY—
A PIONEER OF PROSPERITY—
BY INDUSTRY AND HONESTY HE
ACHIEVED SUCCESS—BY JUSTICE
AND MAGNANIMITY HE WON THE
RESPECT AND LOVE OF HIS FELLOW
MEN—BY FAITH IN CHRIST HE
BUILT A CHRISTIAN CHARACTER.
"AND A MAN SHALL BE AS THE
SHADOW OF A GREAT ROCK IN A
WEARY LAND." ISA. 32.2.[4]

Similar approbation was made explicit on many occasions by ministers and religious periodicals during the period from 1880 to 1915, and to lesser degree down to the present time. From

3. Editorial, "Mr. George A. Gray, Dead," *North Carolina Christian Advocate* (February 15, 1912), p. 2. Numerous other examples of commendation of mill builders may be found in Elliott Wannamaker Hardin, "The Attitude of the Methodist Episcopal Church, South, in North Carolina toward the Textile Industry in North Carolina" (B.D. thesis, Duke University, 1938), to which the writer is indebted for much material.
4. From tombstone of George A. Gray, Gastonia, N.C.

the beginning, textile manufacturers were accepted by the churches as rightful leaders of their communities, and the only concern for their leadership was the hope that it would be both successful and Christian in character. The *North Carolina Christian Advocate* was representative of religious opinion generally in writing in 1896:

The majority of the mills are reported to be under good management. We are glad to note this; as we have learned from observation that the managers of a cotton mill have much to do with the social, moral and religious condition of their operatives. If the manager is a worthy Christian he has a wonderful influence over those who continually look to him for support. Mr. W—— says: "The majority of the mills are managed well, and have at their heads honest, conscientious, Christian gentlemen, who have done much and are still exerting their every effort to better the condition of their help both morally, financially and educationally. The mills are an honor and a credit to the State."[5]

In lauding the achievements of the manufacturers, religious spokesmen often virtually identified religious idealism and the rise of the mills, thereby revealing their own ideals for economic life. An example of identification of the two spheres is found in an editorial appearing in the *Raleigh Christian Advocate* in 1890 concerning a family of textile manufacturers living in a county adjacent to Gaston:

Their great success is a fine exemplification of what Southern brains and energy, devoted to business and consecrated to God, can accomplish. Where such men control you never hear of strikes and mobs among their employees. They not only lift themselves up in the scale of being, but give life to all around and about them. All honor to such noble specimens of the highest type of manhood in our new South. Wherever they plant a mill they plant a church of our God, and thus open the way to better living here and to a brighter life hereafter. May God multiply such men by the thousands all over this sunny land of ours.[6]

5. Editorial, "Cotton Mill Industry of North Carolina," *North Carolina Christian Advocate* (January 15, 1896), p. 1.
6. *Raleigh Christian Advocate* (April 9, 1890), p. 2.

Spokesmen for religious institutions not only praised industrialists but also sanctioned the rise of industry as such. As
early as 1880 Braxton Craven, the president of the largest
Methodist college in North Carolina, publicly dedicated a new
cotton mill to "Almighty God."[7] A Methodist minister present
at the dedication sent the following comment to his denominational paper:

I never saw such a thing in this country before—but I do hope
the example set by this company will be followed by all who succeed them in this bright Southern land. When we, as corporations
and as business men, bring business and religion into daily contact and recognize, formally, our dependence upon divine blessing
for success, we are not likely to fail to realize all.[8]

In the next issue the editor of the paper commended the action
of the founders of the mill in providing employment for so
many women and children, and stated explicitly that capital so
invested should have the divine blessing.[9]

During subsequent years pronouncements from religious bodies sanctioned, almost without exception, the rise of industry in
the region and pointed to the economic advantages resulting.
Religious journals reminded their readers that the cotton mill
workers had larger advantages, better school facilities, more
comfortable housing, more adequate sanitation, and higher income than they had in their previous condition.[10] This general
approval has continued, largely unmodified and unqualified,
down to the present. Criticism of conditions prevailing in the
industry still elicits from ministers in Gaston County a recita-
tion of the advantages brought by the mills to the workers and
the community. A minister in South Carolina expressed this
common feeling more clearly, though hardly more fervidly, than
most of his fellow ministers in a speech made in 1927 which was
widely reprinted in textile magazines:

To those who can read history it is unthinkable that any one fail
to see in it all the hand of God bringing the many thousands from
the bondage imposed upon us by social and economic forces which

7. Hardin, *op. cit.,* p. 51.
8. *Raleigh Christian Advocate* (February 25, 1880), p. 1.
9. Hardin, *op. cit.,* p. 52.   10. *Ibid.,* pp. 64–67.

of ourselves we were powerless to control. . . . It is imperative that we think of Southern industry as a spiritual movement and of ourselves as instruments in a Divine plan. Southern industry is the largest single opportunity the world has ever had to build a democracy upon the ethics of Christianity. . . . Southern industry is to measure the power of Protestantism, unmolested. . . .

Southern industry was pioneered by men possessing the statesmanship of the prophets of God. . . . I personally believe it was God's way for the development of a forsaken people.[11]

Ministers did not confine their approval to speeches and editorials. In a number of instances religious leaders participated personally in the organization and administration of Gaston County mills. Even before 1880 a Baptist preacher in the county had become interested in the industrial development of the region, and in 1873 had begun publication of the *Working Man,* a monthly magazine published in New York City for four years, expressly "to induce manufacturers, mechanics, skilled labor, and capital into the Southern states." To promote this purpose, he maintained an office in New York from 1873 to 1879 and is reported to have done much to attract the attention of Northern capital to Southern possibilities. He persuaded several railroads to offer reduced rates to all settlers coming to the South.[12]

One of the most active promoters of new mills in the period between 1880 and 1900 was a Lutheran minister stationed in the county, who became so interested in textile development that he left the active pastorate in order to devote all his energies to the service of his new enthusiasm. It is reported of another Lutheran minister of the same period that he "was a man much loved by the people of the community, even to the extent of serving as a director of one of the cotton mills."[13]

When opportunity has presented itself, other ministers have followed similar roles in subsequent decades. A Methodist

11. Rev. John W. Speake, "Relation of Church to Industry," published in *Southern Textile Bulletin* (June 23, 1927), pp. 24–25, and in *Textile World* (June 25, 1927), pp. 71–73.

12. Deacon John R. Logan, *Sketches, Historical and Biographical, of the Broad River and King's Mountain Baptist Associations, from 1800 to 1882* (Shelby, N.C., 1887), p. 282.

13. *Gastonia Gazette,* April 9, 1938.

preacher who was pastor of the uptown church in Gastonia for four years, and then presiding elder of that district for four years, made it a practice to organize an industry wherever he went, "for the good of the community." He was instrumental in the organization of several mills in Gaston County, subscribed for stock in several of them, and was regarded as a tower of strength in economic development of the community. That his participation in economic affairs was generally approved is attested by the fact that he was the first and only pastor the Gastonia church ever attempted to retain beyond the customary four-year pastorate.

Comparable action by ministers in the county has appeared recently.[14] The Lutheran minister in Gastonia claims to have instigated the organization of a new hosiery mill there in 1938, reporting proudly, "I have Share No. 5; the officers got the first four." Other Gastonia ministers acknowledge his leadership in this connection. One of the members of the Methodist church subscribed ten shares of stock (par 100; sold at par) for his minister, telling him he wanted him "to be in on it." The minister expressed approval of the project and gratitude for the gift.

In sanctioning the rise of cotton mills, ministers and churches have not been merely pronouncing their blessing upon a *fait accompli*. They have also thereby given impetus to further industrial development. Approval by religious spokesmen of conditions prevailing in the textile industry has been of incalculable service in helping to fend off regulation which might hamper its growth. Religious institutions have been both a source and a sanction of the growth of the mills; in being a sanction, they were also a source. Though public opinion had already been turning away from exclusive reliance for economic welfare on agricultural pursuits, support given by the churches was of

14. Active leadership by ministers in the building of mills has by no means been confined to Gaston County. Several Southern mills grew out of revival meetings, with the evangelist serving as presiding officer and members of his congregation as original stockholders. An evangelist in Salisbury, N.C., proclaimed in the middle 'eighties: "Next to the Grace of God, what Salisbury needs is a cotton mill!" His congregation was "converted" to the idea, and the town got a cotton mill (B. B. Kendrick and A. M. Arnett, *The South Looks at Its Past* [Chapel Hill, 1935], p. 125; see also Broadus Mitchell and George S. Mitchell, *The Industrial Revolution in the South* [Baltimore, 1930], pp. 85–86, for a similar case).

genuine service in crystallizing and extending the new interest in industry. If religious sanction was in part a product of prior economic developments, it was a simultaneous product and a source of further developments along the same line. Certainly it was only one factor in bringing the mills to birth, but few contributions to the growth of industry were of greater importance than the early approval tendered by the churches.

INDIRECT CONTRIBUTIONS

In addition to direct contributions, the churches of Gaston County assisted the growth of the mills through activities more indirect in character, but of equal importance. Typical of these was the part played by the churches in bringing prohibition to the county—an achievement which accelerated the rise of the mills considerably. Almost from the time of settlement, the region embracing Gaston County had an unsavory reputation as a center of distilleries. In 1795 Bishop Asbury wrote in his diary regarding this locality: "My body is weak, and so is my faith for this part of the vineyard. . . . This country improves in cultivation, wickedness, mills, and stills. . . ."[15] A local legend explains a crooked place in the boundary line of the county by the surmise that surveyors went out of their way to go by a still. Advertisements of "corn whiskey" were conspicuous in the earliest editions of the *Gastonia Gazette* in 1880, and for a number of years following. In 1885 the number of licensed distilleries in the county reached forty and a maximum of forty-eight was attained three years later.[16]

Prohibition sentiment had been crystallizing gradually in the churches of the vicinity for several decades. It was by no means unanimous from the outset but had reached virtual unanimity by 1890, and ministers became leaders in a campaign for restrictive legislation. An election in Gastonia township in 1886 resulted in defeat for prohibition, but partial success was achieved a few years later when a Presbyterian minister, irritated by the proximity of several large distilleries to his

15. *The Journal of the Rev. Francis Asbury* (New York, 1821), II, 220. Cf. Clarence W. Griffin, *The History of Old Tryon and Rutherford Counties, 1730–1936* (Asheville, 1937), p. 592. "Mills" referred to sawmills and gristmills.

16. S. H. Hobbs, Jr., *Gaston County: Economic and Social* (Raleigh, 1920), pp. 9–10.

church, organized agitation which secured a law in the North
Carolina legislature prohibiting distilleries within three miles of
certain churches and schools in Gaston County.[17] Further victory was won in 1903 in an enactment by the legislature prohibiting the sale and manufacture of liquors anywhere in the
county. Though small amounts might still be imported, this
legislation dealt a death blow to the industry.

Credit for the eradication of distilleries from the county
should not be given exclusively to the churches. The building
of cotton factories, calling for a steady and dependable supply
of labor and outbidding the liquor business for all available
capital, was also a significant factor. Several pioneer manufacturers were leaders in the fight to make the county dry; one
was a prohibitionist so rabid that he opposed Coca-Cola. Religious leaders introduced an argument for industrial efficiency
into their prohibition propaganda; liquor was denounced as
detrimental to industry and as the "greatest oppressor of the
laboring man."[18]

Attainment of prohibition legislation had several results of
far-reaching significance for the rise of the textile industry in
the county. It provided moral dynamic for the rise of cotton
mills, on the theory that mills displaced distilleries. The building of mills took on the atmosphere of a crusade; the decline of
the whiskey business and the rise of the cotton mills have been
described as "a moral revolution."[19] The two developments occurred in close conjunction; between 1891 and 1900 seventeen
new mills were built in the county, and the number of licensed
distilleries declined from about forty to sixteen. Disappearance
of the whiskey industry also furthered the rise of textile manufacturing through releasing capital; as legislation forced the
discontinuance of distilleries, capital invested in them was
transferred to the building of cotton mills. Most important of
all, the attainment of prohibition helped to discipline textile
workers and to provide a more stable, dependable labor force.

The prohibition fight also had important consequences on the
policies of the churches toward social questions. It taught them

17. *Public Laws of North Carolina, 1899*, p. 882; Mrs. G. A. Sparrow, "The
History of Union Presbyterian Church" (MS. No. 45416 at Montreat Historical Foundation), p. 7.
18. *North Carolina Christian Advocate*, December 18, 1895.
19. Hobbs, Jr., *op cit.*, p. 9; Mitchell and Mitchell, *op. cit.*, p. 177.

to explain poverty and other social ills in terms of drunkenness or personal shortcomings rather than in terms of industrial relations as such. It focused their attention on prohibition as the central social problem, and interest in prohibition legislation became a substitute for nearly all other types of social concern. Prohibition has remained, down to the present time, a social crusade adequate to satisfy the "social conscience" of most Southern churches. Denominational committees for "social service" have been principally concerned with the liquor problem, and have more often than not been called the "Committee on Temperance and Social Service."

The greatest contribution of the churches to the industrial revolution in the South undoubtedly lay in the labor discipline they provided through moral supervision of the workers. From the beginning employers used the churches as vehicles of welfare work and supported church programs, as will be seen, in numerous and substantial ways. The churches, if one may judge by statements of their leaders, were proud of the responsibility entrusted to them, and set out to mold transplanted farmers into stable, contented, sober citizens and industrial workers. Methods used in helping to convert an atomistic assemblage of rural individualists into a disciplined labor force, amenable to a high degree of social control, consisted of the inculcation of personal virtues (stability, honesty, sobriety, industry), provision of a center of community integration other than the mill itself, and emotional escape from the difficulties of life in a mill village. Both as disciplinarian and as safety valve, a village church became a valuable center for the constitution of a new industrial community.

There is no doubt in the minds of employers that churches have succeeded, and still succeed, in providing better workers for the mills. Statements by employers in Gaston County may be taken as representative of employers throughout the brief history of the Southern textile industry. Most of them see no great difference in technical efficiency as between workers who participate in church activities and those who do not. That is, production may be quite as great from an atheist as from a saint, provided the atheist works at his best for the same number of hours as the saint. Managers agree almost unanimously, however, that church members are more stable (a high rate of labor turnover has been one of the most difficult problems the industry has faced) and more dependable (less subject to tardiness or absence from work because of drunkenness, gambling, recuperation from debauches, etc.). They agree, further, that church members are more "reasonable," making less trouble in the mill and in the community.[20] Church members "work together better, and are more coöperative, among themselves and with mill managers, than non-church members." Even if there is no difference between the two groups from the standpoint of industrial production alone, church members are alleged to be better all-round citizens for the mill community. Church membership, to be sure, is generally a mark of integration into community life, as well as a source of such integration. It is, therefore, both a cause and a symptom of the worker's stability, dependability, and docility.

The following direct quotations from mill officials in Gaston County attest to the importance of the role played by the churches in disciplining workers:

The mill feels that the church is for the general good of the community. A worker is a better worker if he attends church. I tell my foremen to watch a man who has stopped attending church, as he will soon show signs of disintegration—and the foremen nearly always report that my warning was correct.[21]

My officials ask every applicant for a job if he or she is a church member. We do not hold it against him if he is not, but find invariably that church members are more dependable workers. That is, they do not get drunk, etc. We had one worker who was absolutely no good. He got religion and is a much better worker now.[22]

Belonging to a church, and attending it, make a man a better worker. It makes him more complacent—no, that's not the word.

20. This fact might be interpreted, from the angle of church influence, as due to the instillation of humility as a Christian virtue, or as a result of disciplinary training imposed by the corporate life of the church, or as consequent upon the diverting of attention, through religious services with otherworldly orientation, from immediate troubles and sources of dissatisfaction.

21. Mill Superintendent D. D, Interview, September 3, 1938. Mr. D asks applicants for jobs whether or not they attend church, and gives preference to churchgoers. He personally notices absences from church on the part of individual workers and reminds the absentees of their negligence.

22. Mill Owner G. G, Interview, July 28, 1939. A Jew himself, Mr. G believes wholeheartedly in providing Christian churches for his workers.

It makes him more resigned—that's not the word either, but you get the general idea. It is good practice in resignation even to sit through most of the sermons you hear! A churchman is more reasonable; he does not "fly off the handle" as easily, but sits down quietly and figures things out. A churchman is also more law-abiding. We think the churches are vital to our community and to our mill.[23]

Eighty-five per cent of our industrial accidents occur on Monday morning. People who loaf over the week end, instead of going to church Sunday morning and Sunday night, eat too much, get drunk, wear themselves out in gadding about, and as a result are not at their best for production until Tuesday morning. Non-church members would be as good producers as church members, if they took care of themselves—but, on the average, they don't take care of themselves as well. I base this observation on ten years of experience with various types of workers.[24]

These comments are typical of many others that might be given. In reply to a questionnaire sent to mill executives by the Southern Combed Yarn Spinners Association on behalf of the writer, a unanimous answer in the affirmative was given to the question, "Do you think church members are better workers, on the average, than nonchurch members?"[25] The churches have afforded "a balance wheel," to use an expression common in the county, for the steady development of industry.

REASONS FOR SUPPORT OF MILLS BY CHURCHES

In one sense, the problem as to why churches and religious leaders supported the rise of a new type of economic life in Gaston County is beyond the scope of descriptive analysis. It is

23. Mill Executive C. C, Interview, September 5, 1938. Note the double standard of judgment in most of these quotations: community welfare and better workmanship. The institution of the mill village tends to make these two standards largely identical in the Southern textile industry.

24. Mill Superintendent J, Interview, September 12, 1939.

25. The Southern Combed Yarn Spinners Association is a manufacturers' organization, successor to the Gaston County Textile Manufacturers' Association. It includes in its membership all mills in Gaston County producing combed yarns—about 65 in number. The questionnaires received poor quantitative response, probably because most of the questions called for information generally kept secret. Of some 50 questionnaires sent out, 8 replies were secured, representing 13 mills employing about 5,000 workers. This questionnaire will be referred to hereinafter as *Questionnaire to Mills,* 1939.

inescapable, however, if a serious attempt to test various theories of the relation of religion and economics is envisioned. Those who interpret religion solely as a sanction of the status quo, for example, would find it difficult to explain the sudden transfer of religious sanction from an agricultural economy to an industrial one, when the transfer occurred simultaneously with the rise of the first mills; they would expect at least a brief time lag. Those who hold, on the other hand, that a new religious impulse underlay the industrial revolution in the South are faced with the problem of explaining the roots of this new religious impulse. It may be pertinent, therefore, to probe more deeply into psychological factors operating in the period of transition.

There is no doubt that Southern churches sanctioned the type of economy prevailing in the Southern states before the Civil War. Actions of various church bodies are unequivocal and unambiguous on that score. As early as 1835, the Broad River Baptist Association, including churches in Gaston County, repudiated the pamphleteering activities of Abolitionists, looking "with indignation and contempt on such efforts to disturb the best interests and peace of our country."[26] At least a hundred books were written by noted Southern divines to justify slavery. Churches and religious leaders pretended to be interested only in the spiritual state of masters and slaves, without concern for the institutional structures in which master and slave found themselves. Their interest passed quickly, nevertheless, into defense of the system as a system, and especially during the Civil War. In 1863 the committee charged with drawing up a "Narrative of the State of Religion" reported to the General Assembly of the Presbyterian Church in the Confederate States of America:

We are glad to note a growing interest in *the religious instruction of our colored population.* We believe that more is done for their spiritual interests now than at any former period. Our ministers generally regard them as a portion of their flocks. There are few churches in the South wholly destitute of this interesting class of worshippers; and most of our larger churches embrace a considerable number of our slaves among their members. . . . The best

26. Griffin, *op. cit.,* p. 588.

vindication of our system of domestic servitude is the generous provision of masters for the temporal and spiritual well-being of their servants, and the faithful, affectionate, and grateful service of those who enjoy their protection and care.[27]

In 1864, a similar report to the same body affirmed even more strongly than before:

We hesitate not to affirm that it is the peculiar mission of the Southern Church to conserve the institution of slavery, and to make it a blessing both to master and slave. We could not, if we would, yield up these four millions of immortal beings to the dictates of fanaticism and to the menaces of military power. . . .[28]

When the war had been lost, the General Assembly appeared to retract its endorsement of the system as a system, though still denouncing the fanatics who had overthrown it:

We would have it distinctly understood that in our ecclesiastical capacity, we are neither the friends nor the foes of slavery; that is to say, we have no commission either to propagate or abolish it. The policy of its existence, or non-existence, is a question which exclusively belongs to the State. . . . Our business is with the duties which spring from the relation: the duties of the masters on the one hand, and of their slaves on the other. These duties we are to proclaim and enforce with spiritual sanctions. . . . The Church has as much right to preach to the monarchies of Europe, and the despotisms of Asia, the doctrines of republican equality, as to preach to the governments of the South the extirpation of slavery.

.   .   .   .   .   .

The lawfulness of the relation [master-slave] as a question of social morality, and of scriptural truth, has lost nothing of its importance. When we solemnly declare to you, brethren, that the dogma which asserts the inherent sinfulness of this relation is unscriptural and fanatical; that it is condemned not only by the word of God, but by the voice of the church in all ages; that it is one of the most pernicious heresies of modern times; that its

27. *Minutes of the General Assembly of the Presbyterian Church in the Confederate States of America, 1863*, p. 158.
  28. *Ibid., 1864*, pp. 291–294.

countenance by any church, is a just cause of separation from it [I Timothy 6. 1–5], we have surely said enough to warn you away from this insidious error, as from a fatal shore.[29]

Nor is there any doubt that Southern churches remained conservative in economic views after the Civil War. Many observers have contended that the churches have been the strongest forces in maintaining a spirit of isolation and in idealizing ante bellum civilization in the region; the Southern churches, it is said, have never been reconstructed.[30] The institution of slavery had been legally dissolved, however, and it was necessary to find new structural forms for the organization of economic life. The desperate plight of the region after the Civil War virtually compelled the churches to share in the quest, if they themselves were to survive. Their profession of relative indifference to social structure facilitated the transfer of religious sanction from an economy which had been overthrown to a new one beginning to emerge.

The sanction given textile entrepreneurs and the rising textile industry by the churches was not based purely on moral and religious grounds, but also on definite economic advantages to be gained. From Revolutionary days, religious leaders in Gaston County had recognized the value of industrial enterprises to the community. After the victory at King's Mountain, at the edge of Gaston County, a deacon had led the devout Lutheran and Presbyterian soldiers in a prayer of thanksgiving in which, among other things, he said: "O Lord, we thank Thee for this victory, but should have been even more grateful to Thee, if Thou hadst not let the enemy destroy Bill Hill's iron works."[31] As industry achieved an increasingly important place in the life of the county after 1880, the churches profited immediately in all numerical and material respects.[32] They grew in membership, in value of equipment, and in money available for the support of church programs. Pastors' salaries increased rapidly. Only a superhuman disregard of material considerations

29. *Minutes of the General Assembly of the Presbyterian Church in the United States, 1865*, p. 385.
30. For example, E. DeForest Leach, "The Old Churches in the New South," *The Christian Century*, XLVI, 1277–1279 (October 16, 1929).
31. *Visions Old and New: A Historical Pageant* (Gastonia, 1924), p. 87.
32. See chap. iii.

could have prevented the ministers and churches from regarding the rise of the mills as a divine blessing.

Two other considerations deserve notice. There was general rejoicing among ministers and churchmen in the county when it became apparent that the rise of the textile industry would mean the virtual displacement of the liquor industry. This rejoicing was widespread among church folk during the 1880's and 1890's, according to older citizens. Another factor, almost decisive in character, was the fact that builders of the early cotton mills were leading churchmen, able to control to large degree the attitudes and actions of churches and ministers. Most pressures on the churches took the form of statements concerning the "good of the community," "the moral welfare of mill operatives," "the improvement of life gained through advantages offered in mill villages," and the like. For such purposes the support of the churches was quickly won.

In summary, religious institutions assisted the rise of new economic institutions by creating opinion favorable to industry and to industrialists, by occasional direct action on the part of religious leaders in the organization of mills, and by helping to mold a more effective labor force. There is no evidence that the churches restrained or hindered the growth of the mills in any way. To the contrary, they provided one source and an important sanction of that growth. Their own views and activities in this connection were to some degree a product of economic forces, but became apparent almost simultaneously with the changes in the economic realm. Neither the religious nor the economic factor was strictly or completely determinative of the other, insofar as the changes in economic foundations were concerned. Of the six types of interrelationship theoretically possible, three are applicable to the part played by religious institutions in the growth of economic institutions in Gaston County: the churches represented a source of economic change and a sanction of the type of economic institution which resulted, while their own role was partly a product of economic change.

CHAPTER III

THE ROLE OF THE MILLS IN THE GROWTH OF THE CHURCHES

It would not be necessary to convince anybody in Gaston County that the growth of the churches there has been closely related to the growth of the mills. Residents recognize, and have done so since 1900, that all aspects of their common life have been tremendously influenced by the development of the textile industry, and are now directly dependent upon that industry for foundation and sustenance. The problem involved is that of delineating spheres and defining types of relations in which this dependence has become operative. Mills have contributed to the growth of the churches both directly and indirectly.

Direct Contributions

The background of direct support of churches by mills is found in the general traditions of paternalism which have prevailed in the Southern textile industry from the beginning. Some of the mills were built in rural locations in order to obtain water power, adequate space on cheap land, lower taxes, and other advantages. It was necessary, therefore, for the employer to furnish nearly all the facilities for the maintenance of his workers, including houses, stores, schools, and often a mill-paid deputy sheriff. The new workers, imported from poverty to the mill villages, were in no position to finance the construction of churches themselves; it was imperative that the mills should contribute largely to this purpose, if churches were to be built. Direct solicitation of mill owners and executives by denominational officials, seeking to extend the work of their particular denominations in the rising mill villages, confirmed this necessity.

The unquestionable church loyalty of the mill builders was also an important factor underlying organization and construction of churches. Most textile pioneers gave time as well as money toward the development of religious institutions in their villages; they were frequently the prime movers in the organization of Sunday Schools and congregations, the importation of preachers, and the erection of church buildings. In the very earliest days the mill executives often lived in the mill villages, and in contributing to the building of a church were helping to provide a place of worship for themselves as for their workers.

Direct financial contributions from mills as corporate entities have been made, for the most part, to churches located in the mill villages themselves, or on the fringes of them.[1] Nearly every mill in Gaston County has donated one or more lots for the erection of churches, and has given appreciable percentages of the costs of construction. Conversely, there are practically no mill churches in Gaston County that were not partially built by mills in their vicinity. The following items indicate the types of help given by mills:

An official of the Loray Mill "voluntarily offered for the mill company to give dollar for dollar for all funds raised by the First Presbyterian Church of Gastonia" toward the erection of a Presbyterian church in the Loray village.[2]

The owner of three mills in the neighborhood helped build a Baptist church, finished in 1919, worth $18,000. He also paid rent on a parsonage for the minister for several months after the church was organized.[3]

The McAdenville Baptist Church was organized in 1886, after the proprietor of the mills there had brought in a Baptist preacher to hold services in his village.[4]

A Presbyterian church was erected in one of the mill villages by the First Presbyterian Church of Gastonia, but on completion of the building the family and a business associate of one of the early

1. These churches will hereinafter be called "mill churches." The contributions of mills to rural and uptown churches have been chiefly indirect in character, though nonetheless important.
2. "History of West Avenue Presbyterian Church" (1938), MS. No. 49972 at Montreat Historical Foundation.
3. Luther Hawkins, "History of South Marietta Street Baptist Church" (1929). MS. in Library of Wake Forest College.
4. "History of the McAdenville Baptist Church" (c. 1930). MS. in Library of Wake Forest College.

mill builders asked to assume the entire cost as a memorial—a cost totaling $20,000. The request was granted.[5]

In 1902, several representatives of the company then building the Loray Mill called on the Bishop at Belmont, and requested him to build a Catholic church in the city of Gastonia, assuring him that if he did so, many skilled workers of the Catholic faith would be induced to move from the textile sections of New England and would be employed in the Loray Mill. This they said would insure the founding of a self-supporting parish.[6]

A brick church costing $20,000 was built in a mill village in 1923, and a parsonage costing $6,000, with the mill contributing a total of $10,000 to these buildings.[7]

Many other examples might be given.[8]

Mill owners, under such circumstances, obviously controlled to large degree the growth of churches as to number, denomination, and location. Because they owned all the property in the villages, their consent was necessary before any church could be established in the new industrial communities. Owners of several mills in the same neighborhood often limited the number of churches to be erected, and deliberately planned their location, in order to avoid duplication of buildings and denominations. Mill owners in South Gastonia, where fourteen mills were erected within a few years, specified that a Baptist church

5. *Gastonia Gazette,* "History of the First Presbyterian Church," January 15, 1938.

6. *Ibid.,* "History of St. Michael's Catholic Church," March 19, 1938. The church was built, but very few Catholic workers have come to the county.

7. Bertha Carl Hipp, "A Gaston County Cotton Mill and Its Community" (M.A. thesis, University of North Carolina, 1930), p. 87.

8. In reply to the *Questionnaire to Mills,* 1939 (see above), eight Gaston County mill corporations reported that they had helped to build thirteen churches and had donated six sites. A list of 161 churches erected by cotton mills either in part or entirely, in South Carolina, is contained in August Kohn, *The Cotton Mills of South Carolina* (Columbia, S.C., 1907), pp. 148–149. By 1902 the 65 cotton mills of that state had spent $90,000 for church buildings; it was estimated in 1929 that the church buildings reworked and built in the preceding five years in South Carolina mill villages could not be duplicated without industrial subsidy for less than $400,000 (R. W. Spears, "The Attitude of the Southern Methodists of South Carolina in regard to the Textile Industry in South Carolina" [B.D. thesis, Duke University, 1936], pp. 50, 83). Subsidies similar to those depicted in these figures would probably hold for Gaston County and for the entire textile region in the two Carolinas.

should be placed at the southern end of the settlement and a Methodist church at the northern end. When a fissure appeared in the Baptist church after a few years, and a group of members withdrew to build another Baptist church in the vicinity, the mills withheld all support from the schismatic group, regarding it as a renegade from the original plan.

Textile manufacturers contributed not only to the establishment of churches in their mill villages but also to the erection of handsome churches uptown. Nearly every uptown church in the county included in its membership several textile manufacturers, who were major factors in the building of pretentious church edifices. Mill owners have contributed also to the building of occasional rural churches, though such assistance has been more sporadic in character than support of mill and uptown churches.

Having assisted in the erection of church buildings, the mills began also to contribute to the current expenses of church operation. Statistics on their contributions to current expenses, which usually have taken the form of direct, semisecret supplements to ministers' salaries, are not available for the past, and are very difficult to obtain for the present. The mills have consistently refused to allow their subsidies to be reported to parent ecclesiastical bodies because, they say, such support might need to be withdrawn at any time, and mill workers might rely too heavily upon mill contributions instead of supporting the churches themselves. Ministers, on the other hand, are wary of giving the sources of their income, especially since there has been some criticism of them as "paid agents of the mills." Contributions by mills to the salaries of pastors are made directly; that is, a check is mailed to the minister or he calls personally at the office of the mill. In the case of the Methodist churches, the amount forthcoming from the mills is specified for a year in advance, and is about the same from year to year. The district superintendent of the Methodist churches calls on the mills at least once each year to secure renewal of their contributions. In addition to this regular visit, he goes to various mill owners for extra sums whenever needed, and generally gets them.

It is common knowledge that mills have subsidized ministers from the very earliest days. Information available concerning the extent of this practice at present may be taken as fairly representative, in proportion to the number of mills and churches involved, of its prevalence during recent years. The sources of the salaries of Methodist ministers in the county in 1938 are revealed in full in Table I. Of twenty pastoral charges, eleven of which were mill charges, six received direct help from mills on the pastor's salary and four received subsidies of other types, such as provision of a parsonage. Gifts from mills comprised only 6 per cent of the total amount received by Methodist pastors in the county, but accounted for 20 per cent of the total amount received by the ministers to whom subsidies were given.

TABLE I

CONTRIBUTIONS BY MILLS TO CURRENT EXPENSES OF METHODIST CHURCHES IN GASTON COUNTY, 1938

| Pastoral Charge Number | Sources of Pastor's Salary | | | |
	Congregation	Mills	Missionary Funds	Other Support from Mills
1	$ 2,400			
2	1,200		$ 300	
3	1,500			
4	1,700			
5	189			
6	1,150	$ 750		Parsonage and $50 gift to minister at Christmas
7	1,500	150		
8	2,500			Water and light
9	1,200	200	100	
10	4,250			
11	1,300	204	150	Parsonage
12	1,500	200		$200 from mill superintendent, personally
13	1,050	300	150	
14	2,000			Parsonage
15	1,800			
16	362			
17	272		300	
18	2,250			
19	1,250		200	
20	368			
TOTALS	$29,741	$1,804	$1,200	

Ministers of other denominations apparently receive less support directly from the mills than the Methodist ministers, though the difficulty of obtaining information renders conclusions somewhat tentative. Probably not more than two Baptist ministers (out of thirty-five) receive a direct subsidy as a matter of regular practice. Three of the Baptist ministers are provided with parsonages by the mills, and several churches receive coal, lights, water, etc. A number of them doubtless obtain occasional gifts from mills; as one admitted, "the mill owner slips me a little on the side when I want to take a trip or something." No Presbyterian church in the county receives assistance on current expenses from the mills at present; several have done so at intervals in the past. The same generalization would hold for Lutheran and Episcopal churches. Failure of these denominations to receive support is due principally to the relative absence of mill churches among them. Nor have the mills contributed to any significant extent to the salaries of preachers of the newer Holiness and Pentecostal sects, though, like roving evangelists, these ministers receive occasional handouts from mill offices. The system of regular contributions has been worked out most fully by the Methodist churches and probably roots in the activities of district superintendents attempting to regularize salaries in order to make annual ministerial appointments.[9]

Although the paternalistic and village systems in Gaston County have been breaking up slowly since about 1925, subsidies to churches have remained almost unchanged. Almost no new mill houses have been built since 1925, and elaborate welfare services maintained by many of the mills during the 1920's were severely truncated during the 1930's. Serious question is being raised at the present time by textile executives as to the

9. At least two Methodist bodies have openly requested larger contributions from mills to the support of churches in the mill villages. In 1910 the South Carolina Annual Conference, pointing out that "the properly manned church is a commercial as well as moral asset of the mills," adopted a resolution urging mill administrations to appropriate proportionate amounts to the salaries of ministers in their villages, and appointed a commission to confer with the Manufacturers' Association of South Carolina on the matter (Spears, *op. cit.*, pp. 53–54). The Western North Carolina Annual Conference, to which Methodist churches in Gaston County belong, adopted a resolution in 1929 calling on textile manufacturers to pay at least one half of the expense of maintaining religious worship in their mill villages.

economic feasibility of subsidies to workers in view of Social
Security legislation and of the failure, under the Fair Labor
Standards Act, to allow for a wage differential between the
Northern and Southern branches of the industry. An increasing number of employers believe that all mill contributions to
employee welfare should be directed into wage and Social Security payments, both for the benefit of the employees and
for the economic welfare of the mills. Little question has
been raised, however, concerning continuation of support to
churches. Methodist churches receiving direct help from mills
were approximately the same in number and in amounts received in 1938 as in 1929. In the Southern textile industry generally, assistance given to churches has remained practically
unchanged.[10] Support of churches is one of the most persistent
holdovers from the direct subsidy system. It is probable, nevertheless, that the larger trend away from such practice will
eventually bring discontinuance.

GENERAL CORRELATION IN GROWTH OF MILLS AND CHURCHES

In addition to direct patronage of the churches, mills in Gaston
County influenced the growth of religious institutions by providing a general background of population growth and economic expansion. In 1880 the county contained 5 mills, the
total white population was 10,188, and the total value of all industrial products of the county was $844,308.[11] In 1930 the
county had 102 mills and a white population of 65,701, and its
industrial products in 1929 were valued at $69,083,052.[12] This
rapid industrial transformation wrought profound changes in
other social structures, including religious organizations.

Industrial expansion was reflected more precisely in the
growth of church membership than in the erection of new
church buildings. Though the building of churches was tremendously affected by the construction of mills, and the num-

10. Cf. Frank T. DeVyver, "Southern Textile Mills Revisited," *The Southern
Economic Journal*, IV, 466–473 (April, 1938)—a report on paternalistic practices in fifty-six Southern mills in 1938.

11. *Tenth Census of the United States, 1880:* "Manufactures," II, 158. Cotton
goods products accounted for $393,170 of the total.

12. *Fifteenth Census of the United States, 1930:* "Manufactures, 1929," III,
389. Cotton goods products were valued at $61,927,806.

ber of each increased rapidly in each decade up to 1930 (as indicated in Table II), the correlation in growth has been rather loose. Growth in church membership, however, has fol-

TABLE II

COMPARATIVE GROWTH OF MILLS AND CHURCHES IN GASTON COUNTY, 1880–1939*

	Number of Mills in Operation	Number of Active Churches
1880	5	41
1890	10	60
1900	27	78
1910	48	98
1920	90	109
1930	102	121
1939	100	145

* This table is foundational to most of those that follow, in that statistics have been collected for individual mills and individual churches known, from careful research, to have been in existence in the county on the decennial years. This procedure has yielded figures considerably more trustworthy in character than the statistics for the county as a whole to be found in general census reports, including those of the *U. S. Census of Religious Bodies.*

For a detailed description of the methodology and sources of the statistical studies contained in this volume, the reader is referred to the original manuscript deposited in the Sterling Memorial Library of Yale University.

lowed closely upon opportunities for employment afforded by the mills, as evidenced in Table III. Correlation has been fairly close between general increase in employment in the mills, total white population, and church membership, though the rates of increase have varied widely as between them. Divergence has been growing wider, especially since 1920; as employment in the mills increased, providing a basic source of livelihood for an increased population, there was a general proliferation of other economic activities capable of supporting an even larger population.

The industrialization of the county brought new opportunities and new problems with respect to growth in church membership. Gaston County was seventy-second in size (363 square miles) and third in density of population (215.1 persons per square mile) among the one hundred counties of North Caro-

TABLE III

COMPARISON OF GROWTH OF MILL EMPLOYMENT, POPULATION,
AND CHURCH MEMBERSHIP IN GASTON COUNTY,
1880–1938*

	Number of Employees of Mills†	Total White Population‡	Number of White Church Members§	Per cent of Total White Population in Churches
1880	352	10,188	3,690	36.2
1890	640	12,927	5,520	42.7
1900		20,661	8,362	40.5
1910	5,808	28,561	13,034	45.6
1920	12,708	42,014	18,639	44.4
1930	16,991	65,701	27,225	41.4
1938	19,805	72,061	35,670	49.5

* Statistics in this table have been gathered in terms of the individual mills and churches represented in Table II. Where figures were not available for all individual units, the average of those available—always a large majority of the total—has been multiplied by the total number of mills or churches known to have been active at the time. No special circumstances have appeared to vitiate the element of estimate thereby involved.

† Derived from data in the respective Federal censuses, the annual reports of the North Carolina Department of Labor, reports of the Southern Combed Yarn Spinners Association and the Gastonia Chamber of Commerce, L. L. Polk's *Hand Book of North Carolina* (Raleigh, 1879), and Levi Branson's *North Carolina Agricultural Almanac*, 1890. The number of employees in mills in the county has increased greatly under the stimulus of national defense production since 1939; a census taken by the Gastonia Chamber of Commerce at the beginning of 1941 placed the total at 24,323.

The number of Negro employees of the mills has always been so infinitesimal that its inclusion in employment figures does not modify comparability with other figures for whites only.

‡ Compiled from the respective Federal censuses, except for the figure for 1938, which is based on the proportionate percentage of the increase from 1930 to 1940.

§ Based on figures reported by individual churches to parent ecclesiastical bodies.

lina in 1930.[13] Relatively high concentration of population would presumably enable the churches to reach people more easily than in sparsely settled areas. Other factors, however, have probably tended to retard the growth of church membership: a high rate of illiteracy, low income levels, and fairly high rates of tenancy in the rural areas and of transiency among em-

13. In 1940 it was fifth in density of population (244.5 persons per square mile).

ployees of the mills. In any event, the percentage of the white population enrolled as church members has remained approximately the same for the last fifty years (Table III). The figure for 1930, 41.4 per cent, was twenty points below the percentage for the Southeast as a whole in 1926, indicating that the ratio of church membership has fallen behind in the most highly industrialized county in the region.[14] This lower ratio may represent only a temporary lag, to be accounted for by inability of the churches to absorb the rapidly increasing population, as the rising ratio since 1930 suggests.

The county differs from the usual Southern picture also in the average membership of its churches. In 1926 the average congregation in the Southeast contained 137 persons, as contrasted with an average of 235 members for each church edifice in the United States.[15] The average membership in Gaston County in 1930 was 225, which suggests that a higher degree of industrialization, along with associated factors, has brought the county more nearly in line with the nation as a whole in this respect than is true of most of its neighbors.

The churches grew not only in membership but also in wealth as the mills developed. If growth in the number of spindles in place in the county is taken as an index of the ability of the mills to produce economic wealth,[16] close correlation results between this factor and growth in the average value of church property, the average salary paid to pastors, and the average total of money raised per annum by the churches.[17] As spindles

14. The regional and national figures are from Howard W. Odum, *Southern Regions of the United States* (Chapel Hill, 1936), p. 141.

15. *Ibid.*, p. 143.

16. No figures are available for the entire period since 1880 on profits of the mills, wages received, the total value of products manufactured, or capital actually invested in the mills during each decade. Growth in spindles is, therefore, the best available index for the growth of the power of mills to create economic wealth. It is not presented here as a completely adequate index of economic development, but as a central and basic one. Technological changes have not disturbed the reliability of the index, except to some degree since 1927. See Boris Stern, *Effects of Mechanical Changes in the Cotton-Textile Industry, 1910 to 1936* (Washington, 1937, Bureau of Labor Statistics, Serial No. R.612), pp. 12–13, for description of technological change in spinning, and Angeline Bouchard, "An Analysis of the Southern Combed Sales Yarn Industry, 1928–1938" (M.A. thesis, Columbia University, 1938), pp. 59–84, for description of the technological efficiency of Gaston County mills.

17. The correlation holds for absolute growth, not for rate of growth, as the churches had a much larger base line in 1880 than the mills.

increased, the wealth of the churches increased (Table IV). The average value of church property per church increased forty-threefold as between 1880 and 1938, the average salary paid to its pastor by each church in 1938 was nine times as large as in 1880, and the average total of money raised per annum by the churches was more than ten times as great in 1938 as in 1880.

The economic expansion of the county has made its churches much richer than churches in the Southeast in general. The

TABLE IV

COMPARATIVE GROWTH OF NUMBER OF SPINDLES AND WEALTH OF CHURCHES IN GASTON COUNTY, 1880–1938

		Average Wealth per Church†		
	Total Spindles in Place*	Value of Property	Salary Paid‡	Total Money Raised
1880	13,332	$ 575	$ 131	
1890	47,540	829	153	$ 293
1900	197,166	1,766	230	669
1910	459,480	4,194	420	591
1920	1,023,114	10,420	807	4,101
1930	1,481,079	26,224	1,140	3,464
1938	1,342,464	24,923	1,207	3,081

* Compiled in terms of individual mills from statistics in textile directories, chiefly the *Official American Textile Directory.*

† Based on figures reported by individual churches to parent ecclesiastical bodies.

‡ Does not include estimated value of rent for parsonages, or supplements to salaries from missionary funds or from mills. This column is not to be interpreted as depicting what the ministers received, but only what the average church paid; many of the ministers have served more than one church at a time, and income from perquisites is not included here.

average value of church houses in North Carolina in 1926 was $8,564; in Gaston County in 1930, the average value of church property per church was $26,224. Erection of more expensive church buildings in the county followed the fortunes of the textile industry, the two most significant periods of church building coming immediately after the two principal advances in the building of cotton mills. Rapid growth in the number of mills from 1890 to 1900 was followed by a period of church building and remodeling from 1900 to 1905, and the expansion of industry during the war years was followed by another period of church building from 1920 to 1924, during which churches in Gastonia alone spent more than half-a-million dollars in new construction.

Ministers also shared in the increasing economic affluence. The average salary paid per church to pastors in 1880 was $131; in 1938 it had reached a high of $1,207. Growth in the ability of churches to pay larger salaries has resulted in a larger amount of pastoral service for most of them. In 1880, only one or two churches in the county had preaching on more than one Sunday each month; each minister served from four to eight different churches.[18] A Gaston County minister reported, optimistically, to the Baptist State Convention of North Carolina in that year: "I am glad to report our church is self-sustaining. The brethren hope by next year to have preaching two Sundays in the month."[19] As late as 1897 the First Baptist Church of Gastonia was the only church of its denomination in the county that had preaching every Sunday.[20] Similar conditions prevailed in all other denominations. In 1938, by way of contrast, only two Baptist ministers in the county, of a total of thirty-five, served more than one church. Comparable concentration of pastoral service has taken place in the other religious denominations. As the average size of the congregations has grown and the wealth of the county has increased, ministers have been enabled to focus their attention upon a single parish, and churches have been able to afford full-time pastoral service.

The average total of money raised by Gaston churches has varied considerably as between the decennial years, principally because of the two periods of building activity noted above. The churches have had larger incomes by far than the average for the Southeast; they averaged $3,464 in 1930, as compared with an average expenditure of $1,749 by Southeastern churches reporting to the 1926 Census.[21] They surpassed in 1938 the average for American churches as a whole, with an

18. *Gastonia Gazette,* June 26, 1880.
19. *Minutes of the Fiftieth Annual Meeting of the Baptist State Convention of North Carolina* (Raleigh, 1880), p. 21.
20. Statistical tables in the *Minutes of the King's Mountain Baptist Association, 1897,* and the *Minutes of the South Fork Baptist Association, 1897.*
21. Regional figure from Odum, *op. cit.,* p. 145.

average expenditure of $3,081 as compared with an average of
$2,214 for the nation.[22]

The churches of the county expanded in other respects, in
rough proportion as the mills grew. Enrollment in Sunday
Schools, contributions to foreign missions and to home missions,
the number of organizations functioning per church, the total
amount contributed to benevolences—all expanded as the textile industry expanded, and in fairly close correlation.[23] In providing a background of opportunity, as well as in direct patronage, the mills contributed immensely to the development of religious institutions in their vicinity.

22. The national figure was computed from H. C. Weber, ed., *Yearbook of
American Churches* (Elmhurst, 1939).

23. The writer studied all these factors statistically, but has omitted tables
depicting their growth, as they seem relatively less important than those already described.

CHAPTER IV

THE EMERGENCE OF SOCIAL CLASSES[1]

THE development of industry not only brought general expansion of population and economic wealth to Gaston County; it also helped to create striking internal distinctions along occupational, residential, educational, and attitudinal lines. The only distinctions of any considerable importance in 1880 were those between white and Negro. Other divisions in the population, including political and theological disagreement, were not based on economic and social stratification; social classes did not exist in any clearly identifiable form. Most of the white residents of the county were small farmers, and were on approximately equal economic footing. Tenant farmers, about 40 per cent as numerous as farm owners, were regarded as somewhat inferior, and the handful of merchants and professional men as somewhat superior. Descendants of early settlers were, in general, better established than newcomers, and veterans of the Civil War carried a certain aura. Economic lines of demarcation were vague, however, and had relatively little influence on the internal organization of the county. The equality of rural poverty which had characterized colonial America lived on in Gaston County, as in many other sections of the country.

The industrial revolution brought to the county, as it had to other regions, the overthrow of agriculture as the prevailing mode of economic life, an increasing urbanization of occupation and of culture, and the emergence of distinct social classes. Many of the patterns which had worked themselves out earlier in England and New England were recapitulated at accelerated speed. Almost before residents of the county knew what had happened—and many of them are still "old-fashioned" and confused—they found themselves in a context of new social relations created by the rise of industry, towns, and wealth.

Three social classes have emerged, clearly separated in geo-

1. The term "social class" has many prejudicial connotations and is used here only because no satisfactory substitute is available. The terms "social group" and "cultural type" are sometimes used instead, but are equally unsatisfactory.

graphic, economic, and cultural terms.[2] There are the small farmers and tenant farmers, fundamentally dependent on agriculture for a livelihood, though sometimes verging toward part-time industrial employment. There are the mill workers, whose occupational ties with their agricultural background have been almost completely severed. Lastly, there is the group which may be classified as "uptown"[3] in occupation and general culture; corresponding to the bourgeoisie of earlier commercial and industrial revolutions, it is composed chiefly of mill owners and managers, professional and commercial groups, white-collar workers, schoolteachers, independent skilled artisans, and the like. Though there is a measure of mobility between these three classes, the lines between them are rather sharply drawn at present. Even a superficial observer can generally see the geographical line of demarcation between "uptown" and a mill village on the periphery, and the distinction is equally clear between a mill village and its surrounding countryside. Natives can see, with equal clarity, the lines of cultural differentiation which separate the social classes.

Relative numerical strength of these classes is difficult to ascertain and can be only approximated. The Census of Manufactures for 1929 reported a total of 18,444 industrial wage earners (average for the year) in the county, 16,991 of whom were in cotton goods industries. Dividing the latter figure by 1.94, the average number of workers per mill family in Gaston County at that time,[4] and multiplying the quotient by 4.72, the average size of mill families in the county,[5] a figure of 43,338 results as an approximation of the total mill population.[6] The total white rural-farm population in 1930 was 10,575. Sub-

2. The Negro population is not taken into account in the analysis that follows. It constitutes a fourth type of population group, with the race factor as crucial. Its peculiar problems lie largely beyond the purview of the present volume.

3. Rather than "urban." As will become evident, categories of "rural" and "urban" do not coincide neatly with those of economic stratification.

4. J. J. Rhyne, *Some Southern Cotton Mill Workers and Their Villages* (Chapel Hill, 1930), p. 84. This book summarizes data from a study of 500 mill families in Gaston County in 1926–27.

5. *Ibid.*, p. 78.

6. This estimate is corroborated by estimates of mill managers to the North Carolina Department of Labor and Printing (*Report, 1925–26*, pp. 44–49), which indicated that approximately 45,000 people in Gaston County at that time were directly dependent on the cotton mills for a livelihood. A study made

tracting these two groups and a Negro population totaling 12,392 from the total population, 78,093, a resultant of 11,788 may be taken to cover, roughly, the uptown population in 1930. Of the white population, then, about 66 per cent was composed of mill workers and their families, 16 per cent of farm families, and 18 per cent of uptown people.

Class formation appears to have rooted largely in economic changes, and especially in the emergence of wide differences in occupational status. Differences in ability and other personal characteristics, if they can be correlated at all with class rank, have been operative within a more basic context provided by economic developments. Social classes appeared, by and large, in proportion as division of labor, and wide disparities in wealth attendant on it, came with industrialization. Even in recent years, when many secondary features have become associated with each social class, the primary test of class status remains that of occupation. One's job is, in most cases, the principal nexus between an individual and the social niche occupied by him and his family.

THE DECLINE OF RURAL DOMINANCE

When the industrialization of the Piedmont section of the South first began, many Southerners urged that the region should attempt to build a dual agrarian-industrial economy, with development in agriculture keeping pace with the growth of industry. It was felt that the best agrarian traditions of the region could be retained alongside the new cotton mills, and that farmers might share proportionately in a new prosperity. This social philosophy became semiofficial in many communities, and is reflected in many of the present-day writings of Southerners. A recent analysis of the Southeastern region pointed out that Gaston County, taken as a whole, "represents one of the greatest concentrations of cotton textile manufacturing in the country; yet Gaston remains predominantly a rural county."[7] The South, it is said, is principally agrarian, has al-

by a Gastonia service club in 1940 indicated that 73 per cent of the persons employed in Gastonia were employed by the mills.

7. Gerald W. Johnson, *The Wasted Land* (Chapel Hill, 1938), p. 37. Cf. R. D. W. Connor, "The Rehabilitation of a Rural Commonwealth," *The American Historical Review*, XXXVI, 44–62 (October, 1930).

ways been so, and will probably remain so, despite the extensive rise of industry.

The choice of Gaston County as an exhibit of the balanced solution of agricultural and industrial development is rather unfortunate, counting too heavily on the fact that a majority of the population (62.9 per cent in 1940) is classified as "rural" under the standards of the Federal census. Even in

TABLE V

RURAL AND URBAN POPULATION OF GASTON COUNTY, 1900–1940

	1900	Per cent	1910	Per cent	1920	Per cent	1930	Per cent	1940	Per cent
Urban	4,610	16.5	5,759	15.5	15,812	31.0	27,709	35.5	32,461	37.1
Rural	23,293	83.5	31,304	84.5	35,430	69.0	50,384	64.5	55,070	62.9
TOTAL	27,903	100.0	37,063	100.0	51,242	100.0	78,093	100.0	87,531	100.0

TABLE VI

GROWTH OF VILLAGES AND TOWNS IN GASTON COUNTY
1880–1940

Towns	1880	1890	1900	1910	1920	1930	1940
Belmont			145	1,176	2,941	4,121	4,356
Bessemer City			1,100	1,529	2,176	3,739	3,567
Cherryville			1,008	1,153	1,884	2,756	3,225
Dallas	417	441	514	1,065	1,397	1,489	1,704
Gastonia	236	1,033	4,610	5,759	12,871	17,093	21,313
Lowell			290	876	1,151	1,664	1,826
McAdenville			1,144	983	1,162	914	887
Mount Holly		472	630	526	1,180	2,254	2,055
Stanley			441	321	584	1,084	1,036
Cramerton							3,280

these terms, there has been a significant trend toward urban residence in the county during the last four decades (Table V), and Gaston has come to have a larger number of towns than any county in North Carolina, embracing within its small area in 1940 nine villages and towns of more than a thousand people (Table VI).[8] Its largest village in 1880 had 417 residents. The

8. A similar trend toward urban residence is indicated in census figures for North Carolina as a whole. In 1880, 3.9 per cent of the population was classified

new towns are almost entirely nonagricultural in occupational character; the 1930 Census reported, for four of them, a total rural-farm population of only 120 out of a total population of 6,491.

TABLE VII

NUMBER OF FARMS AND STATUS OF OPERATORS IN GASTON COUNTY, 1880–1940*

	Number of Farms	Full Owners of Farms	Tenants†
1880		1,093	454
1890		1,062	629
1900	2,213	1,059	992
1910	2,859	1,421	1,424
1920	2,339	1,111	987
1930	2,555	1,090	1,262
1940	2,207	1,175	833

* This table includes figures for Negroes, as it has not been possible in each case to secure figures for whites only. Figures for whites only in 1940 were: number of farms, 1,806; full owners of farms, 1,097; tenants, 530.

Figures often refer to the preceding year, in this table and in those that follow.

† The notable decreases in the number of tenants listed for 1920 and 1940 are doubtless to be explained by the high ratio of cotton mill activity for each of those years, which drew new workers temporarily into the mills.

In more basic terms, farming as an occupation has not increased in proportion with industrial occupations, and the creation of agricultural wealth has not kept pace with the rise of industrial wealth. The number of full owners of farms in the county has remained almost unchanged since 1880, the number of farms in 1940 is practically the same as in 1900, and the number of tenants, though at times it has increased considerably, is still not large (Table VII). Of even greater significance, acreage in farms has been decreasing steadily since 1900 along with the average size of farms, as revealed in Table VIII. The value of farm products has increased greatly since 1880, but to far smaller degree than the value of industrial products. The value of all farm products in 1879 was $625,459 and the

as urban as compared with 27.3 per cent in 1940. From 1920 to 1930 the Southeast showed a larger ratio of increase in urban population than did the nation as a whole (Howard W. Odum, *Southern Regions of the United States* [Chapel Hill, 1936], pp. 68–70).

TABLE VIII

LAND IN FARMS, AND AVERAGE SIZE OF FARMS, IN GASTON COUNTY, 1880–1940

	Land in Farms: Acres	Per cent of Total Acreage in County	Average Size of Farms: Acres
1880			130
1900	201,963		91.3
1910	199,951	84.2	69.9
1920	178,346	76.8	76.2
1930	161,029	69.3	63
1940	159,920*	69.8†	72.5

* With 2,100 farms reporting, 60,103 acres of land were used for crops in 1939 as compared with 63,692 acres reported as so used in 1929. Negro operators are included in this table, but white farmers have far outnumbered Negroes, and accounted for 137,657 acres of the total land in farms in 1940.

† This percentage is higher than for 1930 even though the absolute acreage in farms is lower; the explanation lies in the fact that a new survey in 1940 reduced by 3,200 acres the total acreage reported for the county in 1930.

value of all crops in 1929 was $2,367,039. The value of industrial products in the county in 1880 was $844,308, as compared with $69,083,052 in 1929. It is obvious, therefore, that in respect to production of wealth Gaston County has become overwhelmingly an industrial center, and notions of a balanced social structure and a dual economy are mythical in character.

THE RISE OF NEW CLASSES

A large percentage of the population classified as rural is composed of mill workers dependent entirely on industrial employment for a livelihood. Of the 50,384 people classed as rural in 1930, only 15,298 were specifically rural-farm.[9] Most of the remainder are accounted for by the location of mill villages in rural districts, and the unincorporated character of one mill village large enough to meet otherwise the census requirement for urban places.[10] The industrial transformation of the county has

9. This percentage is much smaller than for North Carolina as a whole; the population of the state in 1930 was 74.5 per cent rural and 50.4 per cent rural-farm. Rural areas of Gaston County are the most densely populated in the state, but because many cotton mills are located outside of city limits rather than because of agricultural factors.

10. Cramerton, with a population of 3,280 in 1940.

brought a new economic class, the mill workers, standing between rural and urban life. Many of them are rural in residence, and nearly all have come out of a rural background.
Their isolation into separate villages has retarded their as-
similation into urban centers socially as well as geographically.
Increasingly, however, urban standards of income, amusement,
education, housing, and the like are normative in their lives.
Considerable envy has tinged their attitude toward the "city
slicker," and he has been replaced by the "country yokel" as an
object of ridicule and humor.

Control over nearly every aspect of life in Gaston County
has passed progressively, as the industrial revolution proceeded, into the hands of a new social class, the uptown people.
The occupational basis for this class has been erected very
quickly. Several hundred mill owners and managers comprise
its dominant group. As population increased, the number of
professional men, public employees, merchants, real estate and
insurance agents, schoolteachers, and the like rose rapidly. In
1872, 18 merchants were listed as having establishments in the
county;[11] in 1939 the number of retail stores was 799, with
nearly 3,000 people engaged in their operation. Service establishments, catering to public needs of various sorts, numbered
231 in 1939 and gave employment to several hundred persons.
A large number of small industrial plants other than textile
mills, but often associated in some way with the textile industry,
have been established, frequently importing or training labor
of a comparatively high degree of skill and income. A survey
in 1940 listed a total of 945 white-collar workers and 540
skilled manual workers in Gastonia alone.[12] In each of the rising
towns in the county, a new class arose to manage the operation
of industries and the distribution of credit, services, and goods.
By virtue of their key positions, members of this class, with or
without design, immediately achieved control over most aspects
of the county's life.

11. Rev. Levi Branson, ed., *North Carolina Business Directory, 1872* (Raleigh, 1872), pp. 99–101.
12. The survey was made under the sponsorship of the Altrusa Club of Gastonia. It put the number of unskilled manual workers in Gastonia at 8,827, of
whom 7,599 were "millhands," and the number of "managers" at 67, with the
grand total of employed persons being 10,379. Domestic servants were not included in the study. Though the categories and methodology of the study were
somewhat ill-defined, the results are suggestive.

DISTRIBUTION OF WEALTH

Wide variance in financial income came to the county with the division of labor attendant on industrialization, and led toward comparable divergence in the ownership and control of wealth. Adequate statistics on income and property ownership of the three social classes are not available, but are not necessary for the simple assertion that extensive differentials have prevailed.

TABLE IX

AVERAGE VALUE OF LAND, BUILDINGS, AND OTHER EQUIPMENT,
PER FARM, IN GASTON COUNTY, 1880–1940

	Land and Buildings	Implements and Machinery	Domestic Animals
1880	$1,187	$ 45	$159
1910	2,660	87	
1920	4,757	230	500
1930	4,602	280	310
1940	3,357	267	

TABLE X

AVERAGE VALUE OF FARM PRODUCTS, PER FARM,
IN GASTON COUNTY, 1880–1930

	Total Value of Crops, including Vegetables	Receipts from Sale of Poultry and Dairy Products
1880	$ 404	
1910	624	$ 34
1920	1,658	113
1930	926	185

The relative equality of economic status which had obtained before the industrial revolution was lost in the unequal distribution of the new wealth brought to the county. The face value of farms and of farm products increased (Tables IX and X), but farm income fell considerably behind that of the industrial family and far behind that of the average uptown family. As late as 1911 farm labor in the county was receiving only 75 c. to $1.25 a day, $15 to $18 a month,[13] and hired hands still fre-

13. W. E. Hearn *et alii, Soil Survey of Gaston County, North Carolina* (Washington, 1911), pp. 11–12. Cf. Ben F. Lemert, *The Cotton Textile Industry of the Southern Appalachian Piedmont* (Chapel Hill, 1933), p. 75.

quently receive wages as low as that. Tenant farmers were often worse off and welcomed the opportunity to transfer to a mill village. Independent farmers have, on the average, retained their independence at the cost of poverty. In 1910, for example, the average farm owner was required to spend about one fourth of the value of his crops for hired help, fertilizer, and feed (Table XI), and had about $500 left for seed, interest,

TABLE XI

CERTAIN AVERAGE EXPENDITURES OF FULL OWNERS OF FARMS IN GASTON COUNTY, 1910 AND 1920*

	Cash for Hired Help	Fertilizer	Feed
1910	$ 68	$44	$ 38
1920	124	94	100

* The average is figured for farms reporting such expenditures rather than for all farms in the county.

TABLE XII

MORTGAGES ON FARMS OPERATED BY FULL OWNERS IN GASTON COUNTY, 1910–1930

	Total Number of Farms Operated by Full Owners	Number Reporting Mortgages	Average Percentage of Value of Land and Buildings under Mortgage
1910	1,421	168	20.7
1920	1,111	225	25.7
1930	1,090	348	29.0

taxes, and other operating expenses, and for the maintenance of himself and his family. A growing percentage of the small farmers of the county have labored under an increasing ratio of debt (Table XII), with attendant dangers of the loss of farm and independence, and absorption into the ranks of "cotton mill hands" or the unemployed. In this respect, as in the others enumerated above, the Gaston County farmer is not untypical of his class throughout the South; his economic condition is somewhat better, indeed, than the average for the region.[14]

14. A study of the farm business of 1,115 farms in various parts of North Carolina in 1927 (reported in the *Report of the Tax Commission of North Carolina, 1928*) revealed an average annual cash income of $556, plus an aver-

Wages in the textile industry, and especially in the Southern mills, have been a subject of controversy for many years. The industry has always tended to follow cheap labor rather than raw materials or markets. For decades it has paid the lowest average wage among the major manufacturing industries, and its cotton goods branch has paid the lowest wage in textiles. Several members of a family have customarily worked in a cotton mill in order to obtain a sustenance income for the family; the average number of workers per mill family in Gaston County in 1914 was 2.11, and had declined to only 1.94 in 1925–26.[15] Mills have traditionally provided housing and some other necessities at greatly reduced rates, thereby raising the real wages of the workers to some extent, and at the same time affording mill managements an argument to use in defense of low money wages.[16]

Despite the long-standing controversy over wages in Southern mills—or perhaps because of it—accurate statistics on the income of mill employees are difficult to obtain and often highly ambiguous in character. Table XIII presents a chronological picture, based on the Federal Census of Manufactures, of the average annual wages of all industrial workers in Gaston County at intervals since 1880, and also affords comparison with the annual incomes of salaried employees in industry, most of whom have belonged to the uptown class.[17] Several mill superintendents in the county at present recall that they began work in the mills, at very tender ages between thirty and forty

age value of $478 for products raised and consumed on the farm. Wide extremes entered into the average; the average cash income per farm for one county in 1927 was $59. Studies of the incomes of white tenant and cropper families in two counties of North Carolina in 1922 (summarized in Rhyne, *op. cit.*, p. 99) found an average daily money income of 9 c. per person in one county, and 14 c. for tenants and 8 c. for croppers in the other. The per capita income for the entire farm population of the Southeast in 1929 was $183, as compared with $535 for the nonfarm population of the region, and $366 for the farm population of the Northeast (see Odum, *op. cit.*, p. 46).

15. E. R. Rankin, "A Social Study of One Hundred Families at Cotton Mills in Gastonia, North Carolina" (M.A. thesis, University of North Carolina, 1914), p. 11; Rhyne, *op. cit.*, p. 84.

16. See chap. x.

17. Nearly all industrial workers in the county have been employees of cotton mills. The statistics on wages in Table XIII do not represent the average wages received by full-time employees, as the Census of Manufactures has included part-time employees and their wages in its totals. This fact, however, does not modify greatly the accuracy of these figures for Gaston County.

years ago, for wages as low as 10 c. a day. The average wage in the early days of the industry, and as late as 1900, was less than $5 a week. A careful investigator in 1914 found the median wage for individuals to be $25 a month and the average $26.86; the median wage for one hundred families was $42.50 a month, and the average $56.67 a month.[18] Extremes ranged from $8 a month for learners to $75 a month for skilled ma-

TABLE XIII

AVERAGE ANNUAL INCOMES OF SALARIED AND WAGE EMPLOYEES IN GASTON COUNTY INDUSTRIES, 1880–1930

	Salaried Officers and Employees	Wage Earners
1880		$159
1890	$ 863	
1900	827	184
1920		692
1930	2,726	691

chinists. An equally painstaking study in 1925–26, after the rise in wages during the first World War, found that individual employees received an average weekly wage of $15.72, with the median being $15.14 and the modal $13.40. For mill families, the average weekly income was $28.65, the median $25.43, and the modal $16.07.[19] Income received by the mill workers dropped considerably during the next eight years, but has approximately made up the loss under the provisions of the National Industrial Recovery Act and the Fair Labor Standards Act. A survey of 7,599 mill workers in Gastonia in 1940 disclosed an average weekly wage of $14.96.[20]

In mill wages, as in farm income, Gaston County has not been exceptionally low in comparison with standards in its

18. Rankin, *op. cit.*, pp. 11–13.
19. Rhyne, *op. cit.*, pp. 95–97. These figures coincide rather closely with those derived from the Census of Manufactures for 1925, if a moderate allowance is made for plant idleness, illness, and other loss of working time.
20. The survey previously referred to, as having been made under the sponsorship of the Altrusa Club of Gastonia. The average weekly wage for all unskilled manual workers in Gastonia was $15.28, if only white workers, 8,175 in number, are included. An average weekly wage of $11.45 was received by 659 unskilled Negro workers.

vicinity. Its wage rates have often been higher than those in districts farther south, though they have always been considerably lower than those prevailing in New England.[21] Apologists for wage rates in the county have compared them with agricultural income and wage levels in neighboring mills, and have attempted to justify the wage differential as compared with New England through arguments over skill of workers, the comparative cost of living, and the like. They have not introduced comparison of mill wages and uptown incomes, though uptown standards are increasingly normative in the lives of mill workers.

Beyond question, the per capita wealth and income of the uptown class have far exceeded that of the farm and mill classes. In general, members of this class have lived in better houses, worn more expensive clothing, eaten more adequate food, provided more extensive education for their children, worshiped in more pretentious churches under the guidance of higher-salaried ministers, played in more luxurious settings, and built up more adequate financial reserves against future hazards. Being more heterogeneous in occupational classification than the members of the other classes, the uptown people as a whole have not been studied as adequately, in respect to those statistical indices most indispensable for an understanding of comparative class status. No information is available concerning the incomes of professional men, merchants, and agents of various types. Annual incomes of salaried employees in industry are depicted in Table XIII; they have ordinarily been several times as high as those of mill workers or farmers. A survey of wages in Gastonia in 1940 revealed the degree to which income differentials have developed among employed persons: 67 managers received an average weekly pay of $40.76, 533 skilled manual workers received an average of $27.37, and 945 white-collar employees received an average of $23.69.[22] Nearly all the members of these groups belong to the uptown class. The average weekly wage for mill workers, as already seen, was $14.96. Though income

21. See Clarence Heer, *Income and Wages in the South* (Chapel Hill, 1930), and the United States Department of Labor Bulletin, Serial No. R.689, *Regional Differences in Cotton-Textile Wages, 1928 to 1937* (Washington, 1938), among innumerable references that might be listed.

22. The Altrusa Club study, referred to above.

has varied considerably as between individuals and groups within the uptown class, averages for the various uptown groups have ranged between extremes of 50 per cent to 5,000 per cent above those for the other social classes.

The most spectacular concentration of wealth in the county came in the rising economic affluence of the mill owners. The property of the richest citizen in Gastonia in 1887 was valued for tax purposes at $10,000; in 1929 one mill owner was receiving an annual salary of $75,000, plus income from dividends and other investments. No great fortunes have been made in textiles, and profits have been amazingly erratic from year to year, because of the highly decentralized, competitive character of the industry. In general, however, profits were very high during the early decades in Gaston County, and the wealth of the larger stockholders increased by leaps and bounds. In 1907 stock of Gastonia mills was advertised as paying dividends of 10, 20, and 30 per cent.[23] One investor relates that he put $5,000 into a cotton mill and received dividends of $5,000 for each of nine subsequent years. During the period of the first World War profits reached unprecedented levels; several new mills are reported to have paid for themselves during the first year of operation, and stock was selling at from 50 per cent to 100 per cent above par before the beginning of construction on projected mills. In 1920–21 one mill capitalized at $150,000, borrowed $300,000, and paid off its indebtedness in one year.

Mill owners put a large percentage of their profits into new mills, and their wealth increased in proportion. Single individuals became officials of a dozen mills, and generally drew salaries as well as dividends from each. Members of their families, including wives and daughters, were sometimes given official positions without responsibility but with remuneration. Annual salaries of mill superintendents often reached $10,000 or more, while mill executives received as high as $75,000 a year. Individuals lost wealth and rank from time to time, but the mill owners as a group retained their favored status in all basic aspects of the county's life.

With the depression of 1921, the rate of development of industry in the county began to decline, and profits in many of

23. *Gastonia Gazette*, October 7, 1907.

the existing mills became uncertain from year to year. A few mills were abandoned; others were consolidated. Ownership of the county's industries has passed increasingly into the hands of outside capital, but natives are still in possession of a majority of them and continue to comprise as a group the pinnacle of the social structure in the county. Though mill officials are as secretive as always about profits, and stock in most mills is held so closely that information about dividends is difficult to obtain, there is ample evidence that in most instances profits have far exceeded losses even during the last two decades. The national defense effort since 1939 has given to some of the less profitable mills an opportunity to recoup their fortunes. Wages of employees have risen slightly, but not enough to threaten seriously the income differential in favor of salaried officers and mill owners.

Differences in Housing, Schooling, and Family Life

If distinctions between the social classes in Gaston County rest especially on differences of occupational status and financial income, they are strikingly reflected in other aspects of social structure, and most patently of all in diversity of housing facilities. As the new mills of the county began to roll up profits, those who profited most, the uptown people, built more expensive houses. Mill officials who at the outset had lived humbly in their villages succumbed to the urge to live uptown, and the major mill official who still resided in his village soon became an anachronism. An illustrated history of Gastonia published in 1906 contained pictures of commodious houses constructed by the new textile manufacturers, and commented: "Within the past ten years quite a number of comfortable and handsome homes have been erected and many of them ranging in cost from $5,000 to $20,000 each. Few indeed are the towns in this state, the size of Gastonia, that can boast of more handsome residences."[24] Fifteen years later some mill owners were build-

24. J. H. Separk, ed., *Illustrated Handbook of Gastonia* (Gastonia, 1906), pp. 65–70. The editor also exulted in the fact that beauty was not being sacrificed before material progress. "It is doubtful," he wrote, "if any town in the state can excel ours in the growing of the rose. . . . Thanks to the aesthetic taste of our city fathers, that they have not followed the example of many towns and laid low, with the ruthless axe, the beautiful trees, in their eagerness to make the town citylike."

ing residences costing $100,000, laying expensive oriental rugs on their floors, and in general demonstrating their status by luxurious living. Restricted residential sections were developed, with names such as "Forest Hills," "Hillcrest," and "Fairmont Park."

Mill workers, meanwhile, continued to live in separate villages, in houses costing anywhere from $700 to $2,000 at the time of construction. In most villages each house was identical with all its neighbors in shape, size, and color. For the most part they were small houses, seldom containing more than four or five rooms, into which families consisting on the average of six persons were crowded.[25] The mills retained ownership and cared for upkeep; in return they charged a rental averaging 25 c. a room per week. Though they operated the villages at an economic loss, the mills were provided thereby with an effective instrument of control over labor, and were also assured a permanent labor supply, as the social isolation of the villages made it difficult for children of mill workers to escape the occupation of their parents.

Obviously, therefore, housing arrangements have helped to create and to symbolize the gaps between the three social classes. Residence in a mill village soon became a distinctive badge of class affiliation, and a stigma in the eyes of independent farmers and uptown people alike. The mill village system also promoted the concentration of social control in the hands of the uptown class, and further guaranteed the dependent status of the mill class. Its prevalence in Gaston County has rendered the percentage of home ownership, a suggestive index to social equality, extraordinarily low. Though figures cannot be computed precisely according to social classes, Table XIV reveals significant variations between population groups. In this particular, the white industrial worker falls below the nonfarm Negro.

Analogous differentiation occurred in the educational facilities provided for the three social classes.[26] Separate schools for

25. Rankin, op. cit., pp. 7–10.
26. The county has developed a passion for public schools, and members of all the groups boast that their schools are the best in North Carolina. In 1900 public schools in the county employed 76 teachers and current expenses totaled $14,600; in 1924, 450 teachers were employed, and it cost $750,000 to operate the school system for the year. See the article by the county school superintendent in *Visions Old and New* (Gastonia, 1924), pp. 38–39. Cf. Oscar Lee

the children of mill workers appeared very early, partly because of the geographical isolation of many villages but also in
those located within the corporate limits of larger towns. The
mills themselves often constructed school buildings and employed teachers; in a few communities direct ownership and supervision of educational facilities by the mills have continued
almost to the present, and transfer to public ownership and
control has sometimes been a subject of considerable dispute.
Each of Gastonia's mill villages contained a school in 1914.

TABLE XIV

HOME OWNERSHIP AND TENANCY IN GASTON COUNTY, 1930

| | White Families | | | Negro Families | | |
	Owners	Ten-ants	Percentage of Owners	Owners	Ten-ants	Percentage of Owners
Gaston County	3,625	9,192	28.0	637	1,839	26.0
Rural-farm	1,182	717	62.0	119	630	16.0
Rural Nonfarm*	1,120	5,008	18.0	170	505	25.0
Gastonia†	774	2,090	27.0	235	555	30.0

* White population in this category is composed almost entirely of mill workers and their families.

† A large number of mill villages are included in the corporate limits of Gastonia.

Generally they carried pupils only through the third grade.[27]
More recently there has been a widespread movement, in mill
villages as in rural areas, toward consolidation of schools; but
consolidation has not cut across lines of social differentiation to
any significant degree. Children of mill workers have habitually
gone to school with the children of other mill workers, and continue to do so. Theoretically they can go, after graduation
from their own grammar schools, to the central high school
along with children from uptown families. Comparatively few
go, however, and those who do are met with strong cultural dis-

Kiser, "The Growth and Development of Education in Gaston County" (M.A.
thesis, University of North Carolina, 1928). The percentage of illiteracy in the
county has been steadily reduced, from 18.7 per cent of persons ten years old
and over in 1910 to 9.5 per cent in 1930. The percentage for Negroes in 1930
was 21.6, for native whites 7.1.

27. Rankin, op. cit., pp. 21, 25.

crimination, often very subtle but sometimes explicit, and find it difficult to make adjustments.

As in the case of separate schools for Negroes, a system of separate schools for the mill villages has posed many peculiar problems, and has helped to perpetuate and augment the differentiation of mill workers from other population groups. Mill schools still experience considerable difficulty from truancy, retardation, and withdrawal of pupils.[28] Their facilities compare unfavorably with those in uptown schools, but have often surpassed those available in rural schools.[29] In this respect, as in many others, mill owners have been correct in claiming that the mill worker has had larger advantages in the mill village than he had on the farm. More recently, however, the disparity between educational opportunities for the children of mill workers and the children of farmers has virtually disappeared.

The division into distinct social classes is reflected in all other aspects of social structure in Gaston County. Even the family institution is affected by it. Relations between parents and children of mill families are in many cases the reverse of those prevailing in the semipatriarchal rural families; young people in the mill village are often the breadwinners of their families, and parents are reduced to the status of housekeepers and "mill daddies."[30] On the other hand, both parents frequently work in the mill, and small children are left to shift for themselves, or else grow up under the supervision of Negro women whose talents cannot command wages higher than mill workers can afford to pay. Under such circumstances, control of parents over children is less rigid, in general, than that found in uptown or rural homes, and rates of juvenile delinquency in mill villages

28. T. L. Looper, "The Causes of Elimination of Pupils in the Elementary Schools in Gastonia, North Carolina" (M.A. thesis, University of North Carolina, 1929); Bertha Carl Hipp, "A Gaston County Cotton Mill and Its Community" (M.A. thesis, University of North Carolina, 1930), chap. iv; J. H. Cook, *A Study of the Mill Schools of North Carolina* (New York, 1925).

29. In 1914 the school term in all Gastonia schools consisted of eight months of twenty days; in rural Gaston County, it consisted of five months (Rankin, *op. cit.*, p. 25).

30. It is the peculiar function of "mill daddies" to carry lunches to their children at work in the mills, and this constitutes almost their only responsibility.

are undoubtedly higher than in rural and uptown families. Desertion appears to be the usual mode of separation in a mill home, while divorce is a more frequent mode in uptown homes.[31] Sexual immorality is discounted to greater extent among mill villagers, and illegitimate children are generally accepted without serious penalty; overcrowding in company houses, intimate contact in alleys of the mills, and absence of adequate resources for amusement all contribute to sexual promiscuity.

GENERAL CLASS DISTINCTIONS

Social stratification has been shaped and reflected not only in the emerging institutional patterns of the county, but also in more general and secondary spheres of culture. Uptown people have progressively become "more cultured" than their mill and country cousins; that is, uptown agencies have become dominant and uptown standards have become normative in the shaping of culture, wresting dominion from rural agencies and standards. A clear illustration is found in the changes occurring since 1880 in the *Gastonia Gazette*, the principal newspaper in the county. Established in 1880, the *Gazette* catered to rural readers during its earlier years, when it had virtually no subscribers of any other type: it ran fiction on the front page, gave prominent position to prices for farm products, and secured most of its advertisements from manufacturers of fertilizers, farm implements, and patent medicines. As a mercantile class began to appear in the county, the *Gazette* courted their interest increasingly, reflecting the shift from rural to urban standards; by 1910 it was explicitly urging subscribers to patronize local merchants for their Christmas shopping, and not mail-order houses.[32] It quickly identified itself with the fortunes of the rising textile industry, and for the last forty years has been regarded as a sort of unofficial spokesman and protector for the mills of the county.

As urban population grew, distinctively urban organizations and culture traits began to emerge. The appearance of such agencies as the chamber of commerce, civic clubs, secret orders,

31. B. H. Smith, "The Social Significance of the Southern Cotton Mill Community" (M.A. thesis, Emory University, 1925), pp. 13–14.
32. *Gastonia Gazette*, December 9, 1910.

garden clubs, music clubs, a private country club, women's clubs, parent teacher clubs, societies based on genealogy, and the like has been indicative of the growth of "civic spirit," leisure time, and urban facilities. Since they have got one step ahead of the wolf, uptown residents have organized, characteristically, to promote further economic welfare and to attain those graces commonly referred to in Gastonia as "the finer things of life." Libraries have been established, lyceums have been brought to town, community pageants have been produced, a poetry group has been organized, and other leisure-time activities have been extended. Farmers have generally regarded them with suspicion and contempt, as being indicative of laziness and "puttin' on airs." Mill workers respond to them more positively, with a mixture of admiration and assumed indifference, and a frequent trace of bitterness.

The mill workers, isolated geographically and socially into separate villages, have developed culture traits peculiar to themselves—traits often despised by farmers and uptown residents alike. Instead of country clubs and garden clubs, they join fraternal lodges with low dues, such as the Patriotic Order of the Sons of America, the Red Men, and the Woodmen of the World. Instead of tea or cocktails, they drink Coca-Cola. Leisure-time activities—since reduction in long hours of work has allowed leisure—include a mixture of rural and urban amusements; such rural sports as hunting, fishing, "blackberryin'," and talking in desultory fashion alternate with attendance at baseball games and, most popular of all, the movies. The Bible, religious papers, pulp magazines, and an occasional rural weekly provide reading matter.[33] "Hillbilly" music is very popular—and, indeed, is still secretly preferred to opera by most uptown citizens. Most mill homes now have a radio and an automobile of one vintage or another.

In respect to "bourgeois virtues," the mill villager is often sadly deficient in the eyes of his uptown neighbor. He is less scrupulous in paying bills, partly because he has less with which to pay them and can less well afford the virtue of honesty. His house and person are often comparatively slovenly and "run down" in appearance, partly because he has less inspiration to

33. Cf. E. R. Hartz, "Social Problems in a North Carolina Parish" (A.M. thesis, Duke University, 1938), pp. 103–104.

care for his house (which is not his) and less training in "citi-fied" methods of personal hygiene. The ineptitude of trans-planted farmers and mountaineers for modern plumbing de-vices is a favorite topic of humor among uptown people.

Finally, and of great importance, class attitudes have de-veloped which tend further to isolate the three social classes from each other. In the early days of the textile industry in the county, cotton mill workers, not yet accustomed to "city ways," used to appear uptown in their work clothes and with cotton lint in their hair; townspeople attached such names as "cotton dodgers," "cotton mill trash," and "millhands" to them, and the designations have survived. The traditions that grew up in England at the end of the eighteenth century which relegated mill workers to the status of an inferior caste have been re-capitulated in the South.[34] Mill workers have been regarded generally by townspeople as being of degenerate stock, and in-ferior in native intelligence. It would be as unthinkable in most uptown homes of Gastonia to invite a "common millhand" to dinner as it would be to invite a Negro. Social distinctions pre-vail likewise between young people from uptown and mill homes; town boys almost never call on cotton mill girls for "honorable" purposes.

Mill workers, in turn, resent the attitudes of "townfolks" toward them, and withdraw into themselves in the face of dis-crimination. Many observers, including most ministers who work among them, agree that mill people are extremely "sensi-tive," due chiefly to a feeling of inferiority generated by their isolated life. The fact that employment in cotton mills repre-sented, for many of them, a last stand against complete desti-tution has also conditioned their attitudes. They resent the names applied by uptown residents, saying defensively, "I may work in a cotton mill, but I'm just as good as anybody." Their sense of repression sometimes leads to abnormal forms of be-havior, such as extreme suspicion of strangers, ecstatic recrea-tional and religious activity, and occasional outbursts of vio-lence. As one mill pastor summed it up: "Mill people are un-predictable. They take funny twists. Everything may seem all right with them, but then something comes along and they blow

34. Harriet L. Herring, "Cycles of Cotton Mill Criticism," *The South Atlan-tic Quarterly*, XXVIII, 114–115 (April, 1929).

up all over the place." Under such circumstances, mill workers guard their small prerogatives jealously, and live pretty much to themselves. Often they decline to mix to any large degree even with residents of a neighboring mill village. As will be seen, they prefer to attend their own church, or none.

Cultural isolation between rural people and mill workers is somewhat less pronounced than between uptown people and mill workers, and appears to have been diminishing during the last several decades. Farmers are much closer to mill workers in economic status than to uptown people. As between uptown people and farmers, and especially independent farmers, even less discrimination prevails; most urbanites have a nostalgia for the farm on which they spent their childhood.

The mill worker, with nobody else to "look down on," regards himself as eminently superior to the Negro. The colored man represents his last outpost against social oblivion. In response to an invitation from the mill management asking for "suggestions for the benefit of the Company and the Employees," two mill workers recently wrote a letter which would have been endorsed by most of their class:

We think unstopping Toilets is out of a White Man's Class of Work, it ought to be done by Negros   You would not Unstop Toilets Your Self   You should have the same Respect for your Employees' You have for Your Self.[35]

In stimulating the emergence of social classes, as well as through direct subsidies and the provision of an expanding population and wealth, the mills of Gaston County profoundly influenced the patterns by which the churches of the county grew. Economic developments not only laid the basis and set the limits for the outward expansion of religious institutions; they also helped to create internal social divisions in terms of which the internal life of the churches would be molded. Examination of the rise of class churches will reveal the degree to which the churches have adapted themselves to the emergence of social classes, and will elaborate further the role of the mills in the growth of the churches.

35. From a collection of grievance letters in possession of a Southern professor of industrial relations; his name and the source of his collection are confidential.

CHAPTER V

THE EMERGENCE OF CLASS CHURCHES

RELIGIOUS ideals in Gaston County do not approve the recognition of class lines within the churches. One minister affirmed: "If we don't get all these social classes together in the church, I don't know how they ever will be brought together. So I try to make no difference as between uptown folks and mill folks." Despite all such sentiments, the churches have adapted neatly to class segregation. Individual churches, when judged by the type of membership attending, have been almost exclusively either rural, mill, or uptown in type,[1] especially since 1900. With five exceptions, the original rural churches of the county have remained predominantly churches for farmers. New churches were built for the mill villages and for the growing towns, and have been distinctive in membership almost from the beginning.

A careful examination of the constituencies of individual churches in the county in 1939 revealed the extent to which economic stratification has been reflected in religious institutions. If a minority type of membership is defined as one comprising at least 20 per cent of the total membership of an individual church, the degree to which different classes have been brought together within single churches is indicated in the following table:

Number of predominantly rural churches	34
with a minority of mill workers	5
with a minority of uptown members	0

1. These terms are used hereinafter with reference to the three social types described in the preceding chapter rather than in accordance with census definitions. Thus, "rural church" means a church attended principally by farmers. Classification of churches has been effected from an internal point of view— that is, from the judgments of ministers, members, workers, and the general community as to the type of church each is and has been. The type of people who attend has been the crucial factor in each instance; rather precise percentages have been obtained on the distribution of the membership between the various types of people—rural, mill, and uptown. Each church has then been classified according to its majority membership—and the majority has generally been overwhelming, as the three types seldom mix in appreciable numbers.

Number of predominantly uptown churches   35
    with a minority of mill workers   17
    with a minority of rural members   3

Number of predominantly mill churches   76
    with a minority of rural members   1
    with a minority of uptown members   8

Only 34 churches in the county included minority groups accounting for at least 20 per cent of the total membership, leaving 111 churches without a minority group of this size. From the standpoint of a majority membership of at least 66.6 per cent, results are even more significant. Only 9 churches in the county in 1939, of a total of 145, failed to have a membership in which at least two thirds of the total was composed of one social type. In brief, only 23 per cent of the churches in 1939 had important minority groups and only 6 per cent lacked a majority group of at least 66.6 per cent. The churches have followed closely the distinctions created by the rise of the mills, and most individual churches are now overwhelmingly affiliated with a particular social class.[2]

There has been significant variance in growth of the number of churches of the three types, reflecting differential growth in numerical size of the three social classes (Table XV). Since 1880, 84 new mill churches have been organized, as compared with 19 new rural churches, and 32 new uptown churches. Twenty rural churches have been abandoned, 9 mill churches, and 2 uptown churches. Between 1880 and 1900 fewer mill churches were organized than uptown churches; mill workers coming into the county often worshiped with rural and uptown congregations, and the number of mill churches lagged far behind the number of mills. Beginning about 1900, however, emerging social stratification began to become manifest in the building of separate churches for the industrial workers. Twice as many mill churches were organized in the first decade of this century as between 1880 and 1900, while the number of new rural and uptown churches declined sharply.

2. The process of segregation has not proceeded as far in the smaller towns of the county as in Gastonia, suggesting that social distinctions tend to increase with the size of towns.

TABLE XV

GROWTH IN NUMBER OF ACTIVE CHURCHES, AND IN TOTAL
CHURCH MEMBERSHIP, BY TYPES, IN GASTON
COUNTY, 1880–1939*

	Rural Churches		Mill Churches		Uptown Churches	
	Number	Membership	Number	Membership	Number	Membership
1880	35	3,290	1	75	5	185
1890	38	3,268	4	316	18	1,980
1900	42	4,158	10	1,110	26	3,926
1910	39	4,212	28	4,172	31	4,836
1920	38	4,446	37	6,549	34	7,786
1930	34	4,726	53	12,985	34	9,928
1939	34	5,338	76	19,456	35	11,585

* Statistics in this table have been gathered from figures reported by the individual churches to their parent ecclesiastical bodies. The membership of a
few churches for which specific figures were not available has been calculated
as that of the average for the social type in which they belonged rather than in
terms of general or denominational averages. Discrepancies between tables,
arising from the use of different averages, are so slight as to be inconsequential,
and each table is rendered more accurate through employment of an average
appropriate to itself.

The Rise of Mill Churches

The appearance of churches especially designed for the working class was the most significant aspect of the social differentiation of churches. A number of reasons for their origin are
given by citizens of Gastonia. It is urged, almost without exception, that the religious segregation of mill workers was not due
to the desire of fashionable uptown churches or conservative
rural churches to exclude them. Though subtle social pressures
may have existed, disbarment of the new workers from existing
congregations was not openly advocated, and was not an important factor underlying the appearance of the new type of
church. Nor was distance from existing churches of crucial importance in a majority of cases; new rural and uptown churches
were often organized for the sake of convenience, but only a few
of the new mill villages were so isolated as to have no churches
in their vicinity. Alternative explanations are advanced. In the
very nature of things, it is said, the lives of mill operatives were
different from those of other people, leading them to desire
churches of their own in which they could feel perfectly at ease.

This interpretation is getting, obviously, at the matter of cultural differentiation. Descendants of earlier settlers in the county, being natives and having acquired some property before the industrial transformation began, constituted a cultural and economic group differing in important respects from the imported, propertyless mill workers. If uptown churches professed a desire to have workers worship in them, it was in a mood of paternalism. If mill workers desired separate churches, it was partly because of a desire for independence and self-respect, possible in the religious realm if not in the economic.

Another explanation places greater emphasis on forces leading to the organization of life in the mill villages, such as the desire of natural leaders among the villagers to exercise leadership in churches of their own. A number of mill churches have been organized through the initiative of influential workers; one of them, more prosperous than his fellows, explained, "I put up [mortgaged] my house to put up [erect] the church." Group life in the mill villages needed focal centers around which to integrate itself; the church had been the most characteristic institution in the rural background from which most of the workers came, and it was quite natural that they should desire a similar rallying point in their new industrial setting.

All these forces figured in the background of the emergence of the mill church as a distinctive type of religious institution. The most important immediate factor, however, has apparently escaped the attention of residents of the county. The rise of mill churches was immediately due, more than to any other influence, to intense denominational rivalry for the enlistment of mill workers. As soon as mill villages began to appear, various denominations hastened to vie with each other in exploiting the new field, which seemed especially promising because of the contiguity of population in the villages as contrasted with the atomism of farms. Interest in home missions had been growing rapidly in the major denominations in North Carolina for some years before 1880; the rise of the factory towns gave it new impetus, and several denominations singled them out as areas for concentration. The Baptists and Methodists were especially concerned, as most of the mill workers had belonged to them previously. The Board of Missions and Sunday Schools reported to the Baptist State Convention of North Carolina in 1899:

. . . with regard to the rapidly increasing factory population in our State. So remarkably has the number of factories multiplied that the condition is rapidly assuming the phase of industrial revolution. The factory population has more than doubled itself during the past five years. An unfortunate feature of this movement for practical remedy is that there is an apparently unavoidable tendency on the part of this population to form a distinct community which can be reached religiously only by the provision of a separate church and a separate pastor. . . .

It is here that Baptists are deeply involved, that the people who are to be and are already effected [sic] by this movement, are those connected directly or by attachment with Baptist churches. It is in the country that our numerical strength is to be found, and it is from the country that the people are moving at the rate of five hundred a month during the year 1899. It is to be noted also that factories are being built for the most part at or near the towns or cities where Baptists are comparatively weaker and less influential than Pedobaptists. So that the problem that presents itself to your Board is that of Baptist population moving into a Pedobaptist atmosphere where the influences are strong to undermine doctrinal conviction, finally resulting, unless remedy is provided, in an absolute loss from our strength. The only practical plan of operation, as your Board sees it now, is for us to provide every such factory community not otherwise provided for with a preacher, a Sunday School and a church. At present we have only fourteen missionaries who are doing work among the factory people, of whom there are in North Carolina more than one hundred thousand.[3]

At the next annual convention this same board reported that "six milling points . . . are asking and expecting missionaries from us next year. . . . It is our judgment that we must specialize the factory mission work and concentrate attention upon it; and must ask God to raise up men who feel called to it, just as for foreign missions."[4] By 1910 the denomination had 148 home missionaries at work in North Carolina.[5] Its interest in factory centers, and support of new churches in them, has con-

3. *Minutes of the Sixty-Ninth Annual Meeting of the Baptist State Convention of North Carolina, December 6–10, 1899* (Raleigh, 1899), pp. 26–28.
4. *Ibid., 1900*, p. 26.		5. *Ibid., 1910*, p. 13.

tinued to the present. The motives advanced have generally been of mixed character. The secretary of the department of missions urged the state convention in 1929 to build a Baptist church at Enka, where a new ten-million-dollar rayon plant was under construction. "A few hundred dollars invested here now," he said, "will yield many thousands of dollars a few years hence to all of our Kingdom enterprises."[6] He reported happily at the next convention that the church had been built.[7]

Similar motives and methods appeared in the Methodist denomination. A special committee on church extension, reporting to the North Carolina Conference of the Methodist Episcopal Church, South, in 1880, advocated that serious consideration be given to the erection and support of weaker churches at home, pointing out that "such aid is especially needed in our own borders where thousands have already been expended, and thousands more will be expended to strengthen those who are seeking to supplant us."[8] A correspondent wrote to the official denominational journal in North Carolina in 1904, urging Methodists to make a special effort to reach mill workers, and warning that "there is unholy competition between the churches in the mill village."[9] In 1910 an article in the journal reported:

The operatives come largely from the country, and in them flows as pure Anglo-Saxon blood as is found anywhere. They are Americans and not aliens. But little has been done by our churches in the way of institutional work, but the field is white with harvest, and many of the mill owners are ready to assist in any well directed effort that commends itself to their judgment.

There are thirty mission churches in the [Western North Carolina] Conference where the gospel is preached to the mill people, and an appropriation of $4,200 was made to this work last year by the Board of Missions.[10]

By 1929 a committee was able to announce to the Western North Carolina Conference that "20 per centum of our churches

6. *Minutes of the North Carolina Baptist State Convention, 1929*, p. 70.
7. *Ibid., 1930*, p. 58.
8. *Minutes of the North Carolina Annual Conference, Methodist Episcopal Church, South, 1880*, p. 17.
9. G. D. Langston, "How to Reach the Mill People," *Raleigh Christian Advocate*, March 23, 1904.
10. *North Carolina Christian Advocate* (April 28, 1910), p. 8.

are composed of textile workers, and those related to the industry. Seventy-five per centum of these receive aid from the Board of Missions. It is a field of prime importance in our development."[11]

Though the Presbyterian denomination has sponsored a Synodical Home Missions Movement since 1881, it appears to have done little, through its General Assembly or the Synod of North Carolina, to reach the mill workers as such. Occasional ministers, nevertheless, have called for special attention to the new industrial centers. A Presbyterian minister wrote, in 1907:

By day and by night the mill people are chained to the looms of our factories, till they themselves are but part of the machinery itself, which enormously increases the wealth of the church, that passes them by in the distribution of the bread of life. . . .

The necessity of a new estimation and emphasis of Home Missions arises from the Industrial Awakening of the South. . . . This . . . calls for a corresponding spiritual awakening of the church, to the fact that Home Missions is the supreme need of the hour. How otherwise shall we contend with the spirit of commercialism, threatening to engulf the entire country in its insatiable vortex of destruction? . . . There are millionaires in the church who have never yet awakened to the possibilities of spiritual good in their vast growing fortunes. Where are the men who will immortalize their names by linking them forever with the great cause of Home Missions?[12]

Lutherans were less ready than any other denomination, apparently, to recognize the new economic type in process of creation in the South. They made almost no effort to build mill churches as such, or to reach the mill population as a distinct group. Such efforts as were made were largely local in origin, and sporadic in character.

Results of denominational programs for reaching the mill

11. *Minutes of the Western North Carolina Annual Conference, Methodist Episcopal Church, South, 1929*, p. 78.
12. S. L. Morris, "Home Missions, the Supreme Need of the Hour (sermon)," in Rev. D. I. Craig, *A History of the Development of the Presbyterian Church in North Carolina, and of Synodical Home Missions, together with Evangelistic Addresses by James I. Vance, D.D., and Others* (Richmond, 1907), pp. 175–176, 179, 181.

workers appeared clearly in Gaston County. Missionary grants from denominational bodies were made to a large number of the mill churches organized there, and missionary support for many of them has continued to the present. Further, wider denominational rivalry for the evangelization of mill workers was reflected in activities of the churches and ecclesiastical associations in the county itself. Around 1900 nearly every convention of Baptist churches in the county called attention to "factory missions" as being of great urgency. Unless adequate funds were provided to send missionaries to such work, one convention was warned, "We are going to lose our own people to the other denominations which are paying more attention to the factory people than we are."[13] Similar interest was demonstrated by other local denominational bodies.

Uptown churches served as focal centers from which efforts at the organization of mill churches in the county radiated, with the period from 1915 to 1925, during which the number of mills in the county increased most rapidly, as the time of greatest missionary activity. The uptown Methodist Church of Gastonia has helped to organize at least six new churches in the mill villages that surround the town, often furnishing pastoral service until the fledgling church was able to support its own ministry, and almost invariably contributing to building costs. In 1919 this church sponsored a campaign for a $50,000 building program for suburban churches and parsonages,[14] and the denomination supported several missionaries in the county between 1920 and 1925. Many tentative mission points were established, and several permanent organizations resulted. Comparable procedure was followed by uptown churches of other denominations. The First Baptist Church of Gastonia was instrumental in the organization of several outlying churches, which in turn sponsored the organization of still other churches.[15] The First Presbyterian Church of Gastonia at one time had seven mission Sunday Schools in industrial sections of

13. *Minutes of the King's Mountain Baptist Association, 1900,* p. 11.
14. *Gastonia Gazette,* March 12, April 11, 1919.
15. "History of East Baptist Church"; "History of Loray Baptist Church"; "History of the Temple Baptist Church"; W. A. Marley, "History of Calvary Baptist Church"—all manuscripts in the Library of Wake Forest College, and all written by local church officials about 1930.

the city, and for several years it engaged an additional full-time minister for local missionary work. Even the Lutherans in the county, whose denomination had evidenced no special concern for the mill workers, operated a missionary chapel in West Gastonia. Sponsorship of missionary efforts by uptown churches has continued, to lesser degree, to the present. In 1939 four mission Sunday Schools were supported by uptown Presbyterian churches, two by Methodist churches, and three by Baptist churches.

Methods employed by the denominations in reaching mill workers have been partly new, partly a carry over from previous evangelistic and missionary techniques. New elements include recognition of the mill village as a separate community and of the mill worker as a special religious problem and opportunity, and direct appeal to mill owners for support of churches in their villages. For the most part, however, old approaches have been extended to cover the new situation. Prior to the rise of industry each denomination had, at least in embryo, a home missions program. After the appearance of mill villages, this approach was enlarged to include them, with the same technique (evangelism), the same purpose (conversions), and the same result (additions to church enrollment). The "revival meeting," often held under movable tents in the mill villages, has remained the basic means of approach, and most of the mill churches were organized following such meetings.

If economic differentiation in Gaston County was basic for the rise of class churches, denominational rivalry was the factor that provided immediate impetus for their organization. Methodist and Baptist churches overlap each other in nearly every industrial section of the county, with an occasional Presbyterian church as well, and with a growing number of churches erected by the newer religious sects. Economic differentiation alone would not have explained the degree to which duplication of churches has occurred; here, as at many other points, the policies of religious institutions were of considerable importance in the shaping of forces that found origin chiefly in economic developments. Any simple theory of economic determinism of religious institutions must be severely modified, if it is to be of explanatory or heuristic value.

GENERAL CHARACTERISTICS OF CLASS CHURCHES

Whatever the sources of differentiation may have been, the churches of Gaston County are divided at present into clearly defined uptown, rural, and mill types. Each type has its own peculiar characteristics, representing a confluence of social and

TABLE XVI

GROWTH IN AVERAGE WEALTH PER CHURCH, BY TYPES OF CHURCHES, IN GASTON COUNTY, 1890–1939*

	1890	1900	1910	1920	1930	1938–39
Average Value of Church Property						
Rural		$ 771	$2,514	$ 4,347	$13,662	$10,754
Mill		843	2,117	7,777	18,761	18,873
Uptown		4,339	8,050	20,975	51,784	55,145
General Average		1,766	4,194	10,420	26,224	24,923
Average Salary Paid						
Rural	$126	166	260	493	842	622
Mill	110	156	238	835	1,145	1,164
Uptown	240	364	704	1,200	2,103	1,972
General Average	153	230	420	807	1,140	1,207
Average Amount of Money Raised						
Rural	208	272	401	1,269	1,297	1,090
Mill	210	379	324	2,475	2,934	2,958
Uptown	532	1,933	1,069	9,070	7,179	5,750
General Average	293	669	591	4,101	3,464	3,081

* Statistics in this table have been gathered from figures reported by the individual churches to their parent ecclesiastical bodies. Only those churches actually reporting—a large percentage in each instance—are represented in this table. If desired, average per capita church wealth may be computed by arriving at the average membership for each type of church from the figures in Table XV, and dividing the results into the appropriate figures of Table XVI.

religious factors. Each ministers to special needs, in distinct accents, with unique results.

Each type of church has tended to grow and prosper in proportion as its respective social class increased in size and wealth. In terms of absolute membership, rural churches surpassed mill and uptown churches until after 1900; uptown churches led in

1910 and 1920; since 1920 mill churches have taken a com-
manding lead and had more members in 1939 than both the
other types combined (Table XV). Average membership per
congregation, which can be computed from Table XV, also has
varied considerably as between the three types, with larger
congregations ensuing on the growing concentration of population and wealth in the mill villages and towns. In terms of
economic affluence, divergence is greater still, reflecting the disproportionate distribution of the new wealth created by the
textile mills.[16] Uptown churches have grown in wealth far out
of proportion to their absolute membership or average membership, in comparison with mill and rural churches, as evidenced in average value of church property, average salary
paid to pastors, and average amount of money raised per annum (Table XVI). In respect to the greater value of uptown
church property, part of the disparity is due to higher land
values in the cities than in mill or rural locations; no observer
could fail to notice, however, the comparative costliness of uptown edifices and equipment.

The furnishings of the rural or mill church are poorer in
quality, the pews are less substantial, colored glass is less profuse but more ornate, the carpet on the floor is less extensive,
the organ is less mighty and less flexible. Uptown churches have
likewise been able to raise considerably more money annually
for salaries and other current expenses; in 1939, for example,
they paid an average salary more than three times as high as
that of rural churches, and almost twice that of mill churches.
This has meant that pastors of rural and mill churches have
either received smaller compensation, or served several churches,
or both. Mill churches have paid higher salaries than rural
churches since 1910, and most of them now command full-time
pastoral service, while many rural churches continue to share
their pastor with other congregations.

Dissimilarity between the three types of churches becomes
even more apparent when "average" individual churches of each

16. Numerous factors which are not strictly economic in character, such as
orientation toward the church, the practice of tithing, etc., affect all indices
of church wealth, but the basic and most constant factor of all is economic
ability to support the church. Other factors seem to become marginal when a
wide sample of churches is studied.

type are closely compared. Table XVII presents the results of a detailed comparison of the membership of one uptown church, one rural church, and one mill church, all belonging to the same denomination. No significant variations are apparent in age grouping; the common notion that "only old folks" are left in the country churches is not substantiated, though the rural church is considerably below the mill church in the percentage of members under sixteen years of age. As might be expected, in view of the recency of industrialization and urbanization in Gaston County, members of the rural church are more often natives of their community than are their uptown cousins, and both groups have been considerably more stable than the mill workers. Though the mill church depicted here is somewhat

TABLE XVII

COMPOSITION OF MEMBERSHIP OF THREE "AVERAGE" CLASS
CHURCHES IN GASTON COUNTY, 1939*

	Rural Church	Mill Church	Uptown Church
Year Established	1835	1897	1911
Membership, 1939	159	310	349
		Percentages	
AGE GROUPINGS:			
0–16 years	13	22	17
17–30 years	27	18	25
31–54 years	40	47	50
55 and over	20	13	8
MARITAL STATUS:			
Husbands	25	28	30
Wives	40	41	38
Adult Single Persons	22	9	15
RESIDENCE IN COMMUNITY:			
Natives	62	11†	70

* These churches were selected as "average" representatives of their respective types through conferences with ministers and other residents of Gaston County. The denominational factor was kept constant—all are Methodist churches—in order that religious differences (such as requirements for membership) might not seriously modify the picture of economic and social stratification.

† This church was badly upset by the events depicted in Part III of this volume and is untypical of mill churches in respect to length of residence of its members.

TABLE XVII (*Cont.*)

	Rural Church	Mill Church	Uptown Church
Over 16 years	27	22	8
5–15 years	8	35	19
Under 5 years	3	32	3
OCCUPATIONS:			
Mill Workers	6	24	4
Housewives and Mill Workers	0	18	0
Housewives only	40	21	32
Mill Owners and Executives	0	0	5
Mill Officials below Superintendent	0	4	2
Students	13	24	17
Merchants and Professional	2	1	8
Farmers	23	0	8
Skilled Craftsmen	1	1	8
White-Collar Workers	8	4	15
Unemployed	6	1	1
No Occupation	1	2	0
EDUCATIONAL ACHIEVEMENT:			
Under 7th Grade	26	45	14
Grammar School Graduate	51	43	35
High School Graduate	14	11	38
College Training	9	1	13
ATTENDANCE AT CHURCH SERVICES:			
Regular	58	41	35
Occasional	23	38	47
Never	19	21	18
LEADERSHIP:			
Percentage Holding Church Office	12	37	31
FINANCIAL SUPPORT OF CHURCH:			
Percentage Contributing	85	86	66
Annual Contribution:			
$1–$26	98	90	80
$26 and over	2	10	20
Average per Contributor	$ 7.28	$13.48	$23.39

untypical in this respect, the rate of turnover within industrial congregations has been notoriously high. Related to this transiency is the fact that 91 per cent of the members of the mill church lived in company-owned houses, whereas 65 per cent of the members of the uptown church owned their homes.

Occupational distribution portrayed in Table XVII clearly verifies that each of the churches is a class church, with membership composed overwhelmingly of one social class. The differentials in economic wealth thereby implied are reflected in the average financial contribution each type of church receives, but apparently are not normative for willingness to support the church, to attend its services regularly, or to accept positions of responsibility in its affairs. The poor may be more devout than the rich. Training for leadership does vary considerably by class, however, as the comparison of educational achievement indicates.

THE RURAL CHURCH

In addition to quantitative distinctions between rural, mill, and uptown churches, qualitative aspects of differentiation are also observable, and though less tangible are no less important. Little attention need be given to the rural church, because it has undergone very little qualitative change under the impact of industrialization in the county. The fact of most importance about rural churches is their gradual attrition, quantitatively, as uptown and mill churches grew. For example, one rural church in the county lost fifty-four of its members in two or three decades to the uptown church of its denomination in Gastonia, including several leaders.[17] As economic opportunities multiplied in the towns, members of the country churches increasingly left the farms and added their membership and leadership to mill and uptown churches. Otherwise, rural churches are much the same now as in 1880, remaining relatively unchanged in type of service, methods of conducting business, congregational organization, and the like.[18] Because their economic position does not enable them to bid, through comparable salaries, for the services of the better-trained ministers, their pastoral leadership is often little different from that of a generation ago, though the standard of education for ministers has been rising steadily and has affected even rural churches to some degree. Many rural churches, furthermore, still find it

17. Rev. George A. Sparrow, *History of the Presbyterian Church of Olney, Gaston County, North Carolina* (pamphlet, Gastonia, 1902).

18. Cf. Frank D. Alexander, "Religion in a Rural Community of the South," *American Sociological Review*, VI, 241–251 (April, 1941).

necessary to share their minister with other churches, in order to insure him adequate support. By and large, the rural churches are regarded as training grounds for young, inexperienced ministers, or else as convenient shelves on which to place old men who have passed the peak of energy and usefulness; as one pastor complained, the rural fields are too large and the salaries too small to prove attractive. Though their absolute membership and economic wealth have risen since 1880, rural churches have failed to keep pace, in terms of any significant index, with uptown and mill churches.

The Mill Church

The mill church is not simply a transplanted rural church or a smaller and poorer edition of an uptown church. Though many of its practices and policies are modeled after those of its rural and uptown neighbors, it is in itself a distinctive type of religious institution. It faces problems peculiar to itself because of the social and economic context within which it functions. Its ultimate fate is largely bound up with the vaster fortunes of a single industry, and its immediate program depends to a considerable degree on the disposition of the local managers of that industry. Like the mill worker, the mill church lives in a perpetual atmosphere of insecurity. Unlike the worker, it cannot move to another community in the hope of improving its lot, but must make its adjustments within its given setting in such fashion that it may survive and prosper.

The mill church is peculiar not only in its social setting but also in the unique problems and needs of its membership. The forces which play upon the mill worker and isolate him into a separate social class operate through him upon his church. The structure and program of the mill church are conditioned in innumerable respects by the occupational requirements, wage levels, educational achievement, housing facilities, recreational needs, and psychological state of mill villagers. The timing and character of religious services, and attendance at them; the quality of lay leadership; the methods of raising money and the amount available; the ideas a preacher may expound and the routine by which he may make pastoral calls—all these, and many more, are affected profoundly by the mode and levels of

life among the constituency of the village church. If the mill
worker is different, his church must be different too.

Many of the special problems of the mill church, for example, root in the social insecurity and instability of the mill
worker. Mill workers have blamed their misfortunes almost universally upon conditions in the particular mill in which they
were working at the moment, and have moved frequently in the
belief that life would be better in another mill.[19] This high rate
of transiency has been reflected in the membership and policies
of village churches. The First Baptist Church of Gastonia, an
uptown church, received 1,116 new members between 1928 and
1938; a mill church of the same denomination in Gastonia received 2,330 additions between 1925 and 1938; yet the two
churches had about the same number of members both at the beginning and the end of the period. That is, the mill church received twice as many new members as the uptown church but
achieved no greater absolute growth. As to church policies, pastors of mill churches complain that it is impossible for them to
stimulate interest in long-range church programs because the
worker often refuses to commit himself to the future of the community. In this respect the mill church is comparable to
churches composed chiefly of sharecroppers and tenant farmers. It is much easier to raise money for current expenses than
for permanent improvements. Programs which promise immediate results arouse interest; revival meetings stimulate greater
enthusiasm than extended programs of religious education. The
mill church must meet the immediate needs of a procession,
whereas the rural or uptown church can plan for an ongoing

19. The rate of labor turnover at one of the mills generally regarded as having a stable working force was 40 per cent for 1929, and much higher in many
mills (Bertha Carl Hipp, "A Gaston County Cotton Mill and Its Community"
[M.A. thesis, University of North Carolina, 1930], pp. 48–49). The recent depression appears to have reduced the rate of turnover considerably; in the
largest mill in the county the rate in 1939 was about 2 per cent a month.

A traditionally high rate of labor turnover is not to be interpreted, as it
generally is, as an indication of "shiftlessness" among mill workers. The rate
of turnover among workers has probably been no higher than the rate of
change in ownership and management of mills in Gaston County. A study of
twelve mill superintendents, based on brief biographies in the *Gastonia Gazette* (May 11–August 10, 1935), revealed that the average superintendent has
been in the industry 29.5 years and has worked in 10.5 mills—staying in each
mill on the average, therefore, less than three years.

program with a settled constituency. At a given moment a mill church more nearly resembles a series of meetings than it does an established institution.

Religious services in a mill church are, correspondingly, more intense in mood than those found elsewhere.[20] Lack of social security is compensated for by fervor of congregational response, and the degree to which all worshipers participate in the service is much higher than that prevailing in rural or uptown churches. A larger number of persons, relatively, sing in the choir, serve as ushers, offer personal testimonies, shake hands with each other. Music is more concrete and more rhythmic; it conjures up pictures rather than describes attitudes or ideas, and it appeals to the hands and feet more than to the head. The entire service in mill churches has an enthusiasm lacking in the more restrained worship of the "respectable people" uptown. The order of service is less formal, more personal. The services on Sunday evening are especially informal and exciting; they attract larger congregations than those held on Sunday morning, whereas the opposite is universally true in uptown churches.

Religious beliefs as well as practices are profoundly affected by the special problems inhering in the social and economic status of mill workers. Their religion is intimately related to the everyday struggles and vicissitudes of an insecure life, and proves useful for interpretation and for succor. It "works" and "changes things." The better-educated pastors of mill churches report that their parishioners hold an extraordinary number of "superstitions" concerning the efficacy of religion, of which the following are representative:

While the manager of a mill was absent from the community on a trip to Europe, the mill was forced to curtail operations because of inadequate orders. The workers thought curtailment was due simply and purely to the absence of the manager. (The manager thinks it was occasioned by poor business conditions.) The mill had run on a full-time schedule ever since he had come to the mill, and workers had associated prosperity with his presence. So the villagers held a prayer meeting, to pray that he would soon return. The arrival of the manager in New York was coincidental

20. Except among Negroes in the South, whose social status and emotional needs are comparable in many respects to those of the mill workers.

with the placement of several large orders for the mill, and the workers were immediately put on full-time employment again. Hearing that the manager had returned to this country, the workers declared that this was the answer to their prayer.

A woman missed a bus twice, caught the third bus, but found that her husband had died while she was enroute home. Missing the busses, she declared, had been "a sign."

A woman who had not been attending church had to go to a hospital; she attributed her misfortune to her sin, saying that the Lord had brought it on her. [Ministers report that such diagnosis is widespread, and that workers vow to attend church regularly when their misfortune passes—but seldom do.]

As evident in these illustrations, a strong admixture of magic is often found in the popular religion of mill workers. They trust devoutly in the power of prayer to get results and believe that the results will be precisely those they pray for. If consequents do not sustain their faith, they attribute their disappointment to their own sinfulness, or to the inscrutable will of the Almighty. When petitions are granted, they mark well the ritual by which they were made; a group of men in one church believe that prayer at "the white spot"—a bare place in an old field—has special efficacy, and go there frequently to pray.

Mill workers show no interest in theological questions as such; they simply accept notions coming from a wide variety of sources and weld them together without regard for consistency. The following statements, taken from "testimonies" made by them at services and from comments in private conversations, illustrate the ideas and phrases that recur when they attempt to describe their religious beliefs:

Jesus saves, and the way grows sweeter.

I'm so glad my name is written in the Book of Life.

When you have more than you can bear, cast it on Jesus, and He will always take it away.

I praise God that I have at last got shet [shed] of the World, so that hit don't bother me no more. I know a feller who tried to git right with God, and threw his cigarettes away but went right away

and bought cigars, tryin' to fool God. You cain't git the Holy
Sperit that way.

In all my trials, Jesus is my refuge. I have been persecuted so
much that I just smile now when somebody persecutes me, and cast
it all on Jesus. I thank the Lord I'm sanctified. I ain't never seen
a talking picture show; people who goes to sech places cain't save
nobody if they want to—you got to be different from the World.
You got to live with Jesus! Me and Him lives alone and has a
good time.

I was a backslider once, but praise God I'm back on the glory road
now.

It's a Christian's duty to speak out for the Master, instead of being too proud to testify. I'm glad I'm different from the World;
the way peoples does today sure cain't please the Lord. I'm glad I
got the old-time religion and am on the way to glory land.

In the theology of the mill worker, the world is a great battlefield on which the Lord and the Devil struggle for each individual soul. The "blood of Jesus" and the reading of the Bible
turn the tide of victory toward the Lord. As one mill minister
summarized it, "You have to carry a bucket of blood into the
pulpit to satisfy these people." The principal sins, in the eyes
of mill villagers, are such uptown "worldly amusements" as
playing cards, dancing, gambling, drinking, and swimming
with members of the opposite sex. Inclusion of mixed swimming
as a sin, found almost universally in the more sectarian groups,
is rather strange in view of the fact that sexual immorality is
discounted to a great extent among mill villagers. A similar
tendency to avow in theory that which is denied in practice is
found in the designation of profanity as a serious sin, though
profanity is both a solace and an art for a great many mill
workers.

As intimated frequently in the preceding paragraphs, the religion of the mill worker is affected at many points by economic
and social conditions in the midst of which he lives. Attempt at
summary of the satisfactions he finds in his church points to
economic influences even more clearly. In general terms, he de-
rives two benefits: the organization of life, and the transvaluation of life—though this terminology, of course, is alien to him.

There is no doubt that mill village churches have been among the most powerful agencies in community organization. Less exclusively than in rural areas, but more largely than in uptown districts, the church in the mill village is a community center; in the comparative absence of other social institutions, it is the focal point around which noneconomic life in the village largely revolves. Natural leaders among the workers find in it almost their only vehicle for expression of leadership; this fact helps to explain the continuing popularity of "testimony meetings" in which a number of worshipers are given opportunity to speak, and the comparatively large number of officers and committees found in mill churches. Those who do not aspire to leadership derive from participation in church activities a "sense of belonging." Church membership is an indication of respectability in the villages, as revealed in the following statement by a mill worker: "Nearly everybody goes to church around here. I go nearly every Sunday. Them sorry folks over there [a despised neighborhood] don't go to church much, but pretty near everybody over here goes, nearly every Sunday. The church is always full, and sometimes there ain't enough room for the congregation." Equation of church membership and respectability is illustrated even more graphically in the remark of a man generally regarded in his village as a worthless renegade: "I'm a damn rascal and can't nobody make me join no church until I get ready." The church is the center of most "worthwhile" community enterprises, including recreational activities. Even practices regarded as religious in character are frankly interpreted as being entertaining and enjoyable. A great many mill churches have as many as four or five prayer meetings weekly; one worker explained, "These prayer meetings are about the only entertainment we have."

But the worker also looks to his church to find transvaluation of life, which may take the form of reassurance or of escape, or both. By affirmation of values denied in the economic world, the church provides comfort and ultimate assurance; in its religious services it often affords escape temporarily from the economic and social situation in which workaday life must be spent. The difficulties of life for the mill worker in this world help to explain the noteworthy emphasis on otherworldliness in his churches. Most of the hymns and sermons in village churches point toward a more placid state and have little concern with mundane economic or social relations. Favorite hymns include: "Beulah Land," "When the Roll Is Called Up Yonder," "Higher Ground," "There Is Power in the Blood," "Revive Us Again," "I Can Hear My Saviour Calling," "I Left It All with Jesus (And Now He Shares My Every Care)," "Jesus Saves," "The Everlasting Arms," "The Home Over There," "Heavenly Sunlight," etc.[21] A well-loved stanza, typical in ideas of many others, says:

> While some live in splendid mansions,
>   And have wealth at their command,
> I'm a stranger and a pilgrim
>   Passing through this barren land.
>
> But God still answers prayer,
> In the same old-fashioned way.

Religious services also help the mill worker to transcend his daily life through providing excitement. All ministers acknowledge that mill workers need a strong emotional outlet because of the damming up of self-expression by the conditions amid which they live. The company-village system preëmpts nearly all their fundamental choices, and jobs in the mills are highly mechanical and routine in character. When his day in the mill is over, the worker frequently feels the need of a vigorous emotional massage; he finds it in hair-raising movies and emotional religious services, among other outlets. Newer sects, indulging in ecstatic religious emotion, thrive in the villages. Revival meetings have retained their popularity, and the tents of roving evangelists dot the mill hills during the summer months. A revival meeting becomes a community festival, and the astute evangelist provides as much entertainment and induces as much emotional response as possible. Saxophones and string ensembles are favorite props. "Special music" nearly always includes undisguised appeal to the simpler emotions of the hearers, with the yearning for home as an especially prominent motif—the

21. Cf. the otherworldly strain in Negro spirituals. For example, the spiritual "All God's Chillun Got Shoes" reflects escape from conditions in which many of the slaves were forced to go barefooted, with the result that their feet were often sore, bruised, torn by rocks and briers. In heaven, everybody would have shoes.

home from which one came to the mill village, or the home to which one hopes to go after the last spindle has been wound. Many of the favorite songs are in the form of ballads reminiscent of half-remembered mountain ballads, telling a story in a succession of from twelve to eighteen stanzas and adding to nostalgic escape. All parts of the revival service are designed to induce the high emotional crisis of "being saved"—saved to a personal security that transcends the troubles of the world.

Thus, whether to make this present life more endurable or to escape from it in otherworldliness and emotional excitement, the religion of the mill worker is heavily conditioned by the economic and social environment in which he lives. The forms assumed by his religious expression are not determined, however, by economic forces; they are largely religious in character and root principally in religious culture. Economic conditions figure prominently in the environment in the midst of which religious variations occur, and the survival of a particular variation appears to depend, to considerable degree, on whether it meets needs coming directly out of the economic background. Overtly, religion in mill churches appears to be indifferent to economic conditions; actually, it is in part a product of those conditions and, by diverting attention from them, is indirectly a sanction on them.

THE UPTOWN CHURCH

As already indicated, uptown churches have profited most of all from the rise of mills in Gaston County, insofar as measurable indices are concerned. By 1900 uptown churches had become the dominating churches in their respective denominations in the county, and they increasingly set the standards and formulated the policies for all their sister churches. Their rise to wealth and influence during the first two decades of the industrial revolution was phenomenal. The First Presbyterian Church of Gastonia between 1883 and 1899 increased in membership from 33 to 301, in total amount of money raised from $1,050 to $11,667, and in salary paid to its pastor from $50 to $1,325.[22] The uptown Methodist church in Gastonia in 1900,

22. *History and Souvenir of Presbyterian Church, Gastonia, North Carolina, 1899* (Gastonia, 1899) at Montreat Historical Foundation.

as compared with other Methodist churches in the county, reported the largest membership, a Sunday School enrollment
nearly twice as great as that of any other, church property
having higher valuation than that of all others combined, a salary nearly twice as high as that paid by any other church, and
an annual budget that exceeded by 50 per cent the total income
of all others.[23] One uptown church was erected in Gastonia in
1923 at a cost nearly equal to the value of all mill churches in
the county, approximately forty in number, at that time.

If religion in the mill villages is largely an escape from economic conditions, religion in the uptown churches is to considerable degree a sanction of prevailing economic arrangements.
Belonging to a church is as much a symbol of respectability
among uptown residents as it is among mill workers; in addition, church membership is often "good business," especially
for commercial and professional people. Uptown churches, in
turn, boast of the "prominent citizens" included in their membership. One minister asserts: "Everybody who is anybody in
this town belongs to my church." Another writes: "Thirty of
Gastonia's leading business and professional men constitute the
boards of the church. . . ."[24]

Major sins in the eyes of uptown church members include
sexual immorality, breaking one's word, not paying one's debts,
engaging in "shady business," and failure to recognize one's
civic and social obligations. Emphasis on economic virtues—
that is, on qualities essential for the transaction of business and
the validity of contracts—is especially significant; uptown
churches are more concerned with them, and less concerned with
personal virtues, than mill churches. In the latter, religion frequently invades the sphere of personal life, especially in the new
sects, prescribing even the amusements one may indulge. In uptown churches, however, religion must not meddle too much in
private life; greater economic security breeds personal independence. An uptown minister who announced that he would
attend a certain dance and then preach on the following Sunday morning against things he saw there[25] was severely criti-

23. *Minutes of the Western North Carolina Annual Conference, Methodist Episcopal Church, South, 1900*, statistical tables.
24. *Gastonia Gazette*, March 12, 1938.
25. *Ibid.*, September 6, 1921.

cized by many members of the uptown community on the grounds that the private life of church members was none of the minister's business and that, further, "they did not have to put up with it."

For uptown people, religion—well, it's just religion—which is to say, it is a set of actionways and thoughtways associated with, and largely confined to, the church, with the minister as exemplar and chief practitioner. Just as citizens of Gastonia believe, in general thoughtways—

that their schools are as good as there are anywhere

that their good roads are an undeniable symbol of progress

that you can tell mill folks by the common way they look

that all Northern writers want to take a slap at the South, when all the time they have worse conditions right there in New York

that a person ought to be a booster, not a knocker

that a mill owner ought to look after his people

that labor leaders are racketeers, and try to mislead the workers, with the result that workers lose their jobs—and you can't blame the mill owners for firing them after they've caused trouble

that they have one of the finest little cities of its size on earth

that several bad strikes have hurt the town, and it will take a long time to get over the black eye they gave

so they believe, in religious thoughtways—

that a man ought to belong to a church, and should attend as often as convenient, and should bear his part of the financial burden

that churches are essential to the welfare of the community[26]

that there is no use in getting all wrought up or emotional about religion

that if a person lives as decently as he can, that's all that God can expect of him

that a minister ought to be a good fellow in his private life, joining civic clubs, attending baseball games, and the like

that a minister ought to be a leader in all community enterprises, such as projects sponsored by the Chamber of Commerce

26. In 1938 the *Gastonia Gazette* ran a series of histories of Gaston County churches under the caption, "What Would Gaston Communities Be without Their Churches?"

that religion ought not to meddle in politics, except where moral
issues, such as prohibition, are involved
that Holy Rollers are ignorant, and are to be pitied
that mill churches meet the needs of mill workers very satisfac-
torily.

The dean of Gaston County ministers, stationed in an uptown church, recently celebrated the twenty-fifth anniversary
of his ministry in Gastonia. On that occasion he gave an accounting of his stewardship which affords considerable insight
into the functioning of an uptown church and into the role of
an uptown minister. He told his congregation that during the
twenty-five years he had preached 2,500 sermons, had delivered
2,500 talks to schools, civic clubs, Masonic gatherings, Bible
classes, men's clubs, and the like, had baptized 790 infants, per-
formed 257 marriages, and conducted 283 funerals, and had
made between 25,000 and 30,000 visits. Five new automobiles,
including the first Chevrolet sedan that came to town, had been
given to him by the people, and a trip to Europe lasting fourteen weeks and costing $2,100, not to mention other trips, gifts,
and favors. During the twenty-five years the church had raised
a total of $740,000, of which half went to missions.

"You have been mighty good to me," he said. "These twenty-
five years have been the happiest of my life. There have been
no discord, no factions, no differences, no splits or quarrels in
the church in this time. No one has said an unkind or cross word
to me in all this time, and harmony and satisfaction have prevailed."

The community joined to pay tribute to the minister. He was
extolled as one of the leaders of community life. The Rotary
Club had a special program in honor of his anniversary at
which he was congratulated on having drawn various members
of the club to church services for twenty-five years, and was assured of the esteem of the entire community.

The minister lives in a large, well-tended manse on one of the
best streets. He is proud that many of the town's leading citizens, including a number of mill owners, are members of his
church, and that they take him into their councils on civic matters. He deplores a violent strike that shook the community and
the nation in 1929. "The people had no cause to strike," he

says. "I happen to know how much the mill owners in my church had done for them." He preaches on theological subjects (i.e., doctrinal questions) almost exclusively.

Uptown churches in the county put an increasing amount of emphasis on religious education and a decreasing amount on revival meetings, which have a tendency, it is felt, to be undignified and fanatical. Their choirs are usually robed and their minister speaks in a well-modulated voice. Most uptown ministers are designated by members of their congregations as "very scholarly" and are automatically called "Doctor"; ministers who bear such traditions convincingly are considered a "credit to the town" and a mark of superiority over rival churches. A minister must not be "too deep" in the pulpit, however, if he wishes to hold his congregation; Gastonia prefers ministers who allegedly are scholars in the quiet of their studies but are "good talkers" in the pulpit, "good fellows" on the street, and sympathetic comforters in time of trouble. In a sermon, personality is more important than brains, and delivery than content. One of the first things a Gastonian will say about his preacher is that he does, or does not, have "a good delivery." The preacher must speak with assurance of those "eternal verities" which everybody believes—or at least was taught in childhood to believe. He may startle his hearers occasionally with some fresh insight, and thereby retain their interest, but the congregation begins to feel uneasy if his viewpoints become too cosmopolitan and remote. The role of the uptown minister, and of his church, is not to transcend immediate cultural boundaries but to symbolize and sanction the rightness of things as they are.

CHAPTER VI

RELIGIOUS DENOMINATIONS AND SOCIAL CLASSES

THE population of Gaston County is divided not only into diverse social classes but also into various religious groupings. Religious differences existed in the county before the industrial revolution brought acute social division, and have continued to exist through the successive decades. They have been both modified and increased, however, by the economic transformation; older denominations have been changed and newer sects have risen to challenge them. As industrialization proceeded apace, religious denominations, as denominations, were affected almost as patently as the individual churches by which they were represented. Wide social differences appeared between Presbyterians and Methodists, Lutherans and Baptists, with each denomination becoming especially identified with one (or at most two) of the emerging social classes. When the older religious traditions proved too inflexible to meet needs arising from novel social situations, new sects arose to fill the gaps: the Church of God, the Wesleyan Methodists, the Pentecostal Holiness Church, and other neoteric cults.

The process of religious transformation was not one of simple, one-sided adaptation. Diverse religious traditions responded variously to changing social conditions: for example, the Presbyterian and Methodist systems alike were remarkably affected by developments in the economic sphere, but their religious dissimilarities were of crucial importance in shaping the way in which each reacted. The presence of varieties of ecclesiastical structure and religious culture modified the process of religious change, rendering it very complex rather than simple in character. New economic forces, in their impact on religious institutions, found semi-intransigent materials with which to work.

In short, denominations as such more nearly preserved a fundamentally religious base of organization than individual churches did, and an analysis of the effect of economic change upon them explicates further the modes by which religious and economic institutions tend to interact.

CLASS AFFILIATIONS OF DENOMINATIONS

Nearly all the older denominations in Gaston County have grown significantly in number of churches (Table XVIII), membership (Table XIX), and wealth (Tables XX and XXI) as industrial expansion provided an enlarged background of population and economic resources, and new religious sects have been given opportunity to appear. Differential rates of growth among the denominations have been far more significant, however, than the mere fact of general expansion. Examination of the relation of particular denominations to the different social classes provides clues for the understanding of their unequal growth and also furnishes a background for interpretation of the emergence of novel religious forms.

No denomination in the county has notably surpassed the others in ability to combine the different social classes within

TABLE XVIII

ACTIVE CHURCHES IN GASTON COUNTY, BY DENOMINATIONS, 1880–1939

Denomination	1880	1890	1900	1910	1920	1930	1939
Presbyterian	8	11	14	16	19	19	19
Lutheran	5	9	12	14	14	13	13
Baptist	8	12	16	23	28	35	37
M.E., South	10	16	22	23	24	26	26
Methodist Protestant	2	2	2	2	2	1	1
M.E., North	4	4	4	3	3	2	2
A.R. Presbyterian	1	2	4	4	5	5	5
Episcopal	1	2	2	3	3	3	3
Roman Catholic	2	2	2	3	3	3	3
Wesleyan Methodist	0	0	0	6	5	5	5
Pentecostal Holiness	0	0	0	1	1	1	4
Church of God	0	0	0	0	1	2	8
Free-Will Baptist	0	0	0	0	0	1	4
Miscellaneous	0	0	0	0	1	5	15
TOTALS	41	60	78	98	109	121	145

TABLE XIX

GROWTH IN CHURCH MEMBERSHIP, BY DENOMINATIONS, IN GASTON COUNTY, 1880–1939*

Older Denominations	1880	1890	1900	1910	1920	1930	1938–39
Presbyterian	627	979	1,208	1,984	2,869	3,119	3,857
Lutheran	645	711	1,068	1,274	1,242	1,357	1,521
Baptist	747	1,140	1,819	3,979	6,384	11,240	12,712
M.E., South	735	1,440	2,824	3,228	4,943	6,758	7,600
A.R. Presbyterian	167	304	419	575	722	899	1,053
Episcopal				181	118	184	230
Newer Sects							
Wesleyan Methodist				636	285	405	300
Pentecostal Holiness						63	178
Free-Will Baptist							852
Church of God							904

* The figures given in this and subsequent tables in this chapter were computed for individual churches from statistics reported by them to their parent bodies. Figures for churches not reporting were arrived at through the denominational (not the general) average. Where no figures were available for a denomination, no estimate has been made.

TABLE XX

GROWTH IN AVERAGE WEALTH PER CHURCH, BY DENOMINATIONS, IN GASTON COUNTY, AS BETWEEN 1900 AND 1938–39

Denomination	Average Value of Church Property		Average Salary Paid		Average Amount of Money Raised	
	1900	1938–39	1900	1938–39	1900	1938–39
Lutheran	$1,628	$22,193			$304	$1,932
Presbyterian			$304	$1,288		
Baptist	1,080	27,035	190	1,268	596	3,547
Methodist, South	2,339	31,608	206	1,154	861	3,717
A.R. Presbyterian	1,550	23,000	272	1,350	542	3,707
Episcopal		24,283				
Wesleyan Methodist		8,000		1,252		2,418
Pentecostal Holiness		2,400		577		1,161
Free-Will Baptist		1,750		226		425
GENERAL AVERAGE	$1,766	$24,923	$230	$1,207	$669	$3,081

its individual churches, as Table XXII reveals. Though Presbyterian congregations have succeeded most fully in incor-
porating small minority groups, they include only one church
in the county which does not have a majority group comprising

TABLE XXI

GROWTH IN AVERAGE WEALTH PER CAPITA, OF DENOMINATIONS
IN GASTON COUNTY, AS BETWEEN 1900 AND 1938–39

Denomination	Average Value of Church Property per Member		Average Salary Paid to Pastor per Member		Average Amount of Money Raised per Member	
	1900	1938-39	1900	1938-39	1900	1938-39
Lutheran	$18.29	$189.68			$3.42	$16.51
Presbyterian			$3.53	$ 6.34		
Methodist	10.46	108.25	1.61	3.95	6.73	12.73
Baptist	9.47	78.59	1.66	3.69	5.23	10.31
Wesleyan Methodist		133.33		20.87		40.30
Pentecostal Holiness		53.33		12.82		25.80
Free-Will Baptist		8.22		1.06		1.99

TABLE XXII

COMBINATION OF SOCIAL CLASSES IN THE CHURCHES OF GASTON
COUNTY, BY DENOMINATIONS, 1939

Denomination	Total Number of Churches	With Minority Groups of 20 Per cent		Without Majority Groups of 66.6 Per cent	
		Number	Percentage	Number	Percentage
Lutheran	13	3	23	2	15
Presbyterian	19	9	47	1	5
Methodist	26	6	23	3	12
Baptist	37	9	24	3	8
Others	50	7	14	0	0

at least two thirds of the total membership. Churches of the
minor denominations are almost completely dominated by one
social class, most of them being exclusively mill churches. Individual churches in the county are mostly class churches, irre-
spective of denominational affiliation.

Each denomination, as well as its individual churches, has

tended to become identified with one, or perhaps two, of the
three social types. No denomination is represented equally or
proportionately among the three classes in number of churches
or distribution of membership, with one possible exception (Tables XXIII and XXIV). Classification according to the pre-
dominant types of membership results as follows: Presbyterian,

TABLE XXIII

CHANGES, BY DENOMINATIONS AND TYPES, IN ACTIVE CHURCHES IN GASTON COUNTY, AS BETWEEN 1880 AND 1939

Denomination	Rural		Mill		Uptown		Total	
	1880	1939	1880	1939	1880	1939	1880	1939
Presbyterian	8	7	0	5	0	7	8	19
Lutheran	5	6	0	2	0	5	5	13
Baptist	6	8	0	25	2	4	8	37
M.E., South	8	9	1	11	1	6	10	26
M.E., North	3	1	0	0	1	1	4	2
Methodist Protestant	1	0	0	0	1	1	2	1
A.R. Presbyterian	1	2	0	0	0	3	1	5
Episcopal	1	1	0	0	0	2	1	3
Roman Catholic	2	0	0	0	0	3	2	3
Wesleyan Methodist	0	0	0	4	0	1	0	5
Pentecostal Holiness	0	0	0	4	0	0	0	4
Church of God	0	0	0	8	0	0	0	8
Free-Will Baptist	0	0	0	4	0	0	0	4
Miscellaneous	0	0	0	13	0	2	0	15
TOTALS	35	34	1	76	5	35	41	145

uptown; Lutheran, uptown and rural; Baptist, mill; Methodist, mill and uptown; Episcopal, uptown; Wesleyan Methodist,
Church of God, Pentecostal Holiness, and Free-Will Baptist,
mill (Table XXIV). The distribution of membership in the
Baptist denomination corresponds rather closely with the relative numerical strength of the three social classes but by the
same token it is overwhelmingly composed of mill workers.
Other denominations fail to approximate either equal or proportionate coverage of the social spectrum.

Similar class alignment becomes evident from examination of
the growth in wealth of the various denominations (Tables XX

and XXI), though special features disturb the neatness of the pattern. The Presbyterian and Lutheran communions, to which most of the earlier settlers and early mill builders belonged, have retained their original advantage in economic wealth per member, but have been surpassed in wealth per church by the Methodists and Baptists whose congregations have come to be much larger on the average because of their extensive influence among mill workers. More important variations occur between the older churches and the newer sects. As might be expected,

TABLE XXIV

MEMBERSHIP OF DENOMINATIONS, BY TYPES OF CHURCHES,
IN GASTON COUNTY IN 1938–39

	Membership of					
Denomination	Rural Churches	Per cent of Total	Mill Churches	Per cent of Total	Uptown Churches	Per cent of Total
Presbyterian	1,019	26	631	17	2,147	57
Lutheran	697	48	104	7	661	45
Baptist	1,715	13	8,470	67	2,570	20
M.E., South	1,278	17	3,339	44	2,983	39
A.R. Presbyterian	431	41			622	59
Episcopal	32	14			198	86
Wesleyan Methodist			223	74	77	26
Pentecostal Holiness			178	100		
Free-Will Baptist			852	100		
Church of God			904	100		

the Wesleyan Methodist and Pentecostal Holiness sects fall far below the older bodies in economic wealth per church, but exceed them, oddly enough, in contributions per member, though their membership is drawn from the lowest income groups. Members of most of the newer sects outstrip members of the older and wealthier denominations in their financial support of the church, thereby disproving a purely economic interpretation of religious institutions. Analysis of the membership of one local congregation of the Church of God, for example, revealed that fewer members (64 per cent) contributed anything than in average Methodist churches of each social type, but that the average annual donation per contributor, $49.98, was more than twice as high as the average in an uptown Methodist church.[1]

Explanation of this divergence between older and newer denominations in per capita financial support of the church illustrates clearly the manner in which economic and religious factors interplay in the life of a religious institution. Among the newer sects rigorous religious requirements for membership have resulted in small congregations, which in turn demand high contributions per member if an institutional program is to be supported. For instance, the total number of Wesleyan Methodists in the county is less than the average membership of a single Baptist church, and yet they operate five churches in separate communities. More important than institutional necessity, however, is the religious requirement by which the necessity is met—namely, the practice of tithing, generally expected of members of the sects. Whereas adherents of the older denominations give to the church in terms of "what they can spare," sect members give a tenth of their income; if the average contribution of members of the Church of God, as listed above, is multiplied by ten, the result approximates the total annual income of the contributors. Of an income of about $500 a year, they give nearly $50 to the church—a percentage which is obviously too high, as contrasted with that of wealthier churchmen, for explanation in simple economic terms. On the other hand economic factors help to shape religious differences even within the newer sects: the Free-Will Baptist congregations are drawn from lower economic groups than those of any other sect, with the result that requirements for membership and insistence on tithing have been considerably relaxed in order to secure enough members to support the denominational program. While exclusive religious requirements impinge upon the economic possessions of church members, they tend to be modified when the economic necessities of religious institutions demand or permit.

The reciprocal character of the relation between economic

1. For details, compare these figures with those in Table XVII. In the rural Methodist church, 85 per cent of the members contributed, with the average contribution being $7.28; in the Methodist mill church, 86 per cent of the members contributed, with the average amount being $13.48; in the uptown Methodist church, 66 per cent contributed, and the average contribution was $23.39.

and religious factors is similarly evident at other points. It has operated, most pregnantly of all, in the efforts of the various denominations to enlist mill workers in their respective memberships. As already seen,[2] most of the major religious bodies sought to capture the new industrial population, and expended considerable effort and money toward that end. The

TABLE XXV

MILL CHURCHES ESTABLISHED, BY DENOMINATIONS, IN GASTON COUNTY, 1880–1939*

Older Denominations	*Mill Churches Established*						
	1881–1890	1891–1900	1901–1910	1911–1920	1921–1930	1931–1939	*Totals*
Presbyterian	0	1	2	2	1	0	6
Lutheran	0	0	1	1	0	0	2
Baptist	1	3	5	5	10	3	27
M.E., South	2	2	2	1	4	0	11
Episcopal	0	0	0	1	0	0	1
Roman Catholic	0	0	0	0	0	0	0
Newer Sects							
Wesleyan Methodist			6	1	0	0	7
Pentecostal Holiness			1	0	0	3	4
Church of God				1	1	6	8
Free-Will Baptist					1	3	4
Miscellaneous				1	3	9	13
TOTALS	3	6	17	13	20	24	83

* Does not include mill churches abandoned—a total of nine. Does not include churches changing from some other type to mill—a total of one.

Baptists, Methodists, and newer sects have succeeded out of all proportion to their Presbyterian and Lutheran rivals, however, and have increased in number of churches and in total membership accordingly. From 1890 to 1930 the Baptists led all other denominations in the establishment of mill churches, and from 1921 to 1930 equaled all other denominations combined (Table XXV). Since 1930 leadership has been taken over by the newer sects, which have organized twenty-one mill churches in the last decade, as compared with three for the Baptists and

2. See chap. v.

none for the other major bodies. The Methodists have more mill churches than rural or uptown congregations but have fallen far behind the Baptists. The Lutherans have been able to establish only two industrial churches, and only five such churches organized by the Presbyterians have survived. The Roman Catholic and Protestant Episcopal churches have never planted any successful missions among the mill workers, though they have been active in Gaston County throughout the period of industrialization and have made several efforts in that direction.

Disproportionate success of Baptists, Methodists, and newer sects in reaching the mill villagers cannot be explained in terms of an initial numerical or financial advantage in Gaston County. In 1880 the four major denominations (Presbyterian, Lutheran, Methodist, and Baptist) were about equal in number of members in the county (Table XIX). The Presbyterians and Lutherans, being descendants of the early Scotch and German settlers, were well established socially and economically as compared with the Baptists. Methodism had entered the vicinity about 1787 and had more churches in the county in 1880 than any of its major rivals. The Baptists, on the other hand, had almost no following there even at the time of the Civil War.[3] They were generally discriminated against in the vicinity and were excluded from the use of school buildings for services in several Gaston communities.[4] The pious Lutheran father of one of the first Baptist ministers in the county, it is reported, "could hardly endure the thought of having raised and educated a Baptist preacher."[5] Less than five families in the uptown Baptist church in Gastonia were pioneers in the town, and in the earlier years the church found it difficult to enlist newcomers, who were told that they had better join the Lutheran and Presbyterian churches if they wanted to associate with the "best people."

3. John R. Logan, *Sketches, Historical and Biographical, of the Broad River and King's Mountain Baptist Associations* (Shelby, N.C., 1887), pp. 556–605; W. A. Graham, *History of the South Fork Baptist Association, or, The Baptists for One Hundred Years in Lincoln, Catawba and Gaston Counties, North Carolina* (Lincolnton, N.C., 1901).

4. Rev. C. J. Black, *A Short History of Sandy Plains Baptist Church* (Gastonia, c. 1923), pp. 6–7.

5. *Ibid.*, pp. 48–49.

Obviously, therefore, the Baptists did not possess favored status or wealth by which to impress the incoming industrial workers. This very fact, of course, worked in their favor in proportion as the newcomers recognized their own inferior status. Because members of Presbyterian and Lutheran churches in the county were descendants of early settlers, had been in residence longer, and had acquired more property, on the average, than Methodists and (more especially) Baptists, the latter denominations were more acceptable to the impoverished mill workers. Methodists and Baptists tended to be "plain folks," whereas Presbyterians and Lutherans were mill owners, merchants, professional men, and independent farmers. Many of the same cultural differences that led to the emergence of separate mill churches likewise made it natural that these churches should belong chiefly to the Methodist and Baptist denominations.

Other theories are advanced in Gaston County in explanation of the popularity of Baptists and Methodists among the mill workers. Baptist ministers in the county argue that their denomination has outstripped all others because it has consistently preached the simple gospel of the New Testament in a way easily understandable by untutored mill workers, and also because the emphasis of the denomination has been intensely evangelistic. Methodist ministers sometimes attempt to explain the growth of their congregations by their system of an itinerant ministry; the limited pastorate, they argue, has insured the circulation of a diversity of ministerial talent among the churches. Neither of these diagnoses is convincing. Baptist preachers have had no monopoly on a simple gospel or evangelistic fervor. The argument from itineracy is likewise inadequate: the average length of pastorates of Baptist ministers has been greater than that of Methodists (see Table XXVII), yet Baptists have outnumbered Methodists.

Another interpretation attributes the failure of Lutheran and Presbyterian churches among mill workers to an antipathy on the part of the latter to ritualistic and liturgical worship services. Workers, it is said, have regarded these denominations as "high-falutin," "cold," "stuck-up," and the like. Mill villagers are not content simply to have the truth expounded and the Word opened to them, a Presbyterian minister complained; unless there is much emotionalism and drama, they think there is little religion.[6] There is no doubt, for example, that the custom of public baptisms on river banks helps to explain the great appeal of the Baptist church to the masses; these were dramatic, impressive spectacles, attended by thousands of people in the days when public spectacles were comparatively rare and amusement was scarce.[7] Nevertheless, arguments affirming universal aversion of mill workers to particular denominations are of minor merit only; one Presbyterian minister in one year enlisted 765 members for a new Presbyterian church organized in a mill village. Such arguments are valid insofar as they point toward previous religious traditions of the workers, most of whom had not been accustomed to the ritual found in Presbyterian and Lutheran churches.

The policies adopted by Presbyterian and Lutheran bodies toward the establishment of separate mill churches militated against the extension of their influence. Soon after the Civil War the Presbytery of King's Mountain adopted a semiparish system, refusing to allow the organization of Presbyterian churches too near to each other, with the result, as one minister complained shortly thereafter, that "churches of other orders" came in and usurped the field.[8] The Presbyterians held too long to the theory that it was best for mill people to worship in uptown churches—a theory defended on the ground that contact with educated persons would provide elevating influences. Though Presbyterian churches in Gaston County modified this view and attempted to do special missionary work in the villages, they have prosecuted the erection of separate churches for mill workers with less vigor than the Methodist and Baptist denominations. Lutherans still follow, with few exceptions, an unwritten policy of putting no churches on mill-owned property, and of accepting no direct subsidies from mill manage-

6. The minister told a story of a Negro who went to a Lutheran church but got nothing out of the sermon. He then went to an Episcopal church but did not like the people. At length he went to a Baptist church and said he liked that, because in the Baptist church "Yo' is dipped and done with."

7. For a graphic description of a "baptizin'" in a river and the excitement attached thereto, see Grace Lumpkin, *To Make My Bread* (New York, 1932), pp. 59–64.

8. Rev. R. Z. Johnston, *Historical Sketch of Goshen Presbyterian Church, Gaston County, N.C.* (Shelby, N.C., 1889), p. 4.

ment; they have insisted that the church must embrace all economic groups rather than allow itself to reflect economic divisions. As a result they have reached few mill workers, and have had no greater success than others in combining different economic groups within their fellowship.

Most significant of all, the mill workers belonged almost entirely to the Methodist and Baptist denominations before they came to Gaston County, and refused to change their previous religious affiliation in their new economic setting. The Methodists and Baptists have prevailed, by a large majority, in the South generally. In some regions of the Carolina mountains as many as 90 per cent of the church members have been Baptists. This circumstance, however, simply pushes investigation back farther and raises questions as to why the workers had belonged to these denominations in the first place and why they did not change their affiliation when offered alternatives in Gaston County.

For clues to a theory which will gather up the elements of truth in all the foregoing diagnoses, it is useful to compare the types of ministers commonly found in the various denominations. Whether as symptom or cause, or both, of his particular religious cultus as it is exemplified in his congregation, the minister is the official representative of his church to the public and typifies the appeal of his institution to the different social classes. He is the supreme custodian and exemplar in a local community of the special religious tradition to which he belongs, charged with preserving the integrity and extending the influence of that tradition. In preparation for the task he has been professionally trained in the history, theology, liturgy, and polity of his denomination. Comparative study of ministerial training, therefore, may clarify the patterns of religious and economic interaction, and the way in which particular denominations and social classes become congenial.

MINISTERS AND SOCIAL CLASSES

In general the influence and extension of a denomination over the masses of the people in Gaston County have tended to vary inversely with the degree of professional education required of its ministers. In terms more appropriate to the county, the more highly educated preachers have not attracted the mill workers, who have come to comprise two thirds of the total population. A denomination has lost influence in the mill villages in rough proportion as its ministerial representatives there became professional religious experts, as a survey by denominations discloses (Table XXVI).

The Presbyterian church traditionally has insisted on an educated ministry and has established theological seminaries in all those regions in which it has been strong. As early as 1819

TABLE XXVI

EDUCATIONAL ACHIEVEMENT OF MINISTERS SERVING GASTON COUNTY CHURCHES, 1938–39

	Presby-terian	Lu-theran	Meth-odist	Baptist	Church of God
Total Number	14	9	20	34	11
Grammar School or Less			1	4	8
Finished High School Only			2	11	3
College Degree	14	9	17	19	0
Seminary Degree, from Own					
Denominational Seminaries	13	8	8	6	0
Elsewhere	0	0	0	0	0

it set aside funds to assist ministerial candidates in obtaining proper training;[9] one of its branches argued some decades later that these candidates, usually being poor, should be assisted in order that they might preach more effectively to the poor.[10] Requirements for ordination have included, for the last one hundred years or longer, a college degree and a three-year seminary course, including the study of Greek and Hebrew. Every active Presbyterian pastor in Gaston County at present except one meets this standard and exceptions in the past have been very rare.[11]

9. *Minutes of the General Assembly of the Presbyterian Church in the U. S., 1920*, Appendix I.

10. *Minutes of the General Assembly of the Presbyterian Church in the Confederate States of America, 1864*, pp. 326–334.

11. I. S. McElroy, *Some Pioneer Presbyterian Preachers of the Piedmont North Carolina* (Gastonia, 1928), contains a number of brief biographies of Presbyterian preachers in Gaston County and vicinity during the nineteenth century, nearly all of whom were graduates of outstanding seminaries, especially Princeton.

Equal emphasis has prevailed in the Lutheran denomination. A system of beneficiary education has been supported for at least forty years, and ministers have been expected to take a college degree and three years of seminary work. Every minister in the county at present, except one, meets this requirement.

As compared with Presbyterian and Lutheran standards, Methodist demands have been relatively low. The Methodist Episcopal Church, South, did not establish a college degree as a prerequisite to ordination until 1934, and it was possible until 1940 to circumvent this requirement. Less than half of its preachers in Gaston County at present have had seminary training; most of them now have college degrees, but several older men, representative of past standards, have only a high school education or less.

The policy of the Baptist churches has been even less exacting. The denomination has never erected an educational requirement for its ministers, or maintained an informal standard, or insisted on a course of study. In 1869–70 there were only two college graduates in the Baptist Association which included most of the churches in Gaston County.[12] In 1903 few Baptist preachers in the county had even a high school education and college men were almost unknown. The tendency in more recent years has been to give preference to better-educated men, but only 56 per cent of them at present have college degrees and only 18 per cent have completed a seminary course.

The newer sects in the county are led by ministers almost wholly uneducated. Several of them find it necessary to have some more literate person read the Scriptures in their services. Others did not go beyond the fourth or fifth grade in the public schools; none have college degrees. Most of them are on sabbatical leave from jobs in cotton mills. There are no established educational requirements for preachers in the sects with which they are affiliated, though there are trends in that direction.

These differences in educational norms for ministers have been of far-reaching significance in respect to pastoral work among mill workers, both before and after the workers came to the mill villages. For one thing the Presbyterian and Lutheran

12. C. J. Black, *op. cit.,* p. 56.

denominations, because of their high and expensive educational requirements, found it difficult to secure enough ministers, especially when thousands of mill workers began to migrate to the county. The Evangelical Lutheran Tennessee Synod, to which Lutheran churches in Gaston County belonged, complained in 1880, and again in 1889, of insufficient pastors to serve congregations in North Carolina, and reported that several large congregations were without pastors.[13] Presbyterian churches in the county faced the same difficulty, and several of them were without a regular pastor on each of the decennial years after 1880. The Methodist and Baptist denominations, on the other hand, were able to commission ministers as opportunity for service presented itself, without long and costly periods of preparation. Further, they were able to send part-time pastors into parishes unable to support the full-time services of a minister; less specialized, Baptist and Methodist preachers were often able to earn part of their livelihood in other pursuits and to follow the ministry as an avocation. As over against the professional standards of Lutheran and Presbyterian ministers, the Baptists and Methodists were able to provide pastoral service on the basis of demand rather than of theological or educational competence.

Of even greater import, the higher educational status of Presbyterian and Lutheran ministers tended to isolate them from the less-educated masses. They were often unwilling to climb the mountains and visit remote farms from which mill workers subsequently were to come, or, after mill villages had been established, to spend any considerable period of their ministry amid the ignorance and squalor of the transplanted villagers. High educational training made it more difficult to live at the level of the mill population or to think and speak in terms attractive to mill workers. As a consequence, mill villagers felt less at home in Presbyterian and Lutheran churches than in those presided over by less-tutored Methodist and Baptist ministers, who were more nearly of the people themselves in standard of living, thought, and speech.

Insistence on an educated ministry also resulted in strengthening the denominational cultus as such, making it less flexible

13. *Minutes of the Evangelical Lutheran Tennessee Synod, 1880,* p. 2; *1889,* p. 35.

to meet new conditions and new demands brought by economic transformation. Ministers trained in seminaries were often more concerned with preserving religious traditions than with adapting them. Presbyterian and Lutheran churches carried on in their accustomed ways, under the leadership of pastors carefully schooled in those ways, and were little influenced in ritual, organization, or ideas by the industrial revolution. Methodist and Baptist ministers, and more recently those of newer sects, have had less training in religious traditions and more experience in the immediate conditions of a culture in process of transformation. They have been more sensitive, therefore, to emerging needs in the changing culture and more flexible in adapting their programs to new conditions. They have thereby been able to interest and lead the mill workers, whose outlook likewise has been obtained in the school of economic realities rather than in theological seminaries.

For example, preaching in Gaston County varies more by denominations than it does by economic type of church, and the theological training of the preachers appears to be the chief factor in explanation. The sermons of uptown ministers resemble those of mill preachers of their own denomination more nearly tnan they do those of other uptown preachers belonging to different theological traditions. Uptown ministers agree in being somewhat more sedate, restrained, and grammatical than their brethren in the mill churches, but there is even wider divergence in degree of restraint among uptown preachers themselves. Even if he preaches in a church valued at $250,000, the uptown Baptist preacher in Gastonia delivers a fervent evangelistic sermon (without benefit of Greek and Hebrew) and calls for repentant sinners to come to the altar at the close (though a decreasing number come). His denominational colleague in a $9,000 building in a mill village at the edge of town does the same, and the sinners come abundantly. They have been coming for at least sixty years, and their names have swelled the membership rolls. Presbyterian ministers, meanwhile, have been more interested in theological topics than in the sorry state of man, and the mill workers have not been able to understand their message.

More recently Methodist and Baptist ministers have become better educated and are tending to lose their influence over the mill villagers to the newer emotional sects in rough proportion as the educational gap widens. One Methodist preacher recently bewildered his congregation of mill workers by declaring in a sermon that "there is no precise and indefectible definition of sin in the Bible, because of the undogmatic state of apocalypse and eschatology as found therein." He also used such terms as "conditional immortality," "sacerdotalism," "entity," "cognitive," and "rational." At the end of his sermon, he bowed to tradition by making a "proposition" that called for repentant sinners to come to the "altar"; when one came, he apologized for the repentant one, telling the congregation that "X is all right; he sometimes slips just a little." After the service he apologized to a ministerial colleague for having made a proposition at all: "You must face people like these with propositions," he said. "An intelligent man can make his own private decisions."

No clear and direct correlation exists in the Methodist and Baptist churches of Gaston County as yet between the degree of education a minister has and the type of church to which he is assigned.[14] Men with seminary degrees are found in rural and mill churches, and one or two uptown pastors lack seminary training. Already, however, ministers without college or seminary backgrounds are confined to mill and rural parishes, and nearly all the more highly trained men tend to shrink from these assignments, or to regard them as steppingstones toward "better" appointments. One young Methodist pastor with a seminary degree reports that it is a terrific struggle to preach on Sunday morning to a congregation whose education averages between the third and fourth grade—a congregation with which he has no cultural contact. Nor does it encourage him, he adds, to see his wife sitting in the congregation with women accustomed to dipping snuff continually and living in terms of low ideals and aspirations. If a trace of snobbery has entered into a complaint of this sort, it is nevertheless representative of a widespread ministerial reaction.

14. Trends toward positive correlation are reported to be evident in wider contexts, with less-educated ministers assigned to rural and industrial parishes. See C. C. Taylor, *Rural Sociology* (New York, 1926), p. 223. Cf. Margaret M. Ledbetter, "The Village Church in North Carolina" (A.M. thesis, Duke University, 1931), pp. 95–106, and B. H. Smith, "The Social Significance of the Southern Cotton Mill Community" (M.A. thesis, Emory University, 1925), pp. 38–41.

Educated ministers almost universally complain of the lack of privacy in a mill village and of the inferior educational opportunities provided for their children. They share most of the attitudes of uptown citizens toward mill workers, generally regarding them as immature children, on the one hand, and as especially perverse and inferior on the other. A mixture of sadness and cynicism often enters into their descriptions of their parishioners, typified in the comment of a pastor as he noted large holes torn in the walls of Sunday School rooms in his

TABLE XXVII

AVERAGE LENGTH OF PASTORATES IN GASTON COUNTY,
BY DENOMINATIONS AND TYPES OF CHURCHES,
1880–1939*

| | Average Length of Pastorate, in Years | | | |
Denomination	Rural Churches	Mill Churches	Uptown Churches	All Types
Lutheran			6.48	6.48
Presbyterian	3.93	3.41	5.83	4.37
Baptist	3.24	3.07	3.50	3.22
Methodist		2.05	2.22	2.13
All four denominations	3.62	2.72	3.82	3.31

* Based on a study of 453 pastorates, of which 76 were in rural churches, 198 in mill churches, and 179 in uptown churches. By denominations, these pastorates were distributed as follows: Lutheran, 33; Presbyterian, 83; Methodist, 151; Baptist, 186.

church building: "You'd know you were in a mill village." Most ministers acknowledge that they have never known a clergyman who would prefer a mill village church to any other type; their judgment is confirmed by the fact that only one ever came to Gaston County and voluntarily dedicated his ministry to mill people in preference to a place in an uptown church. When assigned to a mill parish, ministers generally seek to be transferred after a minimum of conscientious service. Their restlessness is reflected in the rate of ministerial turnover in mill churches, where the average length of pastorates is 75 per cent of that in rural churches and 71 per cent of that in uptown churches (Table XXVII).

In short, almost none of the ministers representing major de-

nominations in the textile villages share the cultural status of
their parishioners or desire to invest there a large part of their
years of service. Whatever their personal social backgrounds
may be—and many of them come from families of economic
status little higher than that of the mill workers—their educational achievements tend to isolate them from the less-educated
masses and to identify them in sympathy and standards with
the uptown class. Given the kind of professional training most
of them have received, they no longer sense or represent the
peculiar needs of their mill parishioners. Ministers of mill
churches, indeed, constitute very important intermediaries for
the transmission of uptown norms to the mill class, and for the
maintenance of the control of the uptown class over other social
groups. The fundamental lines of cleavage between ministers
are denominational rather than social in character; while they
disagree vigorously over theological and denominational matters, they are pretty much the same in social outlook and in
personal aspiration to uptown status. One mill preacher, for
example, used illustrations from the game of golf in his Sunday
morning sermon (though none of his auditors could afford
golf), and urged his congregation to be as regular and punc-
tual in church attendance as directors of a corporation are at
their meetings.

To the degree to which mill ministers of any denomination
lack insight into the special needs of the mill class and the capacity to identify themselves with those needs, a denomination
fails to enlist or retain the support of mill workers. The minister of the mill church is the center around which the institution
revolves; religion for its members is a very concrete affair, demanding a visible symbol and object of loyalty. Mill pastors
universally affirm, often regretfully, that they find themselves,
rather than faith in God or devotion to the church, the focal
point of religion among their parishioners. By the same token
a mill church with a disappointed, condescending pastor is
doomed to disintegration. In contrast, preachers who "side with
the people" and reveal genuine enthusiasm for their work are
rewarded with an increasing number of adherents. So Methodist and Baptist ministers defeated their Lutheran and Presbyterian rivals four decades ago, but in turn are being slowly vanquished at present by "ignorant and disreputable" preachers of

the newer sects, who are of the people and manifest an unfeigned enthusiasm for service to the people.

Despite the years spent in professional preparation, almost none of the mill pastors in Gaston County have had any special training for work in an industrial parish. Under ordinary circumstances they follow conventional, standardized programs in their churches, aping the policies of uptown churches of their denomination and the sermons of the uptown preachers who speak at their denominational gatherings. In most instances their knowledge of economic processes, labor relations, management problems, trade union tactics, and culture analysis is no more extensive or competent than that of their village parishioners, and they are easily convinced by the only persons who presumably do know about such matters—the mill owners and managers. When conflict occurs between the social classes, the mill pastors almost invariably adopt the analyses presented by the "most intelligent" and "best informed" citizens in the vicinity, who always are members of the uptown class. Uptown pastors, though their economic insight is frequently even less acute than that of their colleagues in the mill parishes, give the cues by which all their ministerial brethren are guided, citing mill owners and other persons "in the know" as their source of authority. Lacking economic and sociological perspectives wider than those of their own communities, ministers of all types of churches fail to appraise the opinions of community leaders as being in themselves highly relative; instead, they incline to accept them at face value or to modify them in minor details only. Though they are acknowledged experts in the field of religion and continually profess to be troubled by the gap between ethical ideals and social practice, they do not possess criteria for judging social possibilities, and thus in effect become instruments of social inertia.

Perhaps it is the kind of education rather than education in itself which isolates professionally trained clergymen from the industrial masses in Gaston County. If theological training invariably produces upper-class tastes and dispositions, it renders its subjects less flexible socially while assuming that it makes them more competent religiously. If it is concerned only with religious perspectives and knowledge, its graduates find themselves at tremendous disadvantage in appraising the "secu-

lar" forces which impinge powerfully on their parishes. Where
seminary students are prepared simply to propagate the faith
of a particular denomination, that process in itself helps to
limit the number and social type of churches possible for the
denomination. Though a denomination, a theological seminary,
or an individual minister may refuse to reckon openly with social conditions, the religious effort that follows is shaped and
modified nevertheless by those conditions.

Whatever the pedagogical implications may be, the comparative educational status of ministers constitutes one of the
most useful clues to the economic differentiation of denominations in Gaston County. It is only one, however, and might be
interpreted as being itself a symptom of underlying economic
forces. The economic level of the membership of a denomination helps to determine its demands and facilities for an educated ministry, quite as truly as the level of ministerial education helps to specify the social group to which it will appeal. A
denomination must have attained considerable wealth before it
is able to train and support highly specialized religious leaders. Having attained prestige, it seeks to send out ministers
whose training will further enhance its standing, in a culture
in which education has been something of a fetish. It is possible
to interpret the variation in education of ministers as a symptom of deeper economic cleavages—a symptom varying, perhaps, with the economic affluence of the various denominations.
Even so, it is a tangible and definite index to the affiliation of
denominations with social classes.

CHAPTER VII

PATTERNS OF DENOMINATIONAL DEVELOPMENT: CHURCHES AND SECTS

IN his monumental work, *The Social Teaching of the Christian Churches*, Ernst Troeltsch formulated a distinction, which has become classic, between the Church type and the sect type of religious institution. He defined the Church as being, in essence, an objective institution into which an individual is born, and by which, under the direction of duly constituted ecclesiastical officials, he is trained and disciplined for life in the religious community. Desiring to cover the whole life of humanity and to be coextensive with society, the Church accepts the secular order and becomes an integral part of existing social structures; it correspondingly becomes especially dependent on the upper classes and overwhelmingly conservative in outlook. It vests authority in religious matters in an established ecclesiastical hierarchy, in the precedents of tradition, and in the sacraments, while it seeks to dominate and to use political institutions for authority in secular matters. The sect, on the other hand, was defined by Troeltsch as a small, voluntary community, aiming at the inward perfection and fellowship of its own members, who have joined it by conscious choice. Rather than seeking to penetrate or dominate other social spheres, the sect is indifferent, tolerant, or antagonistic toward secular matters, and attempts to be a moral community separate and sufficient unto itself. Rather than locating religious authority in the religious institution or its officers, it appeals directly to the Scriptures and to Christ, practicing within itself the priesthood of all believers and criticizing the Church for apostasy from the original charter of Christianity. It is especially connected with the lower classes, working "upwards from below, and not downwards from above."[1]

1. Ernst Troeltsch, *The Social Teaching of the Christian Churches* (trans. by Olive Wyon; New York, 1931), I, 331–336. Cf. H. Richard Niebuhr, *The Social Sources of Denominationalism* (New York, 1929), pp. 17–21, for summary of Troeltsch's distinction, with special reference, as the title suggests, to the problems of denominational differentiation.

In numerous respects beyond those already observed, wide variance is discernible between denominations in Gaston County; and a line of division somewhat akin to that of Troeltsch is possible if indices are formulated more precisely, and if it is recognized from the outset that classification of any particular denomination is relative in character. In order to embrace the manifold character of religious culture, indices of comparison and classification must be of several types—economic, sociological, psychological, and doctrinal—without the assumption that any one type of index is purely secondary and completely determined by the others.

Before proceeding to formulation of indices and to classification of denominations, it is desirable to define more clearly the character of relations between sect and Church, summarizing the general results reached from a comparative study of all the denominations represented in Gaston County. Troeltsch appears to have dealt with relations between his two types in static terms, for the most part; he explicitly denied that a sect is an undeveloped expression of the Church, and assumed that it is an independent sociological type which may or may not stand in process of transition away from sectarianism.[2] Changes in religious institutions in Gaston County since 1880, however, indicate that the relation between the Church type and the sect type is to be interpreted, broadly, in dynamic terms. Though many other factors underlie its emergence, the sect arises as a schism from a parent ecclesiastical body, either a Church or a previous sect. It then becomes a distinct and independent type of religious organization but moves, if it survives, increasingly toward the Church type.[3]

A number of factors are associated with this transformation as dynamic agents. On the face of it, the transition from sect to Church appears to lie parallel with a class movement. The poorest mill workers have afforded the invariable starting point of sects in Gaston County, but as a new sect has passed toward churchly status the percentage of mill workers in its membership has correspondingly decreased; roughly, the degree to which any denomination is churchly at a given moment varies inversely with the percentage of its membership which is com-

2. Troeltsch, *op. cit.*, I, 338.   3. Cf. Niebuhr, *op. cit.*, pp. 19–21.

posed of mill workers. Deeper analysis, however, leaves little evidence that the transition is a class movement in the sense that changes in a sect depend upon changes in the economic class, as a class, with which it is especially associated. Rather, some process such as the following appears to take place. A sect, as it gains adherents and the promise of success, begins to reach out toward greater influence in society, whatever the roots of its ambition may be—evangelistic fervor, denominational rivalry, ministerial desire for greater income and influence, the cultural vindication of its peculiar faith, or what not. In the process it accommodates gradually to the culture it is attempting to conquer, and thereby loses influence over those relatively estranged from that culture. It counts this loss a gain as its own standards shift and as it attracts an increasing number of persons who enjoy the cultural and economic privileges of the society. Though at any given moment of transition the rising sect is associated especially with one economic group, it does not necessarily carry that group as it moves on. There is no indication that classes rise as classes but there is proof that denominations do. Perhaps emphasis by earlier sects on the Calvinistic virtues of industry, frugality, and the like resulted in making their practitioners wealthy, as is often averred concerning the Methodists of England. Thus far, however, sectarian asceticism and moral discipline have not caused a majority of the members of any religious sect in Gaston County to ascend appreciably in the economic scale; to the contrary, the teachings of the sects have often been accessory to keeping members in their previous social and economic station. Emphasis on personal virtues produces more efficient workers; it does not necessarily produce owners and managers of the economic system.

As the new sect reaches out for conquest of society, its original identification with those existing at the edges of society is soon modified. The change does not follow an improvement of economic status in its membership as a whole, but is consequent on the growing economic opulence of a small minority of its membership. A few members of any sect are likely to prosper, partly because of personal qualities (not necessarily virtues), but more often because of loose play in the economic organization. In the vernacular, a few members "get the breaks." Becoming more affluent and "responsible," they either desert their sect as their economic status improves or else help to remold it in keeping with their newer position. They are the more easily able to influence the life of an institution after they have attained comparative economic wealth because a struggling sectarian group stands in need of many things money can buy.

A denomination inclines to move and to settle down with its few leaders who become community leaders also, leaving behind the masses of its members and of society. Its position on the scale of transition from sect to Church follows closely after the economic fortunes of its more influential members; its religious character changes as the economic status of its leaders improves. From reflecting the needs of a large group of people, it comes to sanction the position of its more respectable members simply because their position, sanctioned also by the whole weight of existing culture, enables them to control the particular religious institution. As time goes on, the emerging Church either raises up its membership from childhood, finds new members from cultural groups to which its fresh but moderate enthusiasm appeals, or else declines in membership and influence. It cannot go back to sect form because the unique social naïveté and pristine enthusiasm are irrevocably lost. Movement on the scale between sect and Church is, with minor exceptions, in one direction only.[4] A sect may arise through schism from a Church but not through the decline or reconstitution of a Church, according to the evidence available here.

To be sure, the sect is not always clearly aware that it is striving to gain larger control over its cultural environment and that in so doing it modifies its peculiar religious character. More extensive contact with society is forced upon it, however, by the very necessities of institutional existence. No institution, however embryonic in form (and the newer sects are closely integrated from the outset), can escape social responsibilities, as contrasted with sheer religious responsibilities. Children are born to members of the sect, and their relation to the religious contract must be defined; Professor Niebuhr has pointed out that "by its very nature the sectarian type of organization is

4. This does not mean that the movement consists in successive attainment of a series of fixed stages, without possibility for omission of steps or for retrogression at certain points. No neat unilinear pattern is intended here, even by inference.

valid only for one generation."[5] It frequently is not preserved inviolate for even one generation.[6] From the outset there are relatives—careless husbands, aged mothers—who are not signatories to the contract, but for whose religious welfare (especially if a funeral must be held) the new sect has a derived, but inescapable, responsibility. The conventicle becomes a parish almost immediately, and wider social bonds intersect and relax the tautness of religious bonds.

Further, the nature of the religious impulse renders it unable to sustain an institution on purely religious grounds, any more than the sex impulse alone could sustain the family institution. The first fine fervor associated with the appearance of sects begins to fade, and to be replaced by reasoned faith and institutional structures. The religious experience is not synonymous with life on the earth, and imperatives arising from mundane relations reshape perspectives and condition religious association as time goes on. All social pressure is against immoderate deviation from conventional religious patterns, and the members of a sect, who cannot spend all their time in association solely with each other, lose ardor under its restraining influence.

The preservation of association despite diminution of enthusiasm demands horizontal organization. A social institution encysts the institution of Grace. Nightly prayer meetings in a parlor—or anywhere, because place does not matter—lead, after a few months, to the renting of a hall or the erection of a cheap church. Then songbooks and a piano must be bought, and responsibility for the care and use of the building and program must be specified; an official hierarchy begins to develop. In contrast with other churches, the building is nothing to be proud of and so a part-time preacher is appointed "to build up the church," and esoteric monopoly of religious joy is extended into an evangelistic program. The new group begins to compare itself with other religious groups, and to regard others as rivals, especially those which compete with it in terms of its own peculiar religious doctrines. Rivalry between sects ensues, and

5. Niebuhr, *op. cit.*, p. 19.

6. Of the 34 sect groups on observation of which this generalization is based, all are less than forty years old and 21 are less than ten years old. All these latter show clear symptoms, already, of transition toward Church status.

each seeks to outdistance the others—no longer simply in religious possessions but in terms that the entire society accepts and can understand, which are, by definition, qualities that characterize a Church rather than a sect.

The process of transition from sect to Church can be described in evolutionary terms, if it is clearly affirmed that the use of such terms constitutes a parable rather than designation of religious institutions as organisms. New variations occur in the religious realm. Against necessities inherent in their social environment, they compete with each other. As they adapt, they survive and grow strong and stable; if conditions change, they either adapt or decline. All the while, unless the social environment is surfeited with religious institutions, new variations are occurring and old churches are declining, or else surviving in sheltered cultural pockets. The rate of infant mortality is high among the new variations, but they continue to occur so long as the Church is not completely coextensive with culture in fact as well as theory.

Specific aspects of the movement from sect to Church are more tangible and illuminating than general description. After close observation of religious institutions of all types, the following scale has been worked out to indicate the various facets of this transition:

1. *From* membership composed chiefly of the propertyless *to* membership composed of property owners.

2. *From* economic poverty *to* economic wealth, as disclosed especially in the value of church property and the salary paid to ministers.

3. *From* the cultural periphery *toward* the cultural center of the community.

4. *From* renunciation of prevailing culture and social organization, or indifference to it, *to* affirmation of prevailing culture and social organization.

5. *From* self-centered (or personal) religion *to* culture-centered religion, from "experience" to a social institution.

6. *From* noncoöperation, or positive ridicule, toward established religious institutions *to* coöperation with the established churches of the community.

7. *From* suspicion of rival sects *to* disdain or pity for all sects.

8. *From* a moral community excluding unworthy members *to* a social institution embracing all who are socially compatible within it.

9. *From* an unspecialized, unprofessionalized, part-time ministry *to* a specialized, professional, full-time ministry.

10. *From* a psychology of persecution *to* a psychology of success and dominance.

11. *From* voluntary, confessional bases of membership *to* ritual or social prerequisites only (such as a certificate of previous membership in another respected denomination, or training in an educational process established by the denomination itself).

12. *From* principal concern with adult membership *to* equal concern for children of members.

13. *From* emphasis on evangelism and conversion *to* emphasis on religious education.

14. *From* stress on a future in the next world *to* primary interest in a future in this world—a future for the institution, for its members, and for their children; *from* emphasis on death *to* emphasis on successful earthly life.

15. *From* adherence to strict Biblical standards, such as tithing or nonresistance, *to* acceptance of general cultural standards as a practical definition of religious obligation.

16. *From* a high degree of congregational participation in the services and administration of the religious group *to* delegation of responsibility to a comparatively small percentage of the membership.

17. *From* fervor in worship services *to* restraint; *from* positive action *to* passive listening.

18. *From* a comparatively large number of special religious services *to* a program of regular services at stated intervals.[7]

19. *From* reliance on spontaneous "leadings of the Spirit" in religious services and administration *to* a fixed order of worship and of administrative procedure.

20. *From* the use of hymns resembling contemporary folk

7. That is, participation in religious activities becomes more and more compartmentalized and institutionalized, as the denomination trends toward Church status, and thereby takes a relative place in the prevailing culture, rather than continues to assume hegemony over large spheres of time and interest.

music *to* the use of slower, more stately hymns coming out of more remote liturgical tradition.

21. *From* emphasis on religion in the home *to* delegation of responsibility for religion to church officials and organizations.

Classified in terms of the indices contained in this scale, denominations represented in Gaston County fall as follows, in a series ranging from sect type to Church type: Free-Will Baptist Holiness, Pentecostal Holiness, Church of God, Free-Will Baptist, independent tabernacles, Wesleyan Methodist, Baptist, Methodist, Presbyterian, Lutheran, Protestant Episcopal, Roman Catholic. A brief review of salient particularities of these denominations will illumine further the process of transition from sect to Church, and the relation of economic and religious factors thereto.

CHURCHES

The Protestant Episcopal and Roman Catholic churches have never gained any significant following in Gaston County, despite the fact that both have been active there for about seventy years. Though present in the county since 1842, and though they have maintained a fairly large monastery and abbey there since 1884, the Roman Catholics have made little headway among natives, and their church membership in 1939, a total of 396 white and 173 colored members, was only .007 per cent of the total population. They have reached almost no mill workers, chiefly because they have not adapted themselves to the mill village system. Their unwillingness to compromise fully on the race question has also handicapped them; mill workers frequently say, with a scornful chuckle, "Catholics use the same church for white people and niggers." Both the Roman Catholic and the Protestant Episcopal churches have been impeded by the ethnic backgrounds of the early settlers (almost entirely Scotch and German), reaction in colonial years against ecclesiastical hierarchies, and the like. Neither has come into contact with a sufficiently large segment of the population to permit generalizations concerning its adaptation to economic change, or its movement along the sect-Church scale. Both are distinctly uptown in type, however, and their theory and type of organization place them at the other extreme from minority groups such as the Church of God.

Of the major denominations in the county, the Lutherans
and Presbyterians most nearly represent the Church type.
Each is a Church in terms of every index listed above, though
the process of transition in some instances is less complete than
in others. There is doubt, for example, concerning the proximity of the Lutheran churches to the cultural center of the community; in membership and practice, they are associated more
closely with rural traditions than with the new industrialism.
Each denomination retains, moreover, particular traits that
appear to be survivals of earlier sect practices; evidences of
transition away from sectarianism are clearly discernible in the
brief period since 1880. In 1880 and 1890 the Lutheran
churches listed "Expulsions" as an item on which individual
churches should report to the Synod (though none were reported in churches in Gaston County for those years), indicating that they still thought of themselves as exclusive moral communities. Presbyterian churches have continued to emphasize
tithing down to the present, and their women's auxiliaries stress
daily reading of the Bible, membership in intercessory prayer
groups, and family worship in the home.[8]

Despite the survival of occasional sect traits, the Lutheran
and Presbyterian denominations in the county have been largely
of the Church type throughout the period covered in this study.
The impression one gets from reading the Minutes of the General Assembly of the Presbyterian Church in the United States
from 1863 to 1938 is that of consistency throughout the period. Put another way, it is that of conservatism. Committees
are largely the same, attitudes expressed in reports are almost
unvarying, statistical tables still regard the same items as worth
recording. The scope of the church has increased; it reaches
more people and spends more money, but in essence is much the
same. Instead of writing "3½ o'clock" the Minutes now write
"3:30 o'clock"; other modernization is not greatly in evidence.
The same conservatism and sense of tradition prevail among
Presbyterians in Gaston County; older persons among them
"look down on" Methodists and Baptists much as the latter
snub the Church of God. Similar conclusions may be drawn for

8. Of 1,818 members of the auxiliaries in 1938, 630 were reported as daily
Bible readers, 477 were members of intercessory prayer groups, 206 reported
family worship in the home, and 418 practiced tithing.

the Lutheran churches. Lutheran ministers in the county wear pulpit gowns and use the Common Service, and seem to the suspicious mill workers to be pretty close to the Pope.

The Methodist and Baptist denominations are still in transition from sect to Church, with the former much nearer Church status than the latter. Of the twenty-one indices listed above, the Methodists in 1880 were nearer the sect type in ten of them (Nos. 5, 7, 9, 13, 16, 17, 18, 19, 20, 21). Except in continuing emphasis on personal religion and considerable suspicion of rival sects, they are now nearer to the Church type in terms of each index. In 1880 the Baptists were sectarian in every particular; in 1939 the denomination approached Church status in seven indices (Nos. 2, 3, 9, 12, 16, 19, 21), remained a sect in eight (Nos. 5, 7, 8, 10, 11, 14, 18, 20), and was confused in its position on the remaining six. Remnants of sectarian status appear in several significant respects. In 1938, 33 of the 37 Baptist churches reported weekly prayer meetings, and only 3 of them failed to have at least one revival meeting during the year. Exclusions from membership in that year totaled 118, of a total of 12,712 members. Several Baptist churches continue to place considerable emphasis on tithing by their members. As the denomination has grown in wealth and membership, however, it has reached out after cultural conquest, and in doing so has accommodated its own traditions at many points to the general culture. It has changed to greater degree than any denomination in the county during the last six decades.

SECTS

The rise of new religious sects in the last twenty years, and especially in the last ten, has been one of the most significant aspects in the development of religious institutions in Gaston County, as in the United States. Successive invasions by esoteric cults have seriously modified the influence of Methodist and Baptist churches over the mill workers. Generically, the newer sects are often lumped together as "Holy Rollers," but this designation has been specifically repudiated by several of them. In their rise they illustrate the influence of economic conditions on the genesis and growth of religious institutions, and the methods by which religious groups often tend, in their formative stages, to transvalue economic realities. A fairly broad consideration of them is necessary if one is to see economic and religious factors in perspective.

The first notable invasion of the mill villages by newer sects occurred in the first decade of this century, when the Wesleyan Methodists established six churches in the county, all of them among the mill workers. The two cardinal doctrines of this sect, regeneration (conversion) and sanctification ("cleansing of the heart and empowering for service") are typical of the theological bases of most sect groups. The movement was strongly sectarian in 1910 in terms of all the twenty-one indices listed above. More recently it has moved rapidly toward Church status, especially in respect to coöperation with older denominations, comparative growth of wealth, and increasing emphasis upon an educated ministry. In six other respects its position at the moment is confused (Nos. 1, 3, 4, 7, 14, 15), but the denomination is clearly moving away from extreme sectarianism. Whereas most of its membership came through "conversion" thirty years ago, about 80 per cent of it now comes into the church through training in the Sunday School, and the number of revival meetings held annually is decreasing. In the 1920's one of its five churches in Gaston County definitely changed from a mill church to an uptown church, having come to include in its membership a cotton mill superintendent, a number of small merchants and mechanics, and other persons comprising a nucleus of uptown people, who increasingly "set the tone" for this particular church and changed its fundamental character.

The denomination as a whole, however, still belongs definitely in the sect classification. Of 300 members in Gaston County in 1938, a total of 22 were expelled, and 171 were reported as habitual tithers. Major sins in the eyes of ministers and members consist of Sabbath desecration, drinking, and participation in such social amusements as swimming at pools, dancing, and movies. Religious services are more restrained than those of the Church of God, less so than Baptist services. Testimony meetings—a regular mark of the emphasis of sects on "personal experience"—are still held, but have usually been relegated to the Wednesday evening service. Sectarian expressions and ideas crop out in the testimonies offered. For example:

I am glad my sins are under the blood . . .

I love the Lord; pray for me . . .

I want to live like Jeremiah [*sic*] and the men on the wall, working as though it all depended on them, but praying as though it all depended on God . . .

Big preachers and big professors in the seminaries are trying to stop God's work. How? By trying to take away the divinity of Jesus Christ. But God ain't a-goin' to stand for it. How's He goin' to stop it? By the Second Comin' of Christ, a-settin' on a cloud.[9]

A large number of isolated sectarian groups, affiliated with no denomination or constituting the sole representative of a denomination in the county, have appeared since 1920, and especially since 1930, with thirteen of them surviving in 1939. The diversity of their names indicates their variety: the Van Dyke Auditorium, the Church of God Undenominational, the Gastonia Gospel Tabernacle, the Dallas House of God Tabernacle, the Church of the Nazarene, the Tomlinson Church of God. Often these highly atomistic religious units arise from the promotional activities of an individual minister who, dissatisfied with his status in his denomination or expelled from it, has organized an independent group of his own. The most significant and successful religious entrepreneur of this type has built a rude tabernacle in Gastonia and attracts a wide following among the mill villagers. In ideas and methods he resembles the various sectarian movements, but is also close to the type of evangelist often imported by Methodist and Baptist churches. He represents, therefore, a transitional link between sectarian and churchly levels. Many people in Gastonia, and especially the uptown ministers, are skeptical of his sincerity; they point out that his devotion to religion has brought him a beautiful home on one of the town's best residential streets, and more recently, a luxurious Packard limousine. His tabernacle, nevertheless, is well filled with mill workers whenever he preaches. Similar congregations thrive in nearly every town in the county, attesting to the fact that churches of the older denominations are not affording adequate satisfaction to large numbers of the people.

9. These particular testimonials were heard in a service in an uptown Wesleyan Methodist Church, along with a dignified and fairly scholarly sermon by the minister on the objectivity of Grace!

The more significant sectarian movements in the county have come under denominational rather than individual leadership. A large number of new denominations appeared shortly after 1900, often originating in the mountainous regions of North Carolina and Tennessee, and spread quickly through the rising mill towns. A correspondent from one of the mill villages in Gaston County complained in the *Gastonia Gazette* in 1910 of "tongue exhorting" in his village by persons "claiming that they are possessed of gifts of the Holy Ghost," and thereby helping to "lead men's wives astray." Later in the same year he denounced the so-called "holy dance," attributing all such manifestations to "hypnotism" and, therefore, to "demonism."[10] Subsequently the Pentecostal Holiness Church, the Church of God (Cleveland branch),[11] the Free-Will Baptist Church, and the Free-Will Baptist Holiness Church have each established a number of churches in the county.

During the last decade the growth of these groups has been especially rapid, and has provided the most noteworthy aspect of religious development. Since 1920 the older denominations have organized only 20 new churches, while the newer sects have organized 26, of which 21 have been established since 1930. During the same period the older denominations have abandoned 12 churches, while the newer sects have abandoned none. Without exception, the churches established by these sectarian groups in Gaston County have been exclusively mill churches. Growth in membership, though exact figures are not available,[12] has been as rapid in the last two decades as growth in number of churches; from less than 500 members in 1920, the total had grown to nearly 4,000 in 1939. Membership per church unit varies from 8 to 275, with the median at about 100; in addition

10. *Gastonia Gazette*, correspondence from Arlington Mill, April 15, December 6, 1910.

11. At least a dozen small denominations in America appropriate to themselves, in various forms, this name: Church of God, Church of God (Apostolic), Church of God as Organized by Christ, Church of God in North America, Church of the Living God, Churches of God Holiness, Churches of God in Christ, Church of God (undenominational), Tomlinson Church of God, Original Church of God (which was an offshoot of another Church of God), etc. See Elmer T. Clark, *The Small Sects in America* (Nashville, 1937).

12. A minor mark of sectarian status seems to be indifference toward keeping ecclesiastical records. One of the sects explicitly refuses to keep a membership roll.

to the actual membership, however, there is always a large following of persons not technically attached.

A composite and impressionistic picture of the kind of religious service held by extreme sectarian groups may help to lay bare the roots from which they spring:

One traverses a grassless, rutted yard, climbs precarious 2 x 6 steps into a long, bare room filled with crude pews, and takes a seat in the Church of God. It is Sunday night, and the building is filled to overflowing, with about a thousand people present. Many stand in the doors or in the front yard of the church, including a large group of young men watching the girls go in and out. An ice cream vendor has placed his portable refrigerator near the church door, and is doing a thriving business. About 65 per cent of those present are women between the ages of fourteen and fifty-five, many of whom have sleeping babies in their laps. The atmosphere is expectant and informal; members of the congregation move about at will, and talk in any tone of voice that suits their fancy.

A crude pulpit, a piano, and a section of pews for the choir are placed at the far end of the oblong building. Back of the pulpit to the left is a homemade board on which to register weekly attendance; beneath the board, in sprawling letters, the question:

HOW WILL YOUR
REPORT IN HEAVEN BE

To the right of the pulpit is another sign:

GOD IS ABLE

A band, including three stringed instruments and a saxophone, plays occasional music.

The service begins at eight o'clock or thereabouts. Rather, the actions of the congregation become more intense and concerted in character; there is almost nothing by way of formal announcement. The choir, in coöperation with the pastor, breaks into a rhythmic hymn, and the congregation follows suit. The hymn has an interminable number of stanzas, and a refrain, reminiscent of mountain ballads both in music and in narrative form. The hymn looks toward a narrative climax, and the excitement of the congregation increases as the singing proceeds. The stanzas are punctuated with loud shouts of "Hallelujah," "Thank you, Jesus," "Glory," and the rhythmic clapping of hands and tapping of feet. Almost immediately, various members of the congregation begin to "get the Holy Ghost" (as a teen-age boy awesomely remarks). One young woman leaves the front row of the choir and jerks about the pulpit, with motions so disconnected as to seem involuntary, weird. A man's head trembles violently from side to side. Another man, tieless and red-faced, laughs boomingly at odd moments, in a laugh resembling that of intoxication.

Half a dozen songs follow in succession. Then comes a prayer, with everybody kneeling on the floor and praying aloud at the same time, each in his own way. Some mutter with occasional shouts; others chant, with frequent bendings backward and forward; the volume of sound rises and falls, without unified pattern or group concentration. The pastor's voice booms out occasionally above all the others. Then, as if by a prearranged but unobservable signal, the prayer abruptly ends; the onlooker is amazed to see emerging from the confusion a concerted return to a sitting position. The cacophony of prayer is ended as suddenly as it began.

Then the pastor reads "the Scripture," after confessing that he "ain't had no time to study today," and after attempting to induce a layman in the congregation to "say something"—without avail, because the layman confesses that he "ain't had no time to study neither" and insists, "you go right ahead, brother." Reluctantly the pastor begins to read, explaining each verse with amazing exegesis and equally amazing insight. Each verse becomes the subject for a homily, and the reader works up to a climax in its exposition—a climax reflected in increase of rhythmic motions and hortatory shouts from members of the congregation. Having finished the Scripture lesson, the preacher takes up a collection, counts it, announces that he has to have "a little more," and runs around in the congregation to garner proffered contributions, acknowledging each with a receipt "God bless you, brother," and finally emptying the collection plate into his pocket.

Then the service moves toward a climax; the taking of the collection has been an emotional interlude. The preacher begins a sermon; more precisely, he enunciates verbal symbols that arouse immediate response from the congregation. Such motifs play through his shoutings as "sanctification," "the Second Coming," "the world despises and misunderstands and lies about the Church of God,"

"Jesus can heal your body and soul," "Believe the Word," "follow the knee-route." The Church of God is depicted as a remnant of those who have escaped from the "coldness" of the Methodist and Baptist churches. Lay preaching is urged, and personal evangelistic work. Attention is called to a number of prayer meetings to be held at various houses during the subsequent week, and to persons for whom prayer is desired—especially the family of a four-year-old girl who has just died, because "they can't hardly get over it."

Then there is a testimony meeting in which a large number of the more faithful testify to their personal experience and joy in religion, some mutteringly, some loudly, fervidly. One woman defends her right to wear long-sleeved, high-necked dresses in the summer time, because "the Spirit told me to." Nearly all say that they are proud to speak for Christ, and not ashamed to speak out for their Master in church. The man who has been indulging the intoxicated laugh defends his right to laugh in church, saying that his religion makes him feel good all over and is not like the stiff coldness of the Methodist church. Recurring phrases appear in the testimonies: "I'm glad I got over bein' too proud to be a Holiness and get all there was of the Holy Ghost"; "I'm a better wife and I've got a better husband because I joined the Church of God"; "the Baptists are all right, but I wanted more of the Lord than they had." Several testify to marvelous cures of physical illness during the past week, through prayer and the "laying on of hands."

All the while waves of ecstatic rhythm have been sweeping over the congregation, with the actions of the preacher setting the pace. There are patterns to the rhythmic actions: running around the pulpit, holding trembling hands to the sky, very fast clogging of the feet, swinging the arms in sharp, staccato motions. One girl leaps from her seat as though struck by an electric shock, races four times around the aisles of the church, screaming "O God . . . do Jesus . . . O God . . . glory, glory, glory . . . give me more . . . more . . . glory, glory, glory"; falling over backward with hands outstretched, her whole body quivering and rhythmically jerking, she collapses at last in a dull heap on the floor, and stays there in comatose condition for several minutes. Others rise and shout at the top of their lungs for five minutes, or bang on something in staccato rhythm. The same persons respond again and again, with perhaps seventy-five individuals represented. Each responds with an individual pattern of motions, but all motions revolve around a few general types. The motions appear to have been culturally conditioned, whether immediately conditioned by the agent or not. One wonders if some form of mass hypnotism is at work.

About ten o'clock the pastor calls for sinners to come to the front and kneel around the altar (constructed of a bench quickly placed before the pulpit). About ten come, including one five-year-old boy. A hundred members of the congregation gather about, and a tremendous tumult ensues as they attempt to "pray and shout the sinners through," interspersed with wild demonstrations of joy as one is "saved."

It is nearly 11 P.M., but one stays and wonders. They cry out, and cry; they are drunken, but not with wine; they stagger, but not with strong drink. . . .[13]

This description points to several factors explanatory of the emergence of the newer sects. A number of theories have been advanced to account for their appearance. One has made transiency the fundamental factor, holding that there is a positive correlation between instability of residence and membership in the newer sects.[14] This explanation, if true, would only push the investigation deeper, and call for an explanation of transiency. It does not appear to be valid in the first place; a close study of the entire membership of one sect group in Gastonia revealed that 98 per cent of its members had been living in the community for more than five years. Another theory points to ignorance as the fundamental basis, but this judgment is based on an external standard and contributes little to understanding. Still another accounts for the rise of sects in terms of the failure of older churches to meet the religious needs of all groups in the population, and this theory is of unquestionable merit. The Church of God and similar groups consist chiefly of the religiously disgruntled—of those who have fallen out or been dissatisfied in older churches. At least 80 per cent of the members of such groups had previously belonged to established

13. Cf. Isaiah 29. 9.
14. E. R. Hartz, "Social Problems in a North Carolina Parish" (A.M. thesis, Duke University, 1938), pp. 132, 136.

churches in their communities,[15] Baptist churches for the most part.[16] A recurring note in sectarian services condemns the coldness of the older churches, and sect preachers draw much of their support from ridiculing the exclusive, proud, "stuck-up" character of older religious institutions.

A recent interpretation, combining several of the factors enumerated above, attributes most of the phenomena of the newer sects to the "culture shock" involved in transition from a rural to an urban setting.[17] The older urban churches symbolize to the new migrant to the city his exclusion from urban life, and he turns to the "new" churches, which seem to represent defense of his former standards and modes of behavior. This theory is plausible but inadequate for explanation of the growth of sects in small villages and rural areas in other sections of the South, and is in error in assuming that the newer sects uniquely preserve traits of rural religion.

It has been popular more recently to explain emergence of sects primarily in terms of underlying economic conditions. Ordinarily the poorest strata of the community are attracted into membership, and it is urged that an otherworldly emphasis in the newer sects affords compensation for poverty and transcendence of poor estate. The phenomenal rate of growth during the recent depression argues in favor of a theory of this sort; as economic conditions grew worse, newer sects flourished increasingly.[18]

Another credible diagnosis ascribes psychological deficiencies to most members of the newer sects. Frenetic religious services represent release from psychological repression, it is said, fulfilling a need for self-expression and for identification of one's self with a greater power. Life in a mill village is monotonous and dull; production processes in the mills are largely mechani-

15. Interviews with three ministers of the Church of God, Gastonia, July 27, 1939.

16. Not only because of the numerical preponderance of the Baptists in the county but also because most of the newer sects practice baptism by immersion, and thus appeal especially to persons habituated to the Baptist faith.

17. John B. Holt, "Holiness Religion: Cultural Shock and Social Reorganization," in *American Sociological Review*, V, 740–747 (October, 1940). Cf. Grace G. Leybourne, "Urban Adjustments of Migrants from the Southern Appalachian Plateaus," in *Social Forces*, December, 1937.

18. Cf. the simple but brilliant analysis contained in A. T. Boisen, "Religion and Hard Times," *Social Action*, March 15, 1939.

cal in character, and the worker has little opportunity for choice as to any of the basic factors that control his daily life. The new cults are notably lay movements, and the entire membership participates in most of the services and activities of a particular group. The unusually high percentage of women who belong and who appear to be the most active participants in semihysterical religious practices is also significant; of the members of one Church of God in Gaston County, 57 per cent were women, almost all of whom were between the ages of seventeen and fifty-four. A psychologist observing the religious ceremonies of the Church of God might conclude that the sex factor is crucial in explanation. Certainly members of these groups are widely accused of being immoral, and a considerable degree of sexual laxity is undoubtedly a concomitant of their services. An uptown boy explained, standing outside a Church of God while a service was in progress: "It'll get hot in there pretty soon. A lot of women come over here, which is why all the boys are hanging around. I got started out late tonight and all the dates are taken, so I have to take what I can get. Mill girls are the best looking girls nowadays anyhow." Rhythmic music, supported by stringed instruments and saxophones, tendencies toward exhibitionism, and injunctions to "let yourself go" for "possession by the Spirit" are surcharged with sex stimulation.

Ministers of the emerging denominations insist that the explanation of rapid growth in their adherents must be pitched completely on the religious plane. They argue that their rigid teachings challenge people and force them to invest so much in money and in devotion that they necessarily remain interested and become propagandists. "People are gettin' disgusted with professional religion," one of them said, "and demandin' to get results in their religion—so that's why they come to us." They hasten to add that the devotion of the ministers themselves, in contrast with the professional attitudes of ministers of the older denominations, is of great importance. The type of preacher associated with the sect groups does help to explain their rapid growth, though it does not explain their appearance. Many of the preachers are mill workers who preach as an avocation. They have very little education—often no more than completion of the fourth grade in the public schools, plus a few weeks of training in a Bible school maintained by their denomination (see Table XXVI).[19] They are, therefore, much closer to the mill workers than ministers of the older denominations. They also work for smaller compensation, living at the level of the mill workers. One sect urges its churches to pay their pastors at least $12.50 a week aside from rent, that "they may wield a better influence in their communities"—the desire to conquer culture is making itself felt. Another sect limits the salary of its ministers to $200 a month "and expenses"; it is doubtful that many receive this amount. Most of the ministers tithe rigorously, along with their members; one denomination supervises ministerial fidelity in this respect by providing "that all members of the Conference pay at least 75 per cent of their Ministerial tithes into the Conference Treasury or else give a satisfactory reason for not doing so before their character shall be passed."[20]

All these interpretations of the rise and growth of the sects have in them valid elements, and an adequate explanation cannot afford to ignore any of them. They all are gathered up in the general statement that such groups thrive wherever a considerable portion of the population exists on the periphery of culture as organized, whether the index used be that of education, economic status, possibilities for psychological satisfaction, or religious organization. Members of the newer religions do not belong anywhere—and so they belong, and wholeheartedly, to the one type of institution which deigns to notice them. A considerable percentage of mill workers stand on the outer fringes of their communities, and they provide the invariable starting point of sect movements.[21] The rapidity of growth of

19. Preparation in the eyes of God, rather than the schools of men, is emphasized; one sect carries this emphasis to the point of requiring that "the wife of the Applicant for Bishop license must have the Holy Ghost." *Minutes of the Thirty-Second Annual Assembly of the Church of God, 1937*, p. 148.

20. *Minutes of the Twenty-Fourth Session of the Western North Carolina Annual Conference of the Pentecostal Holiness Church, 1939*, p. 19. Each minister's character must be reviewed and approved annually before he is approved for reappointment to a pastoral charge.

21. In other regions, sharecroppers are especially susceptible to this variety of religious program because they occupy in a plantation economy much the same status as mill workers hold in an industrial economy. Similar religious movements, bearing such names as "The Fire-Baptized Holiness Church," flourish among Negroes; a wave of "Holiness religion" was sweeping over the colored population of Gastonia in the summer of 1939.

the sects is a rough indication of the degree to which mill workers recognize their cultural alienation.

The sects substitute religious status for social status, a fact which may help to account for their emphasis on varying degrees of Grace. This emphasis, indeed, forms their most distinctive theological tenet. As over against the lack of religious differentiation within older denominations, the newer sects divide their members, and people in general, into several religious classifications: saved, sanctified, baptized with the Holy Ghost, baptized with water, recipient of the first, second, or third blessing and the like. What matters it, then, if a Methodist has more money but has never been baptized with the Holy Ghost? As over against segregation from the community, the newer sects affirm separation from the world; in the face of exclusion on educational, economic, and religious grounds, they affirm exclusion from their own fellowship of those who engage in mixed bathing, dancing, card playing, bobbing the hair, gambling, baseball, county fairs, drinking, and using tobacco.[22] Because they have no jewelry to wear, they make refusal to wear jewelry, including wedding rings, a religious requirement. They transmute poverty into a symptom of Grace. Having no money, they redeem their economic status by rigid tithing of the small income they do possess, and thus far surpass members of churches of any other type or denomination in per capita contributions, despite the fact that they stand at the bottom of the economic scale. Many of them cannot take baths at will, because of lack of facilities, but they can practice the washing of the feet of the saints, and rejoice thereby at their superiority to older denominations which have come to regard such practices

22. The Church of God stipulates: "All members who appear in public exposing their upper limbs above the elbow or any part of the lower limbs being nude, are dressing immodest and not according to Scripture, and that where violation of this recommendation exists offending parties be called in question and dealt with except in factories where certain uniform dress is required by their employers. However, this order does not apply to children. We further recommend that it shall be left to the pastor and his councillors to decide when in their judgment the offending person is a child" (*Minutes of the Thirty-Second Annual Assembly of the Church of God, 1937*, p. 145. Cf. *Minutes of the Twenty-Second Session of the Western North Carolina Annual Conference of the Pentecostal Holiness Church, 1937*, p. 18). This sect accepts female ministers, but stipulates that a woman who has bobbed her hair shall be advised to cease her activities as a minister until her hair has had time to grow out again (*loc. cit.*, p. 149).

as uncouth and unesthetic. Excluded from secular society, they set up a religious society of their own, in which standards of membership are more rigid than those of the general culture that has ignored them.[23] The inspired Scriptures, rather than general cultural standards, provide the charter of their new community; without exception, the new churches accept the Bible as their sole and adequate authority (in theory), and interpret it with direct literalness.

Not all mill workers, of course, belong to sectarian groups; there are class distinctions among the mill workers themselves— distinctions clearly reflected in religious affiliation. Presbyterian workers feel superior to those belonging to the Methodist and Baptist churches, while members of the latter two denominations regard themselves as definitely higher in the social scale than Wesleyan Methodists. All, in turn, despise the Church of God and deprecate the social status of its members. The attitude of a typical Presbyterian or Lutheran toward the Church of God is different, however, from that of a Methodist or Baptist. The former regard the sect movements with disdain and are often rather happy to see the "upstart" Methodists and Baptists suffering discomfiture at the hands of new rivals only slightly below them in the religious hierarchy. As a Presbyterian minister put it, "the Methodists and Baptists used to care for the ignorant; the Holy Rollers do now, and the Methodists and Baptists are left floundering, wondering what to do." A Lutheran minister expressed pity for the newer symptoms of religious errancy:

The Church of God, Holy Rollers, etc., do not give our people what they ought to have. Ignorance and itch will eat up anything. Those preachers are so ignorant they cannot even pronounce correctly the names in the Holy Word. I heard one of them call Mesopotamia "Mes-o-pot-i-ma." Of course, his congregation did not know the difference.

23. The rate of expulsion from such bodies is very high. In 1938 one Free-Will Baptist Holiness Church in Gastonia received 33 new members and expelled 24 persons, of a total membership of 88. A Church of God with 143 members has expelled 30 in the last two years; another with 95 members has expelled 40; a third with 101 members has expelled 20 in the last four years. Most of the expulsions were based on participation in one or another of the "worldly amusements" listed above.

Rather than regard their new and dangerous rivals as a thoroughbred might survey a dirty mongrel pup, the Methodists and Baptists look on them with mingled fear and contempt, with ridicule rather than pity. "They practice," said one Methodist minister, "the religion of Hurrah and Take-On, of Knock-Down and Drag-Out."

The sects thrive on persecution and exult in the harassment they afford to older denominations. One Church of God preacher announced proudly: "The Baptists look down on us, but we are getting their members; why don't they get ours, if they are better than us?" It is only toward each other that the newer denominations feel real rivalry, as contrasted with their sense of religious superiority to older denominations. Most of them are essentially alike in their fundamental teachings and practices, and therefore are competitors in the religious field. They denounce each other as imposters, thieves, plagiarists, and fanatics. Remarks by a Holiness preacher typify vilification by one sect of another:

Those so-called Holiness Churches are completely different from my kind of Holiness; they are fanatics and bring discredit on the name "Holiness" by their handling of snakes, their offers to sacrifice their own mothers, and the like. All the preachers who handle snakes, etc., belong to the "unknown tongues" group, as does the Church of God. A New Testament scholar went to them to preach, began speaking in Greek, and seventeen people were saved. These folks regard any kind of outward manifestation as a sign of possession by the Holy Spirit—but to live the way they do makes you wonder if they have the Spirit. Those folks have backslid from the true way.

In their desire to surpass rival sects, the newer denominations begin to lose their extreme sectarianism. Increasingly they are building more expensive churches, insisting on greater educational background for their preachers, and coöperating more fully with older denominations and with community leaders, in an effort to achieve prestige and power. One Church of God preacher boasted: "We have the biggest building program in North Carolina, and are growin' so fast we can't hardly get enough preachers to keep up with it." Ministers of the Church of God in the county are very proud that one of their number

was selected to deliver the commencement sermon at one of
the local high schools recently, "with several mill owners and
preachers of big uptown churches settin' right there." One of
the clearest impressions that comes from conversation with sect
preachers is of their desire to extend the influence of their sect
as a denomination, rather than simply as a faith.

Little by little, the newer sects are seeking and winning support from mill managements and are coming to occupy a recognized place in the life of mill communities. Previously, most
employers have discouraged them, on the ground that they upset the routine of the life of workers, and perhaps also lest organization along religious lines among less integrated segments
of the labor force might pave the way for organization along
economic lines, as it has in some instances. More recently, however, subsidies similar to those granted to older churches are being offered a few sectarian groups. One Church of God minister, when asked if he knew an executive of the mill in whose
village he was stationed, replied exultingly: "Know him! Why,
he's my financier! I've got about $1,400 from him in the last
two or three years. You see, I know something about the income
tax, and have had great success with mill officials!" A preacher
of the Pentecostal Holiness Church is planning to erect a new
building soon; he has inquired, for the first time, concerning
possible assistance from the mills, and reports happily that "the
mills will be tolerable to us when we get ready to build." In
many respects the newer sects are tending to make their peace
with the world, seeking to conquer it rather than to transcend it.

The sect, in summary, represents a reaction, cloaked at first
in purely religious guise, against both religious and economic
institutions. Overtly, it is a protest against the failure of religious institutions to come to grips with the needs of marginal
groups, existing unnoticed on the fringes of cultural and social
organization. But as the sect begins to force its way into the
cultural pattern and to become entrenched as an institution
within the cultural fabric, it passes from sect type to Church
type. Then new sects arise, in protest against the failure of old
sects and of society to distribute their benefits more impartially.

PART II
MODES OF CONTROL

CHAPTER VIII

THE CONTROL OF CHURCHES BY MILLS

As the textile industry grew in Gaston County, the wealth and power of its owners increased rapidly, and the relative number of its owners decreased. In the first three decades of industrialization, astute investors with small margins of available capital gathered the stock of the new mills increasingly into their own hands, and the ownership and control of a large percentage of the mills passed from a relatively broad community base into the hands of less than a dozen families. Large profits were realized from the new mills from the outset, providing capital for the construction and operation of additional mills.

Until recently it has been customary in the county to put new capital into a new mill instead of enlarging an old one; a number of chains, each containing several similar units, have been thereby created, with separate units having independent status but overlapping executive administration.[1] Through this system a comparatively small number of employers came to control a large number of mills, each with its own mill village and other appurtenances of the village system. The degree to which concentration of administrative authority has proceeded during the last thirty-five years is indicated in Table XXVIII; while the number of mills increased by 257 per cent from 1900 to 1935, the number of individuals holding offices in mill corporations increased only 23 per cent.

Control by mill owners over the total economic life was extended as the number of mills increased. Manufacturers estimated that about 45,000 people in Gaston County had become directly dependent upon the textile industry by 1925–26, of a

1. Since 1927 this system has been superseded somewhat by vertical types of integration, though a number of chains are still in existence. For a study of the organization of Gaston County mills, see Angeline Bouchard, "The Southern Combed Sales Yarn Industry" (M.A. thesis, Columbia University, 1938), pp. 27–49. Cf. H. S. Davis, G. W. Taylor, C. C. Balderston and Anne Bezanson, *Vertical Integration in the Textile Industries* (Philadelphia, 1938); Ben F. Lemert, *The Cotton Textile Industry of the Southern Appalachian Piedmont* (Chapel Hill, 1933), chaps. iv, v.

TABLE XXVIII
DISTRIBUTION OF CONTROL OVER MAJOR OFFICES IN
GASTON COUNTY TEXTILE CORPORATIONS*

	1880–1900	1935
Total number of mills	28	100
Total number of mill corporations	25	65
Total number of offices in corporations	112	187
Number of individuals holding offices	93	114
Average offices per individual	1.20	1.64
Number of individuals holding one office	77	85
Number of persons holding two offices	13	17
Number of persons holding three or more offices	3	12

* Compiled from data contained in J. H. Separk, *Gastonia and Gaston County*, chap. xiii, secs. A, B. In 1935 three individuals in the county held more than ten major executive offices each, and the twelve persons holding three or more offices accounted for 68 of the total number of offices.

total of about 65,000 persons.[2] Mill workers and uptown citizens alike became heavily reliant for a livelihood upon the successful operation of the mills. Gaston County recapitulated the ante bellum economic policy of the South, putting all her economic eggs into one basket. Just as the Old South devoted its principal energies to the production of a single crop, Gaston County after 1880 applied nearly all economic resources to the construction and operation of spinning mills. The whir of spindles became a foundation and token of unprecedented prosperity, and little effort was made to diversify industry. In a pageant staged by Gastonia in 1924 to celebrate her civic achievements, a herald proclaimed:

> O Gaston, you are rich in spindles,
> And rich in other things;
> We pass not by your other wealth,
> We would not miss a single one,
> But let the other industries
> To spindles make obeisance
> For spindles make the county known
> To all within the nation.[3]

2. North Carolina Department of Labor and Printing, *Report, 1925–26*, pp. 44–49.

3. *Visions Old and New: A Historical Pageant of Gaston County* (Gastonia, 1924), p. 32.

Command over economic structure carried over into all other spheres of social organization. Textile manufacturers became acknowledged leaders in every aspect of community life. They, or their representatives, were elected to many of the political and civic offices. They "set the pace" in houses and automobiles and leisure activities. They made the largest contributions to all "worthy causes." They became unchallenged arbiters of social

TABLE XXIX

CHURCH AFFILIATIONS OF COTTON MILL EXECUTIVES IN GASTON
COUNTY, AS BETWEEN 1880–1900 AND 1935*

Denomination	Number of mill executives	
	1880–1900	*1935*
Lutheran	30	11
Presbyterian	28	32
Baptist	3	15
Methodist	15	21
Miscellaneous	3	5
Jewish	0	7
Nonchurchmen	2	3
No information	12	20
TOTAL	93	114

* A list of officers was compiled from data contained in J. H. Separk, *op. cit.*, chap. xiii, secs. A, B. Church affiliations were specified by a leading churchman of the county.

policy and were regarded as praiseworthy guardians of community welfare.

Mill owners have been leaders in the churches of the county as in other institutions. As already seen, they played an important part in church life and church extension during the early days of the industry, and the role of leadership in religious institutions continued to be a tradition which few executives could ignore. Though denominational affiliations have shifted significantly, the percentage of major textile officials belonging to some church has changed very little as between 1880–1900 and 1935, as indicated in Table XXIX. In more recent years they have often expressed a desire to remain "in the background," lest ordinary citizens leave responsibility for the churches too largely in their hands, but at least half of the mill officials of the county hold important offices in their respective churches at the present time. Replies to a questionnaire in 1939 indicated that, of 78 mill officials from presidents down through overseers, 71 were church members, and 40 held some office in a church. A special study of 11 superintendents, with direct oversight of 15 mills, revealed that every one belonged to a church and 6 held at least one major office in a religious institution, while the 11 superintendents combined held a total of 15 offices in their respective churches.

Mill officials have supported the churches not only in membership and leadership but also through contributions to building funds and to the support of ministers. Financial support has often been interpreted as representing a means of control over the churches rather than a sincere desire to aid religious institutions as such. Mill owners explicitly deny any such intention. The attitude expressed by one mill president is typical of that almost universally advanced:

The mills regard churches as important in their villages, and support this regard with contributions. But the mills are interested in churches simply because the churches stand for decent and honest living. In one sense, of course, this is a selfish motive. The mills expect, however, to receive no direct returns; so far as I know, no effort has ever been made to dictate the attitudes of the churches toward the mills—not a word has ever been said. If any such direct effort was made, of course, the effectiveness of the churches would be crippled among the workers.

Despite disavowal of ulterior purposes, the fact that mills have almost universally contributed to the support of churches and ministers in their villages, whether or not any mill official belonged to those churches, justifies speculation on the real motives actuating such support. The degree to which textile managers have been conscious of an external purpose is a difficult and ambiguous question, to be sure, and is not as important as often assumed. It stresses motives to the neglect of structural relationships and results. Contributions by mills to churches are probably to be interpreted in the light of the general paternalistic background prevailing in the industry rather than as shrewd efforts to use the churches, in some diabolical way, as instruments of industrial policy. Most of the mill owners, under given cultural conditions, have not considered that they were using the churches in any way incompatible with the highest ideals of Christianity. The fact that churches have never challenged or refused their help, but have received it gladly, has confirmed them in their belief that they were philanthropists. Paternalism in industrial relations requires that they shall continue to be philanthropists, charged with the religious as well as the economic welfare of their workers. In playing this role, rationalizations have been made so subtly that neither mill owner nor church has questioned the essential sincerity of mill subsidies to churches.

The philanthropic mood has not prevented judicious discrimination by mill owners between the type of church to be supported and the type to be ignored. Direct subsidies have been allocated by the particular mill owner, almost without exception, to the churches attended by his own workers, whether or not these churches needed his help more than others in the vicinity. Concern simply for the religious welfare of the community has not resulted in an established policy for the support of Negro churches, though the need appears to be greater here than elsewhere. Further, the donor has often discriminated between the churches serving his own employees; until very recently, most employers discouraged establishment of the Church of God and similar groups in their villages, refusing to grant them space for the erection of buildings on mill property, and declining to render financial support to sect preachers. The personal affiliation of employers with older denominations may help to explain this discrimination—though many Presbyterian and Lutheran executives express a preference for Methodist and Baptist churches for their employees. On the other hand, it is well known in Southern mill villages that union organizers frequently obtain a following most easily from members of the newer sects, who have least to lose in an effort to improve their lot. Insofar as they "settle down" and become "stabilizing influences," according to employers, the Church of God and similar groups are receiving help from the mills. Otherwise, they are discouraged, and mill executives rationalize this policy by statements such as the following:

Our workers here in Gastonia are over 99 per cent pure Anglo-Saxon; they are intelligent, smart, educated. There is no use letting them get all stirred up emotionally. I'm a Methodist, but I don't like the old type of revivals, and naturally I express myself to that effect whenever any such question arises in regard to our mills. We don't care what road a man travels to get to heaven, just as we don't care whether a man travels the northern or southern route to get to San Francisco, but why should we let emotional sects get our people all stirred up?

More recently, a younger group of better-educated, more thoroughly secularized executives has begun to appear in the county, and at least a few of them see more clearly than have their predecessors the implications of their patronage of the churches. Most of them continue, nevertheless, to acquiesce in the system of subsidies. The infiltration of a number of executives from other regions of the country, including a few Jews from New York City, has also tended to increase self-consciousness on the part of their fellow executives: the Jewish managers help the churches quite as generously as do their Christian competitors, though they hold neither the same cultural presuppositions nor a common faith. Increasingly during the last two decades, and in a few instances even earlier, subsidies to religious institutions have been used as instruments of economic control—instruments the more effective because disguised in character. Paternalism in the county is becoming conscious of itself.[4]

Considerable debate has taken place as to whether financial support of churches by mill executives, and active leadership of

4. The end of this road may be foreseen in a feature appearing in the *Southern Textile Bulletin,* semiofficial journal of Southern mill superintendents. "Becky Ann's Own Page," appearing in a section designed for separate distribution to mill workers, is filled with religious admonitions, of which the following are samples:

"Those who have suffered most, serve best."

"God is good, friends are true, and somehow we get courage to 'keep on keeping on.' "

Mixed in with these mottoes are plaudits of the cotton mills, such as: "Today, those who have work in modern mills are the most fortunate people I know . . . nice homes . . . coal at reduced rates . . . educational advantages . . . hours are less and wages more . . . radios . . . daily papers . . . a car . . . insurance . . . fraternal orders. . . ." (August 28, 1930, March 5, 1936).

many churches by them, has actually resulted in control of the
churches by the mill owners, whatever their intentions may have
been. A critic charged in 1929, after a wave of textile strikes in
the South, that the churches were "undoubtedly owned and controlled by the mill owners," and that the clergy were "moral
police for the industrial overlords."[5] The charge was denied by
mill owners and violently repudiated by many ministers in textile centers. The pastor of one mill church wrote:

May I give you some of my experience in this matter? First I was
a student pastor at Spartanburg in the Glendale mill village, and
lived just across the street from Mr. Lindsey, the president, and
next door to one of the biggest stockholders in the mill. Never for
one time did they try to meddle in the affairs of the church that I
was pastor of in their village.[6]

At its meeting in October, 1929, the Western North Carolina
Annual Conference of the Methodist Episcopal Church, South,
openly acknowledged the system of mill supplements to some of
its churches, and urged the extension of the system, recom-
mending that manufacturers "should bear at least one-half the
burden of maintaining religious worship in mill communities."[7]
The chairman of the committee which brought this recommendation to the conference was the presiding elder of Methodist
churches in the Gastonia district, and another member of the
committee became the new presiding elder of that district for
the following year. When reminded a decade later of this overt
appeal to mill owners for heavier subsidies, the chairman said:

Amen! I've always believed that. Mill churches serve the mill as
much as they serve the folks; let the mill pay for the service.
Churches help the mills to have a steadier and more intelligent supply of labor. Let the mills give more than they do, and let it all be
perfectly above board. It's worth something to the mills to have
churches work among their people. Why Mr. —— [one of the
largest textile manufacturers in North Carolina], a Jew, helps

5. Remarks by Rev. W. B. Spofford at a conference in New York, October
30, 1929, widely reprinted in Southern newspapers.
6. *Southern Textile Bulletin* (January 23, 1930), p. 11.
7. *Minutes of the Fortieth Session, Western North Carolina Conference,
Methodist Episcopal Church, South* (High Point, 1929), pp. 78–80.

the preachers, and the first thing he does when a strike threatens is to call them up—and the strikers can't win with the preachers against them. So let Mr. —— pay.[8]

The Methodist appeal drew vigorous criticism from various sources. A correspondent wrote to the Raleigh *News and Observer:*

Pastors are very human. . . . They cannot bite the hand that feeds them. . . . In times of stress the employers and the employed clash. . . . What is a subsidized pastor and a subsidized church to do? . . . As a matter of fact they can do nothing. . . . Better have no church at all than to have one that is subsidized. . . .[9]

The editor of the *News and Observer* agreed, writing that "if there is any institution that must be kept free, that ought to be kept above the faintest suspicion of taint, it is the church of Almighty God."
A similar debate over the implications of support of churches by mills has flared on other occasions, with very few of the disputants being as frank (or cynical) as the sponsor of the Methodist recommendation. Ministers, almost without exception, resent the imputation involved in the question itself, and hasten to defend themselves and their colleagues. The standard formula, heard many times from mill pastors, insists that "the mill owners give our church the free use of a nice parsonage and make regular contributions to the support of the church, yet never have they said anything about the policy of the church." Many ministers in Gaston County aver that never, in all their experience, have they seen or heard any evidence that mills in any way have attempted to dominate church affairs.
Regardless of their own intentions and the protestations of ministers to the contrary, mill owners have held and exercised direct authority over many individual churches in Gaston County. It is very difficult to obtain information concerning explicit use of their power, as most pressures have been applied very subtly and quietly. Several incidents during the last sixty years indicate clearly, however, that on occasion particular mill

8. Interview, September 4, 1939.
9. Raleigh *News and Observer*, November 3, 1929.

officials have held determining power over particular churches. The following cases are representative:

The Presbyterian church at High Shoals, title to which had been retained in fee simple by the mill company there, was discontinued by the mill management in 1928 and transformed into a movie; the management said that the Baptists and Methodists had all the people, and there was no need for a Presbyterian church.

The Hebron Baptist Church was largely dependent on the Mountain Island Mill and when this mill was washed away by a flood in 1916 the church was forced to close for lack of support.

The mill management in one village is favorable to Baptists—at least workers think it is and they feel more secure in their jobs as Baptists than if they are Methodists. This feeling poses difficult problems for the Methodists.

In another mill village the management is decidedly pro-Methodist, and Baptists profess that they are discriminated against within the mill. The wife of the Baptist pastor in the vicinity says: "We face persecution worse than the Middle Ages."

Two brothers, each of whom was president of a cotton mill, quarreled over the distribution of offices in their particular church as between their respective sons, and a schism resulted in the church. Efforts have been made subsequently by denominational officials to heal the break, which has resulted in two separate churches only a block apart, but the mill presidents will not hear to it.

The most significant area for study of control by mill managers over churches is found in the mill churches, of course, as contrasted with uptown and rural churches. In churches located in mill villages the threat of domination by mill managers is always present, even if seldom exercised coercively. Several church buildings in the villages are owned outright by mill corporations, and a number of others contain in their deeds a retroactive clause, providing that the property shall revert to the mill by which it was given if it is ever used for nonreligious purposes. The system of direct subsidies by mill executives to salaries of mill ministers is a tool for overt control, if necessary. It is an instrument of covert control, in any case; given the low income level of mill churches, a gift of a few hundred dollars annually is necessarily a factor of influence in the determination of church policy, whether or not any stipulations or conditions accompany the gift.

Managerial authority over mill churches seldom needs to be made explicit, however, because it really inheres in the relations characteristic of mill villages. Description of these relations may best proceed through close analysis of two mill communities in Gaston County rather than through generalizations. Deviations from the patterns represented in these two samples are differences of degree only; most communities in the county are not so closely controlled, but comparable relations prevail in nearly all mill villages. Both villages represent the paternalistic system pushed to full development.

The first village, here called Milltown, is known through the South and nation as a "model mill village." Unincorporated, it is owned completely by the owner of the three mills that provide its economic base. The mill management is the direct and final authority on all matters of village administration, laying down rules and regulations for the inhabitants and employing deputy sheriffs to control their infraction. Six hundred families, and a total population of about three thousand people, live there. Construction of the village, which is located on a semi-island between two rivers, cost about $1,500,000. Workers live in three- and four-room bungalows, which they rent at a rate of $1.25 a week for a four-room house with bath, with water and a minimum amount of electricity furnished. Neat lawns and landscaping have been designed and are maintained by the mill. A mill farm supplies eggs, milk, fowls, and vegetables to employees at cost. The village has a community hall, a golf course, two large school buildings, a boarding house, and several mercantile blocks, all built by the mill.

The mill owner also built the Baptist and Methodist churches in the village, expending $65,000 on the latter, and more recently has aided in the construction of a building for the Church of God. He provides parsonages, with all conveniences included, for four ministers who live in the village. The Methodist preacher receives a direct subsidy of $62.50 each month, in a total salary of $1,900, and an additional gift of $50 from the mill owner at Christmas. The mill retains title in fee simple to all church buildings and parsonages in the village, deeding them to their respective ecclesiastical bodies as "places of worship" but retaining title to them as pieces of real estate. The mill owner is not himself a churchman but has been interested in providing "adequate facilities" for the religious life of his workers. A son of the mill owner, himself secretary of the corporation, summed up as follows the philosophy underlying support of the churches by the mill officials:

We don't believe in overlapping or duplication here, even in the churches. In our organization every responsibility is graded by rank. We have officials corresponding to generals, majors, captains, lieutenants, and so forth right on down the line. We believe in efficiency. We believe in this in the churches, too. We want the churches we have to do a good job, instead of letting too many duplications ruin them.

But the mill keeps its hands off the church situation. It keeps its hands off everything except production. It leaves all welfare, religious, and other such matters in the hands of an informal committee composed of the four village pastors, two mill superintendents, and whoever else they may select. We don't even give the committee a name, as we want to keep it flexible. This committee distributes all welfare funds,[10] passes on applications for special religious services in the community, and in general looks after the common welfare, just as in Charlotte, in the crowd I run with, the country club is a rallying point. If a mill worker wants something, he goes to his preacher first.

We put all responsibility on this informal board and on the ministers in their own churches. We want them to stand on their own feet, to develop a sense of responsibility. The churches are vital as rallying points—we use them for that.

If a minister does a bad job we withdraw support, but we don't try to chase him off, as he will hang himself if we give him enough rope: that is, he loses members, his church begins to go down, and soon his church officials are coming to us and asking us what to do. We tell them to consider in what respects their minister is de-

10. The mill is reported to have given $1,200 to one church recently, telling it to spend it wisely at its own discretion in relief work.

ficient, and then to find somebody who can meet their needs. If we can add inducements such as free rent to the new minister, we are glad to do so.

As for the Methodist church, the presiding elder often comes to see us regarding new ministers. If the last minister did not do a good job, we point out that his church lost members to other churches, that the Methodist Conference is obligated to us for sending such a poor man, and ought to send us a good one—one who will do a good job in his church, which is all that we require.

There is no support of the church as such by the mill as such; all support for several years now has been purely individual. Dad takes care of the Methodist church, my brother takes care of the Presbyterian church, our operating vice-president (who is an Episcopalian) takes care of the Baptist church, and I, not being especially committed to any church, take care of the Church of God. I do not go to see the Church of God preacher; he comes to see me, and we talk things over whenever he wishes. He is trying to hold his crowd down and seems to be doing it, but I don't see how he does it as well as he does—I tell him he can't get away with it. We had trouble with that crowd some years ago but they have settled down now.[11]

Ministers in other mill villages in the county generally agree that the churches in Milltown are completely controlled by the mill owner and his executives. The Methodist church there, they say, is a "one-man church," and "the preacher has to ask the mill owner when he can pray." As a specific example, they point out that the mill owner will not allow one of the churches to build a Sunday School building adjoining its worship auditorium, but says that it can use one of the mill houses, and that he will build a Sunday School annex himself when it is needed.

At least two of the ministers in Milltown are not happy about their situation. One of them reports that he yearns to get out of an industrial church and to have an independent church and freedom. "To work in a mill church," he says, "is to have a yoke around your neck continually. I have to call for my check every month at the mill office, and I have to consult them even about moving a piece of furniture. But the mill never attempts to dictate the policies of my church or to circumscribe its message—

11. Interview, Milltown, September 5, 1938.

not a word has ever been said about that." Another minister in
the village suspects, however, that the support of churches by
the mill is designed to control internal religious policies. "The
mill owners themselves are not church members," he says, "and
I am beginning to wonder if their support of the churches is not
hush money to keep us off the Social Gospel. They won't deed
the church property to the churches, but I think they will have
to if we are to get anything done. As for me, I want to move to
a place where I can be independent and have some freedom."

A few miles away from Milltown lies another mill village regarded as one of the more exemplary manifestations of the paternalistic system. The mill was built in 1917, and it is reported
that the builders, having the record of other mills in the county
to profit by, set out to construct their community along ideal
lines. Houses in the village, though of the same design, are
painted different colors. A community house and picnic
grounds, library, Boy Scout hut, baseball field, and an elaborate welfare program have been established and supported by
the mill. One church has been erected there, and a parsonage.
The total cost of church and parsonage was $26,000, of which
the mill contributed a total of $10,000.

The superintendent of the mill is habitually referred to in
the vicinity as the "dictator" of the village. He exercises supervision over ownership of dogs by his workers, prohibits
drunkenness, gambling, and immorality, and dominates all
other aspects of life. His supervision of moral welfare extends
to the churches. He organized and was superintendent of a
small Sunday School which led eventually to the construction
of the church in the village, and has remained superintendent of
the Sunday School and treasurer of the church ever since their
establishment. At one time or another he has held the following
offices in the church, several of them at one time: chairman of
the board of trustees, chairman of the Boy Scout committee,
teacher of the men's Bible class, steward, and lay leader. He insists that his wife and children shall attend the village church
also, from loyalty to it, though his wife is said to lament missing the cultural values of an uptown church.

The mill superintendent demands similar interest in the
church from his employees. Overseers in the mill are affiliated
almost automatically with the village church and Sunday

School, and chiefly constitute its leadership. In hiring new workers the superintendent asks about church affiliation, and reports that he has had much better results from church members than from nonchurch members.[12] He notices habitual absences from the services of the church, reminds absentees of their negligence, and instructs mill overseers to "keep an eye" on the wayward ones, to see if the quality of their work declines. He has discovered that it generally does. He also allows deductions from the pay envelopes of the workers, after their authorization, for the support of the village church, and about half of the total contributions to the church are secured in this manner. The mill adds $200 a year of its own, and the mill superintendent adds $200 privately, insisting that contributions from himself and the mill must not be mentioned lest the people "lay down" on their own contributions.

The superintendent declares that neither he nor any other official of the mill attempts any dictation to the minister or any stipulation of his message; they encourage and support the church, he affirms, simply for the general good of the community. He professes to belief in encouraging self-reliance on the part of churches, and points to the noncoöperative attitude of many of the church members at Milltown as an example of the effect of too much open support by mills.[13]

Despite his efforts at coöperation, the mill superintendent reports that he has had continual difficulty with pastors of the village church, and that he is disgusted with the denomination to which the church belongs, because of the poor caliber of the ministers it has provided. He was especially embittered by his experience with a pastor who served the church for one year recently. The minister, who may be designated as Mr. A, heard rumors before going to the parish of the support accorded to the church by the mill. On arrival, in his own words—

The superintendent of the mill told me that if my ministry pleased the mill officials they would give me $400 extra on my salary— that is, in addition to that reported in the Conference Minutes. I asked a Conference official about this, and he told me that the superintendent had more money than anybody else in the church and

12. Interview, Gaston County, September 3, 1938.
13. *Ibid.*

had been running it for fifteen years; he advised me to take the money, saying "Let him run it—what do you care?" I thought it over and told the mill superintendent that a straight salary increase would be all right, but that I didn't like two words in his proposition to me: "if" and "give." I had supposed, I said, that my ministry was to serve Jesus Christ, not mill officials.[14]

There is a persistent rumor in the community that Mr. A stood in the pulpit on one of his first Sundays in the community and said that he had heard the church was a "one-man church." "If so," he added, "I expect to be that man." Mr. A himself denies that he made the statement publicly but admits that he told the chairman of the board of stewards, who was a worker in the mill, that the job of the mill superintendent was that of running the mill. He admits further that he challenged the prevailing arrangements within the church in several respects. He differed with the mill superintendent on the system of deductions from pay envelopes for church support. He insisted that four members of the official board of the church were adulterers, and suggested that they should be left off the board, despite the fact that the mill superintendent objected.

The mill superintendent, in turn, began to bring pressure to bear against the new preacher. After sixty days he notified Mr. A that he was not satisfactory, and stopped coming to church. He required Mr. A to come, as previous ministers had done, to the mill office every Monday morning to get his check, paying him in private checks or in cash. He inspected the parsonage every week to make certain that it was being kept in good condition. He raised numerous questions about the use of facilities provided by the mill for church groups over which the new minister had assumed supervision. As treasurer of the church, he reduced Mr. A's salary to a small percentage of the previous level, explaining that income for the church had declined seriously; Mr. A reports that he investigated and found that income was up to the usual level and that all other bills were being paid in full. The superintendent insisted that the preacher should "preach the gospel, not rant." Mr. A had delivered only one sermon, according to his own testimony, that bore directly on industrial problems; in that sermon he had ad-

14. Rev. Mr. A, Interview, September 18, 1939.

vocated collective bargaining, to which the mill was stringently opposed.

Mr. A claims that, in addition to direct harassment, the mill superintendent spread all sorts of charges against him to the effect that he had consistently refused to pay his bills in previous parishes, that he cursed in public, that he held the services of the church overtime, that he was overly familiar with women, especially in swimming parties, and that he had proselyted members from other churches. On such grounds the superintendent demanded that denominational officials investigate Mr. A's character. A committee was appointed to consider the matter; the decision stipulated that the accused must withdraw from the ministry at the end of the church year or else stand trial before his ecclesiastical body. Mr. A claims that the committee found no verification of the rumors emanating from the mill superintendent but ruled that he must withdraw from the ministry because the rumors were abroad, even if untrue. In the face of this ruling, Mr. A had no alternative; at the end of the church year he left the church, the community, and the ministry.

As indicated at several points in this record of altercation, Mr. A challenged existing arrangements by which the mill and its officials appeared to him to be exercising unwarranted control over the church of which he was pastor. His methods of protest were, indubitably, often tactless and, from the standpoint of expediency, ill-advised. There is also some evidence that at least one or two of the charges brought against him by the mill superintendent had foundation in suspicion, and perhaps in fact. With the exception of the mill superintendent, all parties involved in the dispute agree, however, that the crux of the matter lay in the refusal of Mr. A to coöperate without question, as his predecessors had done, with the mill management. Charges brought against his personal character were, at most, used to buttress and to mask deeper objections. As a brother minister observed: "If the mill officials 'get it in for you,' they will use any excuse to get rid of you."

Evidence of direct control by mills over churches in Gaston County is not limited to the two situations which have been described above. Interviews with pastors of mill village churches brought many statements such as the following:

The mill preachers' hands are tied. We know where we get our support, and can't say anything.

Mill preachers know where their bread is buttered (it generally is buttered on only one side), and do not talk of unions.

Mill officials never tell me what to preach, but on several occasions I have felt their pressure.

The X's [prominent textile manufacturers in a county near Gaston] match one dollar with four dollars for anything the church wants to do. I was pastor in their mill village and know. They don't believe in the church no more than nothing; they are Jews, and they would as soon turn your church into a gymnasium or volley ball court as not if they wanted to. They help the church for the advertising—and the mill workers there don't appreciate it no more than they do here.

My relations with the mill officials are purely detached, but friendly. They do not want preachers to discuss labor questions with them: "Do not get yourself implicated one way or the other," they say, "as we do not want to tie strings on you."

A prominent official of an uptown church in Gastonia in the early 1920's was superintendent of three mills around the industrial church I was pastor over. He was a notorious whoremonger, and took girls from the night shift out into the grass nearly every night. Because I knew this, and he knew that I did, he undermined me with the uptown church, and I had to leave the pastorate.

Structural relations between churches and mills in Gaston County mill villages render control of churches and ministers by the mill officials almost inevitable, provided the latter wish to exercise that control. Control is seldom made explicit; it simply inheres in accepted relations. Its manifestation is almost always disguised in terms of the general welfare of the community, over which mill officials have final supervision. Positive and direct coercion appears very infrequently, because opposition does not demand it. When it does appear, the mill management has no difficulty in ridding itself of the troublemaker —for the good of the community.[15]

15. A well-known Southern sociologist tells of an interview he once had with a mill executive in South Carolina. The executive admitted that the mill con-

Control over religious institutions inheres not only in structural interrelations but also in the cultural setting in which mills and churches function. The traditions of mill villages include acceptance of mill executives as the final arbiters of all questions concerning community welfare, including questions that involve the policies of the churches. Pastors seldom protest seriously against these traditions because they recognize the futility of their objections, and because they themselves derive benefits from existing arrangements. Their acquiescence is not habitually self-conscious and uneasy; more often than not, it is accepted as an axiom of ministerial workmanship in situations of this sort. In short, it is taken for granted that the dependence of the mill village church on the mill itself, structurally and culturally, largely circumscribes all possibility for independent action by the church or its minister.

It is sometimes suggested that the control exercised by mill officials over mill churches is no greater than that exercised by them over uptown churches to which they themselves belong, and of which they are the acknowledged leaders. The degree to which independent action is possible appears to be greater in uptown churches, however, than in mill churches. Uptown churches are not controlled by economic institutions as such. Influence over them is cultural and personal, rather than structural, in type. Further, they can lose the support of a few individuals without endangering their institutional life. In an uptown church, as compared with a mill village church, there is a relative heterogeneity of membership, and some diversification of economic foundations is represented; even if all economic activities center around a dominant industry, as in Gaston County, there is nevertheless some possibility for independent action by those not directly employed by the industry. In a mill village, however, the church is composed of persons with a single occupation—an occupation completely dependent upon the fortunes and decisions of textile managers. It has been inevitable that the high degree of social control associated with

tributed handsomely to the support of churches in the mill village, but averred that it did so only for the general good of the community. "We had a young fellow from an Eastern seminary down here as pastor a few years ago," he continued, "and the young fool went around saying that we helped pay the preachers' salaries in order to control them. That was a damn lie—and we got rid of him."

mill villages from the outset should have come to include, as a conspicuous feature, control over village churches.

For the most part, the churches and ministers have adapted themselves to the situation and serve as an arm of the employers in control of the mill villages. Ministers rationalize their position by equating paternalism (though they avoid the word) with Christian principles. Does not the Christian gospel teach parental solicitude and admonish the strong to care for the weak, to practice generosity toward the less fortunate, and to extend the helping hand to mankind? Were not mill workers ignorant, diseased, and living in dirt and filth until the mills came along? Would they not be in that same condition today if the mills had not provided schools, welfare services, better housing, and all the advantages of life in proximity to cities and towns? Though a few younger ministers are beginning to ask whether Christianity does not demand that one shall be his "brother's brother" rather than his "brother's keeper," and to suspect that paternalism is a perversion of fraternalism, most preachers in Gaston County still ascribe untempered benevolence and Christian charity to the mill owners.

CHAPTER IX

THE SOCIAL CONSTRAINT OF THE CHURCHES

MINISTERS and churches played a significant part, as has been seen, in facilitating the industrial transformation of Gaston County. When the cotton mills began to rise, ministers and leading churchmen ventured boldly into the field of economics, lending the moral sanction and active support of the churches to the new enterprises. In numerous and crucial respects, religious institutions encouraged the growth of industry, and were partly responsible for the emergence and expansion of the mills.

Has the sense of social responsibility which characterized many religious leaders in the county half a century ago been modified in character and intensity? Have later ministers significantly altered or lost the social interest of their predecessors? Has the effort to build new economic institutions carried over, in religious circles, into attempts to shape and judge the institutions after they had emerged? If so, what methods have been adopted, and with what success? Answer to these questions involves examination of the attitudes and actions of ministers and churches with respect to social questions generally, and to the regulation and control of the mills in particular.

SOCIAL VIEWS OF MINISTERS

In recent decades very few ministers of Gaston County have demonstrated any interest in the social control or restriction of the mills their predecessors had helped to create. Many of them have maintained the tradition of commending the expansion of industry but have done practically nothing, conversely, to determine what manner of expansion it should be. So far as evidence survives, virtually no preachers in the county have made clear and definitive statements concerning child labor, the mill village system, wages and hours, or other social questions which have been agitated from time to time in wider circles. Various ministers stationed there at present explain as follows their relation to such questions:

Ministers around here let social issues alone—most of us are pretty conservative. We can't help much by discussing politics and economics, except where a moral issue, like prohibition, is involved. The mill here pays good wages, keeps up its houses, and the people are pretty well satisfied. The mill provides paint, nice lawns, hot and cold water, bathtubs and other conveniences. Why, a crew works all the time on village upkeep alone![1]

Ministers in this section do not pass resolutions on economic problems. It is not the business of the church to meddle, but to teach principles, as our Lord did, and let individuals work them out. Equally conscientious opinions differ on social questions. Of course, preaching on social issues is a good way to play to the gallery, if that is what you want to do. On the whole, mills in this section are being run with a real desire to do the right thing for all concerned, and still make a little profit. They have frequently run at a loss simply to provide work for the operatives. They provide good housing and better living conditions than would be possible otherwise.[2]

The ministers of Gastonia never take the initiative on economic and industrial questions. They are opposed only to things downright evil, such as pool rooms. On such matters they take the initiative.[3]

Ministers in the county have seldom inveighed against any practice of the mills. Dozens of interviews with clergymen of all denominations elicited only three specific criticisms of economic policies. One preacher did not see why the general manager of one of the mills should draw a salary as high as $10,000 a year. Another opposed the practice, prevalent among mill owners, of duplicating executive salaries by holding offices in several different mills; he argued that the practice deprives the stockholders of their dividends and also acts against wage levels. A third minister lamented that mill owners sometimes op-

1. Wesleyan mill pastor, Interview, July 24, 1939.
2. Episcopal uptown pastor, Interview, July 28, 1939.
3. Presbyterian mill pastor, Interview, July 27, 1939.

pose community programs such as recreation; when Federal funds provided parks for one of the mill towns, the owners of the mills provided recreation supervisors only after considerable pressure was brought to bear on them. Otherwise, no traces of desire to censure economic practices or to restrain economic power were in evidence. A minister occasionally expressed a sentiment which he himself designated as very "radical," but such statements were always so indefinite and veiled in content that they obviously represented an effort to assert personal independence rather than social dissent. One of the ministers in the county opened a prayer by saying: "O God, we thank thee that Jesus Christ is not a stick of candy, but a stick of dynamite." Many similar statements, purporting to represent Christianity as world-changing, were made, but generally failed to specify what was to be blown up.

Preachers of the newer sects, who are closer to those most disadvantaged under existing economic arrangements and presumably are in better position to see need for changes in economic affairs, display even less interest in the social sphere than ministers of older denominations. Sectarian groups, being more otherworldly in emphasis than Church-type religious institutions, are largely indifferent toward this present world. For the most part they acquiesce in the economic status quo, seeking at the same time through withdrawal to constitute a new community based on religious foundations, with participation in economic life as a sort of necessary evil. As noted, their interest in regulation of the world consists almost exclusively in setting up standards for nonparticipation in it, and these standards are devoted entirely to the regulation of individual rather than social conduct. Members may not engage in mixed swimming, dancing, or any other "worldly amusements." None of their proscriptions has extensive economic implications. When asked about the "social views" of his denomination, a Pentecostal Holiness minister replied that his denomination engages in, and enjoys, Sunday School picnics and young people's "sociables," but does not permit oyster suppers to raise money for the church. The Western North Carolina Annual Conference of this denomination has a standing committee on public morals, which has been concerned entirely with such matters as Bible study, Sabbath observance, prohibition, modern swimming pools, and style of dress.[4]

The nearest approach to a tenet that would impinge on social conduct lies in the extreme pacifism of sect groups, who allow no combatant service in war under any conditions.[5] Aversion to violence is basic in their doctrines concerning all social questions. Most sects permit members to belong to a trade union but forbid them to engage in any sort of "agitation" that might lead to violence. On the whole, the influence of the groups is normally against unionization, though they expressly stipulate that members may join a union if necessity demands but must not take part in "labor troubles" and must be "peaceable until they return to work." As one Pentecostal Holiness preacher summed it up, "We tolerate joining of unions but we do not tolerate activities [i.e., agitation]." Sectarian views on this question, as on most social issues, are ambiguous. At times sect ministers have denounced trade unions as bearing "the mark of the beast," a stigma little understood but fearsome and dreadful for all members of sectarian bodies. At other times members and ministers of the newer religious sects have afforded a nucleus for labor organization. Being relatively less integrated into the larger community, they are the more easily enlisted for campaigns that challenge prevailing conditions. They offered almost the only religious sanction accorded to strikers in Gastonia in 1929. For the most part, however, they favor organization to await the Second Coming of Christ rather than to secure immediate economic benefits. If the Church provides sanc-

4. *Minutes of the Western North Carolina Annual Conference of the Pentecostal Holiness Church, 1937*, pp. 17–18; *1939*, p. 18.

5. During the war of 1914–18 this regulation appears to have been observed in the breach quite as much as in the fulfillment. At a service of the Church of God, shortly after the beginning of the European war in 1939, testimonies by several members touched upon the European situation; one man said that love of the Lord would stop the war, while another thanked God that, though a soldier in France in the last war, he managed to keep from shedding blood.

Whether a member of the Church of God can be an officer of the law, with or without a gun, is left to the conscience of the individual. Sect groups tend to make their peace with the political as well as the economic order, except in the one matter of pacifism. The Annual Assembly of the Church of God, for example, stipulates that "the Church should appreciate the laws that protect public worship and should recognize the officers of the Law as God's ministers, Romans 13.1–6." *Minutes of the Thirty-Second Annual Assembly of the Church of God, 1937*, p. 144.

tion, by and large, for the economic culture, the sects are largely indifferent to it, but their indifference passes occasionally into sharp antagonism.

Social Views of Ecclesiastical Bodies

Gaston County ministers have been little bolder collectively than individually in discussing industrial relations. No ecclesiastical body in the county has ever made any statement or adopted any policy calling for significant regulation of economic conditions. The ministerial association of Gastonia, to which about forty ministers belong, has taken the following actions, representative of its interests, during recent years:

Held a program on the dangers of unemployment (May 2, 1932).

Endorsed support of N.R.A. program (August 3, 1933. The entire community, including manufacturers, endorsed this program, and still believes that it was "the best thing that ever happened to the textile industry").

Pledged support to the United Dry Forces of North Carolina (September 4, 1933).

Protested against pool rooms within the bounds of the city (March 5, 1934).

Commended city officials for banishing slot machines (December 2, 1935).

Held two joint meetings with colored ministers of the city, at one of which a Negro minister spoke "with deep humility" (January 3, 1937, January 3, 1938).

Approved efforts to enforce the truancy law among school children (September 6, 1937).

Praised county officers for their enforcement of laws against roadhouses (November 8, 1937).

Adopted resolutions condemning gambling, the sale of liquor, and prostitution in Greater Gastonia (November 8, 1937).

Sponsored religious services for prisoners on the chain gang (1937), the County Home, neighboring C.C.C. camps, and a nutritional camp for underfed children (1938).

Protested against the flying of airplanes at low altitudes over the city on the Sabbath (May 2, 1938).

Passed resolutions of sympathy for the national campaign against syphilis (June 6, 1938).

Heard a denunciation by one minister of "the marriage of Clark Gable and Carrolle [sic] Lombard, flaunting their adultery before the world" (April 3, 1939).[6]

The programs of the Ministers' Association have consisted principally of talks by various members on theological subjects ("The Nature and Method of Revelation," "The Sovereignty of God," "The Holy Spirit"), papers on the history of the various denominations represented, and similar topics dealing almost exclusively with the religious sphere. In 1920 the Association publicly proclaimed itself as being "closely allied with all the problems directly and vitally affecting the commercial, industrial and civic life of the community."[7] During subsequent years it has given no significant attention to these areas, and can be interpreted as solicitous for them only in that it has attempted to protect the community against "deteriorating and alien influences."

Denominational bodies coterminous in extent with Gaston County, or roughly so, have revealed even less interest in social and economic affairs. Presbyteries, district conferences, and county associations have taken no action, so far as official minutes reveal or the oldest ministers can remember, bearing explicitly on problems of the textile industry. Only one or two of these ecclesiastical bodies have any committee into whose purview such problems might enter, and these have generally been concerned solely with Sabbath observance and temperance. Secular terms like "cotton mill," "textile industry," "labor," and "economics" have almost never entered into the speech of ecclesiastical assemblies.

Certain state-wide ecclesiastical bodies have occasionally displayed interest in the regulation of the textile industry. A rapid survey of denominational social attitudes in North Caro-

6. "Minutes of the Gastonia Ministers' Association" (1932–39; MS. in possession of the secretary, Gastonia, N.C.).

7. *Gastonia Gazette*, June 23, 1920.

lina will indicate the extent to which larger religious organizations have provided leadership in such matters for their members in Gaston County, and will reveal the dominant philosophies underlying the approach of religious bodies in the region to industrial affairs.

Neither the Presbyterian Synod of North Carolina nor the General Assembly of the Presbyterian Church in the United States has ever adopted any resolution or statement of opinion touching the textile industry, so far as careful research could discover. One elderly Presbyterian minister, who is an expert on Presbyterian documents, summed up the attitude of his denomination by saying, "There is practically no material on that; Presbyterian preachers don't talk much on such subjects." No traces whatever have been found of any committee dealing with social questions, or of any pronouncements on such questions, in the minutes of any Lutheran ecclesiastical bodies. Occasional resolutions in favor of temperance are the sole exceptions.

The Methodist and Baptist denominations, on the other hand, have frequently expressed direct interest in the social, economic, and moral problems arising in connection with the textile industry. The Western North Carolina Annual Conference of the Methodist Church, to which churches in Gaston County belong, has occasionally adopted a resolution urging regulation of working conditions in the industry, especially for women and children.[8] After the violent textile strikes in the South in 1929, its committee on industrial relations, of which the presiding elder of the Gastonia district was chairman, presented a report which was adopted by the conference and was widely discussed in the newspapers of the section. It characterized the textile industry as a "sick industry" but insisted that a "living wage" should be paid textile workers, with the cost added to the price of the product. The stretch-out system, wage cuts, longer hours, strikes, and sabotage were condemned, and shorter hours and reduction of night work for women and children were endorsed. Senators and representatives in the

8. A complete description of the pertinent actions is contained in E. W. Hardin, "The Attitude of the Methodist Episcopal Church, South, in North Carolina toward the Textile Industry in North Carolina" (B.D. thesis, Duke University, 1938).

Congress of the United States were urged to secure a Federal study of the entire textile industry in order that wise legislation might be enacted. Employers and employees were entreated "to, in the Spirit of Christ, join hands, minds, and hearts in securing a better industrial order." At the same time employers were requested to subsidize churches in their mill villages more heavily.[9]

The North Carolina Baptist State Convention appointed a committee on social service in 1913, and this committee has been functioning in varying forms ever since. At one time or another it has urged temperance reform, child labor legislation, strict interpretation of marriage and divorce, and Sabbath observance. In 1915 the committee was assigned supervision of the work of the denomination in respect to orphanages, ministers' relief, and temperance; it was allotted two hours for its report at the annual state convention, of which an hour and fifty-five minutes was to be devoted to these three issues. The remaining five minutes might be spent in discussion of other matters. This arrangement continued unchanged until 1927 when a committee on public morals was established; except in 1929, this committee has brought in no resolutions worthy of notice. Meeting in that year just outside the bounds of Gaston County, where labor disorders had kept the region in turmoil for the preceding six months, the Baptist State Convention put itself on record as being troubled over the textile industry. It adopted, with no debate, a report of the committee on public morals which deplored the recent industrial strife, recognized the rights of wage earners to organize, and called for "a fair wage for fair work," with the standard of fairness to be determined by a survey conducted by a state commission. In summing up its cure for industrial ills, the committee said:

A general survey of the business community provides little ground for hope that greed will ever acquire self-restraint or industry put its own house in order. . . . Recent industrial strife, stained with tragedy and the partial failure of justice, within the bounds of this convention, calls for rebuke and a fresh assertion of the inescapable authority of Christ's law of brotherhood in the world of

9. *Minutes of the Fortieth Session, Western North Carolina Conference, Methodist Episcopal Church, South* (High Point, 1929), pp. 78–80. See chap. viii.

business. Wage payers have obligations to face as well as wage earners. . . . Our best and ultimate reliance for industrial justice and peace is the conversion of the men who manage and the men who work to Christ's way of life. . . . Religion is the medicine for industry.[10]

The other state-wide ecclesiastical bodies having significant representation in Gaston County have failed to stimulate any substantial interest in social questions among their constituents. Following the revival of public interest in social reform just after the first World War, to be sure, many of them set up committees to deal with social problems. The fate of most of these committees may be illustrated by two instances. In 1920 the Protestant Episcopal Missionary District of Asheville, through its Social Service Commission, urged that "the time has come when social service is the *sine qua non* of the progress of the church."[11] The report of the commission for 1937 was typical of results that followed: it had held no meetings and done no work, but wished to advise that the finest opportunity for the clergy to do social service work lay in the preparation of young people for marriage and home building.[12] The Methodist Protestant Church in North Carolina also appointed a committee on social reform; in 1929, when most denominations gave some notice to the wave of textile strikes in the South, this committee inveighed against dancing, playing bridge for prizes, buying and selling on Sunday, and "matching coins at the cold drink stand."[13]

Analysis of statements by larger church bodies indicates clearly that churchmen in the section which includes Gaston County have seldom been stirred from a position of indifference toward industrial affairs, and from unquestioning acceptance of prevailing economic arrangements. Denominational bodies have given very little impetus to consideration by their ministers or local churches of the social contexts in which the churches function. When occasional resolutions have been introduced,

10. *Minutes of the Baptist State Convention of North Carolina, 1929*, pp. 46–48.

11. *Journal of the Missionary District of Asheville, 1920*, pp. 32–34.

12. Diocese of Western North Carolina, *Journal of the Fifteenth Annual Convention, 1937*, pp. 46–47.

13. *Journal of the 102nd Annual Session of the North Carolina Annual Conference of the Methodist Protestant Church, 1929*, pp. 44–45.

the principles advocated have been so general in form that nothing has been very much affected by them, and so slight in demands that their complete enforcement would have resulted only in minor regulations of economic practices.

Disinclination of ecclesiastical bodies to deal with social questions is not primarily occasioned, as often thought, by their traditional suspicion of the state and by their insistence on the separation of Church and state. On issues about which they have been especially solicitous, such as prohibition or Sabbath observance, possible interference in affairs of the state has been no barrier to enthusiastic agitation and action. The procedure in such instances has been to designate the question a "moral issue," and to have functional relations with the state while maintaining organic separation. The South has traditionally insisted on translating moral sanctions into statute law, and Southern ministers have been leaders in any number of political campaigns dealing with specific issues. The churches have not, therefore, stood aloof from regulation of economic life because of possible embroilment in political affairs, though this is the reason most often given.

SERMONS AND ECONOMIC RESPONSIBILITY

In the absence of resolutions and public statements concerning the textile industry, sermons of ministers in Gaston County constitute the best available statement of the official (i.e., publicly promulgated, without ensuing challenge) policy of the churches toward economic affairs. Here, as in most other respects, the minister is usually accepted as representative of his church and his public statements are seldom disputed, probably because they generally confirm the ethicways prevailing in the county.

Examination of ideas contained in sermons provides a cross section of the general problem of the relation of mills and churches, and may best proceed with direct reference to the six possible types of relationship. That is, to what degree do sermons delivered in the county indicate that the role of the church in relation to economic institutions is that of source, product, sanction, antagonism, indifference, or irrelevance? A twofold problem is involved in answering this question. On the one hand, what role is envisaged in the sermons themselves? On the other, what institutional interrelationships result from the sermons or from the application of ideas in the sermons? In order to answer the first question, it is necessary to take an internal viewpoint and is illuminating to quote directly from sermons. Answer to the second question demands an external, critical viewpoint in an effort to understand what the sermons mean in social relations, in contrast to what they say.

If judged by their sermons,[14] most of the ministers in the county believe that religion and religious institutions offer the only fundamental hope for a better social order, as the following excerpts indicate:

All the world's difficulties could be settled in twenty-four hours if the nations of the world took the Golden Rule as their guide. [MS. of sermon by a Methodist mill pastor.]

When we all (not just a few) properly adjust our relations to our God and to our fellowman, all other problems, small or great, will adjust themselves around them, or at least will take care of themselves. [Baptist mill pastor, in *Gastonia Gazette*, June 4, 1938.]

Face to face with the problems of life that seem to be perplexing in all their aspects, people are trying to find the solution of these pressing problems in human methods. It is impossible for us to solve them in our own strength. It takes a higher power. The adequacy of the Gospel of Christ seems to have been kept in the background. As the world seeks for plans to solve the problems of civilization why not try the Plan of the Gospel of Christ. Oh, you may say it will not work but why will it not work because we have never tried it? We need faith to proceed. . . . [Presbyterian uptown pastor, *ibid.*, February 19, 1938.]

14. The generalizations that follow are based on approximately one hundred sermons by ministers stationed in the county during 1938 and 1939. In 1938 the *Gastonia Gazette* published a series of articles on various churches in the county, including a brief sermon by the minister of each church represented. A total of fifty-six sermons appeared in the series, many of which were especially valuable for purposes of this present study, as they attempted to define the relation of the churches to the community. (The entire series was captioned "Go to Church Tomorrow: What Would Gaston Communities Be without Their Churches?") The writer also examined a number of sermons in manuscript, and was present at the delivery of approximately thirty, by ministers of practically all denominations.

Problems, the nature of which we have never faced before, are confronting this entire nation and we today are called upon by the Prophet to seek the Lord. This is our greatest need today; this is the greatest need of the world, a direct turning to Almighty God. He is our only Hope. . . . We must seek the Lord and repent of our sins and exercise Faith in Him; then, and only then, can we be saved. [Baptist uptown pastor, *ibid.*, July 2, 1938.]

The churches offer to a confused and selfish world a decalog and golden rule, immortal guides to all human life and business enterprises. . . . The churches propose to all men everywhere a world ruled by the principles of order and good will. . . . The Church is Christ's one supreme institution upon the Earth for its salvation, even the salvation of each individual soul. [Methodist uptown pastor, *ibid.*, February 12, 1938.]

One of today's pressing problems is the gulf fixed between those who fare sumptuously every day and those who eat irregularly. . . . Many who have attained fail to help those less fortunate. Such feeling gives greater tension. In these relationships let us remember the word of Jesus as he said, "All things whatsoever ye would that men should do unto you, do ye, even so to them." [Presbyterian rural minister, *ibid.*, July 9, 1938.]

We need to hold up the eternal things and give them first place in life. Christian character is our need, this will give us Holy ideals to strive for and will give us the right desires and motives in life and is the only thing that can and will save society. Character is greater than wealth, the great desire for wealth today shows that we are material worshipers, and if persued [*sic*] will rob the widow and orphans, will license stealing devices and pretend to operate a government by licensing whiskey, which is the curse of curses that has caused so much poverty and heartaches. What shall it profit a man to gain the whole world and lose his soul? [Methodist mill pastor, *ibid.*, July 23, 1938.]

Most ministers in the county deny that the proper role of religious institutions in relation to the economic and social order is indifference. On the other hand, they assert that the church as an institution must not become embroiled in economic and political affairs but must save the world through "changed individuals" and the extension of the church. Individual conversion and private virtue are demanded as the fundamental requirements for the growth of the church and the correlative correction of social institutions. Practically all exhortation pleads either for personal salvation or for the performance of one's "Christian duty," with the assurance that all problems will thereby be solved. These emphases place a direct sanction on the mores of the county, as the prevailing culture relies on them likewise, and an indirect sanction through diverting attention from examination of existing economic structures. Insofar as it is claimed that this line of attack will lead to the reform of society, most of the sermons probably become irrelevant. It is difficult to see that economic institutions will be appreciably modified by approaches such as the following:

Today there are two questions that should be much in the minds of all thinking people, viz: what's wrong with the world and what's right with the world. . . . One practice which is wrong with the world today . . . is national Sabbath desecration. [Lutheran rural pastor, in *Gastonia Gazette*, May 7, 1939.]

Shall we let God use us to help the church and the Christ in the task of making bad people good and good people better? [Methodist uptown pastor, *ibid.*, October 15, 1938.]

In our relations with the leaders of our community life we should seek a mutual understanding. Let us take time for kindness that the conflict between groups may be lessened. [Presbyterian uptown pastor, *ibid.*, July 9, 1938.]

Good manifests itself in the following qualities: love, kindness, gentleness, longsuffering, humility, temperance, sacrifice, and courage. . . . Evil manifests itself in: selfishness, temper, harshness, hatred, revenge, dishonesty, impure living, and intemperance. . . . One of these powers controls every life. [Baptist mill pastor, *ibid.*, July 18, 1938.]

The bulk of life is spent in domestic and business activities and the greatest thing we can do is to perform these unselfishly and helpfully. . . . [It is too bad when] the employer is interested in great schemes for the uplift of humanity and overlooks his own workmen; husband and wife are interested in religious and charitable work and forget what they owe to each other and their children. [Presbyterian uptown pastor, *ibid.*, March 12, 1938.]

Don't you think that if every member of every church would for-
give everyone who had wronged him, we would have the best
county in the state and the best churches in all the world? If you
think these things, blessed are ye if ye do them. [Presbyterian
rural pastor, *ibid.*, August 13, 1938.]

From the standpoint of direct institutional interaction,
therefore, the strategy of religious institutions is largely irrelevant to economic conditions; seeking to become sufficient within
themselves, the churches do not attempt direct modification of
economic institutions. It is simply assumed that economic problems will be solved, and only so, if the church and its ideals become all-pervasive in society. The tacit premise underlying the
views of Gaston County ministers seems to be that all social
problems would immediately cease to exist if the influence of religion were allowed to mold a perfect society—a tautology of
which they themselves are not cognizant, being so largely dedicated to the service of one particular institution.

Their strategy is also confused. In one breath they urge that
Christians can save themselves only through withdrawal from
the world;[15] in the next that Christianity must pervade all aspects of social life. This confusion was nicely illustrated in a
sermon by a young minister noted in the community for his
straightforwardness:

Nowadays, we can hardly tell the difference between the world and
Christians. But the things of the world keep us from Christ. Be ye
not conformed to this world. It's too bad that even the church has
been largely conformed; why, some churches have even gone in for
bank night and bingo.

.   .   .   .

The trouble is, religion has been too compartmentalized. Young
people are disturbed when they see men who pull shady deals in
business and pass the collection plate piously in Church. If Christ
is in us, He must be in business too.[16]

15. Confusion often results from failure to define clearly what is meant by
"the world." Generally the term is used to designate particular social amusements against which the minister wishes to inveigh.

16. Sermon by Presbyterian uptown pastor, Gastonia, July 23, 1939. This
confusion between strategies of withdrawal and attack, in relation to "secular
affairs," represents oscillation between sectarian and churchly viewpoints.

Confusion exists most strikingly in the theory of the relation of the Christian to material concerns. At one moment the worshiper is urged to surrender all earthly interests and possessions in order to enter the kingdom of God; the next he is assured that success (which is almost inevitably interpreted in materialistic terms) depends upon one's fidelity to Christian principles. The minister of a mill church chose as his topic for a Sunday evening sermon, "Is Your All on the Altar?"; the church bulletin announcing this topic contained several quotations to demonstrate that "tithing pays," including the following:

Five years ago I first became a tither. I tithed for two years. The next year I gave one-ninth. The next year I gave one-eighth. Last year I gave one-seventh. This year I am giving one-seventh. If life be spared next year I want to give one-sixth. As a result I can truthfully say that I am more happy, more generous, and more financially prosperous.

.   .   .   .

When in Sydney, Australia, I knew a man who started tithing, who was then a comparatively poor man; a baker by trade. He prospered wonderfully and gave largely. He used to say he "could not send out of the front door goods and money for the Lord as quickly as the Lord sent them in at the back door."[17]

Though most ministers in the county believe that the church is a mighty force for social redemption, most of their sermons are ostensibly indifferent to all social problems, being concerned with theological, evangelistic, or ecclesiastical subjects.[18] The following topics are illustrative of those chosen for a majority of the sermons:

Christ's Kingdom
Unanswered Prayer
The Decline of Spiritual Power
The Power of Faith in God
The Apostolic Church
The Heresy of Laodicea

17. Bulletin of a Methodist mill church, December 18, 1938.
18. Approximately 70 per cent of the sermons analyzed by the writer contained no direct reference, even incidentally, to any social question.

In His Own Image
Hope in a World of Chaos
From Fight Ring to Pulpit
The A.B.C.'s and X.Y.Z.'s of the Liquor Traffic
How Can Religion Help Me?
What Does It Mean to be Saved?
Is There a Hell?

The most characteristic note in Gaston County preaching might be summed up: "The mission of the church is to do the will of Jesus and to seek to save lost souls. It brings men hope of heaven and comforts them in their sorrows and distresses." Whatever the topic may be, and by whatever excursions the preacher may arrive at his peroration, sermons in the county customarily end somewhat as follows:

We are all sinners. Every person is a sinner. We are all on our way to Judgment: every infant in a mother's arms, every child on the way to school, every person on the highway or in an office— we all are on our way to stand before the Judgment of God. There is no satisfactory substitute for God. He alone can cleanse; only by the power of the blood of Christ can our sins be washed away. That power can save: consider Jerry MacAuley, or Billy Sunday, or people right here in Gastonia.[19]

There is much emphasis on the saving power of "the blood of Jesus," and continual admonition to follow the "Jesus way." There is almost never any direct application of these admonitions to practical problems of economic life; when it is made, references to such virtues as kindliness, forgiveness, and honesty comprise the net result.

If sermons by ministers in Gaston County do not indicate that the church is in actuality a direct source of economic change, neither do they indicate that economic institutions determine the doctrinal structures of religious institutions. Basic ideas in sermons appear to have been changed very little since 1880, though an occasional phrase or illustration is drawn from an industrial environment. One minister referred to the church as "the greatest business in the world," pointing out that it is engaged in "great enterprises that transmute money into saved

19. From a sermon of a Baptist uptown preacher.

souls and treasure in heaven."[20] Another declared: "Time and talents invested in Christian service through a New Testament church will bring finer and richer dividends than those invested through all the other organizations in the whole world."[21] For the most part, however, sermons were largely the same in 1939 as they were before the rise of the cotton mills in the county.

Religious doctrine has been determined more largely by denominational tradition than by economic changes.[22] Older ideas have been retained, on the tacit supposition that they fit one economic order as well as another.[23] The colonial legislature of North Carolina was greatly agitated in 1715 over questions of Sabbath observance, drunkenness, and "profane swearing and cursing," and passed a law to regulate such matters.[24] The ministers of Gaston County are still basically concerned with similar problems, despite the transformation of their economic environment.

In occasional sermons the church is represented as standing in opposition to current economic practices, especially those that fail to display respect for religious traditions. For example:

Today we, as a nation, suffer from a malady which cannot be better described than by one word, soullessness—soul meaning a noble principle. Many railroad companies, many industrial corporations, many business firms, proprietors and employers are soulless in this one particular: they see no value in human flesh except that which is expressed in money and profits. Being soulless, they have no regard for God's Holy Sabbath. Many employees, no doubt, would like to assemble at God's house of prayer and be still a little while before Him on His Holy Sabbath day and feed upon the bread that came down from heaven; but these profane, time-serving, money-grabbing, money-mad employers say to them by word or act that they must either work or give up their jobs.[25]

20. Presbyterian uptown pastor, in *Gastonia Gazette,* January 15, 1938.
21. Baptist uptown pastor, *ibid.,* June 11, 1938.
22. See chap. vi.
23. The retention of former emphases in the churches helps, though certainly not intentionally, to disguise novel characteristics of the industrial revolution.
24. Hugh Lefler, ed., *North Carolina History, Told by Contemporaries* (Chapel Hill, 1934), pp. 48–49.
25. Lutheran rural pastor, *Gastonia Gazette,* May 7, 1938.

The church maintains that all human beings are children of God and possess infinite value. In the face of a world that would exploit individuals for selfish ends, the church proclaims the value of individual personality. Thus the church stands in your community as the source of the social impulse. Back of all social reform, democratic government, crusades against crime, and the agitation for a warless world is the church with its gospel of the value of human beings. Go to church and learn of your infinite capacities and value, think of your present life in comparison, and go home with an inspiration that can help you live a new life in an old world![26]

The two most "radical" preachers in the county are young Methodist ministers, one in an uptown parish and the other in a mill church. The latter, in a sermon published in the *Gastonia Gazette,* decried "unemployment, undernourishment, and child labor," and the fact that "many people must live in tenant shacks not fit for animals." His solution consisted of an appeal to mill owners who, "though called Christians, are detached from God."[27] The young uptown minister on one occasion summed up his hope for economic reconstruction by saying:

Let us suppose that out of the economic chaos of our day we were to see the beginnings of a new society which would be less competitive and more cooperative, whose leaders would be men who would recognize that the old era of selfish profit-seeking must be turned into a new era of profit-sharing. Not sharing equally, to be sure, but with leaders realizing that brains must be used for the good of mankind in a great cooperative adventure in which the individual will have plenty of opportunity for self-initiative and self-development, but less and less opportunity for self-enrichment at the expense of his fellowmen. This is not communism, nor socialism. It is not even controlled capitalism, but simply a Christian spirit of cooperation and sharing—that is the answer to all the "isms" of this chaotic day. This is not day dreaming for there is an undercurrent of thought which has been gathering momentum during this decade which, some day, will outlaw the old economic era where one man enriches the coffers of his own treasury at the expense of his fel-

26. Methodist mill pastor, *ibid.,* August 27, 1938.
27. *Ibid.,* May 28, 1938.

lowmen, while thousands of others live on the ragged edge of subsistence. (MS. of sermon.)

Though sermons occasionally call for social reform, innumerable homiletic passages indicate that ministers regard the church as a sanction of community life, including many of the particular forms in which that life is organized at present in Gaston County. Favorite phrases include: "A good citizen, plus religion, ought to be a better citizen," "the finest people of any and all of our communities are Christians," and the like. Occasionally ministers go into greater detail.

The sound of the spindle is sweet, if we can but realize that we are helping to clothe the people of the world. [Baptist mill pastor, *Gastonia Gazette*, September 3, 1938.]

The church is the protector of our community. Property is more valuable, human life is safer, and virtue less in danger where Christian institutions exist. [Presbyterian uptown pastor, *ibid.*, January 15, 1938.]

Sin is the most expensive thing in the world, and is a fruitful source of poverty. Sin destroys property, destroys health, ruins men's character and degrades nations. . . . [Lutheran uptown pastor, *ibid.*, April 9, 1938.]

I rode today by at least a score of church buildings, each one of them a dedicated house of God. . . . As I rode along I saw many various kinds of industry, shops, and mills, farms and factories, stores, offices, and banks, properties and possessions valued at millions of dollars. As I looked upon these forms of business I said to myself—"All these material concerns are but dust and ashes save for the virtues and morals advocated and propagated by the churches. Take honesty and honor away, leave business in the hands of base men, manage these shops and stores by unscrupulous rascals, destroy their ideals of service and moral value, and then behold a complete collapse of the financial order." The church day by day must protect and shield every dime and dollar by its preaching of true values and by its gospel of redeeming love. The spinning frames and looms, the counters and shelves, the homes and office buildings everywhere must at last be overshadowed by the prayer, the sermons, and the dedicated life. . . . [Methodist uptown pastor, *ibid.*, February 12, 1938.]

No clear picture comes from analysis of preaching in Gaston County. Ideas contained in various sermons represent all possible relationships between religious and economic institutions. The ministers of the county, as represented by their sermons, are primarily concerned with problems that are indifferent to economic welfare in itself. Most of them believe, nevertheless, that the only hope for economic life lies in the saving message of the church—a message calling for individual salvation and personal virtue. From the standpoint of institutional analysis, the influence of religious institutions through their most characteristic instrument of expression is negligible in effect upon economic forms, leaving the latter to go their way unmolested. Through assuming that economic regulation can be achieved by methods other than direct institutional restraint, the churches help to insure, indeed, that economic institutions shall not be restricted.

EXPLANATIONS OF SOCIAL QUIESCENCE

Part of the unwillingness of Gaston County ministers[28] to criticize or attempt regulation of the textile industry roots in their lack of knowledge of economic and social affairs. Almost without exception, they have been trained exclusively (when trained at all) in Biblical, ecclesiastical traditions, and have inadequate background for interpretation of the political, economic, and sociological conditions among which they and their parishioners live. Recognizing the importance of such matters, they appropriate ideas from their immediate environment without clear understanding of their significance or implications. At the same time they retreat to the religious as over against the secular, proclaiming that Christ alone can save the world. Their conception of the differentiation of the secular and sacred is dim, and leads to ambiguities and self-contradiction; a statement

28. The phrase "Gaston County ministers" is used throughout this volume in a generic sense rather than in either a collective or a distributive sense. Judgments involving it, or its equivalent, do not apply with equal pertinence to every individual minister in the county. Notable exceptions to generalizations, however, are pointed out wherever they occur.

that "what this country needs, and all it needs, is a great revival of religion" is followed immediately by a prayer that the
Lord will give his people prosperity. Because the ministers have
no clear understanding of economic relativities and no cogent
analysis of the relation of Christianity to the world, their whole
approach to social problems is set in well-worn, time-honored
phrases which really dismiss the problems.

The average minister has little time for social investigation
or study, of course, even if he had inclination. The pastor of
one cotton mill church has described the job of the minister as
follows:

He must meet the prayer-meeting group, the young people's organization, the fellowship committee, the Sunday morning and
evening congregation with a talk or sermon on each occasion.
Then there are the invalids, the sick, the disgruntled, and those
who have suffered misfortune, to be visited. He is expected to see
all of the new baby arrivals, visit in the homes where relatives from
a long distance have come for a short stay, and sit up with the
deceased most of the night and to speak at the funeral the next
day. Some Potterville church members are offended if the minister
does not visit their homes once a week.

Again, he is expected to assist in getting charity patients in the
hospital, raise money to pay their bill if necessary, and make jour-
neys to the hospital to visit them until they are discharged. He is
to officiate at wedding ceremonies, make talks to the Boy Scouts
and the local school, and attend local plays and community functions. He also must meet with the official board of the church and
spend an entire evening discussing church attendance, finance, etc.[29]

The minister is circumscribed not only by lack of appropriate
training in social analysis and by insufficient time but also by
the attitudes of parishioners and employers toward his role.
Most Gastonia residents expect that their minister shall remain
strictly within the realm usually regarded as religious and resent any excursion into areas not associated with his profession.
People "hide things" from their preacher; even in the more so-
phisticated congregations in Gastonia he is shielded from facts

29. E. R. Hartz, "Social Problems in a North Carolina Parish" (A.M. thesis,
Duke University, 1938), pp. 8–9.

and information which every street urchin knows. Most of the reticence to disabuse his mind of his idealism is due to respect for his devotion "to the finer things," and much of it is due to shame. Whatever its sources, the average church member does not feel free to talk with his minister about problems that involve greed and conflict, and the minister has learned to feel shy about prying. Moreover, employers in the county have generally discouraged investigation of their industry, and have been especially averse to criticism.[30] A young Catholic priest who came to the county a few years ago had done considerable work in sociology and sought to make rudimentary investigations into the social relations of his new parish. He reports that he was severely discouraged and after about a year decided to let his interest in social questions lapse.

Failure to investigate and to deal specifically with textile problems has not prevented ministers and church members from arriving at views concerning the economic realm. Because such matters have been largely ruled out of discussion in religious circles, opinions concerning them have come almost entirely out of the prevailing economic culture. Most ministers and churchmen in the county share the common economic views, therefore, which have been promulgated by mill owners.

Even if he had training and background for understanding of economic questions, it is unlikely that the average minister in the county would engage in criticism of local conditions. An occasional minister stationed there has been widely read in various social sciences; none of them has openly advocated any restraint of managerial power in industrial relations. One minister, prominent in the county for eight years, had a large library of books on social Christianity and had read them all, but was never heard to offer any censure of the economic system under which he lived. Whatever their knowledge, ministers and

---

30. They condemned as "an invasion of private rights" a proposal in 1929 that a special government commission should study the textile industry (James Myers, "Confidential Field Notes on Trip to Charlotte, North Carolina, and Marion, North Carolina [MS.]," p. 6). Textile manufacturers in North Carolina had refused in 1927 to coöperate with industrial experts of the University of North Carolina in a survey of the industry. Similar reticence has been traditional—see Harriet L. Herring, "Cycles of Cotton Mill Criticism," *The South Atlantic Quarterly*, XXVIII, 113–125 (April, 1929). Recently, however, many textile managers have become more coöperative; employers in Gaston County facilitated in many ways the research on which this present volume is based.

churches are seldom in a structural position to reprove accepted views and relations, having received gratefully the benefits showered upon them by mill owners. Paternalistic control has prevailed here as in other aspects of community life. There has been little ministerial cynicism as to the motivation of philanthropy and slight inclination to receive the benefits of philanthropy as being simply one's due. Rather, the churches have accepted gifts from employers in the spirit of children who are grateful for unexpected favors from their parents. Ministers have openly recorded their gratitude, as illustrated in the following excerpts from public statements by them:

[From the pastor of a Baptist church to which a mill owner had given a church and parsonage] For all these generous considerations the church is deeply grateful to Mr. ———.[31]

Mr. W. T. Love provided the seating, has given liberally otherwise to the church, and as an executive of the Ranlo Mills has been a great friend of ours. The Rex Spinning Company assumed the payment of a note of some size due one of our banks and which was a heavy burden on us.[32]

Smyre Methodist Church was named for the late A. M. Smyre [Presbyterian mill owner] who was very generous in his contributions to it. The A. M. Smyre Manufacturing Company has been of great help to the church.[33]

Several mill companies have been very liberal in their contribution to Maylo Church.[34]

Most ministers voice thankfulness likewise for mill subsidies to their salaries. They do not accept them as their due but as generous gifts, placing themselves in filial rather than contractual relations to their employers. Any effort to criticize the system of subsidies, or even to investigate it, is likely to meet with close-lipped hostility. One nonconformist young minister raised objection recently, in a church conference in Gastonia, to payment of pastors' salaries by the mills but was immediately si-

31. Rev. E. V. Hudson, "A Brief Sketch of the Cramerton Baptist Church" (MS. in the Library of Wake Forest College).
32. *Gastonia Gazette,* August 20, 1938.
33. *Ibid.,* September 10, 1938.   34. *Ibid.,* September 17, 1938.

lenced. His denomination publicly acknowledges the system of supplements; at its annual meeting in 1936 the presiding officer said, after reading ministerial appointments for the subsequent year: "Those brethren who see a salary reduction need not necessarily be disappointed; you may be pleasantly surprised, especially those of you who are going to Gaston County." Public statements implying that subsidy eventuates in control of ministers by mill owners have invariably aroused impassioned clerical attempts at vindication of ministers and mills alike.

There is no evidence that members of the churches hold views different from their ministers concerning support of the churches by the mills. Many workers do not know that the mills aid the churches, because of the effort on the part of mill managements to keep semisecret the fact of subsidy lest informed workers lose respect for the churches or their sense of responsibility for the support of their particular church. It is almost certain, however, that only a few of the mill workers who do know of the system of church subsidies object to it, and it is doubtful that a large percentage would object even if all workers knew. The psychological attitude here, as in the case of the ministers, is that of hope for a free gift and of gratitude if it is given. Members of mill churches expect their pastor to take the initiative in efforts to secure contributions from the mills, and consider that his efficiency as a minister has been demonstrated if he succeeds.

Privately, denominational leaders in Gaston County criticize mill managements which refuse to aid churches in their vicinity. Paternal ethicways, plus a desire of ministers for the improvement of their personal and institutional status, lead to condemnation of those occasional manufacturers who decline to grant subsidies to religious enterprises, or grant them in niggardly fashion. Profit is respectable in Gaston County only if it is accompanied by at least a minimum degree of philanthropy. Ministers have a cultural as well as a selfish basis for the censure of mill corporations that seek to produce good yarn without great concern for the production of good people.

As a corollary of their own dependence on the mills, ministers and churches in Gaston County leave wholly to the mill managers all correction of abuses in industrial life. Since the industry first began to appear, ministers have assumed that mill owners were Christian gentlemen who could be counted on to correct imperfections as quickly as feasible. When various conditions have been admitted to be deplorable, the sole strategy of the churches for their correction has been appeal to managers rather than appeal to the entire community or requests for limitation of managerial power.

Ministers and churches have shown no inclination to censure or modify economic conditions in Gaston County, then, for several reasons. Their own social views, coming chiefly out of the immediate cultural context, call for no extensive restraint of the economic institutions. Confusion, individualism, moralism, and evangelism are characteristic of their social outlook and nullify the actual application of a professed desire and ability to create "a better world." Lacking background for interpretation of economic questions, structurally dependent on the mill owners, believing that the mill executives will correct any abuses, and feeling no special pressure from the mill workers or other internal groups in their society, the ministers and churches have failed to stand in opposition to practices of the mills even when challenged to do so.

CHAPTER X

THE CHURCHES AND SPECIFIC ECONOMIC QUESTIONS

THE social quiescence of ministers and churches in Gaston County has been disturbed occasionally by issues so critical that they could not be avoided. The most important of these came in 1929, and considerable attention will be devoted to it. Both before and after that time, however, trenchant criticisms of certain economic practices have impinged on the county and specific challenges to certain social and industrial patterns have confronted local ministers. If preachers have remained apathetic to regulation of the mills in their vicinity, it is not because particular lines of action have never been suggested to them. Several issues have been posed by religious bodies from beyond the confines of the county; others have grown out of economic developments and legislative programs. Salient examples include criticism of the mill village system, the legislative fight against child labor, and the efforts of trade unions to organize workers in the county.

THE MILL VILLAGE SYSTEM

The rise of the mill village in the development of the Southern textile industry was based partly on sheer necessity.[1] The com-

1. It was also, to some degree, a heritage from textile practices in other regions and countries. At least two of the very early Southern textile manufacturers had direct contact with the highly paternalistic mill villages of New England before the Civil War and these New England villages had in turn been influenced by New Lanark and other English model mill villages. The rise of Southern mill villages, however, was greatly influenced by conditions and backgrounds peculiar to the South.

For wider aspects of the development of Southern mill villages and of the special problems created, see C. B. Spahr, "The New Factory Towns of the South," *The Outlook*, pp. 510–517 (March, 1899); Leifur Magnusson, *Housing by Employers in the United States* (Washington, 1920), chap. xiii; Paul Blanshard, "Industrial Problems of the New South: the Southern Mill Village," *Proceedings of the National Conference of Social Work*, 1928; Lois MacDonald, *Southern Mill Hills: A Study of Social and Economic Forces in Certain Textile Mill Villages* (New York, 1928); Harriet L. Herring, "Toward Preliminary Social Analysis: I. The Southern Mill System Faces a New Issue," *Social Forces*, VIII, 351 (March, 1930); Harriet L. Herring, "Social Develop-

parative isolation of many early mills made it imperative that the basic necessities of life should be provided for employees in proximity to the mill itself. As a consequence, the mill builder provided all facilities for the penniless workers he had imported and assumed absolute control over their use. Housing, sanitation, landscaping, marketing, personal hygiene, health, education, and religious welfare came under his supervision. As his interests became more complex and the number of his employees increased, making it impossible for him to retain personal touch with all village problems, he frequently employed social workers to bridge the widening gap between himself and his workers.[2] By this and similar devices, the mill village system and its attendant features remained intact after many of its original purposes had been realized and transmuted. Economic conditions in the textile industry and improved transportation facilities for workers checked the physical expansion of villages in the early 1920's, but textile employers have continued until very recently to maintain the system without appreciable modification, professedly as an indication of solicitude for employees.[3]

Almost from its inception, but especially during the last two decades, the mill village has been the subject of severe criticism. Strictures against it have come from innumerable liberals and labor leaders, and even from textile executives in other regions of the country. In 1925 the managing editor of the *Textile*

ment in the Mill Villages," *Social Forces,* X (December, 1931): Rev. B. L. Smith, "The Social Significance of the Southern Cotton Mill Community" (M.A. thesis, Emory University, 1925); B. B. Kendrick and A. M. Arnett, *The South Looks at Its Past* (Chapel Hill, 1935), pp. 125–127, 149–155.

2. Seventeen community workers were employed by mills in Gaston County in 1924, six of them by one large mill (*Visions Old and New: A Historical Pageant,* pp. 39–40). An able study of programs of this kind in North Carolina is contained in Harriet L. Herring, *Welfare Work in Mill Villages: The Story of Extra-Mill Activities in North Carolina* (Chapel Hill, 1929).

3. Despite all cynicism from outside observers, Southern textile manufacturers continue to represent themselves to the world as kindly benefactors. Mildred Gwin Barnwell's *Faces We See* (Gastonia, 1939), a book published under the editorship of the executive secretary of the Southern Combed Yarn Spinners Association and subsidized by that association, presents an effusive picture of the pleasures derived from living in a mill village, including golfing, shrubbery, tile baths, and flowers, for all of which the residents are represented as grateful to the Heavenly Father. Cf. *Gastonia Gazette,* October 20, 1938; *Southern Textile Bulletin,* March 5, 1936; *Textile World Annual, 1938,* pp. 79–117.

World urged that the operation of mill villages should be put on a strictly economic basis, and that the argument from them in defense of low wages should be discarded and all supplements to the income of workers be placed in pay envelopes.[4] The most direct challenge to the system came in 1927 from a group of forty-one Southern churchmen who signed "An Appeal to Industrial Leaders of the South." Bearing the names of three Episcopal bishops, five Methodist bishops, and prominent pastors of nearly all denominations in the South, the document was widely circulated in the regional press and came to be known as the "Bishops' Appeal." It called for "the improvement of certain social and economic conditions, especially in the textile industry," and specifically mentioned "the isolation of population in the mill villages," long hours and low wages, relative lack of restriction on the work of women and children, and "the general absence of labor representation in our factories." With particular reference to the mill village system, the Appeal declared:

Life in a mill village under company control, while an advance of status in the beginning, is not the best training ground for citizenship in that it does not train residents for participation in government. It has generally been proved in recent years, however it may have been at first, to be unfavorable to education, to religion, and to understanding and sympathy between the citizens of the mill village and those of the larger community. In spite of the difficulty of the problem, we are convinced that these villages should be merged as rapidly as is consistent with safety into the larger community.

The Bishops' Appeal aroused vigorous opposition in Southern textile circles. The signers were denounced as meddling theorists who had no firsthand knowledge of the conditions they were deploring. An editorial in the *Gastonia Gazette* was typical of the reaction:

While local cotton mill men are not saying much about it, the understanding is that they do not think much of the charge of Bishop Cannon and other church dignitaries anent community life

4. *Textile World* (February 7, 1925), pp. 180–181. Cf. Douglas G. Woolf, "What about the Southern Mill Village?" *ibid.* (July 13, 1929), p. 55.

in Southern mill villages. The trouble is that these men do not have their information straight.

Life in the average mill village is far better than it is in many communities from which the villagers come. They have conveniences that were never heard of before. As for the charge that religion is not fostered in these villages, the church men show an amazing lack of knowledge of the real facts in the case. Residents of these communities are the most religious folk we have. The average of church attendance among them is higher than can be found in any other community. Their church is the center of the life of the community.[5]

The response of Gastonia ministers to this criticism, coming from religious leaders, of a system especially characteristic of their county is represented in the following statements from ministers who were stationed there at the time:

The Appeal made no impression on Gastonia. The mill owners here have been mighty good to their folks.

There was no reaction or response among Gastonia ministers to the 1927 Appeal. The ministers there really knew little about it.

The 1927 Appeal had not one iota of effect on Gastonia or on Gastonia ministers. So far as I remember it was never discussed at all.

Ministers in Gastonia were indifferent to the 1927 Appeal, except to resent it.

The reaction of Gastonia ministers to the 1927 Appeal was one of indifference; they paid no attention to it, except to resent it as a case of meddling by outsiders.

The Appeal created little stir in Gastonia. Ministers had an attitude of considered apathy to it, due to the fact that mill owners in the community were leaders in their churches.

A few newspapers in North Carolina praised the document, but most Southern papers denounced it rather bitterly.[6] A representative of textile manufacturers charged that—

5. *Gastonia Gazette,* March 30, 1927.
6. For examples of favorable appraisal, cf. Raleigh *News and Observer,* April 4, 1927; *Twin-City Sentinel,* March 29, 1927; *Greensboro Daily News,* April 8, 1927; *Nashville Christian Advocate,* May 7, 1927. For unfavorable reaction, cf. *Charlotte Observer,* April 1, 1927; *Durham Morning Herald,* April 1, 1927; *Southern Christian Advocate,* April 14, 1927.

This document was inspired and probably drawn by professional agitators who wished to make an attack on the South.[7] . . . A chicken thinks all animals, including people, should eat worms, a hog that everyone should wallow in the mud, and bishops that nobody should work over two hours a day and should draw a fat salary for the same.[8]

The Appeal, despite the prominence of its sponsors, appears to have had no practical effect whatever. Ministers continued to defend paternalism as being both necessary and Christian, and mill owners have continued to point to elaborate villages as an indication of their generosity toward employees.

More recently serious modifications have appeared in the mill village system, due largely to economic rather than moral or religious considerations. Until about 1938 the mill village system constituted a useful tool for control over labor, and was preserved at a net financial loss chiefly for that reason. Most of the reasons given by ministers and employers for its continuation represented a rationalization of economic advantage. Within the last two years it has become economically advantageous for a great many mills to dispose of their village property, and a movement toward sale of mill houses to employees has gathered momentum in the South, with Gaston County as a conspicuous example.[9] Houses in nearly a dozen mill villages there had been sold to employees by September, 1939, and the movement was spreading rapidly.

When the Cotton Textile Code was established under the National Industrial Recovery Act in 1933, a subcommittee of the Code Authority was appointed to consider "the question of plans for eventual employee ownership of homes in mill villages." The committee, composed mostly of Southern textile manufacturers, circulated a questionnaire to textile mills. Its report, submitted on December 28, 1933, concluded: "It is the conviction of this committee . . . [that] it is impracticable at this time to offer any plan looking to home ownership in exist-

7. The document had been drawn principally by an official of the Federal Council of the Churches of Christ in America.
8. *Southern Textile Bulletin*, March 31, 1927. Cf. issues for April 14, 1927, February 9, 1928; *Textile World* (April 16, 1927), pp. 2493–2494.
9. See the excellent survey by Harriet Herring, "Selling Mill Houses to Employees," *Textile World*, May and June, 1940.

ing mill villages by employees. . . . With few exceptions, the employees prefer to live in houses owned by the mills. . . . The mills are unwilling to sell houses in their villages to anyone."[10]

In contrast to this statement of 1933, mill owners in 1939 became willing to sell village houses and to assert that employees were desirous of buying them. As usual, moral considerations were advanced as the reasons underlying the change. For a great many years Southern liberals had criticized the serflike status and social isolation accruing to residence in a mill village and had urged independent ownership of homes by workers as a goal to be desired. Employers announced in 1939 that they would sell village houses in order to make possible this social ideal.[11] Citizens and ministers in the county joined heartily in approval, despite their previous apathy or opposition to the abolition of the villages, and began to praise the joys and virtues of home ownership.

It is probable that Southern manufacturers were selling their houses primarily in order to retain a competitive production advantage. The textile committee appointed under the Fair Labor Standards Act refused to allow a wage differential to Southern mills; other things being equal, it became necessary, therefore, for paternalistic mills to put themselves more completely upon a purely economic base if they were to compete successfully with mills which paid no extra-wage supplements. From the outset, operation of mill villages had entailed an economic loss, with various mills reporting the deficit as follows: $4.02 per house per week, $2.54 per operative per week, 1.7 cents per pound of yarn produced, $1.14 per employee per week, 89 cents per employee per week.[12] When lower wage scales were declared illegal, it became advisable to discontinue extra-wage subsidies wherever possible. Higher charges for rent of company houses to offset the loss on village operation were gen-

10. "Report of Subcommittee on Mill Villages, December 28, 1933, to Hon. Hugh S. Johnson" (MS. at Cotton-Textile Institute, New York).

11. Statement by a leading Gastonia textile manufacturer in the *Charlotte Observer*, September 1, 1939; interviews with a number of employers in the county, 1938–39.

12. Interviews with managers of the various mills, 1938–39. Cf. Bertha Carl Hipp, "A Gaston County Cotton Mill and Its Community" (M.A. thesis, University of North Carolina, 1930), p. 40; Angeline Bouchard, "An Analysis of the Southern Combed Sales Yarn Industry" (M.A. thesis, Columbia University, 1938), p. 109.

erally unfeasible in view of traditions in the industry. Therefore the mills were selling their houses, and talk of encouraging
independence of workers was mostly camouflage.

The method by which the houses were being sold practically
insured, indeed, that employees would be kept under rigid control for the next ten years, even while mill managements were
rendered less suspect of unfair labor practices. Most of the
houses were sold at from $800 to $1,000; mills generally required a 10 per cent down payment, with the remainder to be
deducted from pay envelopes at the rate of about $2.50 a week
for the next seven to ten years. Employers expressed belief that
employees who bought their own homes would spend their wages
on them instead of on union dues, and that home owners would
think seriously before jeopardizing payments already made,
through strikes or other activities that might cost them their
jobs. It was also likely that the rate of labor turnover in the
mills would be further reduced.

While retaining control over labor, the mills derive added
freedom in industrial relations from the sale of their mill houses
to employees. It is easier to discharge a worker who lives in his
own house than to discharge a worker who lives in a company
house. Thoroughgoing rationalization of the mills can be more
easily effected, including either new labor-saving machinery or
further extension of work loads or both. The whole movement
toward disintegration of the mill village system will indubitably
make industrial relations more impersonal in character.

Further, sale of the houses insured that Southern mills would
retain a wage differential over Northern competitors for ten
years, despite the refusal of the Wage-Hour Committee to allow one. From an average wage of $15 a week, for example,
suppose that $2.50 was to be deducted as payment on a mill
house: the mill thereby received a 17 per cent rebate on wages
—or, if it is calculated that two workers, on the average, would
share the cost of each house, a rebate of slightly more than
8 per cent. Several answers could be made to the objection that
payments on houses are not to be put in the same general category with deductions from wages. In the first place many workers had little alternative as to whether they would purchase
houses, or as to price; in some cases the mill had houses ap-
praised and notified workers that they must purchase them at

the prices stipulated or else leave the village and their jobs in the mill. In the second place disposal of village property represented a money-saving scheme insofar as the mills were concerned rather than a sacrifice of valuable property. As noted above, the mills have operated villages at an economic loss, and through disposing of them were disburdened of expenses of upkeep, taxes, and other items.

In the face of this sudden change in traditional economic arrangements the mill workers themselves were reacting rather negatively. Many of them were certain that they did not desire to own mill houses, which were often in comparatively dilapidated condition, and were less desirable anyhow than a house outside the boundaries of a mill village. Though they "stood in line to sign up," workers almost without exception reported that nobody would have bought a mill house if he had not felt compelled to do so. Lack of available houses outside the villages, however, added to the necessity for acceptance of the scheme.[13] As one worker said of the houses in his village, "They ain't worth much, and'll cost more'n $800 'fore we git through, but people purty near had to buy 'em, 'cause they ain't no empty houses they could move into." Another said: "I once said I wouldn't have to do nothin' but die—but I was wrong. I had to buy this house. The super [mill superintendent] said if I didn't, I could leave and take my job with me."

A few ministers among those closest to the workers were dubious of the pose of philanthropy assumed by mill owners in the sale of their houses to employees. These ministers frankly admitted, however, that they could not protest openly because they depended both directly and indirectly upon the mills for support. Uptown ministers praised the movement as being in keeping with traditional American ideals—ideals they had not been greatly concerned to defend, in this particular connection, hitherto. More serious criticism came from mill owners who for some reason were not selling their houses, and would therefore be placed in disadvantageous competitive position, than from

13. The percentage of vacant dwelling units available for sale or rent in Gaston County as of April 1, 1940, was only .8 per cent of the total number of dwelling units, according to the 1940 Census. The corresponding figure for North Carolina was 3.1 per cent.

ministers or other persons presumably interested in humanitarian aspects of social relations.[14]

This rapid change in economic structure illuminates the whole problem of the relation of religious and economic institutions in Gaston County. When some alteration offers economic advantage, the mills adopt it, and only then. Mill executives mask their real motives behind the idealism traditionally associated with their role and confirmed in the religious standards prevalent in the county. Ministers who had not been concerned previously with the application of moral judgments to the particular issue in question, suddenly see its new relevance and sanction the change as being for the general welfare of the community. Those ministers who, being closer to the workers, see the more fundamental implications of the proposed change, are circumscribed by their own dependent relation to the mills and can voice no public criticism. The workers, lacking corporate organization or vehicles for self-expression, are inarticulate except as among themselves, and are often confused in their own minds by the public professions of interest in their welfare. Acquiescence of ministers in these professions really helps the mills to make economic changes without opposition, as it abets the confusion of issues in the minds of those most affected.

CHILD LABOR

With respect to child labor, which has been unusually high in Gaston County throughout the history of the textile industry there,[15] ministers and churches in the county have remained almost completely silent and inert. They could not have failed to be aware of the issue, because their larger denominational bodies, especially those representing the Baptists and Methodists

14. Interviews with several mill executives who were refusing to sell their own houses and were skeptical of the philanthropy of their competitors. Cf. Arnold M. Oland, "The Mill Village: Should We Sell It? If So, to Whom?" *Cotton*, CIII, 55–58 (December, 1939).

15. According to incomplete reports to the North Carolina Bureau (or Department) of Labor and Printing, 578 boys and 655 girls under fourteen years of age were employed in Gaston County mills in 1900, comprising perhaps 30 per cent of the total number of employees. In 1913, according to the same source, 963 children under sixteen years of age were employed (14 per cent of the total); in 1925–26 a total of 587 between fourteen and sixteen years of age. All these figures are incomplete.

in North Carolina,[16] have been more concerned with this particular problem in the textile industry than with any other,
and have frequently passed resolutions calling for regulation.
At the same time, however, church bodies have often opposed
the abolition of child labor, with traces of a "Puritan conscience" creeping in occasionally, as in the following editorial
from a denominational paper:

All we want is to see such regulation as will give all the children a
chance to learn something practical instead of being hedged about
by laws that will enhance their opportunity to join the army of
vicious idlers and swell the ranks of criminals. The early learning
of some trade or craft is the surest safeguard against a life of idleness and crime. Let the reformers be careful how they deal with a
vital matter like this.[17]

One young Methodist minister, stationed for a year or two in
Gaston County at the turn of the century, was a leader in
the fight for child labor legislation. Otherwise, ministers and
churches in the county have remained ostensibly indifferent.
Many ministers, if their present testimony reflects past opinions, have privately favored regulation for the last two or three
decades, but have not taken a public stand or engaged in any
overt action in this direction. Some of them still qualified the
principle itself, even in 1939, declaring themselves as privately
"in favor of the principle of restriction" but urging that—

This thing must not be carried too far. Maybe some mother needs
the earnings of her son. And many boys are better off at work than
idle. Many mill owners have said for years that they lost money on
child labor, but had to retain it because of the desire of parents
for their children's earnings.[18]

Though they have at times professed to be in favor of child
labor laws and compulsory education laws, manufacturers in

16. For example, *Annual of the North Carolina Baptist State Convention,
1914*, p. 92; *1919*, pp. 77–80; *North Carolina Christian Advocate*, May 31, 1899,
February 18, 1903, February 7, 1907.
17. *Ibid.*, February 7, 1907.
18. This statement was made verbatim by one of the more influential ministers in the county, and was reflected, in varying phraseology, by several other
ministers interviewed.

Gaston County have in reality opposed each subsequent step in regulation. In earlier years they frequently used moral and semireligious arguments in defending the right of children to work,[19] moving gradually toward economic arguments with religious overtones. When occasional mill owners issued public statements in favor of restrictive legislation and compulsory education, their mill superintendents, who actually handled problems of employment, often went on employing children.[20] When strong pressure groups succeeded in obtaining restrictive statutes, inadequate provisions for enforcement and new devices of circumvention practically nullified the laws.

Elimination of children in the mills was effected only when economic advantage reinforced considerations of moral and social welfare to decree their dismissal. Since 1912 various ecclesiastical bodies in North Carolina had consistently urged the abolition of night work for children; yet they were still deploring it in 1929, as a widespread evil to be eradicated as soon as possible. A series of economic developments quickly accomplished the result at which ineffectual ecclesiastical resolutions had aimed. The depression which descended on the textile industry in the early 1920's provided a labor surplus in the mill villages and made the utilization of children less important. A workmen's compensation law, passed in North Carolina in 1929, rendered the employment of children more hazardous on economic grounds, as they were more liable than adults to expensive accidents. Creation of a minimum wage for the industry under the National Industrial Recovery Act in 1933 virtually eliminated children from the mills, and in so doing revealed that between six hundred and one thousand workers under sixteen years of age had been retained until then in Gaston County. Even if the N.I.R.A. had not specifically outlawed child labor, the possibility of obtaining adult labor in the mills

19. For example, *Fourteenth Annual Report of the Bureau of Labor and Printing of the State of North Carolina* (1900), pp. 302, 349–350. Cf. Elizabeth H. Davidson, *Child Labor Legislation in the Southern Textile States* (Chapel Hill, 1939), chaps. iii, vi–viii. Miss Davidson's treatment is by far the best study of conflicting forces in the battle over child labor legislation in the region.

20. A study of twelve mill superintendents in the county at present revealed that they themselves entered employment in textile mills, on the average, at the age of 11.5 years. They appear to have assumed on occasion that other children might advantageously do the same.

for the minimum wage specified made it economically impracticable to employ children. Manufacturers proclaimed that child
labor was banished once for all from the mills of the county.[21]
After the invalidation of the N.I.R.A., the North Carolina
General Assembly in 1937 enacted stricter legislation and provided for more adequate inspection and enforcement whereby
children under sixteen years of age were no longer permitted to
work in manufacturing industries.

A report by an observer in Gastonia in 1933 illustrates and
summarizes the relationship of ministers and churches to child
labor from beginning to end:

In Gastonia one of the leading merchants, after August 1st, continued a custom, against which he had been warned, of employing
errand boys under sixteen after hours. He didn't seem to realize
that the New Deal had brought actual enforcement of labor laws
in North Carolina.

He was amazed when he was arrested by a state official. Before
court opened, a friend of the defendant said to the state official,
"Why don't you drop this charge? Mr. Merchant is a Methodist,
the judge is a Methodist, and the prosecuting attorney is a Methodist. They all three are very good friends and belong to the same
church."

"What's the church got to do with it?" asked the inspector.
"We're here to talk about working children after the hour of seven
in the evening."

Whereupon the church-going merchant pleaded guilty to violat-
ing the labor laws; the church-going prosecutor said he was willing to accept the plea and the church-going judge ordered the
prisoner to pay the costs of the action—something less than ten
dollars.[22]

LABOR ORGANIZATION

Labor relations in the mills of Gaston County have been consistently paternal rather than contractual in type. Employers have discussed grievances with employees as individuals,
through an open office door or through welfare workers. Col-

21. William G. Shepherd, "Humanity, Common, Goes Up," *Collier's*, October
7, 1933. Cf. George Libaire, "Gastonia: Outpost of Recovery?" *The New Republic*, LXXVI, 233-235 (October 11, 1933).
22. Shepherd, *op. cit.*, p. 38.

lective organization of the workers has been strongly opposed by employers and uptown citizens and has appeared only sporadically and for very brief intervals. So far as it has occurred in the county at all, unionism has consisted of the construction of a fighting force for a strike; as soon as the strike had been lost (which was the invariable result), the union either disbanded or went underground, where it continued to enlist the loyalties of only a few intransigent workers.

Waves of unionization which swept over the South before 1919 hardly touched the county.[23] Two or three brief strikes occurred in 1919 and 1920 as part of a campaign by the United Textile Workers to organize the South. Postwar unrest among the workers, however, was met by a rising tide of community and welfare work inaugurated by the mills, and by the installation of profit-sharing plans for employees in several of them.[24] Employees were continually reminded of the benefactions granted by their employers, and labor organizers were denounced as "paid agitators." Frequent stories in the *Gastonia Gazette* pointed to the futility of efforts at organization in neighboring counties. With several severe textile strikes in progress in counties adjoining Gaston, the *Gazette* said editorially on July 26, 1921:

Employes of nine cotton mills in Gastonia are to meet in a joint community picnic Saturday, August 6 . . . an old-fashioned all-day picnic such as the country churches still enjoy. . . . It will be held on the grounds of a suburban church. . . . There will be fried chicken, country ham, pickles, pies, and preserves. . . . The mills will furnish many substantial eatables. . . . Mill owners and superintendents will hobnob with operatives. . . . That is one of the answers of Gaston County to McMahon [president of the United Textile Workers] and his kind.

A serious labor upheaval did not occur in the county until 1929; a considerable part of this volume is devoted to a description of that uprising. Since 1929 there have been only three or

23. For the history of organizational efforts in Southern mills, see George Sinclair Mitchell, *Textile Unionism and the South* (Chapel Hill, 1931); American Federation of Labor, *Report of the Proceedings of the Forty-ninth Annual Convention* (Washington, 1929), pp. 237–244.

24. *Gastonia Gazette*, November 1, 1919, January 12, 1920.

four strikes, all of them minor in character except the General Textile Strike in 1934, when "flying squadrons" closed every mill in the county and kept most of them closed for three or four weeks. National Guardsmen were called to duty at several mills at that time and one striker was slain by the soldiers. The strike gained nothing for the workers, however, and practically destroyed the unions that had been hastily organized.

More recently, slight organizational efforts by the Textile Workers Organizing Committee (C.I.O.) and its successor, the Textile Workers Union of America, have met with complete failure in the county.[25] Representatives of the T.W.O.C. were sent to Gaston County in 1937 and worked for several weeks in the large Firestone plant there. A company union was thrown up to offset their activities,[26] and the assiduity of this organization, coupled with acknowledged incompetence on the part of the particular T.W.U.A. organizers sent to the county, soon ended all organizational agitation. About four thousand "blue cards," authorizing the T.W.O.C. to attempt collective bargaining in their behalf, were signed by various mill workers in the county, but nothing came of it. Union officers "decided it was better to abandon work in the county because of the very large number of organizers it would take to prosecute it successfully. It is one of those areas that will have to be left until many successes have been gained elsewhere."[27] No unions were

25. Results of T.W.O.C. and T.W.U.A. efforts in the South as a whole have not been impressive thus far. For description see *Building a Union of Textile Workers: Report of Two Years Progress, To the Convention of the United Textile Workers of America and the Textile Workers Organizing Committee* (Philadelphia, 1939), pp. 44–48; F. T. De Vyver, "The Present Status of Labor Unions in the South," *The Southern Economic Journal*, V, 485–498 (April, 1939); John L. Lewis, "Labor Looks South," *The Virginia Quarterly Review*, XV, 526–534 (autumn, 1939); and files of *The Industrial Leader* (weekly labor newspaper published at Winston-Salem, N.C.) and *Textile Labor* (official monthly publication of the T.W.U.A.).

26. The constitution of this union, called the "Southern Golden Rule Association, Inc.," characteristically denied that it was a company union. One of the purposes announced for the union was that of promoting "the interest of the members in their religious education, athletic and social activities." The constitution also announced: "While we have the right to strike, we know what strikes have cost us in suffering in the past and we expect in all our dealings with our employers to be governed and led by the Golden Rule and do unto our employers as we would have them do unto us."

27. Letter from an official of the Textile Workers Union to the author, January 9, 1940.

in existence in the mills of the county at the beginning of 1941, except two small cells that were of no importance in industrial relations. No bona fide election under supervision of the National Labor Relations Board had been held there.[28]

Though larger ecclesiastical bodies to which they have belonged have occasionally favored the principle of labor organization, and though the Bishops' Appeal of 1927 definitely called for some form of employee representation, ministers in Gaston County have continued to oppose unions, often publicly, or else to qualify the principle so stringently as to nullify their endorsement of it. Some of them admit that there is no more reason why there should not be a labor union, "if properly organized and conducted," than a merchants' association. When questioned about the qualifying phrase, they answer that they prefer some "good American union like the A.F. of L., not the C.I.O. or I.W.W." Others are openly and intensely opposed; one minister dismissed the question by saying, "Baptist ministers in Gaston County are absolutely down on the type of labor unions we have had around here." Most of the ministers are reluctant to discuss the subject. No clergyman in the county has any noteworthy knowledge of the principles or practices of the trade-union movement in general, or of any particular unions. One minister, indeed, when asked about his views on unionism, launched upon a discussion of denominational coöperation, thinking that the term referred most appropriately to problems of church unity. Ministers attempt to justify their failure to discuss the question, privately or publicly, by avowing that it has never been an issue in their vicinity, despite the fact that the strike there in 1929 was so bitterly fought that it attracted national attention.

Union organizers have consistently regarded ministers in Gaston County and in the South generally as among their worst enemies. The president of the United Textile Workers in 1929 attributed the retardation of his organization's progress in the South during the preceding twenty-four years to "preju-

28. An election was scheduled for one mill in 1938; allegedly because management propaganda was prejudicial to the outcome, the Board ordered postponement. Whereupon the management held the election under its own auspices, and won, convincing large sections of the population in Gaston County that workers do not desire unions. Uptown citizens of the county trust the impartiality of the mill management far more than that of the N.L.R.B.

dice and bigotry fostered by the churches." "The pastors would lose their jobs," he said, "if the workers got a ten per cent increase."[29] Organizers in the T.W.O.C. drive complained frequently that "revivalists" branded them as "agents of the devil, with the mark of the beast on our foreheads," and destroyed embryonic unions at a number of places.[30] Efforts have been made occasionally to offset religious antiunion propaganda, as in a special religious edition of the T.W.O.C. *Parade*,[31] and in a letter from the union's public relations representative to ministers in the South.[32] Union organizers have never called on ministers in Gaston County, except on a priest or two at the Catholic monastery, as a preliminary to work there, because they have expected them to be antagonistic.[33]

Economic conditions in Gaston County are not yet ripe for the successful organization of stable trade unions, though probably a majority of the workers are. Formidable obstacles to unionism in the South[34] are especially intensified in Gaston County, and it is not likely that efforts at organization will offset them successfully in the immediate future. If unionization does come, it is likely that it will be due largely to the removal of several economic handicaps and not because of humanitarian or moral sentiments voiced by religious leaders.

Similar analyses might be made of the relation of the churches of the county to any problem involving the regulation of the textile industry. There have been no public statements or discernible private pressures from ministers or local ecclesiastical bodies concerning regulation of wages and hours, changes in working conditions, public accountability of mill managements, distribution of profits, or any comparable question. Structur-

29. Raleigh *News and Observer*, October 31, 1929.
30. Textile Workers Union of America, *Proceedings* (Philadelphia, 1939), p. 130; *The Industrial Leader*, September 15, 1939.
31. September 11, 1937.
32. Letter from Lucy Randolph Mason to Southern ministers, August 25, 1937.
33. North Carolina T.W.U.A. State Organizer, Interview, High Point, N.C., July 7, 1939. The Catholic priests in Gaston County have less stake and little influence there; being more detached, they have found it possible to manifest some interest in labor organization.
34. For analysis of these obstacles, see George Sinclair Mitchell, *op. cit.*, chap. iv; G. T. Schwenning, "Prospects of Southern Textile Unionism," *The Journal of Political Economy*, XXXIX, 783–810 (December, 1931).

ally controlled by the mills and culturally conditioned by traditions and attitudes that sanction the industry without qualification, the churches and their representatives have been in no position or mood to criticize or to render unfavorable appraisal. Institutional pressures from churches on the mills simply have not existed, so far as any question of importance is concerned.

In defense of their failure to render direct, institutional judgments on their economic environment, spokesmen for the churches claim that they have really exercised greater influence through indirect methods. That is, they have relied on a program designed to change individuals and have assumed that through individual conversion they would eliminate whatever social ills might exist.[35] Ministers believe that they have succeeded in this program, as demonstrated in the Christian affiliations and civic benevolence of most employers in the county. There is no evidence, however, that employers in the county in 1939 were greatly different from those of 1880, insofar as their policies toward employees, the churches, and the general community were concerned. Nor were prominent churchmen among them observably different, in industrial practices, from nonchurchmen, though the number of the latter was too small to allow adequate comparison. If employers have been changed by religion, it was in respects that did not involve important relations in the economic realm.[36] Religious convictions have not wrought any profound transformations in economic structures or conditions in the county. The few changes that have come have resulted chiefly from economic factors. Ministers have then either maintained an attitude of indifference, in order to justify their former failure to display interest in a matter which obviously called for attention, or else have avowed that they had been privately in favor of this change all the time.

35. They have, however, engaged in direct institutional action, through sermons, committees, resolutions, and financial contributions, in favor of a program of syphilis control, attainment of recreational facilities, support of charitable agencies, elimination of gambling, prostitution, pool rooms, and liquor, and any number of other enterprises. They have not left such matters to "changed individuals."

36. An organizer for the Textile Workers Union summarized a discussion of this question by saying: "Union leaders and textile owners and managers may all be good church members, but when they sit down around a table to bargain over a contract or over conditions, brotherly love flies out the window" (Interview, High Point, N.C., July 7, 1939).

PART III

STRATEGIES OF DEFENSE

CHAPTER XI

BACKGROUND OF THE LORAY STRIKE: STRESSES IN CULTURE

THE Communist-led strike at Gastonia in 1929 affords an extraordinary instance of cultural crisis.[1] It is not typical of Southern strikes; to date it is the only major industrial protest led by Communists in the South. It has been termed "an anachronism" by a competent historian of Southern textile unionism. Attempts to depict it as typical of Southern industrial relations or an omen of future developments have resulted in distortion—and often in absurdity.[2] The strike was a cultural abnormality, unique in many respects, not likely to be reënacted in similar form.

Gastonia in 1929 affords a remarkable laboratory for the social scientist, not in spite of the unusual elements introduced into the situation there but precisely because of them.[3] As a source of information on Southern industrial relations as such, it is hardly more significant than half a dozen other situations: Henderson in 1927; Elizabethton and Marion in 1929; Danville in 1930; the General Strike in 1934; Greensboro in 1938; High Point in 1939. Indeed, it may even be misleading. But as an experiment which tested and revealed the interrelationships of various institutions in a Southern community it is of unique

1. Essential relations between the factors of a cultural or industrial pattern are often revealed more clearly in times of unusual crisis than in times of "normalcy" and peace. The relations may be exaggerated at such moments, but they are thereby the more easily studied. The careful student must allow for the exaggeration but may also learn from it. In time of real or fancied crisis, the dominant ethicways of a community are highlighted, and the strength of each institutional strand in the cultural fabric is tested not only as to its own resiliency and toughness but also as to its coherence with other parts of the fabric. Hence a close study is undertaken here of a single but crucial episode in the life of Gaston County.

2. As in much of the Communist literature about the strike, such as William F. Dunne, *Gastonia: Citadel of the Class Struggle in the New South* (New York, 1929); Myra Page, *Southern Cotton Mills and Labor* (New York, 1929).

3. American sociologists have been concerned too exclusively, perhaps, with analysis of "typical" situations characterized by "the absence of any outstanding peculiarities or acute local problems" (see Robert S. and Helen M. Lynd, *Middletown* [New York, 1929], pp. 7–9).

value, approximated in some respects, but never duplicated, by crises that have occurred in other communities.

The economic culture of the community was organized in the general form loosely called capitalism. Further, it was capitalism at its peak of control over culture: capitalism extended through paternalism.[4] The capitalist did not merely provide capital; he also established the facilities and set the norms for politics, morals, religion, amusement, and all other major spheres of culture. His control and his moral right to control had hardly been questioned. Regulation of his activities had been minimal. In short, Gastonia was a stronghold, relatively isolated and undisturbed, of paternalistic capitalism.

Then the Communists came to town, suddenly confronting this sort of economic organization with its economic opposite. No chemist could introduce a new factor into a chemical equation more precipitately. Though they began their challenge under the guise of trade unionism, which would, if successful, have resulted only in regulation of the prevailing organization, the Communists soon moved—or were forced—to open challenge of the form of economic organization itself. The Gastonia strike came to represent, for the community at least, open conflict between paternalistic capitalism and radical Communism. Seldom have two opposing economic philosophies and forces come into such clear opposition within a rather isolated social context.

It may be instructive, then, to examine the reaction and interaction of the economic and religious institutions of the community in the face of this challenge. First of all it is necessary to delineate the character of the challenge and ensuing conflict. Analysis throughout will proceed primarily from the economic side, leaving description of the reaction of the churches to the economic crisis until aspects of that crisis have been thoroughly examined. In scientific jargon, the course of the economic crisis is here taken as a variable, with the course followed by the churches as a possible function. Little attempt will be made to trace direct causal relations between churches and mills; if such relations existed, as they doubtless did, evidence of them has largely disappeared, and in any event the complex of factors involved would render any description of them an oversimplification.

4. See Part II.

The mills and churches never exist or react on each other in complete separation from other aspects of community life; their interrelationships are always shaped to considerable degree by broader cultural influences. In subsequent pages efforts will be made to trace these broader influences as they appeared in the activities of Communists, employers, mill workers, the uptown community, and the ministers, in a time of cultural crisis. Whereas analysis in the preceding pages has been primarily vertical in character, tracing the interrelations of two cultural strands over a period of sixty years, treatment henceforth will be more nearly horizontal in scope. An effort will be made to trace the configuration of religious and economic institutions in the larger cultural fabric, over a period covering only a few months. Against this wider background, the interrelationships of mills and churches, as represented primarily in attitudes and actions of employers and ministers, can be seen in truer perspective.

TYPES OF EXPLANATIONS

Several theories have been advanced concerning the underlying causes of the strike in the Loray mill at Gastonia in 1929. One holds that the fundamental causes were internal—that is, they are to be found in the grievances aroused in workers by low wages, long hours, the stretch-out, and arbitrary management policies. According to this view, the role played by labor organizers was purely incidental and did not figure greatly in the background of the strike. A wave of spontaneous and "leaderless" strikes which swept over South Carolina in March and April, 1929, is cited as evidence that Southern workers were ready to rebel without outside leadership; and it is pointed out that revolt had already begun at Elizabethton, Tennessee, and Marion, North Carolina, before organizers of the United Textile Workers arrived to take charge of ensuing strikes. All these disputes flared up in opposition to internal conditions deemed intolerable; they represented revolt against existing practices rather than the fruit of efforts at unionization. The Loray strike, several observers contend, was of a piece with all the others in its background, even though it diverged somewhat, through radical leadership, in its development. Even David Clark, a spokesman for the Southern textile manufacturers and an archenemy of "outside agitators" in Southern textiles, is reported to have said on the second day of the Loray strike that union organizers, though active in the South for the previous two months, had little to do with the strikes that had occurred; instead, "at some mills efficiency has been stressed to the point of being unfair to the employees."[5]

A second type of interpretation holds that internal conditions were immediately responsible for the strikes but that these internal conditions were produced by sectional competition and pressures in the textile industry.[6] The strikes are explained as results of the exploitation of workers by manufacturers, Southern and Northern, seeking a reservoir of cheap labor in order to gain competitive advantages in a depressed industry. This interpretation is similar to the first type, except that it definitely explains internal conditions in terms of external stresses.

A more limited variety of this second type of interpretation explains external influence on internal conditions specifically in terms of the alien stretch-out. Thus, the Loray strike

was made possible when the attempts of mill owners to apply New England standards of efficiency to southern conditions, aroused the hostility and opposition of the worker. By *southern conditions,* we mean the relatively unskilled labor, the low wages, and the long hours as compared with New England. This, it should be noted, was the underlying, the fundamental, cause of the strike.[7]

Josephus Daniels, interviewed in New York on the Gastonia strike, rejected the idea that Communism was responsible, saying that "the root of the trouble lies in the attempt to graft the

5. Quoted from the *Greensboro Daily News* by G. T. Schwenning in his article, "Prospects of Southern Textile Unionism," *The Journal of Political Economy,* XXXIX, 788 (December, 1931).

6. Advanced, for example, by Samuel Yellen, *American Labor Struggles* (New York, 1936), pp. 292–301. Broadus Mitchell and George S. Mitchell likewise hold in the main to this interpretation, saying specifically: "Everyone recognizes, except perhaps the Southern strikers immediately involved, that the recent and current conflicts are really battles between the Northern and Southern branches of the industry" (*The Industrial Revolution in the South* [Baltimore, 1930], p. 159, and the essay entitled, "Frowning at the South").

7. B. U. Ratchford, "Toward Preliminary Social Analysis: II. Economic Aspects of the Gastonia Situation," *Social Forces,* VIII, 360 (March, 1930). Italics in original.

New England efficiency system, that works well enough on a
forty-eight- to forty-six-hour week, on to our people, who work
fifty-five and more hours a week at lower wages."[8] The stretch-
out was not the primary issue, however, in all the Southern
strikes in 1929, and in any case it represented only one source
of dissatisfaction. Strikes did not occur in all Southern mills
that introduced the stretch-out.

A third type of explanation attributes the Loray strike almost entirely to "outside agitators," with little or no reference
to internal conditions. This was the interpretation most widely
publicized and most widely believed by the Southern public. Its
appeal to Southern suspicion of Northerners made it especially
useful as propaganda against the strike, and it is chiefly in this
light that it is to be viewed. The superficial character of this
interpretation, in relation to the facts, is evidenced in the designation of both Communists and Northern mill owners as the
"outside agitators" responsible. The appeal to all Southerners
to work together in harmony against the machinations of New
England mill owners to injure their Southern competitors was
revived.[9] An editorial in the *Charlotte Observer* on the fourth
day of the Loray strike pointed out that a textile publication
in Boston had recently called attention, petulantly, to the fact
that Communist organizers were active in New England textiles but were keeping out of the South; the Communists had
now followed this tip, the editorial continued, and the poison of
Communism among Southern workers would be to the advantage of the New England industry.[10] The Senate Committee on
Manufactures, seeking to transfer a proposed investigation of
the Southern textile industry from itself to the Federal Trade
Commission, attempted to place the investigation in the prov-
ince of the latter body through pretending to believe that
Northern manufacturing interests might have instigated the
Southern textile strikes, and thereby have violated antitrust

8. *Baltimore Evening Sun*, April 20, 1929.
9. It had been used by David Clark against the United Textile Workers'
Southern drive in 1921—see Paul Blanshard, *Labor in Southern Cotton Mills*
(New York, 1927), p. 83—and was used again by him against the A.F. of L.
Southern campaign in 1929–30.
10. *Charlotte Observer*, April 4, 1929. This newspaper, notable for its reflec-
tion of the opinion of Southern manufacturers, is widely read in Gaston
County.

laws![11] This argument on sectional grounds becomes rather absurd, however, when it is remembered that all the major Southern strikes in 1929 took place in mills owned by Northern interests, unless further attenuation of the argument insists that the Southern textile industry was made the battleground for Northern mills fighting among themselves.

Attribution of responsibility for the Loray strike wholly to Communist agitators, who came to Gastonia and misled uneducated mill workers into following them, has been by far the most popular view. A few months after the strike the attorney in Gastonia for the corporation owning the Loray mill summed up the entire affair:

All the trouble that has happened in Gaston county in the last ten months was not from any differences that existed between capital and labor, between employer and employee, but solely and only for the purpose of establishing a Communist party in the industrial section of North Carolina, and this was financed from Moscow, from demented individuals in America, from Socialists and from others who did not know what it was all about.[12]

One still hears this interpretation on every hand in Gastonia, and at least two of the Loray mill pastors, who were there in 1929, profess to believe it without reservation.

A certain amount of evidence supports each of these theories, except the alleged instigation of strikes by Northern mill owners. But the more fundamental causes of the Loray strike lay in the realm of serious social disorganization, and all the theories presented above represent surface manifestations of a deeper cultural malady.

RECAPITULATION: CULTURAL ORGANIZATION IN GASTONIA

To uptown residents the economic life of Gastonia in the late 1920's appeared well organized and free of unusual strains. Though the textile industry had been erratic for several years,

11. Committee on Manufactures, U. S. Senate, 71st Congress, 1st Session, *Hearings on S. Res. 49:* "Working Conditions of the Textile Industry in North Carolina, South Carolina, and Tennessee" (Washington, 1929), p. 6, hereinafter referred to as "Senate Committee on Manufactures, *Hearings on S. Res. 49, 1929.*"

12. *Gastonia Gazette,* February 11, 1930.

the city was proud of its economic achievements and no internal voice became articulate to challenge its satisfaction. Chamber of Commerce literature announced that it was "the combed yarn center of America," and that Gaston County was "the third county in America in cotton manufacturing."

Through fifty years of rapid growth Gastonia had reached what seemed superficially to be a well-integrated community life. Diverse streams had gone into the making of its culture— streams so diverse in source and character that their ready accommodation to each other, on the surface, might easily have aroused the suspicion of an observer trained in the ways of culture. Industrial development had brought new technicways, new groupings of population, the growth of commerce and cities, different living conditions, a wage system, the modification of sectionalism in economic pursuits even while it was largely retained in politics, religion, education, and manners. To man the new spindles thousands of small farmers had given up the struggle against tired and niggardly land, attracted by prospects of working in a cotton mill for "cash money." They brought with them to the mill villages their rural outlook: dull patience; acceptance without question of long hours of work by several members of the family, and a low income even then; orientation around the church as a social center. Later, and in swelling numbers, came the mountaineers, pushed off the land long before by a system that elevated the unquestioning and undemanding obedience of the slave and discounted the independence of the yeoman farmer. Made desperate by efforts to eke a livelihood from patches of ground against the mountainside, and attracted as often as not by enticements from millpaid agents, they likewise came down by the thousands. With them came their peculiar traditions, bred of homogeneous population, poverty, long isolation, and quick violence.

In fifty years the population of Gastonia had increased more than seventyfold. The same passion that built the mills and brought the people had welded together their diverse cultures, sometimes through conscious training or suppression, more often through simple outworkings of propinquity in place and inequality in power. The center around which all the divergent cultural patterns had been fitted together, neatly or as patchwork, was the economic interest of the manufacturer. To that all other interests must be subservient, lest the region and the people fall again into the poverty and barren ways from which they had so recently emerged. Values were defined in terms of their relation to this central necessity; autonomy for other spheres of interest existed only insofar as they were irrelevant to the major business in which the community was engaged.

In return for the right to conduct his business profitably, it was assumed that the manufacturer would "do the right thing by" his employees and the community generally. His responsibility to his workers varied in popular definition as to details but always was referred to the general standard of prevailing paternalistic relations. His obligation to the community was considered to consist of being "civic minded," making generous contributions of time and money to charity and public welfare and the churches, providing a pay roll and taxes for the community, and in general fulfilling the role of public benefactor and "useful citizen."

Up to 1929 the political and moral rights of the manufacturer to dominate the entire community had hardly been questioned. Indeed, the community appeared to be willing to sell its own values even further in order to attract additional manufacturing plants. Southern chambers of commerce and power companies advertised the prevalence of cheap labor in the South, with such recurring descriptions as "all American, native white . . . contented . . . English language . . . plentiful . . . cheap . . . faithful and efficient . . . free from outside influences and consequent labor unrest."[13] The secretary of the Gastonia Chamber of Commerce wrote in December, 1928, in answer to an inquiry as to labor conditions there: "Wages in Gastonia range from 18 cents to 20 cents and 30 cents [an hour] for skilled workers. Children from 14 to 18 years of age can only work 11 hours a day. Females under 16 are not allowed to work at night."[14]

It was felt, of course, that the interests of the community and

13. See letters from Southern chambers of commerce replying to a query addressed to them in December, 1928, by a New York investigator posing as representative of a manufacturer seeking a new location, in Senate Committee on Manufactures, *Hearings on S. Res. 49, 1929,* pp. 24–30, 39–40. Or see advertisements in almost any issue of the *Southern Textile Bulletin* during the 1920's or brochures distributed by the Southern Public Utilities Company.

14. Senate Committee on Manufactures, *Hearing on S. Res. 49, 1929,* p. 26.

of the textile manufacturer were identical, but the interests of
the manufacturer, being more definite and concrete and powerfully represented, were taken as the standard in terms of which
the welfare of the community was to be judged. It was quite
natural that this criterion should prevail in view of the background of paternalism and the recent rise from economic des-
peration. The community still labored, as did most Southern
mill towns, under "the elation and obfuscation of the victory
mind."[15] Within the memory of many persons still living there
had been notable and indisputable "progress." The *Manufacturers' Record*, house organ of the development of Southern industry, had described the Southern panorama of industrial
achievement as one that "will forever stand out as the mightiest
ever wrought by mankind."[16]

At the same time articulate elements of the community looked
to the future with faith that it would bring still greater achievement and prosperity. In 1924 the county celebrated its progress with a pageant, "Visions Old and New." A prominent manufacturer wrote in a preface: "Gaston County, amazed at its
own progress, humbly wonders what the next decade may bring
forth."[17] The Epilogue delivered by a herald admonished:

> O ye, who watched this pageantry
> Of Visions, Old and New,
> Go forth a part of ages past
> And live your part as well.
> Build greater than your fathers built,
> For they have built for you.[18]

Elements in the community that might have challenged the
interests of the manufacturer or questioned doctrines of progress in the past and future were either nonexistent or inarticulate, with the probability in favor of the latter. Lacking adequate channels through which to make grievances known, and
confused themselves as to their status and prospects within the
existing framework of the community, the mill workers had

15. Blanshard, *op. cit.*, p. 8.
16. Quoted by Bruce Crawford in his article, "Whose Prosperity?" *Virginia Quarterly Review*, V, 331 (July, 1929).
17. *Visions Old and New: A Historical Pageant of Gaston County* (Gastonia, 1924), p. 6.
18. *Ibid.*, p. 43.

been almost completely inarticulate. As an observer of labor in Southern cotton mills in 1927 reported, "the mill workers are silent, incoherent, with no agency to express their needs. The great newspapers boom on with the voice of commercial expansion."[19]

Careful observers had seen signs of trouble brewing. Lois MacDonald had detected various indications of discontent in her work in Carolina mills several years before the 1929 strikes: a high rate of labor turnover; complaints by the workers of short wages, long hours, and bad living conditions; an almost universal desire of the workers that their children should escape the life of a mill worker; class consciousness in a social sense, due chiefly to the isolation of mill villages; a lingering desire for unions on the part of most of the workers who had been in unions just after the war.[20] A Southern professor early in 1929 warned capitalists who were attracted into the South by cheap labor:

Those who come into the south will presume upon the present situation at their peril. . . . These people [mill workers] may be ignorant, but they are intelligent. And they are independent of spirit and stubborn. Only let them be made aware that they are being exploited, and there will be a rude awakening.[21]

Effective public opinion in Gastonia, however, did not temper the mood of optimism and satisfaction with existing conditions. When at least 80 per cent of the 2,200 workers in the dominating textile plant walked out on strike on April 1, 1929, apparently the leaders of the community were taken by surprise. The surprise turned into amazement when it was learned that the strikers had Communist leadership. Having perceived no fundamental stresses in the economic life of the city, the uptown community was quickly convinced that the strike was an alien importation due wholly to "outside agitators."

Whatever the articulate elements of the community may have supposed, this protest of the workers, by which they suddenly

19. Blanshard, op. cit., p. 86.

20. Lois MacDonald, "Normalcy in the Carolinas," The New Republic, LXI, 268–269 (January 29, 1930). For more detailed analysis, see Miss MacDonald's study of three Southern mill villages, Southern Mill Hills (New York, 1928).

21. George B. Winton, "Is the South Permanently Conservative?" The Christian Century, XLVI, 424 (March 28, 1929).

became partially articulate, would hardly have occurred unless there had been serious stresses in their own position inside the economic organization. The crisis which developed in the economic culture of Gastonia in 1929 grew in part out of stresses and strains within the culture itself and in part from invasion of the local situation by novel cultural proposals. The character and extent of both external and internal factors must be examined if understanding is to be achieved.

CONDITION OF THE TEXTILE INDUSTRY[22]

The textile industry in the United States was faced immediately after the war of 1914–18 with the necessity for fundamental readjustment. To meet abnormal war demands, the productive capacity of the industry had been tremendously increased. Wages had risen to unprecedented peaks, calling additional workers in from the hills and farms of the South and creating in the minds of all textile workers a new standard by which to judge the adequacy of wage levels. Profits had risen to a point enabling many Southern mills almost to pay for their equipment out of the profits of the first year of operation. The price of cotton yarn had reached fantastic heights, and demand had been so urgent that large shipments were sent from Southern mills to Northern consumers by express.

The boom days continued, with minor recessions, through 1919 and 1920. In 1921, however, the cotton textile industry went into a depression that marked, for it, the end of an era. Since then it has had profitable years and unprofitable years, with the latter predominating.[23] Deflation of the abnormal war

22. Factual information on this question has been drawn chiefly from the following sources: Claudius T. Murchison, *King Cotton Is Sick* (Chapel Hill, 1930); Broadus Mitchell and George Sinclair Mitchell, *The Industrial Revolution in the South* (Baltimore, 1930); Claudius T. Murchison, "Southern Textile Manufacturing," *The Annals of the American Academy of Political and Social Science*, CLIII, 30–42 (January, 1931); Ethelbert Stewart, "The Present Situation in Textiles," *American Federationist*, XXXVI, 689 ff. (June, 1929); a speech by Professor Louis Bader on December 27, 1929, reprinted in Federal Council of Churches, *Information Service*, April 19, 1930.

23. The years 1923, 1927, and 1929 were relatively profitable. Intervening years often brought severe depression. For example, using 1923 as 100, index numbers for opportunity for employment in the industry were 83 in 1924, 84 in 1925, and 83.1 in 1926. Pay-roll totals, with 1923 as 100, were 80.7 for 1924, 81.9 for 1925, and 81 for 1926. These figures and other indices may be found in Bulletin 446 of the United States Bureau of Labor Statistics.

demand was accompanied by other inroads on the market for cotton wares: rising competition from rayon; a sudden change in women's styles that greatly diminished the amount of cotton used in their manufacture; the partial loss of foreign markets because of tariff policies and the development of textile manufacturing in other parts of the world.

Adjustment to problems created by decreased demand was complicated by numerous difficulties. Spectacular fluctuations in the price of cotton made the manufacture of cotton products more nearly a gamble than a business, and led to artificial production or restriction based on prospective cotton prices rather than on probable demand for cotton goods. Many of the mills had been constructed at wartime costs, were often overcapitalized (through the widespread distribution of stock dividends) in terms of the relation of stock outstanding to value of productive equipment, and, in the case of Southern mills especially, often undercapitalized in terms of working capital. All these factors called for high earnings, despite a diminishing demand and declining prices. The stability of prices was vitiated by the highly decentralized and competitive character of the industry, and by a chaotic marketing system that enabled buyers to play one mill off against another. The further fact that many mills had very crude cost accounting systems, if any at all, resulted in the flooding of the market with yarns for sale by haggling. Add to all these the presence of many marginal mills, whose days of operation had been lengthened only by the war boom and could be continued only through substandard wages and cutting of prices, and the picture of the chaos which descended on the industry in 1921 is fairly complete.

The year 1923 marked a turning point in the expansion of the industry. Each subsequent year brought a decrease in the number of active spindles operating in the United States. The number of active spindles in the South continued to increase yearly, however, attesting to the manufacturing advantage, estimated in 1926 at about 14 per cent,[24] enjoyed by Southern

24. Charles T. Main and Frank M. Gunby, "The Cotton Textile Industry," *Mechanical Engineering*, XLVIII, 999–1004 (October, 1926). This article, by two industrial engineers, contains detailed comparisons of the costs in textile manufacturing as between New England and the South. See also George E. Newby, Jr., "The Cotton Manufacturing Industry: New England and the

manufacturers. The shift of cotton mills southward in the 1920's was one of the major developments of the decade in the textile industry. In the last half of the period New England lost about one third of her spindles and perhaps half of the additional spindles set up in the South were transplanted from New England. Southern towns offered alluring enticements to mills seeking a quiet place to recuperate, the most attractive being a bountiful supply of cheap and allegedly tractable labor. By 1927 Southern mills were producing 67 per cent of the yardage and 56 per cent of the dollar values of the cotton-goods output in the country, as against 54 and 44 per cent, respectively, in 1921. By 1929 the South had 54.9 per cent of the industry's spindles and accounted for 69.8 per cent of the total spindle hours in that year.[25]

Southern mills also suffered from the general depression in the industry but to smaller degree. While the price of New England mill shares had declined by 1929 to one fifth of their value in 1923, the price of Southern shares had declined to one half.[26] If dividends from New England mills declined 80 per cent during these years, probably half of the Southern mills were paying no dividends on their common stock by the end of 1929 and many of them had gone into bankruptcy or into the hands of their perennial creditors, the New York selling houses. Spindlage continued to increase in the South, however, because exploitation of particular lines profitable at the moment generally resulted in erection of new equipment for production rather than in adaptation or conversion of existing facilities, and because Southern towns were as ready as ever to subsidize new enterprises. The traditional practice in the Southern branch of the industry has been that of building new plants to take advantage of immediate situations rather than utilization of existing plants that would require alteration of equipment.

Faced with a general decline in profits, textile employers and managers, North and South, might theoretically explore several possibilities. Overhead costs might be reduced and additional capital obtained through consolidations and mergers of mills; if the mergers represented vertical rather than horizontal

South" (M.A. thesis, University of North Carolina, 1925), a careful study summarizing previous estimates and making calculations of its own.

25. Murchison, *op. cit.*, pp. 30–31.   26. *Ibid.*, pp. 34–35.

integration, distribution of profits between several converters and distributors could be also averted. This approach was used to considerable extent.[27] Diversification of products and exploration of new uses for cotton were theoretically possible but called for capital to make changes in equipment (and it was easier to get capital for a new mill than to transform an old one) and for retraining of labor. Further, the new uses must be discovered before production for them could be instituted, and the industry had few facilities for research or promotion of sales. Diversification appeared to some extent in Southern mills, with increased tendencies toward introduction of knitting, weaving, and finishing processes rather than continuation of preoccupation with spinning.[28] Costs per unit of production might be reduced through increased use of equipment; the speed at which spindles were operated increased steadily during the 1920's, and probably half of the Southern mills continued to run night shifts. From the standpoint of the industry, of course, this was nonsense, as it flooded a declining market with an increasing amount of goods, further depressing prices. The contradictory policy of curtailing production through part-time operation was also widely used, but this device increased the unit cost and thereby also lowered profits.[29] Regulation of production and ar-

27. It was used in Gaston County, where several large combinations were effected between 1920 and 1931 (*Gastonia Gazette*, March 8, 9, 12, 1928). All but one, however, consisted of horizontal combination of a number of spinning mills, which economized somewhat in administrative expense but from the angle of production represented chiefly a pooling of weaknesses.

The same forces at work in American mills were felt to varying degrees in the textile industry throughout the world, and many of the same devices were used in an effort to offset the textile depression. In England, for example, a mammoth merger of one hundred mills, controlling about seven million spindles, was effected in 1928–29 (National Industrial Conference Board, *A Picture of World Economic Conditions at the Beginning of 1929* [New York, 1929], pp. 17–18).

28. Douglas C. Woolf, "South Continues to Expand and Diversify despite Depression of 1924," *Textile World* (February 7, 1925), p. 180. Gaston County had confined its textile operations almost entirely to spinning, allegedly in order to avoid contrasts in wage levels which introduction of more skilled labor would bring. In 1924 the county contained only about four thousand looms; nearly seventy times that number would have been required to care for the output of her spindles. Knitting and finishing processes have likewise been introduced into the county to small degree.

29. Occasional curtailment of operations had begun in Gaston County as early as 1919, when a majority of the mills reduced their schedules to four days and three nights a week, explaining the reduction in terms of the disorganiza-

tificial maintenance of prices through voluntary agreement might provide a way out of the dilemma, if the Federal Government would wink at possible violation of the antitrust laws, and if enough textile manufacturers could be persuaded to coöperate, and if the demand for cotton goods could be maintained. The Cotton–Textile Institute was established in 1926 to explore possibilities along this line and to "educate" its members toward the acceptance of rational policies through research and dissemination of information.[30] Such regulation was necessarily a slow and imperfect technique, however, really giving immediate advantage to noncoöperative producers, even if the dubious proposition were granted that the interests of the industry would at length take precedence over short-range personal interests in the minds of most manufacturers.[31]

From the standpoint of immediate management economies, the most flexible item of production costs appeared to be labor. For the individual mill other costs tended to be relatively fixed. Though the percentage of manufacturing costs which went to labor was not unusually large (anywhere from 25 to 35 per cent),[32] many managers attempted to effect economies on this item. Three possibilities were open: direct wage cuts, location in a region affording cheaper labor, or a disproportionate in-

tion of the industry in transition from war to peace (*Gastonia Gazette*, February 10, 1919).

30. B. M. Siniavsky, "The Cotton-Textile Institute, Inc., A Stabilizing Agency in the Cotton Textile Industry" (M.A. thesis, University of North Carolina, 1931).

31. The Cotton-Textile Institute suffered loss of prestige when it volunteered to act as a policeman over the industry under the N.I.R.A. code. Though most textile managers admit that the N.I.R.A. was "a wonderful thing for the industry," they are still dubious as to whether they desire a substitute. The fight made by many Southern employers against the textile provisions established under the Fair Labor Standards Act indicates their dread of regulation more nearly than it does their inability to meet those provisions.

As one mill executive explained concerning adherence to the production recommendations of his trade association, "They don't pay my bills, so I don't always let them run my business" (Interview, Gaston County, September 12, 1939).

32. This percentage is for Gaston County mills, arrived at from interviews and from information in Bertha Carl Hipp, "A Gaston County Cotton Mill and Its Community" (M.A. thesis, University of North Carolina, 1930), p. 16; Angeline Bouchard, "An Analysis of the Southern Combed Sales Yarn Industry, 1928–1938" (M.A. thesis, Columbia University, 1938, based on field work in Gaston County), pp. 101–102; Mildred G. Barnwell, *Faces We See* (Gastonia, 1939), p. 106.

crease, in relation to wages, of productivity per worker. Exploration of these possibilities provided the immediate background for a wave of textile strikes in New England between 1926 and 1928 and in Southern mills in 1929, of which the strike at the Loray mill in Gastonia was one of the most spectacular.

THE LORAY MILL

Ever since its erection the big Loray mill at the west end of town has been both the pride and despair of Gastonia. Organized in 1900 as Gastonia's seventh mill, it had an initial authorized capital of $1,000,000, representing a stupendous enterprise in the 'Southern textile picture of its day.[33] Its construction and equipment are reported to have cost several times the amount of this original capitalization, with practically all the money furnished by local capital. About $500,000 was subscribed, however, by a Northern woman; from the outset the mill had a slightly "foreign" taint, in ownership as well as in size. By 1907 it had a capitalization of $1,500,000 and equipment of 57,000 spindles and 1,660 looms, designed for the manufacture of print cloth and export sheetings. During subsequent years it underwent numerous reorganizations, passing finally into the hands of the Jenckes Spinning Company of Rhode Island in 1919. It thereby became the first mill in the county to be owned and operated by "outside capital"—a fact often introduced by residents of the county in mentioning it thereafter.[34]

During the first twenty years of operation the labor policies of the Loray managements had been much like those of other mills in the section, with the usual mill village appurtenances and the customary paternalistic relations. The very size of the mill, however, intensified the labor problems existing under a system of this sort. Because of its wide reputation as a big mill, it attracted many recruits fresh from the hills, and soon became noted as a training ground for textile workers. It is reported to have had, as a result, the highest rate of labor turnover in the

33. The tendency in the South was toward smaller mills, seldom more than 20,000 spindles at the outset. When the Loray was built, it was said to be the largest textile plant under one roof in the South.

34. See, for example, the *Gastonia Gazette,* Gaston County Industrial Edition (September 10, 1926), 3d Sec., p. 6; 4th Sec., p. 1.

county. The size of the mill, further, necessarily made relations between the principal executives and the workers more impersonal than was customarily the case in the county, and frequent changes of management compounded this impersonality. The Loray village was less compactly organized than most mill villages and many of the workers there were never really integrated into community life.

The Loray mill, because of these conditions and its dominating position in Gastonia, was selected by the United Textile Workers of America as the logical place to begin operations in the county in a Southern drive just after the first World War. A local union of the U.T.W. was formed there in the summer of 1919,[35] and over 750 employees of the mill walked out on October 28, giving Gaston County its first strike of any importance.[36] The strikers made no complaint of their wage scale or the 55-hour week, but expressed dissatisfaction with the mill superintendent and with refusal of the management to recognize the union. The strike began when seven or eight union men were discharged. It continued for several weeks with no disorder, though the management resorted to the familiar device of bringing ejectment suits against several strikers living in company houses.[37] The strikers returned to work on November 18, having gained nothing. The seeds of unionism, however, were definitely planted in the community.

The Jenckes Spinning Company immediately launched an expansion of mill facilities and an extension of community services. Weaving was discontinued, the looms were sold, and the mill was converted into a yarn mill for the manufacture of automobile tire fabrics.[38] Spindlage was increased from 57,000 to 90,000, and the number of employees grew to approximately 1,400. Of $1,000,000 spent in enlargement, about half went into new facilities for the village, presumably with a view to counteracting labor disaffection as well as to providing housing for additional workers. Two large dormitories, a cafeteria, a

35. *Gastonia Gazette*, July 30, 1919.   36. *Ibid.*, October 28, 1919.

37. *Ibid.*, November 14, 1919. This strategy had been employed by Southern textile manufacturers in several previous strikes; see George S. Mitchell, *Textile Unionism and the South* (Chapel Hill, 1931), pp. 30, 36, 37.

38. After expansion and conversion of the mill's equipment, it was reported to be the largest single-unit automobile tire fabric mill in the world (*Charlotte Observer*, January 23, 1924).

laundry, and 150 new houses were erected and the Loray Community House was enlarged.[39]

In 1923 the Loray mill was included in a merger of the Jenckes Spinning Company and the Manville Company, another Rhode Island chain, forming a corporation operating 551,672 spindles and 9,781 looms.[40] The Loray Division was enlarged and made the principal unit for production of tire fabric, in which the new corporation specialized. The fortunes of the mill were thus bound in with those of seven mills in Rhode Island and one other in Gaston County at High Shoals. More important, the stock of the new corporation appears to have been increased considerably at the time of the merger, while the amount of productive equipment in operation was somewhat decreased. Authorized capitalization was increased from a total of $28,300,000 for the two separate companies to a total of $39,000,000 for the corporation, while spindlage decreased from 664,652 to 551,672.[41] The stock of the merging companies had already been increased considerably out of proportion to spindles, through stock dividends,[42] and this further in-

39. S. H. Hobbs, Jr., *Gaston County: Economic and Social* (Raleigh, 1920), pp. 22–23.

40. *Official American Textile Directory* (New York, 1924), p. 528.

41. The figures presented here were compiled from information in the *Official American Textile Directory, 1920, 1922, 1924*, and *Moody's Analyses of Investments: Industrial Investments, 1922, 1924*. Stock may not have been actually watered as much as these figures for authorized capitalization would indicate. No figures are available for stock outstanding in 1922; the total outstanding in 1924 was $23,188,200, of which $12,000,000 represented common stock and the remainder 7 per cent cumulative preferred stock divided into two classes. The Jenckes Spinning Company alone had stock listed at $7,694,100 outstanding in 1921, while the authorized capitalization of the Manville Company was $8,300,-000. If it is assumed that the Manville Company stock was fully subscribed, the total stock outstanding in 1921 was $15,994,100 as compared with $23,188,-200 in 1924—an increase of 45 per cent, while spindlage decreased 17 per cent.

Robert W. Dunn and Jack Hardy (*Labor and Textiles* [New York, 1931], pp. 59–60) claim that the stock-watering process was considerably more serious than the figures given above indicate; their figures show an increase from about $20,000,000 to $39,000,000. It is probable, however, that some confusion between stock authorized and stock outstanding has occurred here, as also in the mind of a witness before a Senate committee investigating the textile situation in the South in 1929 (Senate Committee on Manufactures, *Hearings on S. Res. 49, 1929*, p. 59).

42. The Jenckes Spinning Company had declared stock dividends of $300,000 in 1917 and $1,800,000 in 1920, according to *Moody's Analyses of Investments: Industrial Securities, 1924*, p. 1403.

Profits doubtless appeared to justify such dividends. Profits of the Jenckes

crease in capitalization imposed on the mills a heavy demand for profits in the face of a depressed industry.

As the textile depression continued, the strain on Manville-Jenckes's productive resources increased. Spindlage was steadily reduced, having declined to 412,756 by 1929, while capitalization remained the same.[43] Regular quarterly dividends were paid on the 7 per cent preferred stock up to October, 1929 (except for "B" stock in 1924 and 1925), but no dividends were reported on common stock, which comprised over half of the stock outstanding.[44] From the outset the corporation's common stock had been listed as speculative in character, and the textile depression helped to reduce its market value still farther.[45] Faced with the alternatives open to textile manufacturers generally and having already tried the procedure of consolidation, the management of the corporation sought other methods of retrenchment.

The Loray Division of the company had always operated at a profit,[46] and had run two shifts steadily during the years from 1923 to 1928, when most mills were forced to curtail operations at various seasons. The number of employees had increased to approximately 3,500; the spindlage had been raised to 118,400. Steady increases in welfare work and community services had been effected in an effort to keep labor satisfied. In 1926 the mill supported a staff of seven full-time welfare workers, a playground, a nursery, and the operation of the village and community house. In that year the *Gastonia Gazette* com-

Spinning Company had been high: $2,089,189 in 1919; $4,032,488 in 1920; $869,723 even in the depression year of 1921. As of July 2, 1921, the company had a surplus of nearly half a million dollars, and total assets of $22,728,368. *Ibid., 1922*, pp. 1056–1057.

43. Reduction of spindlage, especially of inferior type, might very well lead toward more rational and economical operation of the corporation's equipment, of course. It nevertheless imposed an added burden on the equipment kept in operation, on the supposition that the demand for profits, represented in stock outstanding, remained constant.

44. *Moody's Manual of Investments: Industrial Securities, 1924, 1926, 1930.*

45. In 1929 Manville-Jenckes preferred (par 100) ranged in price from 70 to 60, while common stock (no par; originally 100, later reduced to 50, and then put on a no par basis) ranged from 27 to 10. In 1930, after the Loray strike and Wall Street market collapse, $2 was bid per share of common; in 1932 $6 was asked per share of preferred (*ibid., 1931*, p. 2761; *1933*, pp. a32, 2860).

46. Robin Hood, "The Loray Mill Strike" (M.A. thesis, University of North Carolina, 1932), p. 24, report of interview with the superintendent of the Loray Division in 1930.

mented: "The work done by the Loray Mills . . . might serve as a model for any industrial community in the country. This company has spared no pains or money in providing for the education and welfare of their employees. The results are evidenced in the loyalty and support shown to the mill."[47] By 1929 welfare services had been even farther extended and had come to include a company doctor, several additional staff workers, a company store, a sick benefit association, a baseball team, a summer camp in the mountains for employees and their families, a bank, and the other services previously mentioned.[48] The village had reached a population of about 5,000.

Wages at Loray appear to have been, in 1925–26 at least, about equal to those in other mills in the vicinity. Complete information is not available but wage extremes reported by mill managers to the Commissioner of Labor and Printing of North Carolina for 1925–26 indicate that the highest wage at Loray was somewhat lower than usual in Gastonia and the lowest was somewhat higher, as indicated in Table XXX. The steady operation of the mill insured steady wages. Hours were long— fifty-five a week for each shift—but no longer than those in surrounding mills, and more than half of the mills in the county were operating sixty-hour shifts.

In short, in 1927 there were few unusual problems in the life of the Loray community. Several deviations from the usual Southern industrial picture, however, might have been taken as tokens of possible trouble in the future. For example, Manville-Jenckes had built a fence around the mill soon after acquiring it, and is alleged to have locked employees in during working hours, with the result that the mill came to be known among textile workers as "the jail." It was inevitable, further, that the management of Manville-Jenckes, because of the size of the corporation and the operation of the Loray mill from a distance, should be less interested personally in community life than the

47. For this quotation and a rather complete description of Loray welfare activities, see the *Gastonia Gazette,* Gaston County Industrial Edition (September 10, 1926), 3d Sec., p. 1.

48. J. W. Atkins, "Crimson Tide in Dixie: Being a True Story of the First Invasion of the Cotton Textile Manufacturing Section of the Piedmont by a Communist Labor Union, Resulting in Floggings, Murder and a Long List of Lawless Deeds," pp. 18–19. This manuscript, containing 174 pages, is in the possession of its author, in Gastonia.

Southern employer was expected to be, and more impersonal in labor policies. The elaborate welfare program was designed to offset such deviations, but it became increasingly an impersonal force for labor discipline rather than a positive force for social organization. Checking up on absentees from work was one of its major functions, and welfare workers worked so closely with company police that they came to be identified as such in the minds of many workers. A minister who served one of the vil-

TABLE XXX

DAILY WAGE RATES IN REPRESENTATIVE MILLS IN GASTON COUNTY, 1925–26*

Mill	Highest Paid Men	Lowest Paid Men	Highest Paid Women	Lowest Paid Women
Loray	$4.36	$2.54	$3.27	$1.81
Arlington	7.19	1.99	3.22	1.93
Gray	4.79	2.40	3.60	1.99
Dunn	2.20	1.47	2.48	.98
Flint	7.04	2.40	3.60	2.40

* North Carolina Department of Labor and Printing, *Thirty-fifth Report, 1925–26* (Raleigh, 1926), p. 47. This was the last report in which information was given on individual mills.

The Arlington and Gray mills adjoin the Loray mill.

As compared with 69 Gaston County mills reporting, the Loray mill ranked as follows: to highest paid men, 55 mills paid more and 13 paid less; to lowest paid men, 8 paid more and 60 paid less; to highest paid women, 48 paid more, 3 paid the same, 17 paid less; to lowest paid women, 47 paid more, 2 paid the same, 19 paid less (compiled from *ibid.*, pp. 44–49).

lage churches for several years after 1925 reports that under Manville-Jenckes management the mill cared nothing for the workers and they in turn cared nothing for it, that there was much transiency and unrest for several years before 1929, and that living conditions in the village were miserable.

The traditional tendencies of the Loray village toward transiency and lack of community organization were accentuated under absentee ownership. Trouble was avoided so long as labor management, though impersonal, was fairly lax, allowing the worker some autonomy as to speed of operation, employing a generous supply of supplementary workers, and allowing fairly moderate standards of production per worker. The installation of a stretch-out in 1927–28, coupled with further disorganization of the community, carried previous tendencies in the village to their logical conclusion and imposed on disciplinary agencies such as the welfare program a strain greater than they could bear.

THE STRETCH-OUT AT THE LORAY MILL

The multiple loom, extended labor, or stretch-out system[49] was first introduced into the cotton textile industry in the early 1920's. A new application of older doctrines of scientific management in industry, its introduction in New England cotton mills proceeded rapidly during the middle years of that decade and had become a widespread movement by 1928. Writing of "Progress in Textiles" during 1928, the Textile Division of the American Society of Mechanical Engineers reported that notable progress had been made during the year in multiple-machine operation. While used (and abused) previously to some extent, the report continued, "it is only during the last year that its real value has been recognized by both employer and employee. . . . Every mill will be forced to use it or else forego a large part of possible profits."[50]

By 1929 the movement for rationalization in industry was proceeding rapidly in many fields and had reached the Southern textile industry in the form of the stretch-out. Always a bone of contention between management and workers, extension of labor has had an especially hostile reception from Southern workers. Southern managers have often been arbitrary and uninformed in its introduction,[51] and workers have generally

49. For discussion of various aspects of labor extension in the textile industry, see Richmond C. Nyman, *Union-Management Coöperation in the "Stretch-out"* (New Haven, 1934); Elliott Dunlap Smith, in collaboration with Richmond C. Nyman, *Technology and Labor: A Study of the Human Problems of Labor Saving* (New Haven, 1939; a study based on field studies in eighteen cotton mills, several of which were in the South); H. J. Rehn, *Scientific Management and the Cotton Textile Industry* (Chicago, 1934); numerous articles in *Mechanical Engineering* and similar journals during the last ten years, etc.

50. "Progress in Textiles," contributed by the Textile Division, in *Mechanical Engineering*, LI, 53 (January, 1929).

51. Francis Gorman, international vice-president of the United Textile Workers, repeated at the A.F. of L. Convention in 1929 a story describing with hyperbole the methods used in introducing the stretch-out in many Southern mills. A boss, on giving a man a job, put him through a test by giving him a

lacked organized channels of protest other than strikes. Until
recently the Southern worker had an eleven- or twelve-hour
day, which in itself, as some managers recognized, made efficiency systems dangerous and irksome. Further, he has retained
an individualism which leads him to resent encroachment upon
his "personal liberties" in his job, and a "chivalry" which
causes him to resent even more deeply such efficiency studies as
timing his wife while she goes to the toilet. The sight of a
"furriner" nosing around with a stop watch, "a-spyin' " on
him, makes him fidgety and is enough to stir his fierce antagonism.

Introduction of the stretch-out at the Loray and High
Shoals plants of the Manville-Jenckes Company constituted
one of its first applications in the Southern textile industry.
Though the Loray Division was probably already the most
profitable unit in the corporation, the Manville-Jenckes management attempted to reduce costs of production there still
farther in order to maintain the competitive position of the unit
and to bolster the financial position of the company. Several
large tire companies had built their own fabric plants by 1927;
further, the demand for tires was shifting from cord to balloon,
necessitating expensive changes in equipment at Loray.[52] The
pay roll at Loray was undoubtedly "padded," due to haphaz-
ard labor policies that had prevailed for a number of years and
to the general expectations of Southern workers.[53]

A new superintendent was appointed to Loray in the summer
of 1927, given full powers and, it is alleged, orders and incen-
tives to reduce the costs of production there at least half-a-million dollars a year. He made necessary changes in equipment
and immediately inaugurated a policy of retrenchment. Without benefit of time studies, carefully established job stand-

hand brush and telling him to throw it as far as he could. The new worker, having been a baseball player, threw the brush the entire length of the weave shop.
"All right!" said the boss. "The job is yours. You run all these looms." American Federation of Labor, Report of the Proceedings of the Forty-ninth Annual
Convention (Washington, 1929), p. 274.

52. Hood, op. cit., p. 47.

53. A textile manufacturer declared in 1939 that every yarn mill in the South
could dismiss a considerable percentage of its employees, if management
would dismiss old workers and others "being taken care of." Paternal relations
militate here, as at numerous other points, against strict economic efficiency.

ards,[54] or serious consultation with workers, he arbitrarily increased work loads, sometimes even doubling them.[55] A loom fixer reports that his assignment was increased from twelve to eighteen looms and the speed of the looms was increased—an assignment which permitted him to do only temporary patchwork jobs and in the long run would have resulted in serious breakdowns in machinery. Similar extensions were made throughout the mill. Workers, including foremen, were dismissed arbitrarily and replaced with cheaper labor or with redistribution of tasks, or both. Within fifteen months the superintendent reduced the number of workers from about 3,500 to about 2,200,[56] at the same time keeping production up to its previous level.[57]

Wages did not keep pace with increased work loads for those workers who were retained. To the contrary, two general wage reductions of 10 per cent each were arbitrarily imposed within twelve months after the stretch-out began. Much of the work was put on a piecework basis, further increasing tension on the part of the workers. One observer reported that wages in the card room before the stretch-out averaged $20 a week, and $13 after the stretch-out; similarly, spinners averaged $18 to $21 before and $10 to $15 after.[58] Whatever the reductions may

54. Determination of proper work loads on some fairly objective and mutual basis is the crucial factor in successful extension of labor. See Smith, op. cit., pp. 7, 83; Rehn, op. cit., p. 107.

55. The following description of the introduction of the stretch-out at Loray is necessarily somewhat incomplete and inexact, as the plant passed in 1935 into the hands of the Firestone Rubber Company and no records of the years under consideration are available. This description is based on interviews with workers, ministers, and a few mill officials who were working at the Loray mill during the period.

56. Gastonia Gazette, April 2, 1929.

57. See copy of letter from the president of Manville-Jenckes to the Loray superintendent, in Hood, "The Loray Mill Strike," p. 28. With the help of such tactics the Manville-Jenckes Company operated profitably in 1928 and 1929, reporting net income for 1928 (financial year ending June 30) of $2,692,206 and for 1929 of $2,116,427. This meant earnings of $24.06 per share of preferred stock (par 100) in 1928, and $18.92 in 1929, and earnings per share of common stock (no par) of $7.95 in 1928 and $5.56 in 1929. The company reported, in a statement dated June 29, 1929, that it had total assets of $39,459,775, current assets of $10,245,154, and current liabilities of $4,009,517, leaving a working capital of $6,235,637 (Moody's Manual of Investments: Industrial Securities, 1930, pp. 402–403).

58. Louis Stark, "The Meaning of the Textile Strike," The New Republic, I.VIII, 323–325 (May 8, 1929).

have been in particular, the superintendent reduced the total pay roll of the mill during his first three months there at a rate which would have resulted in a saving of between half a million and a million dollars for the year.[59]

Lower wages appear not to have been crucial in the background of the Loray strike, however, and there is some evidence that they were as high, even after the reductions had been made, as those of several other mills in the county.[60] Nor was the fact of a stretch-out in itself of supreme importance; various methods of labor extension were adopted extensively, but carefully and after consultation with workers, in other mills in the vicinity, without labor trouble.[61] So far as internal mill policies were concerned, the impersonal and arbitrary methods of the superintendent appear to have been the most significant factors underlying the strike.[62]

Though he himself was a staunch churchman[63] and a steward in the uptown Methodist church, the superintendent filled the Loray village with workers who had little connection with the churches. He brought in many workers from South Carolina[64] and Georgia, apparently as cheap labor. The old tendencies of the village to high turnover and lack of community integration were thereby intensified; many of the workers had never become identified with community institutions other than the mill when the 1929 strike began. The presiding elder of the Methodist churches in the county estimated that not more than one in ten of the Loray workers attended any church regularly.[65] A vil-

59. See copy of letter from the corporation president, *loc. cit.*

60. For figures for near-by mills, see the Raleigh *News and Observer,* April 24 and 26, 1929.

61. Hipp, *op. cit.,* pp. 14–30; Rehn, *op. cit.,* p. 111.

62. The superintendent told an investigator in 1930 that he had simply tried to make the Loray workers more efficient and to pay them good wages (Hood, *op. cit.,* p. 27).

63. In his earlier days the superintendent, a big two-fisted man, used to stand on a street corner in Connecticut to protect his parson from the village bullies while the parson, now a prominent Methodist bishop, preached in favor of local option. The superintendent is reported to have agreed with the townspeople in disliking local option but was willing to defend against all comers the right of his minister to preach in favor of it.

64. Gastonia uptown people insist that workers from South Carolina are generally "inferior" and often "bad eggs." Loray is said to have had an unusually high percentage of bad eggs just before the strike.

65. James Myers, "Field Notes on Textile Strikes in the South" (MS., 1929), p. 3. White church membership in Gaston County in 1930 constituted 41.4 per

lage minister told an investigator in 1930 that they were a "bad lot" and not "as excellent type of people as might be found in other village communities." He complained especially of petty thievery, bootleggers, and immoral women, and asserted that the village had reached its lowest ebb under "the stretch-out superintendent," who was interested only in getting cheap labor.[66] A neighboring manufacturer believes that the underlying causes of the strike in 1929 root in the fact that only mill workers who could get jobs nowhere else would work at Loray.

The situation at High Shoals, where the other Manville-Jenckes mill in the county was located, was even more revealing of management policies. Established residents of the community and leading church members were dismissed under the stretch-out there, and their places were taken by cheaper workers brought in from outside. A minister stationed there in 1929 declares that "the mill cleaned up South Carolina towns to get cheap labor, and ran all the steady people out of the village." Less subjective is the evidence secured in a house-to-house survey of High Shoals by this minister in 1929–30: of a total population of slightly over 1,200, there were less than 100 persons who claimed to be members of any church anywhere. Because of the influx of newcomers, the active membership of the Methodist church in the village dwindled from more than 100 to approximately 30, and that of the Baptist church from 300 or 400 to less than 50. The mill executive told officials of the Presbyterian church in the village that there was no longer any need for their church, as the Methodists and Baptists had all the members; he therefore took over the edifice, title to which had been retained by the mill, and converted it into a movie house.

Though low wages, long hours, poor living conditions, and the stretch-out all figured in the background of the strife at Loray in 1929, they were of significance primarily as symptoms and harbingers of deeper maladjustments. The deeper causes of strife were not simply economic but cultural in a broader sense. Alien methods of industrial relations had been introduced into an industrial situation which had come to depend, for unity

cent of the total white population, and church attendance is almost universally a prerequisite and indication of "respectability" in Southern mill towns.

66. Hood, *op. cit.*, pp. 20–21.

and peace, on paternal relations, and to expect emphasis on community welfare rather than on productive efficiency alone. Emphasis by Manville-Jenckes managers on the latter goal to the detriment of the former led to the importation of workers who were often outcasts from other communities, and largely ignored the problem of creating of these heterogeneous elements a new community. In addition, the older residents of the village were alienated from loyalty to the mill by the unfamiliar tactics of an arbitrary superintendent, and from pride in the community by resentment over the sudden influx of new and cheaper labor. At the end of 1928 the Loray village was an industrial camp, not a community, and its inhabitants resembled, in terms of social organization, a mob more nearly than an organized society.

It was comparatively easy, then, for the loyalties of the workers to be organized around a new center and to be turned directly against an institution which treated them as mere instruments of economic production. Impersonal management policies and possibilities for the independent organization of workers appear to vary directly with each other.

Reaction of Loray Workers

Signs of trouble brewing were obvious in the Loray village even before "outside agitators" appeared. The entire weave room force of the mill, comprising about fifty men, went on strike on March 5, 1928, in protest against reductions in wages. The strikers claimed that wages had been gradually reduced until they were making only $15 to $18 a week, or about half as much as formerly. Their spokesman gave a terse statement to the press:

We were making $30 to $35 a week and were running six to eight looms. Now we are running 10 and 12 looms and getting $15 to $18 a week. We can't live on it. All we are asking is simple justice. A weaver cannot run 10 or 12 looms at any price. It is more than a man can stand let alone a woman. There used to be women weavers in the mill but when the number of looms was increased the women all had to give up the work.[67]

67. *Gastonia Gazette*, March 5, 1928.

The mill superintendent declined to comment except to say that the strike "didn't amount to much and would soon blow over."[68] He set loom fixers, girls, and second hands to running the looms, and is reported to have increased the number of guards around the plant.[69] No further record of this strike appears[70] and many residents of the community cannot even remember it. No union was represented; this strike took place nine months before outside organizers entered the village.

Some time later in the year a group of Loray workers staged a parade down the main street of Gastonia, bearing a coffin in which lay an effigy of the Loray superintendent. At intervals of about fifty yards the effigy would sit up and shout: "How many men are carrying this thing?" The marchers roared: "Eight." To which the effigy answered: "Lay off two; six can do the work."[71] The workers hid a frowning face underneath a boisterous countenance.

There were no organized channels in Loray industrial relations through which workers could route their grievances. Even the "open office door," of which most Southern manufacturers boast, was closed at Loray: the superintendent, residents of the village say, was "the sort of man you had to send your name in to, and then wait for two hours." Workers came to hate him and the Loray village came to be known as "a bad place to work."[72] Many workers are reported to have left the village voluntarily. Workers who remained grew increasingly bitter, if the testimony of the few who gave public utterance to their reactions is representative:

It used to be you could git five, ten minutes rest now and then, so's you could bear the mill. But now you got to keep a-runnin' all the time. Never a minute to get your breath all the long day. I used to

68. *Charlotte Observer*, March 6, 1928.

69. *Gastonia Gazette*, March 6, 1928. On March 9, 1928, the superintendent contributed $500 to the endowment fund being raised for Rutherford College, a Methodist institution—*ibid.*, March 9, 1928.

70. *Gastonia Gazette*, March 6–26, 1928.

71. This episode was described by several óbservers, with details always substantially the same. The story may, nevertheless, be apocryphal.

72. The village acquired a bad reputation both as a place to work and a place to live. Observers all agree that it became the center of much more extensive immorality than is customary in Gaston mill villages, because of the infiltration of bootleggers and prostitutes.

run six drawing frames and now I got to look after ten. You just kain't do it. A man's dead beat at night.[73]

The superintendent put in the stretchout at Loray all right. And overseers probably got a cut of wages saved through the stretchout.[74]

Boy, was that some stretchout. They didn't figure out what a man ought to be able to do; they jist decided what they'd make him do, and told him to do it or git out. And wages got down to nuthin'— why some spinners wuz makin' only three-four dollars a week, and that's the truth! And they'd work you jist as long as you'd work.[75]

Other overt forms of hostility to the Loray superintendent were engaged in by Loray workers, ending with a noisy celebration when announcement of his dismissal was made toward the end of 1928. An eyewitness describes the celebration as follows:

Several trucks, loaded with workers from the Loray, mostly young people, paraded through the principal streets of Gastonia. The occupants of the truck were shouting, laughing, singing, blowing horns, beating tin pans, shooting fire crackers, and in general, staging a genuine spontaneous celebration. They looked very much like one of the picnic parties that are frequently organized for outings into the country, except that they were somewhat more boisterous. They continued through the city and out about two miles eastward into an exclusive residential section. Here they turned into the driveway of the home of a Mr. —— and continued their celebration, with increased volume, in the driveway, on the lawn and around the house. Mr. —— finally was forced to summon the sheriff and deputies to disperse the crowd and stop the demonstration. The crowd then returned through the city, con-

73. Statement by a Loray worker, in Margaret Larkin's article, "Tragedy in North Carolina," *North American Review*, CCXXVIII, 687 (December, 1929). Compare, with reservations as to authenticity (though many of them appear, from style of expression and provincial usages, to be authentic), numerous letters alleged to have been written by Loray workers to the *Daily Worker*, April 15, 26, 1929; see also Ella Ford, "We Are Mill People," *New Masses*, V, 3–5 (August, 1929).

74. Textile Worker W. Y, who was "loyal to the company" during the 1929 strike, Interview, Gastonia, September 7, 1939.

75. Textile Worker J. A, who was an active striker in 1929, Interview, Gastonia, August 30, 1939.

tinuing the celebration. Mr. —— had been for a number of years the general superintendent of the Loray Mill, and had been instrumental in introducing the "stretch-out" system. This meant, of course, that he had incurred the intense dislike of the workers. On the date of the demonstration it had been announced that he was being transferred to another mill and the workers took the occasion to express their elation at his going.[76]

A new superintendent was appointed for the Loray mill in December, 1928, and a new policy was inaugurated. In contrast to his predecessor, the new manager gave attention to the human equation in cotton manufacturing and was more nearly of the traditional type the workers had come to expect. The stretch-out was temporarily discontinued, and management policies were put on a less arbitrary basis. Especial attention was given to further development of community programs and the coöperation of the churches was enlisted to improve the community.[77]

Disorganization in the community was too prevalent, however, to permit immediate remedy. Before the alleviative policies had been introduced effectively, organizers of the National Textile Workers Union had diagnosed the community as a promising point at which to launch the union's Southern drive.

Role of the Churches

As seen above, prestrike developments in the two villages controlled by Manville-Jenckes in Gaston County had serious effects on the churches. Membership, attendance, and influence declined tremendously; at least one church was closed as a direct result of the new policies of the mills. The churches had not been able, before the outbreak of the strike in 1929, to absorb new elements in the two communities. Nor had they been able, lacking active management coöperation, to prevent rather extensive growth of two vices against which Southern churches always inveigh without reservation: traffic in liquor and sexual immorality. In brief, so far as evidence is available, the place of the churches in the cultural fabric depended largely on the policies of the mills; lacking active coöperation of the mills, they

76. Ratchford, *op. cit.*, p. 361.   77. Hood, *op. cit.*, p. 31.

tended to shrink in size and influence. The influence of religious institutions, at least for the brief time and limited locale under consideration, depended in large part on the policies of the economic institutions.

There is little evidence that the churches aided in the execution of the new policies of the mill managements or approved the methods being employed. To the contrary, there is one item of evidence—a very important one—that the churches disapproved strongly, though their disapproval appears to have been aroused by the deleterious effects of the new policies on the churches rather than by sympathy for the mill workers. The presiding elder of the Methodist churches in the district, incensed at the callous treatment given his churches at Loray and High Shoals, wrote to the chairman of the board of the Manville-Jenckes Company, asking him to intervene. An extensive correspondence followed, and the presiding elder claims that the change in management at Loray was finally effected through his protest.[78]

Other ministers in Gaston County approved of this protest against the Loray superintendent's methods. Resentment against him and his policies appears to have been fairly widespread among preachers in the community; they still speak of him in disapproving manner. They mention most often the fact that he brought in a "class of workers" who were indifferent or hostile to the churches, and that he seemed to care nothing about community welfare. Their hostility to him, covert as it was for the most part, is to be interpreted as a protective response, a protest against departure from the role which had generally been followed by textile manufacturers in relation to the churches. The Loray management had broken the cultural fabric by its emphasis on making good yarn at the expense, if need be, of making good people. The function of the churches in the Loray community was thereby minimized, and it was this fact, rather than desire to regulate the economic institution as such, that led to ministerial protest. As usual the individual manager, not the situation, was singled out as responsible for the difficulties; a personal rather than a social strategy was accepted as the way out.

78. Interview, September 4, 1939; Hood, *op. cit.*, p. 30; James Myers, "Field Notes on Textile Strikes in the South (MS.)," p. 3.

If the churches displayed no other active participation in shaping prestrike developments, it is nevertheless significant that the background of the 1929 strike included, as one of its salient features, a diminution of the influence of the churches over the workers. This fact is not, of course, to be interpreted as a primary cause of the strike; it is only a symptom of the effect of economic policies on the composition of the community. It is, nevertheless, one of the most significant symptoms it would be possible to find, indicating a high degree of social disorganization. Forced to withdraw increasingly into themselves, the churches were less powerful as forces for community organization, and the task was thereby shifted, because any community must be organized in order to survive, to the mill, the welfare services, and the workers themselves. The mill management was more concerned with production than with such intangibles as community welfare; even the extensive welfare services represented largely an effort at more efficient production. Lacking other centers around which to organize, it was easy for workers to accept leadership calling for organization as workers. That leadership presented itself in the form of organizers for the National Textile Workers Union, and stresses within the culture of the Loray community developed into open conflict between two opposing types of culture.

CHAPTER XII

THE LORAY STRIKE: A CLASH
OF CULTURES

INTERNAL frictions between management and workers in the
Loray community made possible the strike there in 1929. These
internal frictions rooted, in part, in external conditions in the
textile industry and in alien labor practices imposed on the local situation under absentee ownership. Open conflict ensued
when forces external to the community arrived to organize the
grievances of workers into collective protest. The appearance
of "outside agitators" was by no means wholly responsible for
the Loray strike, but the form assumed by the protest of the
workers, and the consequent conflict entailed, must be ascribed
chiefly to the intervention of the National Textile Workers
Union.

THE COMMUNIST CHALLENGE

Organized in September, 1928, around a nucleus of Communist
organizers who had participated in the Passaic and New Bedford strikes, the National Textile Workers Union was one of
the first national dual unions established by the Communists.[1]

1. As is well known, the policy of dual unionism was adopted by the Communist party in 1928–29 to replace the technique of boring from within existing A.F. of L. and independent unions. The Trade Union Unity League was
organized on August 31, 1929, to serve as "a trade union center for the militant
new unions" (*Daily Worker,* March 27, 1929), just as the Trade Union Educational League had served as a center for the former policy. The new unions
stressed militant tactics, political and class aspects of labor organization, the
six-hour day and five-day week, the organization of the unorganized, and racial, social, and political equality for the Negro (see report on the Trade Union
Unity League in the *Daily Worker,* September 3, 1929. See also Extract from
House Report 2290, 71st Congress, 3d Sess., Pursuant to H. Res. 220: "Investigation of Communist Propaganda" [hereinafter cited as *Report of the Fish
Committee, 1931*], pp. 22–25—a report of the Fish Committee, often accurate
in factual information but drawing highly colored conclusions).

For detailed information about the activities of the N.T.W.U. prior to the
Gastonia strike, and the trade-union methods advocated and employed by it,
see R. W. Dunn and Jack Hardy, *Labor and Textiles* (New York, 1931), pp.
206–211; Albert Weisbord (secretary of the union), "Passaic–New Bedford–
North Carolina," *The Communist,* VIII, 319–323 (June, 1929); Charles G.
Wood, *Reds and Lost Wages* (New York and London, 1930), pp. 22–25, 54–63
(strong anti-Communist bias).

In order to make it national in scope, the delegates at the organization convention felt it especially necessary to organize the South.[2] Immediately after the convention, therefore, a few organizers were sent to the Carolinas.

Until the Loray strike began on April 1, 1929, no overt evidence of Communist activities in Southern mills had appeared, though the *Daily Worker* claimed that partial credit was due the N.T.W.U. for instigation of several spontaneous strikes in South Carolina in March[3]—a claim without apparent foundation. Meanwhile, however, one of the more seasoned organizers, Fred E. Beal,[4] had been working secretly in Charlotte and vicinity. Having been told by workers that he could organize the South if he could accomplish unionization of the mills in Gastonia, and that conditions at the dominating mill, the Loray, were ripe for organization, he went there in mid-March, 1929, and immediately began the formation of a secret union.[5] He reports that he had no trouble in organizing the workers but, to the contrary, was unable to postpone a strike until more nearly ready to conduct it.

The Manville-Jenckes management had been warned of the presence of Communist organizers at Loray through spies in the workers' ranks and through information supplied by Federal agents. Toward the end of March several union members were dismissed from employment in the mill. Beal then decided to come into the open and called a public meeting of all Loray workers for March 30. At least one thousand attended and several hundred joined the union. Beal and a strike committee

2. Dunn and Hardy, *op. cit.*, p. 207. After the Southern drive had begun, Albert Weisbord stressed especially the fact that this drive was making the N.T.W.U. a *national* union—*op. cit.*, p. 323.

3. *Daily Worker*, March 27, 29, 30, 1929.

4. A child of Lawrence textile workers, Beal had begun work at an early age in the Lawrence mills. He successively belonged to the I.W.W., the One Big Union, and the Socialist party, and joined the Communist party while acting as one of the leaders in the New Bedford strike of 1928. See his autobiography, *Proletarian Journey: New England, Gastonia, Moscow* (New York, 1937).

5. Fred E. Beal, Interview, Caledonia Prison, September 20, 1939. Beal was here following the same logic as that of the U.T.W. organizers in 1919 and the T.W.O.C. organizers in 1937. As one of the leaders of the strike in 1929 put it, "North Carolina is the key to the South, Gaston County is the key to North Carolina, and the Loray Mill is the key to Gaston County" (quoted by E. W. Knight, "The Lesson of Gastonia," *The Outlook and Independent,* CLIII, 46 [September 11, 1929]).

were given authority to proceed immediately with a strike. On April 1 practically the entire working force of both shifts walked out.

Having thus secured a foothold, the N.T.W.U. rushed additional organizers to the scene. From the outset serious differences over questions of strategy arose between the Communist leaders. Beal was interested primarily in trade-union objectives —shorter hours, higher wages, better working and living conditions.[6] He professes, from his later vantage point of disillusionment with Communism, to have feared from the outset that the Communist party might use the strikers as "cat's-paws for the world revolution which every Communist sees just around the corner," and to have had difficulty throughout the strike with other Communist representatives who wished to transform the strike into a political revolt.[7] He claims that he did not stress the Communist affiliations of his union during the first part of the strike, and various observers confirm this assertion.[8] The demands presented by the union to management on the third day of the strike, though extravagant and more nearly in line with the general objectives of the N.T.W.U. than with possibilities in the immediate situation, were primarily of trade-union character:

1. Elimination of all piece work, hank or cloth systems, and substitution of a standard wage scale.
2. A minimum standard weekly wage of $20.
3. Forty-hour, five-day week.
4. Abolition of all speeding and doubling up of work.
5. Equal pay for equal work for women and youth.
6. Decent and sanitary working and housing conditions.
   (a) Immediate installation of baths without extra charge to workers.

6. Beal, *loc. cit.* Beal claims to have joined the Communist party because of his interest in industrial unionism—an interest that could not be satisfied in the American Federation of Labor.

7. *Proletarian Journey,* p. 129, *et passim.* Beal's fears, if genuine, were well founded; the *Daily Worker* had said editorially on March 18, 1929: "The new proletariat of 'The South' becomes a mighty recruit for the class war that must end with victory mounting the standards of the whole working class."

8. Thomas Tippett, *When Southern Labor Stirs* (New York, 1931), p. 85; George Mitchell, *Textile Unionism and the South* (Chapel Hill, 1931), p. 74; *Charlotte Observer,* April 2, 1929.

(b) Screening of all homes without extra charge to workers.

(c) Repair of toilets in mill.

7. Reduction by 50 per cent of rent and light charges.

8. Recognition of the union.[9]

From the beginning, however, Beal and the other organizers made it clear that the N.T.W.U. was quite different from the U.T.W. and other "reactionary" unions with which the strikers had experience, and under whose leadership previous strikes were alleged to have been "sold out" to employers. Ridicule was heaped on U.T.W. methods in strikes going on concurrently at Elizabethton,[10] and the union-management coöperation policies of the U.T.W. were denounced as "class collaboration." The organizers spent a large part of their speeches in denouncing the A.F. of L. and U.T.W. as being composed of "labor fakers," and by contrast pointed to the N.T.W.U. as a "militant, fighting union."[11]

The strike passed quickly from trade unionism to Communism, and from a challenge of particular economic arrangements to an indictment of the general economic system. Employers immediately convinced the community that Communism was threatening Gastonia, and the union was forced to accept battle on those terms. From the beginning the officials of the Communist party in New York demanded a policy of "no compromise" on general party aims, and some of the Communist leaders at Loray needed no goading to inspire them to proclaim their revolutionary intent to all who would listen. Before the strike was a week old, George Pershing, representing the Young

9. *Ibid.*, April 2, 1929; Beal, *op. cit.*, p. 136. An almost identical set of demands had been adopted for the textile drive by the N.T.W.U. at its organization six months previously; even earlier the same general platform had been adopted by the Textile Mills Committee (forerunner of the N.T.W.U.) in the New Bedford strike (Dunn and Hardy, *op. cit.*, p. 207). External formulation of these demands helps to account for the presence of the "forty-hour, five-day week" item, which was unique in demands presented by Southern textile workers.

10. W. F. Dunne, *Gastonia: Citadel of the Class Struggle in the New South* (New York, 1929), pp. 42–44 (hereinafter cited as "W. F. Dunne, *Gastonia*"); *Daily Worker*, March 15, 18, 27, 28, June 3, 1929; Myra Page, *Southern Cotton Mills and Labor* (New York, 1929), pp. 79–91; Mary Heaton Vorse, "Elizabethton Sits on a Powder Keg," *New Masses*, Vol. 5, No. 2, p. 6 (July, 1929).

11. James Myers, "Field Notes on Textile Strikes in the South (MS.)," p. 7; Tippett, *op. cit.*, pp. 81–82.

Communist League, idealized the Russian system to reporters in Gastonia and became specific in application:

Communism has worked successfully for 11 years in Russia and it can work successfully here. . . . We do not demand that uneducated labor be given control, but we do demand control by educated labor. . . . This Loray mill and every other mill under the Communist plan would be operated by a general committee made up of one representative from each department. They would elect a sort of manager who would be responsible to the general committee.[12]

Strike leaders, including Beal, predicted a general strike in Gaston County under N.T.W.U. leadership within a few days, and then in the entire Southern textile industry, announcing that the Loray strike was but the opening aspect of a drive to organize all the 300,000 textile workers of the South.[13] Albert Weisbord, the national secretary of the union, is reported to have told the Loray strikers:

This strike is the first shot in a battle which will be heard around the world. It will prove as important in transforming the social and political life of this country as the Civil War itself. These yellow aristocrats have ground you down for centuries. . . . We have come to Gastonia to help you in your struggle for existence. Make this strike a flame that will sweep from Gastonia to Atlanta, and beyond. . . . Extend the strike over the whole country-side. We need mass action![14]

As the strike went on, Gastonia became a rallying point for most of the agencies connected with the Communist party, and revolutionary aims and strategies increasingly supplanted

12. *Charlotte Observer*, April 4, 1929. This newspaper gave Pershing's utterances an enormous headline on the front page. Beal confirms the fact that Pershing made such statements (*Proletarian Journey*, p. 137).

13. *Charlotte Observer*, April 3, 5, 1929; *Daily Worker*, April 6, 8, 10, 1929. Between April 1 and June 7 the Communists made extravagant claims concerning the spread of the strike and prospects for its further extension. For example, on May 4 the *Daily Worker* asserted that the N.T.W.U. had branches in 65 mills throughout the South, and on June 3 it claimed that the union had members in more than 70 mills in Gaston County. Actually, the Communists were instrumental during this period in only four or five strikes in the region, and all except the Loray strike were minor affairs, quickly settled. In Gaston County three mills other than the Loray were slightly affected.

14. Quoted in Tippett, *op. cit.*, p. 81.

trade-union objectives. Representatives of the Workers' International Relief set up a commissary for the strikers and the organization launched an extensive drive for relief funds. The International Labor Defense, the *Daily Worker*, the Young Communist League, the Young Pioneers, and one or two other Communist organizations also sent representatives and conducted membership drives.[15] At least twenty-three outside representatives of Communist organizations were in Gastonia during the strike.[16] Copies of the *Daily Worker* were widely distributed there.

If Communism was brought to Gastonia, Gastonia was brought to the world. The various Communist organizations made innumerable appeals, through Communist publications, leaflets, tag days, mass meetings, and the like, for money to carry on the class war in Gastonia.[17] Six delegations of emaciated strikers were brought to New York and other Eastern cities to speak at mass meetings and lead parades. Communist periodicals carried horror stories about the plight of Southern mill workers, describing Southern mill towns as "little hells of sweat and blood where babies come and grow and go into the mills to die yet live."[18] Letters purportedly from Loray workers appeared in the *Daily Worker* at regular intervals, depict-

15. W. F. Dunne, *Gastonia,* p. 21; Beal, *op. cit.,* p. 129; Myra Page, *op. cit.,* p. 76; *Daily Worker,* April 5, or almost any other issue during the strike.

16. A list was compiled and checked with Communist officials in New York in 1939.

17. C. G. Wood, Commissioner of Conciliation for the Department of Labor, contends that the main purpose of the Communists at Gastonia, as in other textile strikes, was raising money—see his *Reds and Lost Wages,* p. 22 *et passim.* He was contemptuous of Communist practices of using trade-union façades for the accomplishment of ulterior (i.e., political) purposes, and his interpretations must be viewed in this light. There is more than a shadow of substance, however, in his contentions. Large sums were collected for the relief of the strikers, and Beal charges that much of the money was diverted to the salaries of party officials, while practically none was sent to Gastonia for organizational work (*Proletarian Journey,* pp. 156–157). A high official of the party estimated in 1939, however, that $7,000 or $8,000 went into organizational efforts at Gastonia from Communist sources (Interview, New York, March 31, 1939). In addition, the Workers' International Relief spent from $300 to $400 a week for relief of Gastonia strikers, over a period of several weeks. There is no possibility of checking the amount of income received for these various purposes; the Garland Fund contributed $1,000 for relief, and the high-pressure campaign inaugurated by the Workers' International Relief and the N.T.W.U. must have brought in considerable sums. See the *Daily Worker,* May 1, 29, 1929.

18. *New Masses,* V, 23 (June, 1929); *Daily Worker,* April 2, 1929.

ing unbearable conditions, bursting into balladlike poetry, and crying for help.[19] The Gastonia campaign was interpreted as an integral and important aspect of the Communist struggle against imperialist war and for the defense of the Soviet Union, and as irrefutable proof of a world crisis in capitalism.[20] International Press Correspondence, the Communist international news agency, featured news of Gastonia, and the name of the obscure Southern town was made a rallying cry for Comrades everywhere. Metropolitan newspapers sent special reporters, and the Loray strike became headline news.

The challenge to Gastonia's culture included attack on "white chauvinism" in the matter of race as well as attack on the economic front. The official party policy refused to allow for racial bars in Communist unions. Recognizing that organization of Negroes and whites into a single union might alienate white workers, the N.T.W.U. organizers at Gastonia tended at first to compromise on the issue. Beal thought it somewhat irrelevant, as only a small percentage of the Loray workers were Negroes,[21] but he was taken to task immediately by national officials, who insisted that the Negro question be made paramount.[22] Albert Weisbord was sent to Gastonia to enforce adherence to the party line in this respect, and made two speeches openly demanding admission of both races into one union without segregation or differentiation.[23] The role of Negroes as po-

19. For example, see the *Daily Worker*, April 15, 26, May 17, 1929. Loray strikers wrote numerous "po'ms" to celebrate the strike, in keeping with their mountain background, and a number of the verses printed in the *Daily Worker* and *New Masses* have the authentic style of mountain ballads. Some of the letters, however, are so stylized in form and contents as to indicate formulation by persons other than strikers.

20. W. F. Dunne, *Gastonia*, pp. 10, 50. Dunne was one of the leaders of the Communist party in the United States.

21. The superintendent at Loray, in an interview later in the year, placed the number at about 1 per cent of the 2,200 employees of the mill; most estimates set the figure at 100 to 125. For Beal's attitude, see *Proletarian Journey*, pp. 140–142—a view confirmed in an interview with him.

22. See articles by Cyril Briggs in *The Communist*, VIII, 324–328, 391–395 (June, July, 1929). The *Daily Worker* had said editorially on March 18, 1929: "Negro workers must everywhere be drawn into the leadership as well as into the membership of every Southern strike struggle."

23. *Daily Worker*, April 11, 12, 1929; *Charlotte News*, April 9, 1929; Hood, *op. cit.*, p. 106. Weisbord later ("Passaic–New Bedford–North Carolina," *The Communist*, VIII, 319–323 [June, 1929]) referred to the Negro question as "the most difficult and at the same time the most vital and fundamental problem we have to solve."

246 MILLHANDS AND PREACHERS

tential strike breakers was emphasized, and Negro organizers were sent from New York to lead them into the union. On May 10, after an internal fight, the executive committee of the Gastonia local voted to promote an organizational campaign among Negroes.[24] A fish fry was planned but failed to entice Negro workers; financial overtures are reported to have been made to colored leaders in Gastonia, without avail.[25] A careful reporter learned on May 18 that only seventeen Negroes had secured union cards.[26] Despite almost complete failure in this respect, Communist ideologists continued to agitate the question. Their program appears to have failed chiefly because of Negro reticence and fear rather than because of active opposition from white workers.

The challenge of the Communists to organized religion in Gastonia was less pronounced than their policies with respect to economic conditions and the Negro question. Occasional antireligious references were made in the *Daily Worker*, copies of which were distributed in Gastonia, and the phrase "religious dope" occurred frequently. Neither Beal nor other organizers had attempted to establish relations with any local ministers; they assumed that the preachers would be against them, having been told that they were hired by Manville-Jenckes.[27] But the Communist leaders did not openly attack religion at the outset; despite some pressure from party officials to the contrary, they encouraged the strikers to hold their own religious services. Beal had once been a Sunday School teacher, and this fact was announced as a concession to the mores of the strikers. When employers publicly charged the strike leaders with atheism, Beal distributed a circular, signed by the secretary of the Gastonia local, stating that

24. Robin Hood, "The Loray Mill Strike" (M.A. thesis, University of North Carolina, 1932), p. 106.

25. J. W. Atkins, "Crimson Tide in Dixie (MS.)," pp. 94–95. The Communist organizers, like A.F. of L. organizers before them, were nonplussed as to the proper strategy to be adopted toward the Negro in the Southern trade-union movement.

26. Raleigh *News and Observer*, May 19, 1929. A Loray striker who is now a Communist organizer claims that at least 95 per cent of the Negroes employed at Loray joined the union, but the evidence is overwhelmingly against him. (Interview, High Point, N.C., July 20, 1939.)

27. Beal, *loc. cit.* Beal was told that some of the Loray preachers had designated bathtubs as sinful, to obviate pressure on Manville-Jenckes for their installation in village houses.

No attack of any kind against religion has been made by our leaders at any time. To the contrary preachers have spoken from our platform. The manufacturers are spreading this propaganda as a smoke screen to cover up the miserable conditions now existing in their plant.[28]

In brief, the Communists presented, during the strike itself, practically no challenge to the religious institutions of the community and voiced little or no public criticism of them. Their silence in this respect was doubtless based on a policy of expediency as they sensed the deeply religious background of the workers. In later phases of the struggle Communist opposition to religion became more explicit.

The chief area of challenge and contention became increasingly that of the relation of the Communists and strikers to the civic and political authority of Gastonia and the State of North Carolina. With the aid of adroit propaganda from the employers, the Communists were forced from their original position of opposition primarily to the employers, into a position of open conflict with the community and the police power. The strike moved from the economic sphere into the political sphere and assumed the character of a revolt.

A division of opinion appeared among the Communist leaders as to attitudes toward violence, just as disagreement had appeared over the aims of the strike and the policy toward Negro workers. Beal appears to have advocated peaceful measures fairly consistently at first, though he permitted an armed guard of strikers to protect him continually.[29] Other organizers, however, were more militant, advocating and preparing for violence if pacific measures failed.[30] On the second day of the strike Organizer Pershing told the strikers: "We are not going to let

28. From copy of the circular reprinted in the *Charlotte Observer*, April 5, 1929. Failure to attack religion was not as complete, however, as this circular indicated. For example, one of the organizers, when questioned by a worker as to his religion, displayed a receipted grocery bill and designated it as his religion (Raleigh *News and Observer*, April 6, 1929). As the position of the Communists in the community became more precarious, materialism and antireligious tenets were increasingly unmasked.

29. *Proletarian Journey*, pp. 146–148; Hood, *op. cit.*, pp. 113–114; *Charlotte Observer*, April 4, 1929; Ex-strikers A. J and R. H, Interviews, 1939.

30. Hood, *op. cit.*, pp. 113–114; James Myers, "Confidential Field Notes on Trip to Charlotte, North Carolina, and Marion, North Carolina (MS.)," pp. 19–20 (report of discussion on this question by Communist leaders).

these people go back to work. We may have to punch noses and use force, but it's all right. We have plenty of money to bail you out."[31] Strikers were advised to offer "mass resistance" to eviction from company-owned houses. Mass picketing was employed from the outset of the strike, with several hundred persons on the picket line at times. On the second day a tug of war between strikers and sheriff's deputies took place over a cable with which the officers were attempting to keep open the entrance to the Loray mill, and the strikers won. This evidence of disrespect for authority gave Gaston officials an excuse to appeal to the governor for intervention, and five companies of the National Guard were sent to the scene. The Communist organizers immediately tried to create disaffection in the ranks of the soldiers. An organizer told reporters:

This call of the national guard was the final step of the mill people to keep us from organizing. I am glad to see them here though. It makes our job of picketing easier. Just like we've done in other places, we can win many of them over to our side, and if our people get hungry, the soldiers can give them food. That has often been done in our strikes.[32]

At least two handbills appealing to the working-class solidarity of the members of the National Guard were distributed to the soldiers; one denounced Governor Gardner of North Carolina as a "slave-driving capitalist" and called on the guardsmen to mutiny: "Fight with your class, the striking workers, against our common enemy the textile bosses. Join us on the picket line and help us win the strike."[33] Albert Weisbord, in a speech to the strikers, advocated a more personal strategy:

This militia question is very easy. You girls and women go in a body to these soldiers. . . . Ask these boys, "Do you mean to shoot us down and stab us and our children?" Fraternize with them. Urge them to create trouble in their ranks so when the order comes to shoot us down they won't obey.[34]

Mass picketing continued and arrests were numerous.

31. Raleigh *News and Observer*, April 3, 1929.
32. *Charlotte Observer*, April 4, 1929.
33. Raleigh *News and Observer*, April 9, 1929; see also the *Daily Worker*, April 5, 1929.
34. *Daily Worker*, April 12, 1929; Raleigh *News and Observer*, April 9,

Though the Loray mill was virtually at a standstill during the first two or three days of the strike, it slowly began to recruit workers from outside and many of the strikers drifted back to work. By April 15 the strike as a strike was defeated. By May 1, the number of strikers had dwindled from about 2,000 to approximately 200.[35] On the same day the *Daily Worker* announced that the fight would be to the finish. Gastonia had been selected as the spearhead of a great drive, and Communist leaders were unwilling to admit defeat. Instead, they became more desperate in strategy; as the economic aims of the strike receded, the political aims of the Communists came rapidly to the fore and revolutionary tactics supplanted usual strike methods. Agitation increased after the possibility of bargaining with the Loray management had disappeared,[36] giving credibility to the belief in Gastonia that the Loray disturbance represented a revolution rather than a strike. The strikers continued to hold mass demonstrations, consisting of parades and rallies at which "Solidarity" was sung, placards were displayed, and fighting speeches were made by the organizers. When the city council of Gastonia passed an ordinance forbidding parades, the Communist leadership capitalized on the restriction by staging parades noisier than ever, and succeeded in keeping their movement alive through the publicity that attended dozens of arrests.[37]

The diminishing band of strikers was soon isolated from the

1929. Observers report that the coquetry of girl strikers had little effect on the National Guardsmen; to the contrary, women who resisted commands were manhandled on several occasions.

35. Hood, *op. cit.*, p. 102; *Gastonia Gazette*, May 1, 1929; Ex-striker S. E, Interview, Gastonia, September 11, 1939. By May 18 production at Loray was up to 450,000 pounds of fabric for the week—only ten or twelve thousand pounds short of the record weekly output before the strike (Raleigh *News and Observer*, May 18, 1929).

36. Beal argues that the strike was not lost, even though the mill was back on a normal schedule of production. He claims that many of those working in the mill were strikers who had been sent back to work for a week or so, in order to propagandize the strike inside the mill and to earn funds for the maintenance of the strikers, with a view to a succession of walkouts from the mill (Beal, *Proletarian Journey*, pp. 159–161). The evidence will not admit this interpretation as warranted. Management had instituted a spy system before the strike began and was remarkably successful from the outset in isolating workers who might cause trouble if taken back into the mill. (Interviews, Beal, *loc. cit.*; Ex-spy S. P, Gastonia, September 11, 1939.)

37. *Daily Worker*, April 22, 23, 24, 1929, *et passim;* Atkins, *op. cit.*, p. 87.

community and became a community within the larger community. This isolation and reorganization came to physical expression in a tent colony erected by the strikers after their headquarters had been destroyed by a mob and a number of strikers had been evicted from Loray houses. The colony was established at the edge of the Loray village, and consisted of a wooden building as headquarters and fourteen tents capable of housing about fifty families. The colony was organized as a commune, with its own committees for administration and judication.[38] It also took into its own hands the problem of its defense against intruders and mobs, as rumors were abroad that agents of Manville-Jenckes had said the new colony would not stand for three days. An armed guard was organized for the sole purpose of defending the new union center.[39] On May 16 the strike committee wrote to Governor Gardner:

The textile strikers of Gastonia are building with their own hands a new union headquarters to take the place of the one demolished by thugs, while the state militiamen were looking on. The new building is about to be finished and the dedication will take place next Saturday evening, May 18th before thousands of workers.

It is rumored about Gastonia that enemies of the workers, inspired by the mill owners, are plotting to wreck our new headquarters within three days after completion.

The strike committee took the matter up today and decided that it was useless to expect the one-sided Manville-Jenckes law to protect the life and property of the many striking textile workers of Gastonia. Every striker is determined to defend the new union headquarters at all costs.[40]

By "the one-sided Manville-Jenckes law" the Communist leaders apparently meant not only special deputies hired by Manville-Jenckes but also all police authority of Gastonia and of Gaston County. Beal is reported to have referred to officers habitually as "tin-star deputies," and to have encouraged dis-

38. *Daily Worker,* June 7, 1929.
39. *Daily Worker,* May 17, 28 (including a picture of the guard, composed of about a dozen men with shotguns), 1929; Myra Page, *op. cit.,* p. 77.
40. Photostatic copy in W. F. Dunne, *Gastonia,* p. 40; see also *North Carolina Supreme Court Cases,* CXCIX, 282 (spring term, 1930).

respect for their authority.[41] Children in the tent colony were taught that

It is clear where the government stands. The government stands with the bosses against the strikers. The government stands for slavery for the workers, misery and starvation for the workers' children. The government stands for child labor. The government is the tool of the bosses against the workers.[42]

Communist doctrines were preached openly within the colony, and Soviet Russia was held up as the ideal for American workers.

The presence of this odd community became increasingly a source of trouble to the larger community against which it was erected. Rumors of sexual misconduct, contempt of religion, and other departures from accepted mores swept over Gastonia. The strikers, on the other hand, redoubled their preparations to undertake personally the defense of their new base of operations. On the night of May 28 guards fired ten shots at prowlers in the vicinity.

The erection of the tent colony, which Beal described as having "the aspect of a military camp,"[43] set the stage for a climax to the conflict between Gastonia and the Communists. The break came on June 7. A report from union officials to the *Daily Worker* on that date carried the following item:

Guards around the Workers International Relief Tent Colony and the National Textile Workers Union headquarters were doubled today when rumors of another raid on the strike center came to the attention of the workers. . . . The workers' guard are determined to prevent the destruction of the tent colony at all costs. . . .[44]

A stormy strike meeting was held at the tent colony on that night, after which a picket line started toward the Loray mill, presumably to greet workers who had been persuaded to stage a

41. From testimony of the Communist organizer of the Young Pioneers in *North Carolina Supreme Court Cases*, CXCIX, 287–288 (spring term, 1930).
42. *Ibid.*, p. 290.   43. *Proletarian Journey*, p. 157.
44. *Daily Worker*, June 8, 1929.

second major walkout.[45] Halfway to the mill the picket line was turned back by Gastonia police officers with considerable violence. A carload of officers, allegedly in answer to a call from neighbors reporting trouble at the tent colony,[46] proceeded to the union headquarters to investigate. When challenged by guards as to their possession of a warrant, one of the officers answered by taking a gun away from a guard. Shooting followed, apparently coming from guards and policemen alike. When it ended, one striker and four policemen, including the chief of police, had been wounded. The chief died on the following day.

The Communists' challenge to Gastonia was almost completely ended by this event. Thenceforth their activities in the region were largely defensive in character and their problem was one of resisting expulsion rather than of making positive gains. Between April 1 and June 7, however, they had offered battle to economic, racial, and political arrangements in the community. Responses evoked by this challenge must be examined before the final phase of the struggle is considered.

REACTION OF EMPLOYERS

The reply of Gaston County textile employers to the Communist challenge was swift and vigorous. Interpreted in the most general terms, it consisted of an attempt to drive a wedge between the strikers and the remainder of the community, thereby forcing strikers to choose as to loyalty, and also thereby isolating intransigent strikers from the support and protection of government and the public. Success in this attempt enabled the employers to use governmental power and public opinion in direct frontal attacks on the strikers themselves.

There was no pretense of bargaining with the leaders of the strike. On the day after the walkout the superintendent of the Loray mill told reporters:

Our attitude will be that we will not pay any attention to the strike, whatsoever. We will continue to operate, and if necessary,

45. Fred E. Beal, Interview, Caledonia Prison, September 20, 1939. The *Daily Worker* had announced on June 3 that the N.T.W.U. was concentrating on calling a second strike in the Loray mill immediately.

46. Strike leaders claimed that the police represented an advance guard for a citizens' committee which was gathering to destroy the tent colony on that night.

we will get workers immediately to replace those who have walked out. We are asking the strikers to vacate our houses.

No demand has been presented to us as yet. I will listen to our employees, but under no conditions will I discuss the situation with the union organizers. . . . From the best information I have, the union is an I.W.W. bunch. . . .

I think the situation will be over in a few days. Our home office at Pawtucket, R.I., is not worried at all.[47]

When a committee of strikers presented demands to the superintendent, he simply terminated the interview, refusing to discuss grievances except with individual workers.[48]

The mill management immediately branded the strikers as un-American and atheistic and appealed to the community to rid itself of the "dangerous foreign agitators" who were responsible for misleading the workers. Eleven different kinds of circulars were distributed on the second day of the strike; one of them warned:

Our Religion, Our Morals, Our Common Decency, Our Government, and the very Foundations of Modern Civilization, all that we are now and all that we plan for our children IS IN DANGER. Communism will destroy the efforts of Christians of 2,000 years. Do we want it? Will we have it? No!! It must Go from the Southland.[49]

Another handbill listed a number of foreign names as belonging to leaders of the strikers and asked: "Do You Want Foreigners to Lead You?"[50] The handbills were followed by a series of full-page advertisements in the *Gastonia Gazette*, on April 3,

47. *Charlotte Observer*, April 3, 1929.
48. Atkins, *op. cit.*, p. 68; Hood, *op. cit.*, p. 45. A company spy was one of the most influential members of the committee that waited on the superintendent.
49. *Ibid.*, p. 37. Two thousand copies of each kind of handbill were distributed. Samples of the content of other handbills may be found in the *Charlotte Observer*, April 3, 1929, and in Paul Blanshard, "Communism in Southern Cotton Mills," *The Nation*, CXXVIII, 500–501 (April 24, 1929).
50. Beal, *Proletarian Journey*, pp. 133–134. All the names but one were fictitious, according to Hood, *op. cit.*, p. 37. This sort of appeal would normally be rather effective, in view of the widespread suspicion of "furriners" among the Anglo-Saxon mill workers. Names that would have been familiar to the workers—Beal, Pershing, Dawson, Reid—were omitted from the management's handbills.

4, and 5, paid for by "Citizens of Gaston County," appealing to the community mores with respect to religion, race, the family, and law and order. One advertisement was captioned: "RED RUSSIANISM LIFTS ITS GORY HANDS RIGHT HERE IN GASTONIA." It described the Communist party as

a party that seeks the overthrow of capital, business, and all of the established social order. World revolution is its ultimate goal. It has no religion, it has no color line, it believes in free love—it advocates [the destruction of]⁵¹ all those things which the people of the South and of the United States hold sacred.

Another advertisement urged:

LET EVERY MAN AND WOMAN IN GASTON COUNTY ASK THE QUESTION: AM I WILLING TO ALLOW THE MOB TO CONTROL GASTON COUNTY? THE MOB WHOSE LEADERS DO NOT BELIEVE IN GOD AND WHO WOULD DESTROY THE GOVERNMENT?

THE STRIKE AT THE LORAY IS SOMETHING MORE THAN MERELY A FEW MEN STRIKING FOR BETTER WAGES. IT WAS NOT INAUGURATED FOR THAT PURPOSE. IT WAS STARTED SIMPLY FOR THE PURPOSE OF OVERTHROWING THIS GOVERNMENT AND TO KILL, KILL, KILL.

THE TIME IS AT HAND FOR EVERY AMERICAN TO DO HIS DUTY.

The employers were able without difficulty to bring the organized force of local and state government to bear against the strikers; their appeals for "protection of property" and restoration of "law and order" were heeded with alacrity, giving the Communists further opportunity to designate the state an "executive committee of the capitalist class." Five companies of the National Guard, comprising about 800 men, were sent in by the governor at the request of city officials.⁵² At a meeting of the Gaston County Textile Manufacturers' Association on April 3 an official representative of the adjutant general of

51. An unfortunate typographical error left out these three words in the advertisement!

52. The first request for troops was made to the governor by the attorney in Gastonia for Manville-Jenckes and was endorsed by the mayor and the sheriff. The mayor of Gastonia told the governor on the day that the troops arrived that "he no longer feared violence and that he expected most of the employees to return to work" on the following day (Raleigh *News and Observer*, April 4, 1929). The troops were fed by the Loray mill, according to the *Charlotte Observer*, April 4, 1929.

North Carolina "assured the manufacturers that the State of North Carolina was ready to extend further assistance in national guard troops."[53]

Under protection of the troops the Loray mill was able gradually to resume operations. It had not closed at any time during the strike; even during the first few days, when probably 80 or 90 per cent of the workers were on strike, the plant was kept open, the lights burned all night, and the superintendent announced that a majority of the workers were at the machines.[54] The mill was in danger of losing valuable contracts and the superintendent offered a bonus equal to a 100 per cent increase in the old wage scale to good spinners and weavers.[55] Even so he got workers only slowly, and rubber companies in Akron canceled their contracts with Loray—contracts which had called for nearly the total output of the mill.[56] Becoming more desperate, the mill management began importation of strikebreakers from outside[57] and adopted a more vigorous policy toward the strikers. A citizens' committee, the Committee of One Hundred, was formed, almost certainly under the aegis of employers, and became a focal point for acts of violence against the strikers. The strikers' headquarters was destroyed by a mob on the morning of April 18. A "dynamite plot" was uncovered early in the strike, with the evidence indicating that the "plot" had been made in the interests of the mill and in an effort to discredit the strikers. Strike leaders were arrested on slight provocation,[58] and an antiparade ordinance was secured from the city council making it illegal for strikers to picket. Special

53. *Charlotte Observer*, April 4, 1929. The Association expressed to the Loray superintendent "its sympathy, and extended the resources of the association to him and offered to aid him in any way possible."

54. These stratagems obviously represented a bluff—see Atkins, *op. cit.*, p. 20.

55. *Ibid.*, p. 63.   56. Hood, *op. cit.*, p. 53.

57. See a document supposedly written by one of the strikebreakers, in W. F. Dunne, *Gastonia*, pp. 56–58. James Myers found evidence that several professional agencies had attempted to sell their services to the mill management, but apparently none of them were successful (MS. "Field Notes on Textile Strikes in the South," p. 7). The mill had its own spies continually among the strikers. There was little need for professional strikebreakers, as a vast reserve of labor was available in surrounding counties.

58. For example, one of the lackeys of the mill management brought suit against Beal for "depriving him of the services of his wife," who had been sent to New York with a delegation of strikers. Another organizer was jailed as being an alien illegally in the country.

deputies were substituted for National Guardsmen after the
strike had continued for about three weeks, and observers all
agree that the deputies were considerably more vigilant and
brutal in breaking up gatherings and parades of the strikers
than the troops had been.

Eviction from company-owned houses was a trump card in
the strategy of the mill management. On April 5 workers "who
do not wish to continue in our employ" had been told in a
leaflet: "You must understand that you cannot continue to occupy our houses, nor remain on the premises of the company."[59]
Actual evictions did not begin, however, until May 7. Eviction
orders were secured against eighty families, many of whom
moved of their own accord, with new employees taking over the
houses. Other tenants resisted and had to be evicted forcibly;
they doggedly set up housekeeping beside the street in front of
their former homes. Though the company physician accompanied the deputies serving eviction orders, several persons who
were ill, including one child with smallpox, were put out on the
street.[60] Rain and cold weather set in on May 9, causing further
hardships for those evicted, including by that time some thirty
families. Additional eviction orders were secured and were
served gradually during subsequent months. It was this policy
on the part of the employers that led to the erection of a tent
colony by the strikers.

It is interesting but somewhat futile to speculate on whether
the reaction of the employers would have been different if the
American Federation of Labor had been leading the strike. In
the early days of the Gastonia strike there was much praise of
the A.F. of L. by newspapers, mill owners, and the public generally, by way of contrast to the Communists. It seemed for a
time that the villain of earlier strikes might become the hero of
the new drama. But the mill owners were still noncommittal, as
evidenced in the statement of one of the leaders among Gaston
County employers: "Undoubtedly the manufacturers would
prefer the American Federation of Labor if they have to have

59. *Charlotte Observer*, April 6, 1929.

60. Parents of the child with smallpox, Interview, Gastonia, August 30, 1939;
Senate Committee on Manufactures, *Hearings on S. Res. 49, 1929*, p. 16; Raleigh *News and Observer*, May 7, 1929, *et sqq.; Daily Worker*, May 3, 1929, *et
passim*. Employers had used the device of eviction in previous Southern textile strikes (George Mitchell, *op. cit.*, pp. 34–36).

either, but whether they will go so far as to let them into their mills is a question which only time can answer."[61] Time brought the answer: efforts of the United Textile Workers to organize Southern mills in 1929 and 1930 brought vigorous opposition from employers. One observer wrote that the U.T.W. was honored as hero at Gastonia in 1929 because it was weak and absent.[62]

The real issue in all the Southern strikes in 1929, so far as employers were concerned, was that of the right of workers to limit, through collective action, the control of the employers. In Gastonia, however, this issue assumed special significance in the fact of Communist leadership of the collective action. Employers fought trade unionism and collective bargaining wherever they appeared, but in no other situation did they fight so effectively, and with such complete victory, as at Gastonia. It was easy for employers there to convince the community that the strike represented not simply an effort at modification of the employers' power but a threat to the entire community as then conceived and organized. Whether or not employers at Gastonia regarded the Communist challenge as serious—and there is considerable evidence that they did—they succeeded in provoking community reaction more violent in character than that found in any of the other Southern strikes.

REACTION OF WORKERS

Any discussion of the response and reaction of Gastonia mill workers to the Communist challenge must consist partly of objective facts and partly of evaluation of contradictory opinions. In general, it may be said that the workers reacted favorably and in large numbers to the Communist leadership at the beginning and gradually reacted negatively as the real character of Communist proposals became more evident and the opposing pressure of community opinion and action more severe.

Several thousand workers attended the strikers' first mass meetings, of whom probably 2,000 were strikers. The number of strikers remained the same for perhaps a week, after which it began rapidly to diminish, until by the end of the fourth

61. Raleigh *News and Observer*, April 8, 1929.
62. Blanshard, *op. cit.*, CXXVIII, 500–501 (April 24, 1929).

week only 150 to 200 remained. The actual membership of the
N.T.W.U. local at Loray is disputed; even the union leaders
disagree, with figures varying from 1,500 to 2,600 members enrolled at one time or another.[63] Many strikers never joined the
union; after remaining away from work for a few days, they
drifted back to their jobs. Their primary interest was not that
of building a union but of joining in the excitement and pro-
testing against their condition. Few of them had ever belonged
to a union or participated previously in a strike; ignorance of
trade-union practices led some of the union members, even, to
pass through their own picket line and go back to work for a
few days.

Most of the active strikers were young, between eighteen and
thirty-five years of age.[64] As one former striker remembers,
"not many of the older folks took an active part, though a
great many come and listened and went back home." Perhaps
half of the strikers or strike sympathizers were women and children; special Communist organizers were sent to Gastonia to
organize them. Women are reported to have been the most out-
spoken and determined of the strikers; they ordinarily were
placed in the forefront of the picket lines and parades, and on
several occasions they used clubs on militiamen and deputies.

The percentage of church members among the more active
strikers was rather low; one of the Communist organizers estimated it at 30 per cent. Of 35 native strikers about whom this
information could be obtained in 1939, 17 belonged to no
church, 14 were members of the Baptist church, 3 of the Methodist church, and 1 was a Holiness member. Only 8 of the 35,

63. Interviews with four leaders of the strike, 1939. The minimum figure may
be approximately accurate, as membership requirements in the union were
very loose. The initiation fee was fifty cents, and dues were fifty cents a
month, but neither was a requirement for membership, according to Beal.

64. A list of 91 active strikers was compiled from reports of arrests, reports
in the *Daily Worker* and local newspapers, etc. It was possible to get information as to several indices concerning 46 of these through a number of interviews with persons who participated in the strike. For these 46 the average
age at the time of the strike was 31 years, and the median age was 30; only 4
were over 40.

Many of the workers had entered the mill at an early age; figures gathered
by one of the organizers from 100 strikers indicated that 48 per cent had begun
working by the time of their fourteenth birthday and an additional 30 per cent
by their fifteenth birthday (Clarence Miller, in the *Daily Worker*, May 28,
1929). There is no reason to believe that these figures are inaccurate.

however, were designated as "active" church members—that is, as regular attendants or officers. The two pastors still in the Loray community who were there during the strike report that almost none of their church members who were "any account" (i.e., who were regular attendants at church services, steady contributors, etc.) played any active part in the strike. One church in the village, with approximately a hundred members, contained only one active striker—and he was a spy for the management. The pastor of another reports that his church, with a membership of about 900, stood against the strike "like a storm wall," though 25 or 30 of its less active members became associated with the union. For the most part, he thinks, the strikers who continued to support the strike after the first few days were composed of "lower-class mill workers who never came near a church." A newspaper reporter who visited strike headquarters on the first Sunday of the strike asked 27 strikers there if they had attended church that day; none had, nor were any regular attendants at any church. Nineteen of the 27 had no church affiliations whatever. The reporter found "general indifference" when religion was mentioned.[65]

The questions of importance in connection with the response of the workers to the Communist leaders are two in number: first, why did the workers respond favorably and almost unanimously at the outset? and secondly, why did they gradually desert the union leadership and return to work? The answer to each question is difficult, as it involves motives, and the analysis must depart here from an institutional level, though institutional and cultural factors continue to be dominant forces in the background.

The factors underlying the strike have been examined at considerable length already; here it is necessary only to recapitulate them as to their manifestation in worker reactions. The workers were ready to rebel against conditions under which they worked and lived; they were fighting against something, not for something. A letter written to a newspaper a month after the Loray strike began by a secret lodge composed of

65. *Charlotte Observer,* April 8, 1929. The reporter may have been attempting to prejudice opinion against the strikers, but the report was fairly objective in tone.

Gaston County textile workers reveals something of the mood the workers were in:

Dear Sir i wont to say right here we are not no union and dont think we will. but we are people just the same the way Gastonia office [police officers] is treating the peoples up there it is going to cause truble, we mill peoples ant going to stand for it. we were promest 55 hours week beford the election and we did not git it. we have good peoples to work for at Belmont but the long hours is all we are kicking about . . . if the good peoples wonts to know what we mill people pay [if respectable, fair-minded people desire to know what our wages are] tell tem to go to Lowell N. C. and ask them poor folks and you will see about. $9 and $12 per week and they say Loray mill is a good place to live why is it just like a state prisen a fince around it and it lock and a armed gard at the door and they work the help like a slay [slave] i no what im talking about go to south Gastonia and see what they pay and you will see that the gazette has told lyes we mill peoples is going to stop his paper after this thing is over . . . we are going to rember sherieff Lingbarger at the next election a man that will put a croud of fools to gard good people like he did. we dont need him for a officer and he will never be sherieff again after his time is out.

   We are

                   THE RED MEN OF BELMONT, N. C.[66]

Another sample, coming from a worker in a strike meeting, is equally significant of hidden resentment which had awaited only a favorable opportunity to burst into open revolt:

I never made no more than nine dollars a week, and you can't do for a family on such money. I'm the mother of nine. Four died with the whooping cough. I was working nights, and I asked the super to put me on days, so's I could tend 'em when they had their bad spells. But he wouldn't. He's the sorriest man alive, I reckon. So I had to quit, and then there wasn't no money for medicine, and they just died. I couldn't do for my children any more than you women on the money we git. That's why I come out for the union, and why we all got to stand for the union, so's we can do better for our children, and they won't have lives like we got.[67]

---

66. *Ibid.*, April 30, 1929.
67. Margaret Larkin, "The Story of Ella May," *New Masses*, Vol. 5, No. 6, p. 3 (November, 1929); cf. Beal, *Proletarian Journey*, pp. 193–194.

Effective channels through which workers might express and secure redress for such grievances were almost wholly lacking in Gastonia mills, and at Loray even the policy of the employer's "open door" was severely modified by reliance upon a professional welfare staff. The Communists came, therefore, at a moment when some channel for expressing resentment was needed, and many of the workers accepted blindly the aid proffered. It is doubtful that any considerable number of the Loray workers knew clearly at the outset that the N.T.W.U. was a fighting unit of Communism, or, if they did know, that they understood clearly the aims and strategies of Communism. The fact that it was a union leading a strike was more important to them than its political complexion; Southern textile workers have habitually thought of unions as fighting units in time of strike rather than as bases for continuous industrial relations.

The very prospect of a strike offered to the mill worker release from the ennui of life in a mill village.[68] The strike was a "holiday," something new and different.[69] It offered a new sense of communal participation to those who had little connection with the regular community institutions: a membership card of the union signified that one "belonged," and persons who had never had places of leadership found in this new adventure a chance for self-expression. An observer described the transition that came over one worker: "She gloried in the vivid strike. . . . She learned to speak; she worked on committees; she helped give out relief; she organized for the defense of imprisoned strikers."[70] The strike became a center of loyalty for numerous workers who had lived on the fringe of their communities. It had its leader, Beal. It had several poets, writing strike songs after the model of mountain ballads.[71] It had its aims and pur-

68. H. L. Mencken suggested many years ago that the organization of a brass band in every Southern village would serve as the most effective deterrent of lynching parties. The monotony of work in a cotton mill plus the monotony of life in a mill village where all the houses are the same and the routine unvarying may lead to the selection of many diverse channels of emotional outlet—ecstatic religious services, drunkenness, sexual promiscuity, a strike, a lynching.

69. Atkins, op. cit., pp. 6–11.

70. Larkin, op. cit., Vol. 5, No. 6, p. 3 (November, 1929).

71. For samples, see Margaret Larkin, "Ella May's Songs," The Nation, CXXIX, 382–383 (October 9, 1929); New Masses, Vol. 5, No. 3, p. 14 (August, 1929).

poses. Toward the end it had its own housing facilities. It had even its heroes and martyrs.

As the fundamental opposition of this new center of loyalty and the older community became increasingly apparent, however, most workers who had roots in the older culture withdrew from the strike. The propaganda of employers brought tremendous cultural pressure to bear, and the Communist leaders, unversed in Southern mores and opposed to them in any case, were unable to offset it. By tradition rather conservative in outlook, and suspicious of the new and strange, the mill workers were easily brought back into the familiar fold. Inability of Communist leaders to redeem their promises quickly and lack of funds for carrying on the strike and providing extensive strike relief hastened the process of defection.

Apparently the factor which more than any other alienated the majority of the workers from the Communist leadership was the indifference, and occasional open contempt, of the organizers for religion. Only a few workers withdrew from the strike because of the union policy toward Negro workers; a great many appear to have slipped out because of the Communists' attitude toward traditional religion. The Communists themselves did not exploit their views on the subject; the employers, however, lost no time in branding them as atheists, and the Communists did not deny the charge with sufficient conviction to set the mill workers' minds at ease. At the outset of the strike a new departure appeared imminent: when a preacher mounted a box at one of the first strike meetings and implored the strikers to do nothing hasty or violent, he was forcibly pulled down and ejected—a novel method of treatment for a preacher in the reverent South.[72] But the strikers held their own religious service, led by a lay preacher who had joined them, on the first Sunday after the strike began. They brought their religious convictions with them into the strike and pronounced it right in the eyes of God.[73] Many of the lay strike speeches were re-

72. The preacher in question, Interview, September 4, 1939.
73. Report of the strikers' service on Sunday, April 8, in the *Charlotte Observer*, April 9, 1929. The strikers at Elizabethton referred to their union as "God's union." Textile strikers in South Carolina in 1929 always opened their meetings with prayer.

ligious in tone, and "Praise the Lord!" was a characteristic exclamation of approval from workers at strike meetings. Though the strikers learned to sing "Solidarity Forever," they continued also to use spirituals and hymns at strike meetings.[74]

Inability of the Communist leaders to use this religious heritage convincingly and to conceal their own attitudes toward religion was a serious handicap to retaining the loyalty of the workers. As an astute observer of Southern life analyzed the situation, "superstition lingers on after faith departs," and even though a majority of the strikers were nonchurchmen, they reacted unfavorably to a possible challenge to religion. A reporter who visited the tent colony wrote of the inhabitants he found there: "Of all the teachings of Communism which they undoubtedly had heard for the first time in their lives in this summer of 1929, the matter of atheism seemed the most heavily impressed on their minds."[75] Other observers believed that the antireligious tendencies of the Communists did more than any other single factor to divorce them from continued leadership of the workers.[76]

A small minority of the strikers was more independent of community reaction and more impervious to propaganda from the employers. It consisted chiefly of transient, less stable workers who could hardly be said to belong to any established community. Attracted by publicity on the Loray disturbance, and perhaps in a few cases by prospects of excitement and free food, drifters had come in from near-by villages and states to join the strike.[77] One older textile worker described the inhabitants of the tent colony as "the motliest mob I ever saw in my life." These unionists were not impressed by propaganda which appealed to established cultural standards. They had a certain cultural objectivity:

"What do we care what the union leaders think, as long as they stick up for us," they said. "And talk about religion—who are the

74. Fred E. Beal, Interview, Caledonia Prison, September 20, 1939.
75. Raleigh *News and Observer*, September 24, 1929.
76. Hood, *op. cit.*, pp. 97, 130.
77. Of a list of 91 strikers compiled in 1939, only 38 had worked in the Loray mill, and 45 could not be identified by long-established members of the Loray community, including several of the former strikers.

people that run this town to talk? If all the religion in Gastonia was nitroglycerin, it wouldn't be enough to blow one man's nose."[78]

Even those who remained loyal to the union to the end, however, did not necessarily accept their leaders as Communists. Probably most of them were participants in a movement they never understood. One of them looks back across a decade to say of the strike leaders, dubiously but wistfully: "They may have been Russian Reds, but I don't believe they were."

In contrast to this continuing group of strikers, the attitude of workers who withdrew from the strike passed into opposition to the whole episode. On April 29 the *Gastonia Gazette* published an appeal from 1,360 Loray workers to the mayor, asking "protection from insult as we go about our duties" and denouncing Communism. Though perhaps instigated by the management of the Loray mills, this petition probably expressed the real desires of a majority of the workers after they had deserted the union. The continuation of the strike constituted a nuisance to their peace and a challenge to the employment they had reassumed. Further, the union had come to be composed chiefly of persons regarded by many of the workers as "lower class," and rumors of loose and infamous practices in the tent colony must have stirred opposition among the mill workers as well as among uptown people. Nevertheless, violent opposition to the strikers found supporters among only a few of the mill workers who had gone back to work, though several men who had been leaders of the strike at the outset were among those indicted later for acts of violence against strikers.[79]

REACTION OF UPTOWN COMMUNITY

The reaction of the uptown class of Gastonia to the Loray strike is easily depicted. This class possessed definite agencies of expression and there is universal agreement in description of the part the uptown people and the agencies played. In general they moved from apathy or a slight tendency to sympathize

78. Jessie Lloyd, *Gastonia: A Graphic Chapter in Southern Organization* (pamphlet, New York, 1930), p. 15. See also Ella Ford, "We Are Mill People," *New Masses,* Vol. 5, No. 3, pp. 3–5 (August, 1929).
79. Don Wharton, "Poor-White Capitalists," *The Outlook and Independent,* CLIII, 252–253 (October 16, 1929).

with the strikers (the mill owners and officials are excepted, of course) to strong opposition, and to acquiescence in policies of open violence against the union and especially against the union leaders.

The general population of Gastonia reacted to the Communist challenge rather slowly. Manville-Jenckes had never been popular in Gastonia[80] because it had introduced alien attitudes into the industrial scene, placing on efficient production an overt emphasis distasteful to natives, whose mores stipulated that economic interests should always be masked under the guise of public welfare. There is some evidence that the Manville-Jenckes management had not been held in favor even by the native members of the Gaston County Textile Manufacturers' Association.[81] Many Gastonia citizens undoubtedly felt that the workers had considerable provocation to strike. Few of the citizens knew anything about Communism. These and other factors rendered public opinion rather apathetic, or even slightly sympathetic to the strikers, at the beginning.[82] The *Gastonia Gazette* said editorially in the early part of the strike: "The union is coming to southern mills and the fact might as well be recognized. . . . The mill operatives . . . have just grievances, and they ought to be righted. . . ."[83]

Several events coming in rapid succession aroused the opposition of the uptown people to the strikers—or, more precisely, to the strike leaders. The National Guard came, lending support to rumors of violence at Loray. The arrival of the troops attracted widespread attention and Gastonia began to receive unfavorable publicity—the bugaboo of all citizens who profit by industrial and commercial expansion. Some of the Communist leaders, as already seen, made front-page copy for the newspapers by declarations of far-reaching radical purposes. Additional Communist organizers came to Gastonia almost daily, arousing increased suspicion. Most dramatically of all, Charles G. Wood, conciliator of the United States Department

80. The terms "Gastonia" and "public opinion" will be used here as pertaining especially to the uptown class.

81. Hood, *op. cit.,* pp. 18–19.

82. Beal, *Proletarian Journey,* p. 138; interviews with many representative citizens, 1938–39.

83. April 9, 1929.

of Labor, surveyed the Gastonia scene and on the fourth day of the strike issued a strong denunciation of its leaders:

It is not a strike as strikes are defined; it is a form of revolution created by those committed to revolutions by mass action. There is not here any existing common ground upon which employer and employee can stand. No conciliation is possible until the misled workers divorce themselves from their communistic leaders.[84]

Officials of the American Federation of Labor and the United Textile Workers repudiated any connection with the Gastonia strike, commenting that "no communistic movement is conducted under the sanction of the A.F. of L." and declaring that they had no intention of entering the strike areas unless invited by the employers.[85] Public opinion, skeptical even of the A.F. of L., could conclude only that the N.T.W.U. was infinitely worse.

The *Charlotte Observer*, traditional spokesman for textile interests in the Carolinas, with a wide circulation among uptown people in Gastonia, denounced the Loray strike from the outset. It said editorially on the fourth day of the strike:

[The N.T.W.U. is] related to the Communists and the I.W.W., which have nothing in common with the splendid trades unions which have the respect and confidence of the public in North Carolina and throughout the Nation. . . . No greater affliction could be wished upon the textile operators [i.e., workers] in the South than that they should come under the dominating influence of the foreign agitators. They might well pray to be delivered from the distress visited upon the New England operatives through the activities of "organizers" of the character now at work in Gastonia, for it would mean a farewell to the contented life the Southern operatives have been living, to enforced occupation in working to pay the agitators, instead of taking their weekly wages home for self-support. The pay envelope of the New England operative

84. *Charlotte Observer*, April 6, 1929. As noted previously, Wood was rabidly anti-Communist; see his *Reds and Lost Wages*.

85. *Charlotte Observer*, April 4, 1929; Raleigh *News and Observer*, April 16, 1929; *Daily Worker*, April 12, 1929. For statements of William Green and T. F. McMahon, president of the U.T.W., with reference to their attitude toward the Communists, see Senate Committee on Manufactures, *Hearings on S. Res. 49, 1929*, pp. 17, 69.

in recent years has gone about 75 per cent into the pocket of leaders of these communistic "unions," with 25 per cent left for subsistence. That is, when New England workers have a pay roll to draw upon, for the agitators keep them away from earning a weekly envelope the greater part of the year.[86]

This newspaper continued in the same vein in each subsequent issue. Similar editorials appeared in other newspapers throughout North Carolina. Only two newspapers[87] made any serious effort to defend the strikers or to condemn mob actions occurring later in the strike; those two newspapers, instead of helping to influence opinion toward moderation, really served to remind the residents of Gaston County and of North Carolina that the strike was bringing "unfavorable publicity" to the region and should therefore be ended as quickly as possible.

The Gastonia manufacturers' handbills and advertisements defined the Communist menace in frightening terms. The *Gastonia Gazette*, sole local newspaper, became excited. It had denounced the Bolsheviki and the Communists in America during the threatening days of 1919, praying editorially: "God save our country from the red-handed Bolsheviki, by whatever name he [is] known. It is anarchy of the worst sort and no crime is too dark for it to perpetrate. . . ."[88] When "Red Russianism" suddenly began lifting "its gory hands right here in Gastonia," the *Gazette* rallied valiantly to the defense of American institutions. When the Communists called it "The Nassy Gazoot," and charged that it was only a mouthpiece of the employers, it reacted more violently still. A cartoon appeared on its front page, depicting a serpent coiled about the staff of an American flag, tilting it over; the cartoon was labeled "Communism in the South," large letters proclaimed "KILL IT!" and the caption read, "A Viper That Must Be Smashed!"[89]

While the National Guard was in town, Gastonia left control

86. *Charlotte Observer,* April 4, 1929. That this analysis of the "plight" of the New England mill worker was absurd is beside the point in this present context; the important thing is that not one Southern citizen in a thousand knew it to be absurd, and it was especially calculated to stir up resentment against the agitator, while subtly reaffirming the traditional conception of the proper status of the Southern mill worker.

87. The Raleigh *News and Observer* and the *Greensboro Daily News.*

88. January 1, 1919; cf. November 14, 15, 1919, *et passim.*

89. April 11, 1929.

of the strikers largely in the hands of the soldiers. Except for a few arrests and occasional rough treatment of a striker, there was little violence during the first two weeks of the strike. Communist demonstrations grew in fervor as they diminished in size, however, and became increasingly hateful to the citizenry. Between April 15 and 21 the militiamen were withdrawn and replaced by special deputies selected by local authorities. Acts of open violence against the strikers, and particularly against their leaders, increased in frequency and intensity. Public opinion had shifted to open hostility toward the organizers and had come to place on them virtually all the blame for the strike. Not adept at abstract economic reflection or analysis, the public personalized its hostility and implemented it with acquiescence in violent treatment of the strike organizers. The strategy of the employers, aided by the various factors enumerated above, was successful: the strikers were isolated from the general community and their position in the vicinity became more and more precarious.

Within two weeks the original character of the strike, as representing presumably a dispute between management and workers, had been largely lost sight of, and the conflict shifted to a conflict between the Communists and the general community. More precisely, it became a struggle between the culture organized around paternalistic capitalism and an alternative culture proposed by the Communists. The fact that the Communists really faced insuperable obstacles and were foredoomed to failure from the outset is of little significance for examination of public reaction. That the citizens of Gastonia thought their community was in very grave danger and that they accepted the challenge seriously are facts beyond dispute.[90] Only so can their overt actions be explained.

The *Gastonia Gazette* continued to react vigorously against the various challenges of the Communists to Gastonia culture. When the union leaders repudiated a policy of racial division within the union and sought Negro members, the *Gazette* took advantage of the move to discredit the union in the eyes of Southern white workers, refurbishing old battle cries concern-

90. In scores of interviews ten years later, only one person was found who did not describe the conflict as a very serious matter—and that person passed quickly to discussion of it in excited tones.

ing racial equality and intermarriage.[91] The appeals of the
Communists to the National Guard to mutiny stirred the *Gazette* to a call to action:

Some of this Bolshevik talk among the strike leaders has gone
about far enough. Just how far does the U. S. government or the
State of North Carolina permit seditious utterance? . . . If officialdom does not soon take notice, somebody else will.[92]

When local deputies began to replace the Guardsmen, the *Gazette* warned:

Here is one thing for your notebook.
    With the deputized home guard from among the members of the
American Legion on duty in the strike area, the more riotous
among the strikers might as well get set for some sore heads and
bruised noses. The former service men are not going to put up
with much foolishness and you can lay to that. The militia was
forced to stand up and take quite a bit of razzing from the boisterous element among the strikers, but let some of them try to get
fresh with an old 1917–18 top sergeant or redleg who saw service
in Belleau Wood or in the Argonne.[93]

Two days later the editor openly urged the expulsion of the
Communists from the community. This was clearly an invitation to a tar-and-feather party, at the least, and the cue was
soon taken. On the morning of April 18 a band of masked men,
variously estimated at from fifty to two hundred in number, destroyed the equipment and building which had constituted the
strike headquarters, and then emptied into the street, defiled,
and burned all the contents of the strikers' relief store. Remaining units of the National Guard, stationed a couple of
hundred yards away, did not arrive until after the damage was
done and the mob had gone.[94] They arrested a number of strik-

91. Cf. *Labor Unity*, June 22, 1929.   92. April 10, 1929.
93. *Ibid.* Such utterances lend credibility to the claim of the Communists that
the National Guardsmen were withdrawn because they were not vigorous
enough in subduing the strikers.
94. Responsible Gastonia citizens believe that the officers of the National
Guard had prior knowledge of the impending destruction of the headquarters.
The last of the troops were withdrawn on the following day; a representative
of the governor explained that they were needed longer only to protect the
lives of the strike leaders, not to protect property (Hood, *op. cit.*, p. 88).

ers who had been sleeping in the headquarters, on the theory that they had destroyed their own equipment in order to win public sympathy.[95] This theory was endorsed by the *Gazette*[96] but received no following elsewhere. An attorney for the strikers dictated a statement:

The outrage perpetrated by the mob upon a group of defenseless strikers is a logical sequence to the campaign of denunciation which has been conducted by a certain newspaper and the organized Babbittry of Gaston county—including those in command of the troops who were sent there to keep order. There have been constant and persistent appeals to violence and these appeals have been made in the name of God and religion.[97]

Several North Carolina newspapers denounced this manifestation of lawlessness, and the governor sent a special representative to investigate. This representative and the grand jury of Gaston County investigated the affair but reported inability to secure evidence sufficient for presentment. No indictments were ever made. Responsibility for the episode is generally attributed to "The Committee of One Hundred," a citizens' committee formed "to restore law and order."

City and county officials were stimulated to action against the strikers. The sheriff provided a corps of deputies, many of whom are admitted to have been of dubious character. The city council passed an ordinance on April 19 forbidding parades without a permit; Communist leaders capitalized on it, and parades were broken up daily, often with considerable violence, by deputies and city police officers, and dozens of marchers were put in jail.[98] Civic clubs staged a mass meeting, importing a well-known editor to lecture against Communism.[99] Sympathy

95. Strikers claim to have found Manville-Jenckes tools and the badges of deputy sheriffs in the wreckage.

96. April 19, 20, 1929.   97. *Greensboro Daily News,* April 19, 1929.

98. Only one policeman was disciplined for unnecessary brutality; he was relieved of his job and fined because he had mistakenly beaten a reporter for the *Charlotte Observer* into unconsciousness, thinking him to be part of a parade the police were breaking up. This officer was immediately hired by the Manville-Jenckes management as a special officer.

99. The meeting was held at the county courthouse on April 26 and a large attendance was secured, but sponsors feel that it did not turn out well as the speaker did not "rise to the occasion." The Communists applied for permission to use the building for a mass meeting to present their case and were refused.

was created for the position of the textile manufacturers; it was rumored around town that the Loray mill had been losing money and that a stretch-out had been necessary if the mill were to continue to give employment. The public was reminded that textile manufacturers had been great benefactors of the Southern people and Southern civic life.

The erection of a tent colony by the Communists served both to isolate the strikers further and to focalize community resentment against them. As a counterstrategy to the care of strikers by the Communists, the *Gazette*, with the coöperation of the City Welfare Department and the Chamber of Commerce, launched a campaign for funds for strikers' relief, stipulating that "none of this money will be used . . . to feed or help in any way people who continue to remain idle from choice or who continue to have part in disturbances of any kind."[100] The strikers had been pretty well segregated, however, by the time this appeal was made, and only about $250 was raised in the opening days of the campaign.

When the shooting occurred at the tent colony on the night of June 7, a mob of approximately two thousand citizens gathered at the courthouse, and community feeling ran very high. Under the leadership of the local attorney for Manville-Jenckes raids were made on the tent colony and the homes of strikers, with other strikers being used as shields to protect citizens entering the tent colony. The strikers, on their side, appear to have been terrified; many of them were hiding under the tent platforms, probably expecting a wave of lynching parties. More than seventy strikers were arrested and taken to the county jail, where most of them were held for about a week. After preliminary investigations fifteen, including Beal and six other Communists, were charged with conspiracy leading to murder.

When news of Chief of Police Aderholt's death came on the following day, excitement in Gastonia reached fever pitch. Beal narrowly escaped lynching. The dead chief became a symbol of a community outraged. The *Gazette* sponsored a fund for his family[101] and demanded vengeance. Editorials on the day after

100. *Gastonia Gazette,* May 2, 1929.
101. It announced on July 26 that the amount of the fund had reached $3,072.70.

the shooting called for immediate expulsion of all Communists in the vicinity. One editorial entitled "A Deep-laid Scheme" announced that the murder had been planned deliberately by the Communists, and that the original plan had included the murder of the editor of the *Gazette*, for deliverance from which the editor "gives Divine Providence credit." Another, with direct reference to the police officers who had been shot, was entitled "Their Blood Cries Out," and said:

The blood of these men cries out to the high heaven for vengeance. This community has been too lenient with these despicable curs and snakes from the dives of Passaic, Hoboken and New York. For weeks and weeks we have put up with insult and injury; we have tolerated their insults and abuses. Our officers have taken unspeakable abuse from these folks day after day. We have put up with it, hoping that they would wear themselves out, although fingers were twitching to get at them. . . .

No one but those who have experienced the abuse heaped on officers and citizens can know what this community has suffered from the presence of these vipers in our midst.

And now they have made good their threats of violence. They have shot down as brave and as good a man as ever lived. Chief Adderholt had no ill feelings toward these folks. He pitied rather than censured them. After he had to use desperate methods to keep his men from resorting to violence in the face of unspeakable epithets and vile abuse from this gutter scum who have come South to prey on the ignorance of a deluded people, it was the very irony of the fate that Chief Adderholt should be the victim of unjustifiable violence at the hands of these very people. . . .

The blood of these officers shot down in the dark from behind cries aloud. This display of gang law must not go unavenged.[102]

On the day after Chief Aderholt's funeral, at which six thousand people had been present, the *Gazette* carried a seven-column headline insinuating that the Communist International had picked Gastonia as its bloody battleground in the United States; news stories alleged that the Communists had imported a dozen or more dangerous gunmen who were "scattered in all parts of Gastonia." Several fires during the last few days were

102. June 8, 1929.

attributed to the incendiary work of Communists, and the *Gazette* urged that "it is high time they were run out of town."[103]

Gastonia was on edge. An observer reports that the people were "wild," standing on the streets in little groups, speaking quietly but tensely—a bad omen. All strangers were viewed with suspicion; a Brookwood Labor College professor and a Smith College girl writing a thesis were both escorted out of town. The strikers' tent colony was razed, though Beal and other leaders had refused permission for its removal. As a resident describes the mood, "authorities took the view that they were justified in using whatever means might be necessary in order to remove from the community these Soviet-inspired Communists, law or no law."[104]

Most of the remaining strikers were in jail, however, and the others were in hiding. There was little opportunity for mob violence. Imprisoned strikers alleged rough treatment, including beatings by the police and the hurling of a gas bomb into one of the cells, the effects of which miscarried and killed a detective. Public feeling slowly subsided, and by the time the first group of strikers was released the attention of the community had been turned toward the forthcoming trials of those held for murder.

REACTION OF MINISTERS AND CHURCHES

Insight into the reaction of Gaston County ministers and churches to the Communist challenge is of crucial importance. Attempts to gain such insight proceed on the theory that reactions in a time of cultural crisis reveal fundamental relations, often unobservable in times of cultural peace, between institutions in a community.

The reactions of religious institutions must be studied largely, here as elsewhere, by observation of the ministers, as it was through them that the institutions most often became articulate. Their statements and actions may be taken, roughly, as representative of the churches of which they were pastors. So far as anybody can remember, no minister was challenged or restrained by any appreciable group of his church members concerning his activities in this connection. Churches as

103. June 10, 1929.   104. Atkins, *op. cit.*, p. 119.

churches (i.e., as organized bodies) engaged in no public pronouncements or actions bearing directly on the crisis in the
community. None of the religious associations or organizations
in Gaston County adopted any resolutions or engaged in any
institutional action with regard to the strike.[105] The Gastonia
Ministers' Association discussed the affair at one meeting but
took no official action as a body. The Gastonia District Conference of the Methodist Episcopal Church, South, met in Gastonia on May 21 and 22, in the very midst of the struggle, but
no reference to it was made.[106] No mention of it was made in
sessions of the Kings Mountain Presbytery, local ecclesiastical
unit of the Presbyterian church, during the year; one Presbyterian minister explained the silence by saying, "Presbyterians
sort of keep out of politics or anything on that order."[107] The
same generalization as to absence of official discussion or action
holds for Lutheran, Baptist, and all other church bodies.

Ministers, individually and in small informal groups, did
participate directly, through word and deed, in the crisis. The
line of division between Gastonia ministers who in some way opposed and those who in some way countenanced the Loray strike
is simple of definition. Salaried ministers of "respectable"
churches, with assured status in the prevailing culture, universally opposed the strike; a few ministers of the newer sects and
a few lay preachers and ministers without churches supported
the strike.[108]

As previously noted, speeches at the strike meetings often became religious in tone; Beal writes that "home-made poets and
lay-preachers . . . made something of a spiritual revival of the
strike."[109] A newspaper correspondent reported that the "real

105. Several ministers of each denomination, who had been stationed in the
county at the time, were questioned on this score, and examination was made
of most of the minutes of the various denominational and ministerial bodies
dominated by churches in the county—i.e., presbyteries, district conferences,
county associations, etc. None of the minutes contained any reference whatever
to the strike.

106. Interview with the presiding officer, September 4, 1939.

107. This minister was subsequently chairman of a special committee of the
Chamber of Commerce, created for the express purpose of fighting Communism
in the community!

108. Several strike leaders, and all the Gastonia ministers of 1929 who are
still there, drew this line of distinction in interviews.

109. *Proletarian Journey*, p. 156.

hits" of the strikers' meeting on the first Saturday afternoon were two regularly ordained Baptist ministers, who had no pulpits at the time but had been working in the Loray mill and also "doing religious work" until the strike came along and they joined it. One of them declared that all the strikers were good law-abiding Americans, and pleaded for the Constitution and for religion. He heartily supported the strike leaders but in his prayer asked "that our leaders may quit the one thing of taking Thy name in vain." Of the employers he said: "We are not revolutionists but we are revolutionizing against the capitalists who stand behind their pocket books and say we are slaves. . . . It is not men we are fighting today, not the owners or operators of the mills, some of whom are fine men, but the conditions under which we do not get living wages."[110]

On the following day, Sunday, the "Billy Sunday of Loray" held services for the strikers under their own auspices. After opening the service with a song, "Mother's Hands," he took his text from Malachi 3.8: "Will a man rob God?" A reporter describes the service as follows:

In a very short time he had taken off his coat, and veins in his throat were like ropes and huge beads of perspiration were falling from his brow.

"I ain't never begged no widder for help. I ain't never asked nobody for no help. I've mighty near starved, and guess I would but somebody helped me, but hit wasn't nobody from Loray; hit was somebody on the outside."

This brought cheers. . . . "But," said he, "you needn't think that this here fighting to git something to wear and eat is gonna git you to heaven, for it ain't. You've got to be just as good a soldier for the Lord as you are chasing around here fighting for a living. Yes, some of youse are hot a-standing out there, but don't you ferget that there's a hotter place than this awaiting for them that stays at home and goes to hell."

The striker-preacher asked for a showing of hands of those who had been "saved by the Blood of Christ," and only about 10 raised

110. Raleigh *News and Observer*, April 7, 1929. On April 13 this preacher announced that he had decided to oppose the strike because of "my obligation, which is to put the Anglo-Saxon race first and to have no mixing of colors." He added further that he thought there were a number of Ku Klux Klansmen in the Loray village (Raleigh *News and Observer*, April 14, 1929).

their hands. He told of his many varied experiences, and mentioned that he had seen as many as three fellows killed all at onect. He made frequent references to his text, and in a very subtle manner remarked, "I'd hate to be in the shoes of men I know in Gaston county who are robbing God." This brought profuse applause.

When he had finished his sermon and the crowd was dispersing, a young fellow jumped in and yelled for the crowd to wait, that he had something to say. He had a severe nervous twitch, and looked to be a complete physical wreck, but his voice could be heard for at least a block away. He had appeared there suddenly from Atlanta, and was a "Holiness," he declared. He was dressed well, but announced, after his testimonial, that he had only 75 cents, and would appreciate five or ten-cent pieces from the crowd. Men and women were seen to take out coins from their slim purses and pockets to give the young preacher.[111]

Other preachers of similar type spoke to the strikers during subsequent weeks. Ministers of Holiness churches and the Church of God frequently defended the strike, despite their sole emphasis, presumably, upon personal salvation, their opposition to action which might lead to violence, and their traditional designation of labor unions as branded with "the mark of the beast." They were more completely identified with the economic and social status of the workers than any other ministers were, and the opportunities of the immediate situation took precedence over doctrinal considerations.

As a final sample of the homiletical support of the strike by preachers of this type, a report from the Baltimore *Sun* when the strike was a month old appears to be representative:

The strikers today went back to the fundamentals which they brought with them from the mountains. Kneeling on an old store counter, salvaged out of the wreckage of the strikers' headquarters, H. J. Crabtree, minister of the Church of God, prayed for divine guidance of the strike. As the old man prayed a group of strikers stood with bowed heads and as he came to the close fully a dozen joined in the "Amen." . . . Brother Crabtree then preached. His text was, "Deliver me, O Lord, from the evil man; preserve me from the violent man." "I call God to witness who has been the violent man in this strike," the preacher said. "But we

111. *Charlotte Observer,* April 8, 1929.

must bear it. Paul and Silas had to go through with it and today they sit a-singing around the great white throne. In a few days you will be a-singing through the streets of Loray with good wages. God's a poor man's God. Jesus Christ, Himself, was born in an old ox-barn in Bethlehem. He was kicked about, speared about and finally nailed on a cross. And for what? For sin. It's sin that's causing this trouble. Sin of the rich man, the man who thinks he's rich. . . .

"All the wealthy men in this here crowd hold up their hands. I'll hold mine up for one. My father owns this whole world. He owns every hill in this world and every tater in them hills."

Brother Crabtree took no collection. He asked, "if they's a man among you who's got two dollars and a half to buy your wife or daughter a dress with tomorrow, hold up your hand." Not a hand went up.[112]

Only preachers who stood largely outside the economic and religious privileges of the Gastonia community, as then organized, supported the strike in any way.[113] They composed a very small minority—probably including not more than two or three ordained ministers (and these were mostly members of the newer sects) and an equal number of recognized lay preachers. The vast majority of the ministers, those with "recognized stand-

112. Baltimore *Sun,* April 29, 1929.
113. There are two possible exceptions to this generalization. The pastor of the Loray Wesleyan church appears to have demonstrated publicly some disposition to favor the strikers, or at least to criticize the mill's treatment of them, and to have preached a sermon to this effect. Evidence on this question is not clear. In any event, the Wesleyan churches are closer to the sect type than to the established churches. One of the other ministers in the village sums up the matter by saying: "He may have had a good many strikers in his congregation; anyhow, he didn't last long after the strike!"
The attitudes and actions of the presiding elder of the Methodist church in the district were vacillating and unpredictable, and appear to have been due to the erratic character of the man rather than to any set of convictions. He professes to have been sympathetic with the strikers at the outset but to have been disillusioned quickly by the Communist leadership. He later became one of the most active agents in strategies that helped to break the strike. At the same time he made public statements which antagonized employers; members of a Rotary Club in the county felt it necessary to apologize publicly for a speech he made to their club, in which he appeared to sympathize with the Communists. There is no doubt, however, that in general he was opposed to the strike; in 1939 he summarized his attitude toward the whole episode by saying, "Strikes never gain anything; I am opposed to strikes. The time to stop a strike is before it gets started" (Interview, September 4, 1939).

ing,"[114] opposed the strike and took various types of action against it.

The reasons for their opposition appear to have been more subtle and fundamental than immediate financial self-interest— the reason most often ascribed to them by their critics. Few if any of the ministers owned stock in any of the local mills, or in any mill; comparatively few were subsidized directly by any mill company, though those who were may reasonably be assumed to have considered the probable cost of favoring the strike. All ministers, of course, recognized the power of the employers in the community and the hazard to their own status that might be involved in opposing them.

Most of the ministers, nevertheless, appear to have been sincerely opposed to the strike apart from questions of personal advantage. They were constrained by general culture much more powerfully than they could have been by fear or financial self-interest. They shared the general presuppositions of the community as to proper industrial relations. They endorsed, as they still do, the tradition that the mills represent a blessing without qualification, and therefore should be carefully protected, and that mill workers should look up to their employers in gratitude and patience. If an individual were not satisfied, they believed, he should seek to better his lot through individual action; a strike never does any good and causes trouble for everybody. That mill workers should be willing to follow Communists proves that they are children, easily misled, who must be cared for. It stands to reason that the employer, living in the same community with the workers, knows better how to take care of them than these "outside agitators" who are after their money, and who are teaching them all sorts of doctrines that run diametrically contrary to the Christian religion.

With such presuppositions, supported by the propaganda of the employers and sharpened by the extravagant statements and tactics of the Communist leaders, the ministers could hardly have taken a stand other than that adopted, unless the influence of cultural background and cultural pressure is to be considered of no consequence. Support of the strike would have constituted, for them, unsocial behavior; diatribes levied against

114. This phrase, used in this connection by the "dean" of Gastonia ministers, is very revealing.

them, on the tacit presupposition that they were consciously
tools of the employers, are deficient both in understanding of
the ministers in question and in estimate of cultural conditioning. Having received most of their training, value standards,
and self-realization from the type of culture being attacked by
the Communists, it was to be expected that they would defend
that culture against all open onslaughts. Further, not one of
them had training in economics which would have enabled him
to transcend the relative character of the prevailing pattern of
economics in his region; though certain minor aspects might be
regarded as relative (for example, dependence on textiles
rather than furniture manufacturing), Gaston County economic relations, in their fundamental aspects, constituted for
the ministers economic absolutes.[115]

Evidence that practically all the ministers were opposed to
the strike in personal views is so abundant and unchallenged as
to represent, beyond question, the real fact of the case. Representatives of all the conflicting forces in the struggle agree on
this one point. A sample of ministerial reaction was observed by
Dr. James Myers, industrial secretary of the Federal Council
of Churches, who attended a meeting of the Gastonia Ministers'
Association on April 11, at which about a dozen ministers were
present. Dr. Myers asked for information on the strike situation. He writes as follows of the response:

The attitudes revealed were defensive, cold, unresponsive to a degree I have never met before in a group of ministers. Evidently
they have not yet thought of any connection between the mind of
Christ and low wages or night work for women or child labor. A
number of mill village ministers were present. They especially felt
called on to defend the system.[116]

In reply to specific questions, Dr. Myers was told, as to married women who work at night: "there are some who were un-

115. According to a Methodist minister—one with exceptional knowledge of
wider social patterns—who came to serve a church in Gaston County three
months after the strike ended, there was not a single Methodist minister in the
county during the strike who might be classified as "liberal" in social views—
i.e., as antitraditional in any significant respect. The generalization appears to
hold also for all the ministers serving Presbyterian, Baptist, Lutheran, and
Episcopal churches in the county.
116. James Myers, MS. "Field Notes on Textile Strikes in the South," p. 5.

fortunate in their selection of a husband." The Loray strike "is merely the result of Communist agitators." In contradiction, another opinion held that "the quarrel at Loray is between the Northern owners of the mills and some Northern agitators." As for wages, "the girls dress fit to kill." Child labor is sensible: "children would rather go to work than go to school." Mill people move so frequently "because they are lazy," or "to escape paying furniture and grocery bills." As for the mill village as a system, "the mill village has done great service for the hill people. . . . The signers of the 'Appeal' were all theorists who had had no practical experience. . . . There are no strictly paternal types of villages around here."[117]

Two of the ministers present at the meeting showed traces of a liberal viewpoint toward the strike, one being the Methodist presiding elder and the other an Episcopal rector. They told Dr. Myers that the ministers present had stated their true attitudes, and that mill village pastors had especially defended their system because of a kind of inferiority complex in the presence of their uptown ministerial brethren. Being entirely out of sympathy with the strike, "they wished to have nothing to do with it[118] or with any inquirer into it." Their job, they thought, was to "preach the gospel" and "run a church."[119]

The types of implementation given by ministers to their views are difficult to describe, as they must be disentangled from a mass of conflicting testimony and recollections which may be distorted. In general, there appears to have been little action by way of direct approach to Communism. The strategy was largely that of an indirect approach and was pitched chiefly on the religious level. With the arrival of the troops and the growing reaction of the community and its authorities, direct action on the part of ministers, even if it had been desired, was rendered largely superfluous. Besides, the ministers could work more effectively through religious approaches than by economic or political action.

Sermons denouncing the strike were few in number; several

117. *Ibid.*, pp. 5–6. These reactions are much the same as those an investigator gets from Gastonia ministers at present.

118. This phrase, as used provincially in the South, carries in its meaning an overtone of positive opposition rather than mere avoidance.

119. Myers, *op. cit.*, p. 6.

observers have exaggerated the one or two sermons that were preached into an unwarranted generalization that most ministers preached against the strike.[120] Sermon topics announced in the *Gastonia Gazette* between April 1 and June 15 were strictly religious—mostly theological or Biblical—in character; anti-strike references, if any, must have been introduced incidentally. At least one Methodist minister was restrained by his presiding elder from making a public reply to the charge of the Communists that the mills controlled the preachers; the elder advised him that the Communists would merely ridicule any reply.

The ministers of the four churches in the Loray village held a meeting early in the strike to plan a strategy against the uprising.[121] It was decided that the approach should be that of telling the mill workers to "behave and do nothing rash, and especially to avoid criminal acts," on the conviction that Beal and the other Communist leaders would certainly lead the workers into illegal action. "We knew all the time," says one of the ministers present, "that the Communist leaders were all bad, and dangerous as leaders. They were the rottenest crowd you ever saw, using all sorts of profane and obscene language."

The pastor of the Loray Baptist Church was the leader of ministerial opposition to the strikers. During the first week of the conflict he told a reporter:

My sympathy is with the people; their cause is just but their methods are all wrong. . . . They could have a committee to appear before . . . the superintendent of the Loray mills. He is just and reasonable enough to give full consideration to any appeal,

120. For example, Tippett, *op. cit.*, pp. 78, 92; Hood, *op. cit.*, p. 71.
121. Information based on interviews with two of the ministers present at the meeting.
Three of the four Loray pastors were provided with parsonages by the mill company in 1929. Apparently there was no direct subsidy by the mill to their salaries, though the general practice whereby preachers can call on the mills in cases of emergency doubtless led to occasional contributions from mill officials. The mill had a policy, of long standing, of offering to pay half the costs of any improvements in church property. Title to the church buildings rested in the churches themselves, or in their appropriate ecclesiastical bodies, with a clause providing for reversion of the property to the mill if it ceased to be used for religious purposes. The mill furnished lights and water to the churches.
The reaction of the ministers at Loray would probably have been little different even if no such support from the mill had been available.

though not to demands. . . . I think the whole thing is going to fizzle out in a very few days. These folks know that I or any of the ministers would have advised them right, and that we are their friends and would have given them help.[122]

This same minister, pastor of the largest church in the village, secured a copy of a Communist booklet and announced that he would preach on Communism the following Sunday. Some of the Communist leaders claimed that he misrepresented them, but he reports that there was little criticism of his sermon otherwise, as he was simply reading from their own publication the views of the Communists toward racial equality and atheism —views which they had kept in the background up until that time.

Otherwise, the strategy of the ministers consisted in attempting to divert the attention of the workers from the strike to religion. The Methodist presiding elder sent one of the region's most popular evangelists into the Loray village to begin a revival meeting about a month after the strike began—"not," he says, "to stop the strike, but to restore its native leaders to sanity." He reports that the revival had the desired effect, really breaking up the strike through bringing native leaders of the people back to their senses. The Wesleyan church at Loray followed the same line of attack, bringing in the Gastonia preacher most admired by the mill workers to hold evangelistic meetings for two weeks.[123]

One other positive strategy of the ministers deserves brief mention. Under the leadership of the Methodist presiding elder,

122. *Charlotte Observer,* April 8, 1929.
123. *Gastonia Gazette,* May 18, 1929.
H. L. Mencken had predicted, in the Baltimore *Evening Sun* of May 13, 1929, that religious forces would settle the Southern strikes by diverting the attention of workers from their strikes to revivals, from the troubles of this world to the horrors of hell. He listed nineteen revivals just closed, in process, or announced for the textile belt in the Carolinas, and predicted an invasion by evangelists paid by mill owners. He pointed out that strikebreaking by force, as carried out by employers in other states through professional strikebreakers and gunmen, was very dangerous in the South, where workers have traditions of independence and resistance to tyranny in the Revolution (and, Mr. Mencken might have added, numerous squirrel rifles and shotguns with which to carry on these traditions). "The gospel scheme," he said, "is far more humane. More, it is far cheaper." He figured that it would cost $10,000–$15,000 to put down by force a strike of 400 men, whereas a good (i.e., hell-blazing, trombone-playing) revival would cost only $400–$500.

a relief fund for "worthy workers" victimized by the strike was raised and distributed through the churches in the Loray village. Even the mill owners and executives contributed to it, despite the fact that it was publicly designated as a fund to be used for the relief of strikers.[124]

Except for these few evidences of open opposition, the action of the ministers against the strike consisted of statements of personal opinion and of refusal to coöperate in any way with the strike. Tactics of this sort were even more effective, of course, than public pronouncements would have been. Most of the members of the Gastonia community, including the mill workers, expect religion to keep itself undefiled by things of the world; if the ministers had entered openly into the economic conflict, they might have lost prestige. Instead, they did all things decently and in accepted religious order, and thereby served as a rallying point for return to "normalcy."

The failure of the ministers to condemn mob terrorism and police brutality against the strikers is more significant of their reaction than the positive steps they themselves took against the Communists. Several ministers recall pleasantly stories such as the one of a Baptist minister who was accused, jokingly, of leading a tar party during the strike; he replied that he did not lead it but had said "Amen."

On the night when Chief Aderholt was shot a minister was one of the leaders in the general roundup of strikers that followed. The following day a visiting clergyman interviewed a number of the local ministers; he received from them all similar expressions of indignation against the strike leaders, with one minister summing up clerical opinion in saying that the "organizers ought to be tarred and feathered and thrown into the lake." At the funeral of the chief, however, each of the several preachers having a part advised the use of sane judgment during the days immediately ahead. One of the preachers reminded his hearers that the Lord had said, "Vengeance is mine, . . . I will repay."[125] Sanguinary citizens had urged the ministers to use the occasion to denounce the Communist murderers, but the

124. It has not been possible to secure information revealing how the fund was really used, except the statement that "nobody suffered." One suspects, of course, that the project was a strikebreaking device.

125. Atkins, *op. cit.*, pp. 116–117.

ministers refused. They only "comforted the family" of the "splendid man and officer . . . shot down in line of duty," thereby really personalizing all the more the injury done to the community.

Religion figured prominently in the trial of the strikers indicted for the murder of Chief Aderholt, and ministers and churches played significant roles in the final expulsion of the Communists from the community and in the reorganization of cultural and institutional relationships. These developments must be examined before a final effort is made at assessment of the relation of religious institutions to economic culture in crisis. Here again the processes of expulsion and reorganization will be examined from several angles, in order that the part played by religious institutions may be seen in context and perspective.

CHAPTER XIII

EXPULSION OF THE COMMUNISTS

WITH Beal and fourteen other strike leaders in jail and the strikers scattered and demoralized, Gastonia appeared willing to allow the final expulsion of the "Communist menace" by due judicial process, rather than take matters further into its own hands. There seemed little doubt as to the verdict of any jury that might be selected; it was just as well, therefore, to observe established forms if the end result would be the same. Besides, the prospect of a big trial, as always in small towns, intrigued public interest and provided a relish for conversation in days before its opening. A chronicle of pretrial days in Gastonia says that "it was the one big event [Gastonians] in every walk of life were looking forward to. They wanted to see [Beal] and his co-conspirators die in the electric chair—the sooner, the better."[1]

Public opinion in Gastonia was tempered, further, by the fact that the dramatic circumstances leading up to and attending the shooting of the policemen had attracted the attention of newspapers throughout the nation, and correspondents from nearly thirty of the leading metropolitan dailies of the country were beginning to converge on the scene. Liberal journals like the *Nation* and the *New Republic* were demanding a fair trial, and several North Carolina newspapers, notably the Raleigh *News and Observer*, joined in the demand.[2] It was good strategy, therefore, for Gastonia to concur in preparations for a trial concerned only with the issue of murder; the town had already received more unfavorable publicity than it relished.[3] On

1. J. W. Atkins, MS. "Crimson Tide in Dixie," p. 124. At least some of the citizens of Gastonia, however, and especially among the mill workers, were in favor of acquittal for the defendants. (See Jessie Lloyd, *Gastonia*, pp. 6–7.)

2. See the editorial, "Gastonia and the Honor of the South," *The New Republic*, LIX, 299–300 (August 7, 1929); editorial, "A Just Judge," *New York Times*, August 3, 1929; Nell Battle Lewis' columns, Raleigh *News and Observer*, June–October, 1929. Miss Lewis' column served as a clearinghouse for the opinions of Southern liberals on the Gastonia case. She also sponsored through her column a fund for the legal defense of the defendants.

3. Forrest Bailey, director of the American Civil Liberties Union, noticed this change in public mood in Gastonia between the time of shooting and the

August 26, when the first trial began, the *Gazette* announced: "It is to be a straight murder trial."

The real issue all the while, nevertheless, was the expulsion of the Communists from the community. A North Carolina newspaperman wrote:

To the resident Gastonian there is but one issue. By all the sacred bugs and beasts of ancient Egypt he is determined that no organization which denies God, defies the American flag, and makes a mock marriage shall gain a foothold among 18,000 of the "most contented workers" in the country. All else about the industrial disagreement is as a snowflake upon the river. The resident Gastonian knows that he is defending his home, his God and his country.[4]

The Charlotte *News* echoed the attitude prevalent in Gastonia and revealed the superficiality of local attitudes favoring a trial concerned only with guilt for murder, when it wrote a few days before the trial began:

The leaders of the National Textile Workers Union are Communists and are a menace to all that we hold most sacred. They believe in violence, arson, murder. . . . They are undermining all morality, all religion. But nevertheless they must be given a fair trial, although everyone knows that they deserve to be shot at sunrise.[5]

The city of Gastonia retained Clyde R. Hoey[6] (the most famous lawyer in the region), Major Bulwinkle[7] (the local attorney for Manville-Jenckes), several distinguished Charlotte lawyers, and most of the "leading" attorneys of Gastonia to assist the solicitor in the prosecution. The defense charged that all the lawyers in Gaston County had been retained by the prosecution; the prosecution countered by saying that there were more than forty lawyers in the county. Only one of the

trial, and commented on it in an article, "Gastonia Goes to Trial," *The New Republic,* LIX, 332–334 (August 14, 1929).

4. Quoted by E. W. Knight, "The Lesson of Gastonia," *The Outlook and Independent,* CLIII, 45 (September 11, 1929).

5. Quoted in Paul Porter, "Justice and Chivalry in North Carolina," *The Nation* (August 28, 1929). Also quoted in numerous other accounts of the trial.

6. Later Governor of North Carolina.

7. Formerly, and subsequently, a member of the House of Representatives of the United States Congress.

forty, however, accepted a place on the defense staff. Several Charlotte attorneys, Arthur Garfield Hayes, Dr. John R. Neal (of the Scopes evolution trial), and Leon Josephson were members of the defense staff in one or another of the trials that finally took place.

The trial had been scheduled to begin in Gastonia on July 29, with Judge Barnhill appointed by Governor Gardner as presiding jurist.[8] On July 29 and 30 the judge heard more than 150 affidavits bearing on the possibility of a just trial in Gaston County. Attorneys for the defense produced more than a hundred, supporting their contention that overwhelming prejudice would militate against their clients if the trial were held in Gastonia. They read parts of twenty-four issues of the *Gastonia Gazette*, revealing strong bias; defense attorneys had been threatened on the streets; the long record of violent episodes preceding the murder was reviewed. The prosecution produced sixty-seven affidavits[9] supporting the possibility of a fair trial in Gaston and read articles from the *Daily Worker* which claimed the overwhelming support of Gastonia citizens in the effort to free the defendants. Judge Barnhill granted a change of venue to Charlotte, twenty miles away, and set August 26 as the date for opening the trial.[10]

The major efforts of the Communist party, meanwhile, were shifted from the immediate situation in Gaston County to the remainder of the country, in an effort to raise money for defense of the prisoners. The party depicted the Gastonia case as a crucial test between diabolical forces of imperialistic capitalism and the upward surge of the toiling masses. "Free the Gas-

8. Barnhill had a wide reputation for fairness and impartiality, and was usually dubbed a "liberal." Shortly before the Gastonia trials he had ruled that Negroes must be furnished seats in public buses—a radical decision in the eyes of most North Carolinians.

9. The *Daily Worker* (August 5, 1929) analyzed their sources as follows: 12 real estate and insurance men; 8 professional men; 2 public officials; 40 businessmen; 1 wealthy farmer; 2 workers. The affidavits supporting the defense came mostly from workers, small merchants, and defense attorneys.

10. In a speech made later in the year Judge Barnhill said he discovered, on first going to Gastonia, a surface attempt to keep down feeling and try to maintain that a fair trial would be possible in Gaston County, but that his personal investigations convinced him to the contrary (Raleigh *News and Observer*, November 10, 1929). The city to which Judge Barnhill moved the trial, Charlotte, was likewise dependent chiefly on cotton manufacturing, but was nearly five times as large as Gastonia, having a population of 82,675 in 1930.

tonia Defendants!" and "Smash Imperialist Capitalism!" became coördinate slogans in Communist literature.[11] Mass meetings were held in principal cities throughout the nation and
demonstrations were staged by Communists in the larger cities
throughout the world. Communist propaganda depicted the issue as closely parallel to the Sacco–Vanzetti case, and pleaded
for support lest history be repeated.[12] Money-raising activities
were intensified by the International Labor Defense, which
appealed for funds through advertisements, circulars, postal
cards, tag days, and other such devices.[13] A campaign was
launched for a million signatures of protest against conviction,
at ten cents a signature.

Disagreement arose between party leaders as to the proper
strategy to be pursued in the Gastonia defense. One group
thought the charges should be fought as a capitalist "frame-up";
another insisted that the basic line of defense should uphold the
constitutional right, guaranteed in the Fourth Amendment, of
the strikers to defend their premises "against unreasonable
searches and seizures."[14] On the one hand it was urged that "no

11. *Daily Worker,* June 11, 24, 26, August 14, 16, September 19, 1929; Dunne,
Gastonia, p. 10.

12. See, for example, the *New Masses,* Vol. 5, No. 3, p. 2 (August, 1929),
and Vol. 5, No. 4, pp. 2, 5 (September, 1929).

13. A posttrial report on the funds raised in behalf of the Gastonia defendants set the total at $99,827.16, of which $38,326.80 was reported spent in
courtroom defense, $11,959.64 in relief for strikers and prisoners, and $39,-
506.85 in miscellaneous administrative expense, leaving $10,033.87 unaccounted
for (*Labor Defender,* April, 1930). Matthew Woll told the Fish Committee
that money raised for the Gastonia defense was spent for purposes other than
that for which it was contributed (*Report of the Fish Committee, 1931,* pp.
25–26).

14. Beal, *Proletarian Journey,* p. 185; W. F. Dunne, "Gastonia: A Beginning," *New Masses,* Vol. 5, No. 2, pp. 3–4 (July, 1929); *Daily Worker,* editorials on June 24, 1929, and August 5, 1929. At a conference of party leaders
in New York on June 26, the right of defense of one's premises was selected,
apparently, as the basic line of defense in the trial (*New York Times,* June
27, 1929).

Even in defending the right of the strikers to resist unlawful entry by the
police, however, the Communist leaders brought in political preconceptions.
The following excerpt from an editorial in the *Daily Worker* on June 11 is
representative of the official attitude: "Militant workers the nation over will ap-
plaud the success with which the Gastonia strikers defended their tent colony.
They had not organized their Workers' Defense Corps in vain. Instead of
many men, women and children of the working class massacred, as has too
often been the case in the past, . . . the only fatal casualty was on the side of
the would-be assassins, the attacking police."

worker can receive justice in a capitalist court," and "mass action" of workers was depicted as the only power capable of stopping the "legalized murder" of the Gastonia defendants;[15] on the other, efforts of the prosecution to introduce "extraneous issues" into the trial were denounced, presumably on the assumption that the trial could be a trial for murder only. The party urged support of the defendants in order that the verdict might free them for future leadership; at the same time it held them up as martyrs for the Communist cause.[16] The problem, in short, was whether the trial should be regarded as a judicial process or an opportunity for propaganda, and failure to agree on a solution hampered the defense throughout. In practice, the defense attorneys attempted to confine the trial to legal issues involved, while the Communist leaders used it as a vehicle for party aggrandizement. Thousands of copies of Communist leaflets and pamphlets, attacking the presiding judge, the "fundamentalist" jury, and the "bourbon" prosecutors, were distributed in Charlotte and surrounding territory while the trials were in progress, and mass meetings of textile workers and Communist leaders were projected for the vicinity. A "labor jury," including two Negroes, was sent to the trial to sit in judgment on the case, further antagonizing public opinion.[17] National Textile Workers Union organizers continued to agitate in the region, with numerous arrests and stormy episodes resulting. The struggle now lay, however, almost completely in the political sphere.

Between the propaganda of newspapers in Gastonia and Charlotte and that coming from Communist sources, it was virtually impossible to select a jury for the trial, which began in Charlotte on August 26. The selection of a jury required nine days and the examination of 408 veniremen. Prospective jurors were examined as to their beliefs about trade unions, God,

15. Presumably "mass action" was to be effective either through open revolution in North Carolina or through frightening the capitalists who controlled the courts; Communist statements on this score are extremely hortatory in character but vague in specification of techniques.

16. Compare statements in Dunne, *Gastonia*, p. 9, and Fred E. Beal, "I Was a Communist Martyr," *The American Mercury*, Vol. XLII, No. 165, pp. 32–45 (September, 1937).

17. The final verdict of this jury, of course, was, "Not guilty of anything besides organizing the workers."

Northerners, and the sanctity of the family and of private property. Most of them expressed belief in the guilt of the defendants, "especially Beal." Nearly all those examined belonged to some church, and several ventured the opinion that a person who has no religion would be more likely to commit murder. North Carolina law required that jurors must be property owners. Of the veniremen questioned, about 60 per cent admitted prejudice against the defendants, about 15 per cent were dubious as to their guilt, and about 25 per cent had no definite opinions on the question, despite the barrage of propaganda that had been laid down by each side.[18] Even those veniremen whose apparent lack of prejudice made them eligible for jury service on the case were carefully scrutinized and usually dismissed by peremptory challenges, of which the state used 54 (of 58 allowed) and the defense 128 (of 168 allowed). The jury finally selected was composed of 7 workers (1 was a textile worker; 2 belonged to trade unions), 4 tenant farmers, and 1 grocery clerk; all but 2 were married, and all but 2 were church members.

A mistrial was declared on September 9, when a juror, previously suspected of mental deficiency, went insane. The solicitor had brought into the courtroom a life-size wax model of the murdered chief of police, in the clothes he had worn at the time of the shooting and, though immediately ordered by the judge to remove it from the room, had exploited its features and wounds before the jury, amid the weeping of the chief's family. This stratagem, perhaps inspired by a similar episode in a movie which had been shown in the vicinity shortly before, is generally given credit for driving the weak-minded juryman insane.

Several of the jurors, interviewed by the press, declared that in view of the evidence presented thus far they had been in favor of acquittal. This fact, coupled with the temporary thwarting of the desires of Gastonia citizens for speedy execution of the defendants and the fear of Gastonia taxpayers that the ex-

18. One cannot help but speculate as to the "intelligence" of any jury that could be chosen from this eligible 25 per cent. At least one of those chosen had never heard of Aderholt, despite wide publicity and discussion of the case. Another was generally regarded in the community as being mentally unbalanced.

tension of the judicial process would add to taxation, led to a new outbreak of mob violence on the night of the mistrial and during subsequent days.[19]

EXPULSION THROUGH MOB VIOLENCE

The Communists did not accept the roundup of strikers and destruction of the tent colony after June 7 as an evidence of defeat in their campaign among the mill workers of Gaston County. New organizers were sent into the county to take the place of those in jail, and a new tent colony was erected on another site, at which remnants of the strikers were gathered. Numerous attempts were made to hold union meetings in mill communities, especially in South Gastonia, leading on several occasions to minor conflicts between Communist organizers and the police or agents of the employers. Communist views on racial equality and religion were displayed more flagrantly than formerly.[20] Thousands of leaflets and copies of the *Daily Worker* and *Labor Defender* were distributed in Gaston County between June 7 and October 15, capitalizing on the interest in various courtroom proceedings during that period. Southern conferences of the National Textile Workers Union were held in Bessemer City (in Gaston County) on July 28, the day before the first hearings before Judge Barnhill were scheduled, and in Charlotte on October 12, during the last trial of the Gastonia defendants.

For reasons already noted, further acts of violence against the Communists were avoided by Gastonia citizens while the legal process against the strike leaders was pending. When the original process ended in a mistrial, however, Gaston employers and citizens felt that the Communists had gained a temporary victory, at the very least, and proceeded to take the effort at

19. Gaston County commissioners had already set aside $50,000 to cover the expenses of troops, deputies, and legal investigations, and it was feared, when the original process ended in a mistrial, that even this amount would not suffice to see the business through (Robin Hood, "The Loray Mill Strike" [M.A. thesis, University of North Carolina, 1932], p. 135). For Gastonia's reaction to the mistrial, see also Atkins, *op. cit.*, p. 138.

20. One day, for example, one of the organizers kicked a Bible out of the hands of a resident of the new tent colony and said, "No one believes that book now" (Hood, *op. cit.*, p. 131). Another organizer announced at a meeting in Charlotte that he would rather have his sister marry a Negro than some white men.

expulsion again into their own hands.[21] On the night of the mistrial about a hundred automobiles filled with citizens of Gastonia staged a caravan through Gaston and adjoining counties, wrecking N.T.W.U. and I.L.D. headquarters and terrorizing organizers. Singing "Praise God from Whom All Blessings Flow," the mob rushed into a boardinghouse in Gastonia, seized three N.T.W.U. organizers, and carried them into an adjoining county, where they were beaten and abandoned. Another part of the caravan visited Charlotte, seeking for additional organizers and for attorneys for the defense in the trial just ended, but found that their intended prey had been forewarned. The *Charlotte Observer* reported that two carloads of Gaston peace officers accompanied the caravan, and it was charged, though it is disputed, that the solicitor and at least one other attorney for the prosecution were among its leaders.[22] Counsel for the State subsequently termed the outbreak most unfortunate, but the *Gastonia Gazette* asked, "Is it so unlawful to protect . . . one's children?"[23]

The Communists immediately called a mass meeting of textile workers for South Gastonia on the following Saturday afternoon, September 14. On Wednesday, September 11, the *Gastonia Gazette* took notice of this announcement and warned: "They [the Communists] have been warned to stay away. If they persist in coming, they do so at their own risk. That is the word from the good people of that community [South Gastonia] who have been law-abiding about as long as they can stand it." Members of the American Legion were deputized to close all roads leading to South Gastonia on the date set. Seven N.T.W.U. organizers were thrown into jail in Charlotte over the week end, allegedly for "insurrection to overthrow the government of North Carolina," but really to confine their movements, apparently, as they were dismissed for lack of evidence the following week. Several incidents of violence marked the prevention of the meeting set for September 14. Communist organizers still at large were arrested on slight legal pretexts. A

21. Atkins, *op. cit.*, p. 138.
22. *Ibid.*, pp. 138–143; Beal, *Proletarian Journey*, pp. 190–191; *Charlotte Observer*, September 10, 1929; *Daily Worker*, September 11, 1929. Affidavits and counteraffidavits were filed concerning the alleged presence of the two attorneys in the mob.
23. *Gastonia Gazette*, September 12, 1929.

truck filled with workers from a neighboring village was turned back as it approached South Gastonia,[24] and was subsequently pursued and forced off the highway by an automobile filled with "faithful employees" and minor officials of the Loray mill. Shots were fired into the truck and at occupants who had deserted the truck and were fleeing across the fields, and Ella May Wiggins, favorite ballad maker and songstress of the Loray strike, was killed.

The reign of terror continued in Gaston County for about ten days.[25] Freedom of assemblage was suppressed. Another N.T.W.U. organizer was kidnapped and taken into South Carolina, where he was beaten and warned not to return to Gaston County. A speaking platform used by Communist organizers was destroyed by dynamite. Not until September 20, when the union suspended all activities in the county, did the wave of violence end. By September 27 the tent colony had been abandoned, union leaders had officially pronounced the Loray strike at an end, and workers who had accepted Communist leadership were scattered throughout neighboring counties and states. One or two isolated incidents involving Communist organizers occurred in the county later in the year but were of no importance. Reaction against the Communist invasion was, at last, completely successful; the "troublemakers" were expelled from the county.[26]

No open criticism of the methods by which they were expelled was forthcoming in Gaston County. No convictions were ever obtained for the floggings of organizers; in one instance where arrests were made acquittal was easily obtained on the general theory that the Communists had fabricated the entire affair as a publicity stunt. A Gaston County Grand Jury failed to

24. A Gastonia minister was one of the embattled citizens who turned back this particular truck. An American Legionnaire reports that he and other members of the Legion had been instructed by the mayor of Gastonia to "preserve peace and protect themselves, shooting if necessary."

25. For a graphic description by an observer close to the situation, see Nell Battle Lewis, "Anarchy vs. Communism in Gastonia," *The Nation*, CXXIX, 321–322 (September 25, 1929).

26. Though offices and organizers were maintained for a time in larger cities, the Communists' drive in the South was temporarily broken by the failure at Gastonia. The publicity accruing to their efforts there had effectively warned Southern workers against them; attempts of N.T.W.U. organizers to inject themselves into the Marion strike late in 1929 and the Danville strike in 1930 were unsuccessful.

return true bills of indictment against anybody in connection with the murder of Ella May Wiggins. Severe criticism followed throughout the state and nation, and six weeks later, on October 26, Governor Gardner assigned a special judge and prosecutor to reopen investigations into the outbreak of lawlessness and the death of Mrs. Wiggins.[27] Five employees of the Loray mill were indicted for the murder of Mrs. Wiggins; the Manville-Jenckes Company furnished bail for them. The *Gastonia Gazette* and attorneys for the defense protested vigorously when the presiding judge moved the Wiggins trial to Charlotte, saying that this procedure intimated that Gaston County would not give justice. On March 6, 1930, all five defendants were acquitted. Though the murder had been committed in daylight, with at least fifty persons present, no conviction was ever secured.

So far as memories are reliable, no minister in Gaston County commented publicly on the death of Mrs. Wiggins or on the failure to secure conviction of the parties responsible. Privately, one of them reports, the ministers thought her murder was "a calamity, as it was bad publicity for the town." Ministers figured, nevertheless, in the Wiggins case. Two Methodist ministers announced at her funeral that her five unkempt children would be received into a near-by orphanage the next day. This move represented a defeat for the Communists, who had planned to take the children to the North as Southern Textile Exhibit No. 1; a newspaper correspondent wrote that Wesley had outgeneraled Marx. Workers spoke at her funeral, one of them saying: "You all knew our sister, Ella May. She was one of our best workers, and we'll feel her loss, I reckon. Her death is on Manville-Jenckes and on North Carolina, too. She died for us and the union. We must go on fighting. . . ."[28] Instead of a hymn, one of the strike songs Ella May had composed was sung. But an orthodox Baptist minister had the last word; he abstained from all reference to the circumstances of

27. Edwin Gill, compiler, *Public Papers and Letters of Oliver Max Gardner* (Raleigh, 1937), pp. 492–494, 496–497.

The American Civil Liberties Union offered a reward of $1,000 for information leading to the conviction of the murderer of Mrs. Wiggins, and also employed a special investigator, according to its pamphlet, *Justice—North Carolina Style* (New York, 1930).

28. Margaret Larkin, "Ella May's Songs," *The Nation*, CXXIX, 382–383 (October 9, 1929).

Mrs. Wiggins' death but read from the Bible, "In my Father's house are many mansions. . . ." The same correspondent wrote that thus Roger Williams vanquished Marx.[29]

The Wiggins trial ended the long series of criminal actions growing out of the Gastonia strikes, though several appeals were still pending. A North Carolina newspaperman wrote in summary: "In every case where strikers were put on trial strikers were convicted; in not one case where anti-unionists or officers were accused has there been a conviction."[30]

THE FINAL TRIAL

With the Communist campaign in Gaston County at an end, the second trial of the strike leaders was rather an anticlimax. At its beginning, on September 30, the solicitor announced that the State would ask for a verdict of guilty of not more than second-degree murder against seven defendants, including Beal, and would grant a judgment of nol-pros with leave against the remaining eight defendants, among them the three women who had been under indictment. With the women out of the way, and the reduction of the number of peremptory challenges available for the defense from 168 to 28 (because of the reduction in the number of defendants), and the indictment reduced from first- to second-degree murder, the prosecution dropped its former mask of "fair play" toward the defendants and pressed for a sure conviction. The legal issue, as in the first trial, was that of an unlawful conspiracy among the strikers, out of which the murder of Aderholt was alleged by the State to have grown.[31]

Analysis of the economic alignment of the witnesses who appeared on each side of the case reveals to some degree the character of the forces opposing each other throughout the Gas-

29. Atkins, *op. cit.*, pp. 153–154.

30. Weimar Jones, "Southern Labor and the Law," *The Nation,* CXXXI, 16 (July 2, 1930). For a similar résumé of the discrepancies between justice for strikers and for their opponents in the Gastonia strike, see Frederic Nelson, "North Carolina Justice," *The New Republic,* LX, 314–316 (November 6, 1929).

31. *Transcript of Testimony of "State v. Fred Erwin Beal, W. M. McGinnis, Louis McLaughlin, George Carter, Joseph Harrison, K. Y. Hendricks, Clarence Miller, et als." for Review by the Supreme Court of North Carolina, Spring Term, 1930, No. 456.* A mimeographed document of 419 pages, this is a record of the testimony of the second trial.

It will be referred to hereinafter as *Trial Transcript.*

tonia strike and trials, whether or not it indicates anything as
to the credibility of the evidence offered. The prosecution presented a total of 49 witnesses, of whom 14 were law-enforcement
officers or members of their families, 10 were professional people
(including 1 minister), 8 were merchants, 10 were skilled workers and craftsmen, and 5 were ordinary mill workers. Ten of the
49, including 4 of the mill workers, were in the employ of the
Manville-Jenckes Company at the time of the trial. Only 1 of
the 49 had belonged to the union; he had subsequently withdrawn from it, and gone back to work at Loray. The defense
presented 22 witnesses, of whom all but 2 were, or had been,
mill workers or organizers for the N.T.W.U. Thirteen of the
22 had been active members of the union.[32]

It is not surprising, in view of this alignment of witnesses,
that the evidence presented by the two sides was highly contradictory in character. No clear impression comes from a reread-
ing of the evidence, except that there was shooting on the night
of June 7, in which the strikers admittedly participated. The
source of the shot, or shots, that struck Aderholt was never
specified.[33] As to the basic charge of conspiracy, the State
proved that the strike leaders had advised their followers to resist officers, while the defense proved that the defendants had
done nothing of the kind but had been perfectly within their
rights in defending their property against an unlawful invasion by police officers.

The real issues on which the trial was fought, however, were
not those of conspiracy or murder but the Communist attitudes
toward politics, race, unionization, and religion. The jury had
been drawn altogether from outside the industrial township of
Charlotte, with a resultant composition of nine farmers, one
rural mail carrier, a Ford employee, and a retired businessman.
When the contradictory character of the evidence began to be
apparent, the prosecution adopted tactics of attempting to dis-

32. Analysis made from evidence contained in the *Trial Transcript*.
33. To this day there is a persistent rumor among mill workers to the effect
that Chief Aderholt was shot by a policeman who coveted his job. The effect of
only two of the shots in the general shooting on the night of June 7 was specified at the trials, and neither of them struck Chief Aderholt. Most Gastonians
will admit now that the chief may quite easily have been shot accidentally by
one of his own men, in the semidarkness and confusion of the general shooting.
Two of his officers are known to have been drinking fairly heavily a few hours
before they accompanied him to the tent colony.

credit defense witnesses and the defendants themselves by appeal to the culture prejudices of the jury. Attorneys for the State sought to bring in the issue of Communism, citing the Sacco–Vanzetti case as a precedent for the admissibility of such testimony. They attempted to exploit alleged sexual irregularities of defense witnesses, and had a field day when one striker, a former divinity student, admitted that he had once inquired as to the symptoms of syphilis. Communist teachings on racial equality were introduced, as were attitudes toward the overthrow of the Government of the United States and the substitution of a Soviet form of government.[34] When counsel for the defense objected, Judge Barnhill ruled that such testimony, though irrelevant and immaterial to the charge of murder, might be brought in to help determine the credibility of the witnesses.

The issue arousing most controversy concerned the admissibility of evidence about Communistic atheism, and in this connection the prevailing religious mores became heavily involved.

RELIGION IN THE TRIAL

Attempts to establish religious unbelief, as one of the issues for which the Gastonia defendants would be tried, had appeared at a habeas corpus hearing in Charlotte on June 18, when several Communist witnesses had been interrogated by prosecution attorneys as to their belief in God.[35] The disposition to include religious heresy among the crimes of the Communists had subsided by the time of the hearings on August 26; on that day the *Gastonia Gazette* approved the policy of resisting the injection of "the matter of beliefs, religious, political, economic, or of any other type," into evidence. The presiding judge ruled that there would be but one issue before the court: "Are the defendants guilty as charged?" All would come into court on an equality, he said, and none has "any right to expect to be either exalted or condemned, to receive either more or less than is just, on account of his race, color, or condition in life, or by reasons

34. Beal answered "No" when asked if he advocated the overthrow of the government by force. Mrs. Edith Saunders Miller, Communist leader from New York, followed Beal on the stand, however, and flaunted undiluted Communist doctrines before the jury (*Trial Transcript*, pp. 252–256).

35. Raleigh *News and Observer*, July 30, 1929; *Daily Worker*, June 19, 1929; Beal, *Proletarian Journey*, pp. 175–176.

of his convictions upon social, economic, industrial, political or religious matters." Liberals rejoiced at such tokens of an impartial, judicial temper; a reporter wrote approvingly that "God and Karl Marx are not to be tried." The Communists continued to scoff at such patent deceptions and "cheap capitalist tricks."[36]

Extraneous issues—if such issues as religion and politics are extraneous—were kept out of the first trial for the most part, though they figured prominently, as has been seen, in the selection of the jury. Between the time of the mistrial and the opening of the second trial, a judge sitting in a criminal procedure in a neighboring county completely excluded the testimony of a Communist who declared himself an atheist.[37] When the prosecution needed additional support in the second Gastonia trial, therefore, it had a precedent on which to press for the admissibility of evidence concerning religious views. After consideration, Judge Barnhill ruled that such evidence might be introduced for purposes of impeaching the credibility of testimony, but not to exclude it.[38] He is reported to have said: "If I believed that life ends with death and that there is no punishment after death, I would be less apt to tell the truth."[39]

One defense witness had no reticence in airing her scorn of religious beliefs. The following exchange took place between an attorney for the prosecution and Mrs. Edith Saunders Miller, who had worked with the Loray strikers' children:[40]

36. See the *Daily Worker,* June 24, August 1, 4, 5, 6, 16, 22, September 2, 1929, for denunciation of alleged "fairness" in Judge Barnhill's court as a liberal snare and delusion, perpetrated to hide the real class nature of the issue involved. Liberal publications and individuals deplored the attitude of the Communists toward the trial, feeling that it prejudiced the chances of the defendants; e.g., Forrest Bailey, "Gastonia Goes to Trial," *The New Republic,* LIX, 332–334 (August 14, 1929) and Joseph Shaplen, "Strikers, Mills, and Murder," *Survey Midmonthly,* LXII, 595–596 (September 15, 1929).

37. This decision was based on the North Carolina "Statute of Oaths" of 1777, which stipulated that a witness must believe in divine punishment after death to qualify as a witness.

38. *Trial Transcript,* p. 315. In a speech later in the year Judge Barnhill deplored the insistence of the state on introduction of such evidence (Raleigh *News and Observer,* November 10, 1929).

39. The *Christian Century* said, concerning 'this statement: "As a confession of the type of motivation by which his own conduct is controlled, this statement is not without interest. . . ." (XLVI, 1335 [October 30, 1929]).

40. Beal charges that Mrs. Miller was instructed by Communist party officials to use the witness chair as an opportunity to spread Communist propa-

Q. Have you not taught in Gastonia that there is no God?

COURT. I am admitting it as it may tend to impeach her testimony, and for that purpose only.

Q. Mrs. Miller, I ask you this question—Do you believe in the existence of a Supreme Being who controls the destiny of men, who rewards their virtue, or punishes their transgressions here or hereafter?

Objection; overruled; exception.

A. No, I believe that man controls his own destiny.

Q. Therefore, taking an oath and appealing to this Supreme Being would have no effect on you?

A. I say any oath I take to tell the truth has a binding effect on me.

Q. When you take it on the Bible and appeal to God, would that have any effect on you?

A. Yes, it is an oath. Any oath will have an effect on me.

Q. You might take it on an almanac just as you would on a Bible and it would have the same effect on you, wouldn't it?[41]

A. Yes—I'd tell the truth.[42]

ganda (Fred E. Beal, Interview, Caledonia Prison, September 20, 1939). The Communists claim, to the contrary, that Mrs. Miller was instructed to discuss such issues freely in order that the defense might have better grounds on which to appeal to a higher court, in case the defendants were found guilty.

41. This question represents a curious historical irony. Zeb Spencer, after whom one of the small mountains in Gaston County is named, was a prominent Tory in the county during the Revolutionary War. Captured by some of his more patriotic neighbors, and condemned to be shot, he promised allegiance to the Revolutionary cause if he were spared, and took an oath to that effect. In the absence of a Bible, he took the oath on an old almanac, and was allowed to live. (O. L. Kiser, "The Growth and Development of Education in Gaston County" [M.A. thesis, University of North Carolina, 1928], pp. 4, 5; *Gastonia Gazette,* April 1, 1910, p. 6.) The attorneys who denied, by implication, the legitimacy of similar procedure 150 years later apparently knew nothing of this Revolutionary precedent.

It is also somewhat ironical that Gaston County should consent to persecution on account of religion, in view of the fact that the county was named after William Gaston, who, as associate judge of the Supreme Court of North Carolina, made a famous speech in 1835 against religious distinction as a basis for officeholding. His speech was largely instrumental in causing a religious disability clause to be stricken from the state constitution.

Communists who testified before the Fish Committee during the subsequent year consistently refused to take an oath, disavowing belief in a Supreme Being and refusing to concur in "bourgeois hypocrisy" by taking an oath unsupported by belief. They were allowed to affirm (*Report of the Fish Committee, 1931,* p. 53).

42. *Trial Transcript,* p. 262.

Leaders of the Communist party rejoiced in this testimony, arguing that it proved the trial to be really a class fight, in which desperate mill owners would use all available weapons to send the union organizers to prison. On October 19 an editorial in the *Daily Worker* exulted:

The working class and its vanguard fighters, the Communists, . . . glory in the opportunity to use the sounding board of the court-room to convey a real Communist, a real proletarian challenge to the fascist reaction, knowing that only by so doing can the pro-letariat receive the enlightenment that equips them for struggle to victory. Such was the clear-sighted attitude of Comrade Edith Saunders Miller. . . . This Communist working woman sought to tear off the blindfolds of religion and capitalist ideas from the masses. In so doing she did her Communist duty. . . . Nor did she hesitate to declare her disbelief in the superstition of religion in the center of "fundamentalist" ignorance, upholding the scientific view held by all Communists that mankind is master of its own destiny with no room for god, angels and devils and that no threats of hell or hopes of heaven, but a social ethic, was the only consid-eration shaping her testimony.

The admission of testimony concerning religious belief aroused criticism from numerous sources throughout the na-tion. The *New Republic*, which had hitherto supported Judge Barnhill against the jibes of the Communists, deplored this de-fection, and asked, with respect to fear of hell as an inducement to telling the truth, "Should a man who believes in a forgiving God be allowed to testify in North Carolina?"[43] The New York *World* pointed out that under Barnhill's ruling the testimony of Unitarian Chief Justice Taft, Jefferson, Lincoln, Emerson, and all Universalists and Christian Scientists would be im-peachable.[44] Heywood Broun argued that "the Christianity of the Carolina lawyers . . . would make God an instrument of legal procedure, like a writ or an injunction. After all, theirs was the greater blasphemy."[45] Lawyers discussed the legal

43. *The New Republic,* LX, 280 (October 30, 1929).
44. For a summary of opinions, see *The Literary Digest,* "Can Atheists Be Believed under Oath?", CIII, 22–23 (November 9, 1929).
45. In his syndicated column, "It Seems to Me," on October 31, 1929.

points involved.[46] The *Christian Century* designated the judge's ruling as "bad justice and bad religion," pointing out that the prestige of hell has waned in the last century and a half as a deterrent to lies, and that a Universalist may be as trustworthy as a Southern Baptist. It called on the churches of North Carolina to make it their "instant business" to repeal laws which made a decision of this sort possible.[47]

No protests came from churches or ministers in Gaston County, however, and no action to change the situation. No records or memories survive of ministerial comments of any type. Editors and "liberals" looking at the situation from a different cultural angle could hardly understand how completely logical it was, from the standpoint of cultural interrelationships in Gaston County, that the atheism of the Communists should be used against them. Whether logical or not, of course, this procedure would doubtless have been employed by the prosecution if its use promised to be advantageous. It was all the more effective because it seemed perfectly reasonable. In terms of the cultural standards by which the jurymen[48] and the citizens of Gaston County necessarily judged culpability, the religious, political, and economic orthodoxy or heterodoxy of persons accused was a matter of considerable importance.[49] Na-

46. J. Crawford Biggs, "Religious Belief as Qualification of a Witness," *North Carolina Law Review,* December, 1929; "The Gastonia Strikers' Case," *Harvard Law Review,* XLIV, 1118–1124 (May, 1931).

47. Editorial, "Religion as a Cloak for Injustice," *The Christian Century,* XLVI, 1334–1335 (October 30, 1929).

Another North Carolina judge, sitting on a case involving Communist witnesses in a county adjoining Gaston, reversed Judge Barnhill's ruling a few days later, on the ground that the Fourteenth Amendment had abrogated all common-law provisions nullifying oaths for disbelief. Could a murderer not be prosecuted, he asked, if the only eyewitness were an atheist?

48. Eleven of the twelve jurymen were described by observers on both sides of the case as "staunch churchmen." All of them were necessarily property owners and taxpayers.

49. The assumption that such matters should not figure in a trial for a specific offense is comforting to individuals and minority groups, but often makes little sense from the standpoint of a dominant culture. One strand in the American tradition holds that all such matters are of purely individual concern, and shall not be infringed upon by external compulsion unless, according to the judicial modification enunciated by Justice Brandeis in 1927, revolutionary utterances may be put into effect so imminently that drastic changes occur before there is opportunity for full discussion (J. M. Landis, "Freedom of Speech and of the Press," *Encyclopaedia of the Social Sciences* [New York, 1931], VI,

tives resented criticism by "busybodies" from New York who
"did not understand the local situation." A cartoon that appeared in *New Masses* shortly after the trial ended would have
appeared logical to Gastonia citizens as well as to Communists,
but from the opposite standpoint: a judge and jury were depicted leaning over a witness in the witness chair, while a frock-
coated, pin-striped, high-collared lawyer[50] asked him: "Do you
believe in God and good roads?"[51] God and good roads and cotton mills and contented labor and legal justice were all closely
connected in the culture of Gaston County in 1929.

Whether justly or not, the trial of the Gastonia defendants
turned into a heresy trial. The decision of the judge to allow
religious testimony helps to account for the refusal of the defense to put several other defendants, especially those who were
avowed atheists, on the stand, and the trial was considerably
shortened.

Religion entered prominently into the final summations by
attorneys for the prosecution, and especially into the speech to
the jury by the solicitor, a resident of Gastonia. Wide latitude
is allowed in summations in North Carolina courts; the solicitor
took full advantage of it.[52] He impersonated the dying chief.
He canonized the dead chief. He knelt and prayed and sobbed
before the jury, as if at Aderholt's deathbed.[53] He seized the
hand of the weeping widow, handed her the shot-torn coat of
her husband, and in a broken voice, freighted with all the empti-
ness of the future, told her to take it home. He spoke of "scenes

458). But there is little difficulty in understanding why, from a cultural point
of view, "private" beliefs of this sort are continually used against persons who
have infracted other mores of a community. Religious, political, and economic
orthodoxy seem no less important to a community than the lives of a police
officer or two.

As William Graham Sumner put it,. "He who adopts the mores of another
group is a heinous criminal" (*Folkways* [Boston, 1907], p. 103). Sumner's dic-
tum is false only in a society having a high degree of social mobility and cultural flexibility, or in a society in process of rapid cultural disintegration. Gastonia in 1929 was in neither of these positions.

50. A caricature of an "old school" Southern lawyer.

51. *New Masses*, Vol. 5, No. 7, p. 5 (December, 1929).

52. His speech to the jury has been referred to subsequently by the North
Carolina Supreme Court as the mode of summation especially likely to prejudice a jury.

53. One North Carolina newspaper—the *Greensboro Daily News*—still refers
to the solicitor habitually as "Wallowing John."

of debauchery" at the strikers' headquarters, and referred to mill owners, policemen, and other "respectable" citizens of Gastonia as "God-fearing, upright, Christian gentlemen."[54] As to the yarn made in Gastonia,

Why, you could wrap it around the sun sixteen times, around the moon thirteen times, around Mercury, Venus, and Saturn, stretch it from San Francisco to southernmost Africa and right back to Gastonia. . . .

Biblical references were numerous:

Moses paid for his act by wandering and doing penance for forty years. Do your duty, men. Make these men do penance for their crime by thirty years in the penitentiary. . . .

I'll ask you to send these defendants to the penitentiary for thirty years in order that they may repent and find light in the Word of God before they come to the end of the trail. . . .

Believing in God, believing in Paul, the God-fearing, law-abiding prosecution of this district of North Carolina gives to you [the jury] its bleeding heart and tender sympathy. . . .

In an impassioned appeal the solicitor summed up the charge against the defendants, saying to the jury:

Do you believe in the flag of your country, floating in the breeze, kissing the sunlight, singing the song of freedom? Do you believe in North Carolina? Do you believe in good roads, the good roads of North Carolina on which the heaven-bannered hosts could walk as far as San Francisco? . . . Gastonia—into which the union organizers came, fiends incarnate, stripped of their hoofs and horns, bearing guns instead of pitchforks. . . . They came into peaceful, contented Gastonia, with its flowers, birds, and churches . . . sweeping like a cyclone and tornado to sink damnable fangs into the heart and lifeblood of my community. . . . They [the people of Gastonia] stood it till the great God looked down from the very battlements of heaven and broke the chains

54. He specifically included the two policemen known to have been drunk shortly before they arrived at the tent colony. He repudiated as absurd the contention of the defense that another of the policemen involved had "slept in a church one night with a horse."

and traces of their patience and caused them to call the officers to
the lot and stop the infernal scenes that came sweeping down from
the wild plains of Soviet Russia into the peaceful community of
Gastonia, bringing bloodshed and death, creeping like the hellish
serpent into the Garden of Eden. . . .[55]

Counsel for the defense objected several times to this summation, and on at least one occasion the judge stopped the solicitor and directed him to stay within the record.[56] Court was re-
cessed for the week end as soon as this ringing speech was
finished. When the jury was sent out on Monday, October 21,
to arrive at a verdict, no one doubted, according to a Gastonia
observer, which way it would decide.[57] It returned in less than
an hour with a verdict of guilty. The judge imposed sentences
of seventeen to twenty years in state's prison on the four defendants from the North, including Beal, sentences of twelve to
fifteen years on two of the others, and a sentence of five to seven
years on the remaining one.[58]

Counsel for the defendants had taken a total of 159 exceptions to the rulings and interpretations of the court during the
trial, and these were used as a basis for appeal to the Supreme
Court of North Carolina.[59] This body handed down its decision
in August, 1930, finding no error: "The State made out a
prima facie case of conspiracy against the defendants. . . . We
are convinced that substantial justice has been done."[60] As to
the permissibility of questioning a witness about religion in order to impeach testimony, the court said that North Carolina
had no statute covering the exact question, and referred it back
to the lower courts. While admitting that "many sins have been
committed in the name of religion," the justices felt that the
testimony admitted in the Gastonia case had not brought appreciable harm to the defendants. At the same time the court
revealed its own disposition in saying: "Ours is a religious
people. This is historically true. American life everywhere, as

55. For summaries of this speech, from which these excerpts were taken, see
the *New York Times,* October 19, 1929.

56. *Trial Transcript,* p. 376.   57. Atkins, *op. cit.,* p. 166.

58. *Trial Transcript,* pp. 15–19.

59. The Exceptions are recapitulated on pages 381–419 of the *Trial Transcript.*

60. *North Carolina Supreme Court Cases,* CXCIX, 294, 305 (spring term,
1930).

expressed by its laws, its business, its customs, its society, gives abundant recognition and proof of the fact."[61]

The defendants forfeited the bail which had been posted for them and fled to Russia.[62] Four are presumably still there, one has died, and one has returned and served his sentence—the shortest imposed. Beal spent several years in the Soviet Union, was disillusioned, and returned to the United States. After several years as a fugitive he was captured and taken to prison in North Carolina in 1938. Application for a pardon was made in his behalf in June, 1939,[63] but was denied by the governor.[64] There was no organized protest from Gaston County against Beal's release, except a resolution from one civic club; most citizens were simply noncommittal. Most newspapers in North Carolina have been disposed favorably toward parole, if not pardon;[65] the most unequivocal statement in opposition has

61. *Ibid.*, p. 300.

62. Bail had been set at a total of $27,000 for the seven defendants, and had been posted chiefly by the American Civil Liberties Union, which opposed its forfeiture. The Central Committee of the Communist party in the United States also opposed, publicly, though it must have condoned the flight privately, as the defendants were welcomed in Russia.

The *Southern Textile Bulletin* had expressed inability to understand the "exceedingly small bonds" required by the court and had predicted that the defendants would forfeit them (October 24, 1929). Beal professes to believe that the authorities in North Carolina purposely set the bonds at a low figure in order to encourage the defendants to get out of the state (*Proletarian Journey*, p. 209).

63. MS. "Application of Fred E. Beal for a Pardon: Brief in Support of Petitions. Submitted June 8, 1939, to his Excellency, The Governor of North Carolina" (Typewritten, pp. ii, 107. On file in the office of Edwin Gill, Parole Commissioner, State of North Carolina, Raleigh, N.C.).

Several hundred signatures, only two of which represent residents of the South, are appended to the application, including fifty well-known ministers (one from the South) and a number of famous writers, educators, A.F. of L. leaders, and prominent citizens. Opinions are quoted from Professors Gardner Murphy of Columbia, Gordon Allport of Harvard, Ernest R. Hilgard of Stanford, psychologists, and Drs. Walter Bromberg and Sandor Lorand, practicing psychiatrists, indicating that an average American jury would not be able to decide a case strictly on its merits if issues of unpatriotism, Communism, and irreligion were prominently brought into the case (pp. 23–28). The petition ends with Scripture: ". . . joy shall be in heaven over one sinner that repenteth"—Beal has repented of Communism (p. 107).

64. The governor, Clyde R. Hoey, had been a member of the prosecution staff in the trial. Before leaving office in 1940 he cut seven years off the sentence imposed on Beal but refused either parole or pardon.

65. See, for example, editorials in the *Greensboro Daily News*, June 10, 1939; *High Point Enterprise*, June 9, 1939; cf. Jonathan Daniels, "A Native at Large," *The Nation*, December 14, 1940.

come from the *North Carolina Christian Advocate,* official organ of the Methodist church in the state:

Beal discovered some years ago that the times were out of joint over about Gastonia and that he had been born to set them right. And he began by murdering a brave officer of the law "who was in line of duty." Then this murderer hied away to Russia, which to him was "The Paradise of God." But he learned that prison life in this country is to be preferred to life in Soviet Russia. So Beal from choice returned to America and is now serving his sentence in the Raleigh prison. And according to our judgment he should serve full time. If Governor Hoey cuts a day from his term we will be unable to credit him with the good horse sense that we have been accustomed to think that he possessed.[66]

With or without "good horse sense," the next governor paroled Beal in January, 1942, after the prisoner had served about four years of his sentence.

66. *North Carolina Christian Advocate,* LXXXIV (No. 22), 3 (June 1, 1939).

CHAPTER XIV

CULTURAL REINTEGRATION

POSTSTRIKE developments in the Loray mill village and in Gaston County do not permit precise delineation of the final effects of the strike on the community, as the depression of 1929–33 came soon after the Communists had been driven from the county, disturbing normal processes of readjustment. Certain lines of evidence are significant, however, for an understanding of the interrelationships of the churches and the cotton mills in cultural reintegration.

THE LORAY MILL AND VILLAGE

As already noted,[1] executives of the Loray mill had begun to moderate the harsh and arbitrary methods of the stretch-out before the strike began, and their efforts to regain control over labor were renewed after its conclusion. These efforts followed traditional patterns and presuppositions. A company union was thrown up, giving the pretense of industrial democracy without its actuality. A recreational camp for employees was completed on a lake a few miles from the village, to which employees might take their families for week ends and outings. Most significantly of all, the mill changed its employment regulations after the strike, enlisting the services of the ministers in the village in what the mill superintendent described as an effort to develop "the finest and most efficient group of operatives in the South."[2] Each applicant for a job in the mill was required to submit recommendations from his minister and from other responsible parties (usually his grocer and his last employer), attesting to his moral character and honesty. Ministers in the Loray village were used as intermediaries for securing information about each applicant from his former minister. This system worked so well, according to mill executives and

1. See chap. xi.
2. Robin Hood, "The Loray Mill Strike" (M.A. thesis, University of North Carolina, 1932), p. 175, report of an interview with the mill superintendent in July, 1930.

Loray ministers, that it was continued for nearly ten years.[3] In addition, a full-time employment manager—a man who had been a spy in the union throughout the strike—was appointed by the mill to make sure that no "troublemakers" found their way back into employment there, and a system of physical examinations and personnel records for all applicants was instituted.

The mill management also attempted through publicity to convince its workers of its good will toward them. In the Golden Anniversary Edition of the *Gastonia Gazette*, published a year after the strike had ended, the mill was represented by a full-page advertisement which designated it as—

LORAY
"The Mill With a Purpose"

. . . . . .

Where the Boss Is the Workers Friend

A paragraph of the advertisement said, in answer to the question, "What Makes the Spirit of Progress?"

Many and varied answers come to the mind, but we believe that the full co-operation of one man with another; of one organization with another; of one community with another; of one state and section with another, builds the great finished fabric known as modern civilization, with its tremendous spirit of progress. It is the intimate connection of the various units in accord with the Golden Rule principle that builds it into a complete whole.[4]

At the same time the mill sponsored an essay contest on the subject, "Why I Enjoy Working at the Loray," offering prizes of five, ten, and fifteen dollars for the best essays.[5]

Such tokens of good will were not always confirmed in practice. About August 1, 1929, the mill discontinued the bonus it had promised to strikebreakers and to employees returning to

3. More complete description of this scheme, based on interviews with mill executives and the four contemporary village pastors, will be found below.

4. *Gastonia Gazette*, p. 12–C (September 30, 1930).

5. R. W. Dunn and Jack Hardy, *Labor and Textiles* (New York, 1931), p. 170.

work, and reduced wages to prestrike levels. It likewise began again to "tighten up on the work," though its methods were somewhat more objective as to job measurement and considerate as to employee welfare than in the previous stretch-out.[6]

Nor were tokens of good will adequate to solve the financial problems of the mill as the depression began to deepen. Loss of its chief customers during the strike had posed serious problems. Demand, and consequently production, fell off sharply. Early in November, 1929, mill operation was reduced to a four-day week. The financial position of the Manville-Jenckes chain of mills, which had depended heavily on profitable operation at Loray, was too precarious to finance readjustments, and the company filed a voluntary petition in bankruptcy early in 1930.[7] During the subsequent year or two the number of employees at Loray steadily declined as the hours of operation of the mill declined; by the beginning of 1933 the mill was practically idle and less than 200 of the 625 houses in the village were occupied.[8] Programs of physical upkeep and welfare work were increasingly reduced, and the village "ran down" physically and morally; it became known again in Gastonia as a favorite haunt of "loose women," bootleggers, juvenile delinquents, and other "undesirables." Despite careful selection of employees for good moral and religious character, with the active coöperation of ministers, the moral tone of the community was lowered when disorganization appeared in the economic realm. Social tendencies similar to those consequent upon economic disruption introduced into the village by the prestrike superintendent reappeared under the economic confusion brought by the depression. Twice within a period of six years, therefore, the influence of economic changes upon moral standards was demonstrated.

6. J. W. Atkins, MS. "Crimson Tide in Dixie," p. 134.

7. A receiver was appointed in February, 1931. The value of Manville-Jenckes stock had fallen by 1932 to one tenth of its price in 1929. All dividend payments ceased after 1929 (*Moody's Manual of Investments: Industrial Securities, 1930, 1931, 1933*). The company was reorganized in 1933 and continued in operation on a greatly reduced scale, controlling two mills in Rhode Island.

8. Firestone superintendent, Interview, Gastonia, December 31, 1938; William G. Shepherd, "Humanity, Common, Goes Up," *Collier's Magazine*, p. 8 (October 7, 1933). According to *Moody's Manual of Investments: Industrial Securities, 1930, 1931*, the total number of employees of the Manville-Jenckes Company had declined from 4,508 on December 31, 1929, to 2,118 on December 31, 1930.

The churches in the village were not able to prevent moral deterioration.[9] To the contrary, they themselves declined in membership and income, as they had under the prestrike economic difficulties. Evidence of their dependence upon the mills is especially clear in poststrike developments. Their membership since 1929 has kept in close, though not precise, correlation with employment figures for the mill. For example, in 1939 the mill employed 22 per cent fewer workers than in 1929, whereas the four churches in the village had 15 per cent fewer members. If the names of nonresident members were expunged from the church rolls, the correlation would be even closer. At one time during the last ten years the advisability of abandoning the Methodist church in the village was seriously considered by denominational officials, as it had dwindled to a few families in membership.[10] In 1939, however, it reported 310 members, most of whom have joined it within the last five years. Other churches in the village showed similar fluctuations. The Presbyterian church, having a small membership of 135 to 150 of the better-paid, more secure employees of the mill, has been most stable of all.

A boom under the National Industry Recovery Act in 1933–34 offset the general decline in the village, and in 1935 the mill and village were bought by the Firestone Rubber Company. The new owners spent several hundred thousand dollars in installing new machinery, and in repairing and adding to the facilities of the village. Special police officers were detailed to the community to restrain vice and crime. The population at present consists to large degree of families admitted during the last five years. Traditional paternalistic modes of industrial relations have been rebuilt; an effort at organization of employees there by the Textile Workers Organizing Committee (C.I.O.) in 1937 proved fruitless.

9. The Baptist church at High Shoals, where Manville-Jenckes management also prevailed, ascribed blame for the moral turpitude of the community to the mill management, just as churches had done before the strike. The Baptist church clearly revealed its dependence on mill support when it reported in 1935: "The mill management has recently changed and our people are looking forward to greater things for the Lord in our community" (Gaston County Baptist Association, *Gaston County Baptist Church History* [Gastonia, 1935], p. 52).

10. *Gastonia Gazette*, May 28, 1938.

Among the Mill Workers

Strikers who persisted to the end of the 1929 strike at Loray disappeared almost completely from the community after the Communist leaders were expelled. From fragmentary data, they seem to have become distributed almost equally between mountain farms and cotton mills in neighboring towns and states. Several have become Communist organizers in various parts of the country. Of a sample list of ninety-one strikers who had persevered to the last, only nine are now living in Gastonia or vicinity, though one is told in mysterious tones that others are still near by. Those still living in the neighborhood are to be found mostly in "the hollow," a collection of hovels across the railroad tracks, literally and figuratively, from the Loray village, where the human driftwood of Gastonia has congregated. Workers active in the strike are extremely reluctant to talk of their part in it or to identify other persons involved; the Loray management has not only refused to give them jobs (under the expert eye of its ex-spy employment manager) but has also refused to recommend them for employment elsewhere, and has actively attempted to stamp out seeds sown by the Communists among them. It is almost impossible now to secure samples of handbills or pamphlets distributed by the Communist leaders. As one striker said, after a futile search of her premises and inquiry among other ex-strikers, "the mills was pressing everybody so hard that gettin' caught with any of that literature was as bad as gettin' caught with a gun." The wife of another ex-striker warned her husband, when he began to talk of the strike: "Looks like that thing has caused you enough trouble, without gettin' mixed up in it some more." Her husband agreed, and added: "Why, for a long time you couldn't get a job in any mill if you told them you was from Gastonia."

A few strikers have remained faithful, if silent and unlearned, Communists; an uninitiated inquirer would judge from their conversation that Gastonia is on the brink of a proletarian revolution. Phrases from Communist leaders survive among them ("stick together to make brotherhood," "race equalities"), and Beal has become a legendary figure, surviving in strange stories of ways in which he outwitted "the law," and inspiring the certainty that "he's too smart to stay in jail long."

The fact that these few persons represent an isolated "Communism" is illustrated in this abiding reverence for Beal, whose name has been anathema to all orthodox Stalinists since he denounced the Soviet Union in a series of articles published in the Hearst newspapers.

Because of the virtual stoppage of the mill during the depression, the majority group of the workers, who at first joined the strike but soon returned to work, have also left the community. Reports of observers, checked by personal interviews, indicate that they too, however, faced problems of readjustment and reintegration after the strike was over. These problems were based on partial disillusionment with both the old system and the new alternatives represented, however fanatically in 1929, by collective protest of the workers. For the first time many of the workers began to see their comparative status in a wider perspective. Comparisons of wages and hours as between New England and Southern textile workers were emphasized by the Communist leaders and left an impression on many workers who deserted the strike. Further, some of the traditions of trade unionism came into their purview, even if badly distorted in presentation by the Communists.

The Communist analysis of political realities, supported by the excesses to which policemen and deputy sheriffs went in suppressing the strike, stirred many workers to new thoughts. As one worker remembers, with a trace of bitterness, "that was the meanest law [i.e., law enforcement] I ever seen; us people didn't have no rights." The most somnolent mentality could easily deduce that justice in the North Carolina strikes of 1929 was Janus-faced, with violence by strikers always leading to conviction while violence against strikers issued without exception in acquittal. Similar suspicion was engendered in the minds of many workers concerning the impartiality of the press, the disinterested benevolence of welfare programs established by the employers, and the merits of traditional reliance upon individualism and good will for improvement of status. The "class struggle" probably came as near being a reality in Gastonia in 1929 as it has ever been in America, and though the majority of the workers were not ready to accept its sharp alternatives, the issues it posed were not quickly dismissed from their minds.[11] The claim of the Communists that the Gastonia struggle symbolized "the emergence of the Southern working class as an integral part of the American proletariat," possessed of new political as well as economic aims,[12] is extravagant; it does point to the fact that the struggle tended to give many workers a new appraisal of their status, their employers, and their communities.

The workers, by and large, were likewise disillusioned with the fruits of collective action as represented in the strike, and this disillusionment did not always clearly differentiate between action under radical leadership and unionism of other sorts, despite diatribes of Communist leaders against A.F. of L. unions. The outcome of the Loray strike has been one of the chief factors preventing subsequent union activity in the county. It brought complete victory to the employers, confirmed the public in its suspicion of unions and strikes, and, most important of all, likewise made many workers skeptical of affiliated unionism[13] of any brand, and especially of Communism. In any discussion of unionism with workers in Gaston County the 1929 strike is likely to be brought up, accompanied by a shaking of heads that seems to indicate skepticism and a desire to avoid similar recurrences. When a strike occurred in Bessemer City, about ten miles from Gastonia, in August, 1930, N.T.W.U. organizers appeared on the scene. The strikers themselves tied the organizers together with a rope, drove them out of town, and burned their literature.[14] A.F. of L. representatives were also

11. This analysis, necessarily subjective in character, is based on conversations with a number of workers who had abandoned the strike, and on the reports of observers soon after the strike had ended, including especially the following articles: Harriet L. Herring, "The Metamorphosis of the Docile Worker," in a pamphlet, *Worker and Public in the Southern Textile Problem* (Greensboro, N.C., 1930); E. T. H. Shaffer, "Southern Mill People," *The Yale Review*, Vol. II, No. 19, pp. 325–340 (December, 1929); E. W. Knight, "The Lesson of Gastonia," *The Outlook and Independent*, CLIII, 45–49, 76 (September 11, 1929).

12. W. J. Dunne, *Gastonia*, pp. 41, 50.

13. They had not been as skeptical previously as is sometimes supposed. A survey of 463 family heads of mill families in Gaston County before the strike had found 43 per cent "favorable" to the unions, 27.1 per cent "opposed," and 29.9 per cent "unconcerned and generally indifferent" (J. J. Rhyne, *Some Southern Cotton Mill Workers and Their Villages* [Chapel Hill, 1930], pp. 205–206).

14. *Gastonia Gazette*, August 21, 1930; Thomas Tippett, *When Southern La-*

asked by the strikers to leave the vicinity,[15] and the Southern
campaign waged by the United Textile Workers in 1930 met
with no success whatever in the county.[16] The Gastonia strike
and subsequent trials, rather than hastening the advent of bona
fide trade unionism in the region, had really retarded readiness
of workers to enter a policy of collective representation. Comparison of the Gastonia strike with the Haymarket riot and
massacre, which seriously handicapped labor progress for a
number of years, is not inapt.[17]

Subsequent efforts to effect labor organization in mills in
Gaston County have proved futile. By November, 1929, unionism was a dead issue there and with the exception of two or three
sporadic outbursts has remained so ever since. Workers have
joined occasionally in collective action, largely spontaneous in
character, as in the General Textile Strike of 1934; they have
manifested little disposition to build stable unions as regular
channels for collective bargaining or even as organizations to
prepare for victory in problematical strikes.

By and large the workers have returned tentatively to prestrike types of industrial relationships, with some disillusionment as to advantages possible thereunder, but with little faith
in the alternatives offered. The depression, placing a greater
premium on jobs, put even their former status in jeopardy, and
discouraged risks looking toward positive advance.

bor Stirs (New York, 1931), p. 171. Several employers, and the *Gastonia Gazette,* approved this strike, which was staged against wages so low and living
conditions so miserable that the paternalistic ethicways of the public could not
countenance them (*Gastonia Gazette,* editorial, August 19, 1930).

15. Hood, *op. cit.,* p. 178.

16. Its success in the South generally, despite much advance publicity, a
triumphal speaking tour by President William Green, and the advent of about
a hundred organizers, was very slight. Employers fought the A.F. of L. almost
as vigorously as they had the Communists and used many of the same weapons.
The union campaign lacked both money and mood to fight, and the depression
was curtailing employment rapidly. When a major strike at Danville in 1930
was lost, the campaign practically ended. Hopes of the A.F. of L. leadership
that the employers would encourage their own "moderate" policies, after the
harrowing experiences with Communists at Gastonia, were quickly shattered.
For fuller description, see Tippett, *op. cit.,* chap. ix; George S. Mitchell, *Textile Unionism and the South* (Chapel Hill, 1931), pp. 81–83.

17. This comparison has been made in Broadus Mitchell and George Sinclair
Mitchell, *The Industrial Revolution in the South* (Baltimore, 1930), pp. 173–
178. The strike has also been compared to Harper's Ferry, in Don Wharton,
"Gastonia: Another Harper's Ferry," *The Commonweal,* pp. 104–106 (November 27, 1929).

AMONG THE EMPLOYERS

Mill owners and managers in Gaston County, though completely successful in overthrowing the Communist challenge to their power, felt it desirable to adopt specific measures looking toward consolidation of their control over the workers.[18] The most definite of these measures consisted in a general reduction of weekly hours from sixty to fifty-five, effective during the first week of August, 1929.[19] Weekly wages remained the same for the time being, and thus represented a 9 per cent increase per hour. The North Carolina law still allowed a sixty-hour week, and the employers felt that they were making a concession to their employees. The Communists arrogated credit to their own efforts in the county,[20] but employers claimed to have been contemplating reduction of hours for some months before the strike began, and insisted that the step had been delayed because of the strike.

There is no evidence that any fundamental change took place in the policies or attitudes of employers as a result of the strike. Their policies had triumphed in the struggle and therefore were proved correct. They deplored the unfavorable publicity which had been brought to the county, and joined with civic officials in an effort to offset it. Certain techniques, especially that of eviction of strikers from company houses, had produced a reaction so unfavorable that their subsequent use must be carefully handled. But the primary approach was to be that of a reconsolidation of paternalistic control so that "outside agitators," a term now extended to include all labor organizers, might not again be able to "mislead" the workers. When every mill in the county, nevertheless, was closed by the General Textile Strike of 1934, led by the United Textile Workers of the A.F. of L., employers in Gaston County again secured the services of the state militia and in general used the same tactics against the A.F. of L. as against the Communists. They resorted again to full-page advertisements in the *Gastonia Gazette*, denouncing "outside agitators," proclaiming that local

18. Interpretations in this section have grown out of about forty interviews with mill owners and managers, most of whom have been operating in Gaston County since before the strike of 1929.

19. *Gastonia Gazette,* August 9, 1929.   20. *Daily Worker,* August 14, 1929.

industry would be ruined if wage increases were granted, and pleading for coöperation and a spirit of mutual good will between employers and employees.[21]

Views of Communist leaders concerning the relations of the mills to other community institutions, notably the churches and civic authority, apparently left no sediment in the thinking of employers; practices with respect to support of churches, direct employment of deputy sheriffs and police officers, and the like were not modified as a result of the strike. To the contrary, employers attempted to extend and strengthen their control over all aspects of community life. In ideology, they continued to appeal to principles of good will, coöperation, and paternal (though they now became cautious of the word itself) responsibility as the proper norms for industrial relations. Within the context of their cultural background, there was nothing incongruous between this ideology and a distribution of power between employers and employees so uneven that noble sentiments were, in practice, reduced to the status of an epiphenomenon of the advantage of the stronger. So much the better: appeals to coöperation, good will, and Christian principles helped to maintain peace and to convince the workers of the Christian benevolence of their employers; but if ungrateful employees contravened this level of industrial relations by making selfish demands, the employers had power to enforce return to higher levels of thought and action.

A pioneer Gastonia cotton manufacturer and banker was one of the speakers at the funeral of several strikers killed at Marion, North Carolina, in October, 1929. He had previously served as mediator between management and labor, and was regarded as an unusual employer in that he was friendly toward the United Textile Workers. Among other things, he said in his speech at the funeral: "I am glad to see the spirit of Jesus here today. Only the Christian spirit can solve our labor problems. I have told my associates who own mills in Gastonia that they must coöperate with me and the United Textile Workers to combat Communism and atheism. God bless you."[22] His espousal of the United Textile Workers fell on deaf ears among

21. *Gastonia Gazette,* September 22, 26, 1934.
22. *Labor Defender,* November, 1929, p. 218.

Gastonia employers, but his endorsement of "the Christian spirit" was echoed, in ideology, in their poststrike strategies.[23]

The depression, not the Loray strike, was chiefly responsible for a decline in certain paternalistic practices, notably the maintenance of extensive welfare programs. Trends toward abandonment of welfare services, and more recently of company housing, grew out of the necessity for economy rather than from a recognition by employers of the desirability of granting greater independence to workers.[24] This latter insight was beginning to appear in theory but it was not applied in practice until economic necessities favored retrenchment in expenditures. The theory that workers should be "independent" was then used by employers to rationalize economic necessity and to convince the public of the continued benevolence of employers toward their employees.

Though an occasional textile employer in the country was stirred by events of 1929 to an appeal for internal regulation of the industry in order to forestall external regulation,[25] the industry continued on its chaotic course until provisions of the textile code established under the National Industrial Recovery Act restored it to temporary prosperity and abolished some of its much-criticized labor policies, such as child labor and comparatively long hours and low wages.

THE UPTOWN COMMUNITY

During the earlier phases of the Loray strike it had appeared that public opinion in Gastonia might come to favor some form of responsible labor organization, in contrast to the Communists. The *Gastonia Gazette* called on mill owners to make pub-

23. In application the elder brother, rather than the forgiving father, prevailed at the homecoming of the prodigal workers, and set the norms for subsequent relations between the members of the "one big family."

24. See chap. x.

25. For example, Henry P. Kendall, "Cooperation or Coercion?" in *Textile World,* February 1, 1930, and a second article, "The Textile Industry Can Control Its Own Conditions," *ibid.,* April 12, 1930. Mr. Kendall, president of a large chain of mills including units in the South, advocated voluntary agreement among textile manufacturers to reduce hours to fifty a week without reduction in weekly pay, and to eliminate nightwork for women and minors. He designated these as "practical, common-sense proposals," pointing out that "night operation for women and minors has been abolished in every civilized country except the United States."

lic their own position on this question. After the shooting of Chief Aderholt, however, and the tension created by subsequent events, opinion reacted against all labor organization and all other forms of "agitation" that might lead to trouble. On October 22, 1929, the *Gazette* said: "It will not be safe for any so-called labor agitator to be caught nosing around here any time soon. The folks here are simply not going to put up with it any longer." Any activity that might raise disturbing questions was discouraged. A representative of the American Civil Liberties Union attempted to organize a meeting on civil liberties in the county, without success. To the contrary, the *Gazette* urged on February 3, 1930, that North Carolina should enact criminal syndicalism laws "similar to those working so well in California."

A year later the Gastonia strike was still sufficiently alive in the public mind to merit discussion at a session of the North Carolina Legislature, in which a representative from Gaston County urged that the pay of National Guardsmen should not be reduced, as proposed, because "nobody knows when a virtual revolution may occur in great sections of our State. It takes armed troops with rifles and bayonets to keep people within reasonable bounds in a time like that."[26] The same specter was abroad five years later, if one may judge from the experience of an organizer for the Emergency Peace Campaign in 1934. Charlotte was the only town in which he could make absolutely no headway; citizens there refused to coöperate with his efforts in any respect, telling him that they "knew what a Communist uprising was!" A similar mood prevails in Gastonia now; any movement can be stopped by comparing it with the Communists of 1929. The public quickly forgot the grievances underlying the Loray strike; it has not yet forgotten the "outside agitators" who presumably were wholly responsible.

Among themselves, however, citizens of Gastonia apparently saw the necessity for minor readjustments in industrial relations, though within the former framework.[27] Public opinion,

26. Raleigh *News and Observer*, February 4, 1931.
27. Beyond the borders of Gaston County, a number of Southern liberals were stirred by the strikes of 1929 to call for more drastic regulation, by legislation, of industrial relations in the South. For example, Professor Frank P. Graham of the University of North Carolina wrote a document which was signed by 390 well-known citizens of the state, calling for new protection of

including employers and the *Gastonia Gazette*, approved of a small strike in Bessemer City in 1930—a strike directed against conditions deplored by most citizens who had knowledge of them.[28] Memory of excesses committed by police officers in the name of law and order in the Loray strike, and of the unfavorable attendant publicity, has tended to temper the actions of public officials in subsequent industrial disputes. Opponents of the General Textile Strike in 1934 lamented the fact that local police and deputies "wouldn't do anything" to protect "loyal workers" in their "right to work," and that as a result the National Guard had to be called in again.[29]

Primary efforts of Gastonia citizens after the strike were directed toward eradication of all seeds of Communism that might be germinating in the community. Attention was given only incidentally to positive changes in the economic pattern. The need for a "return to normal," rather than for change, was regarded as paramount. As already seen, strikers who had been most influenced by the Communists were practically expelled from the community, and were made afraid to voice any radical sentiments or to be caught with any tokens of Communist influence. The Chamber of Commerce set up a special committee to fight Communism.[30] The American Legion sponsored an extensive program of Junior Baseball as an offset to Communism among boys in the mill villages. The Rotary and Kiwanis clubs had no specific projects but gave their moral and financial support to other anti-Communist projects.

The uptown community of Gastonia was also greatly con-

civil liberties, for collective bargaining, for a sweeping survey of the textile industry, and for immediate legislation to restrict hours (Raleigh *News and Observer*, February 16, 1930). Very little was effected, however, until the N.I.R.A. was enacted. Public opinion in Gastonia was not discernibly influenced by any of the liberal proposals.

28. The owner of the mill in question was a Jew, and was generally regarded in the county as a grasping mill owner who took every advantage of labor.

29. See the *Gastonia Gazette*, September 12–17, 1934. The *Gazette* had predicted that workers in Gaston County would not join the General Textile Strike, and had urged: "We do not want a repetition of the 1929 troubles." Nevertheless, the strike closed every mill in the county, with Belmont (ten miles from Gastonia) as its focal point. One striker was slain by National Guardsmen, seven companies of whom were called in. A "Vigilantes" group of three hundred "loyal citizens of Belmont" was formed, and the patterns worked out by the uptown community in 1929 were repeated in other respects.

30. See below.

cerned with counteracting the unfavorable publicity the community had received as a result of the strike and the trials. The Loray strike attracted greater nation-wide attention than any Southern labor dispute in history.[31] Citizens of Gastonia felt that most of the newspaper reports were exaggerated and distorted,[32] and would militate against the industrial and commercial development of the city. The Duke Power Company omitted all reference to Gastonia in a prospectus extolling industrial sites in the section.[33] The commercial interests of the community resented discrimination of this sort and sought through an advertising program and radio broadcasts to remove the stigma. Extracts from a series of radio speeches by civic leaders illustrate the attitudes that prevailed after the strike, as before:

Gastonia, the South's City of Spindles, is a forward-looking town, a hospitable town, an optimistic town, a good town and a growing town. . . .

. . . It is what you are that counts in Gastonia and in many respects no city can more proudly boast of a phenomenal development of her citizenship than can our city.

A more solidly united town could scarcely be found in all the land. We have never had any factionalism. Our political differences have never interfered one iota with the concerted efforts of our people. . . .

Last but not least are the churches of the town. One can hardly get from under the shadow of their towering spires. It can be truly said that Gastonia is a church-going city. The fine spirit of co-

31. Miss Harriet Herring has analyzed the factors that made the Gastonia strike front-page news throughout the nation, and the reaction of Southern citizens to the glare of unfavorable publicity, in her article, "Toward Preliminary Social Analysis: I. The Southern Mill System Faces a New Issue," *Social Forces,* VIII, 350–359 (March, 1930).

32. Stories still abound in Gastonia that depict the false notions the remainder of the country received. A Gastonian who bought a railroad ticket for Gastonia during the strike was advised by the ticket agent in Washington to take along a gun, as "they sure are shooting it up down there." It is reported that tourists drove many miles out of the way to avoid going through Gastonia for months after the strike, and that Gastonia citizens were insulted in other states when their city automobile plates were noticed. Many residents still believe that people in other parts of the country think it is dangerous to walk down the streets of Gastonia. Visitors are urged to correct the impression that Gaston County is like Harlan County.

33. Hood, *op. cit.,* p. 176.

operation on the part of the different denominations is very beautiful indeed.

The religious training that is given our young people in the auxiliary organizations of these many churches will be to them in the future a mighty bulwark. . . .

In no city does the sun shine brighter, or the birds sing sweeter, or the grass grow greener than in GASTONIA, NORTH CAROLINA.[34]

Otherwise, Gastonia has been attempting to forget the events of 1929 and is somewhat suspicious of any person who might bring them again to light.[35] The Golden Anniversary Edition of the *Gastonia Gazette*, published a year after the strike, contained exhaustive accounts of the history of all aspects of the city's life but no mention of the Loray strike.[36] Histories published subsequently by natives of the county have likewise omitted all reference to the most exciting episodes the county has known.[37]

Gastonia is aware, however, that the bad name she acquired in 1929 has not been left behind. The Loray strike became one of the most celebrated industrial incidents of the decade, and has remained but little less famous than the Sacco–Vanzetti case. A plethora (from Gastonia's standpoint) of novels based on the strike appeared within the next few years, with varying degrees of fidelity to actual happenings.[38] One of the novels, Grace Lumpkin's *To Make My Bread*, won the Maxim Gorky award for the best labor novel of 1932 and subsequently was made into a successful Broadway play, *Let Freedom Ring*, by Albert Bein. The name of Gastonia became a

34. "Gastonia, North Carolina, 'The South's City of Spindles'" (Three Radio Talks Made Over Station WBT, Charlotte, N.C., May 14, 1930, printed in a leaflet distributed by the Gastonia Chamber of Commerce).

35. A stock question asked of investigators in Gastonia is, "Are you one of these magazine writers?"

36. *Gastonia Gazette*, September 30, 1930. The Sixtieth Anniversary Edition, published on October 10, 1940, likewise failed to discuss the 1929 strike, though it covered other aspects of the county's history rather completely.

37. J. H. Separk, *Gastonia and Gaston County, North Carolina: Past, Present, Future* (Gastonia, 1936); Minnie Stowe Puett, *History of Gaston County* (Charlotte, 1939).

38. Grace Lumpkin, *A Sign for Cain* (New York, 1935); Fielding Burke, *Call Home the Heart* (London and New York, 1932) and *A Stone Came Rolling* (New York, 1935); Mary Heaton Vorse, *Strike!* (New York, 1930); William Rollins, Jr., *The Shadow Before* (New York, 1934); Myra Page, *Gathering Storm: A Story of the Black Belt* (New York, 1932).

symbol, far and wide, of the confluence of plantation feudalism and a new boisterous industrialism, of underfed, unkempt children and lank, mute mill workers, of sudden violence in the night and quick death on the public highways.

The Role of the Churches in Cultural Reintegration

The part played by the churches in cultural reintegration was carried out, for the most part, subtly and indirectly, and has escaped the notice of all investigators. In addition to reasserting their influence, through their regular programs, as instruments of community coöperation, the churches undertook several projects directed specifically against the continuation of the Communist influence, or any counterpart of it.

One of the projects, limited to the Loray churches, was neither subtle nor indirect. Late in 1929 the Manville-Jenckes management at Loray, with the approval of the four ministers in the village, inaugurated a scheme whereby any applicant for a job in the mill must present a recommendation from his former minister. Loray ministers accepted the responsibility of acting as intermediaries between the employment manager of the mill and the former minister referred to by each applicant. The village preachers were thereby given a direct voice in the selection of residents of the village, as they were entrusted with complete responsibility for interpretation of the information received, and simply forwarded to the employment manager a positive or negative vote on each applicant. A negative vote from the village minister to whom the application had been referred was not always conclusive, though the mill has hired very few workers over a ministerial veto, and the employment manager reports that over half of the vetoes overridden have been proved subsequently to have been correct judgments.[38a] Nor was an affirmative vote always determinative, as other favorable recommendations, and especially that from the applicant's last employer, were required also.[39] The employment

38a. Employment manager, who has been at the mill since the system was instituted, Interview, Gastonia, August 30, 1939.

39. One minister reports that one of the best recommendations he ever received concerning an applicant was of no avail because the mill management learned that the applicant had participated in a strike some years before, and would not give him a job.

manager has noted, however, that persons passed favorably by the ministers have turned out to be good citizens of the community in the vast majority of cases. The mill superintendent thinks that the churches in the village are largely responsible for the improvement in the type of workers employed.[40]

New workers have also turned out to be, for the most part, good church members. Forms used by the Loray pastors in making inquiries concerning applicants contained several questions about previous loyalty to the church, as expressed in membership, attendance, and support, as well as asking about personal habits (use of alcohol, cleanliness of person and premises, etc.), coöperative spirit, and general reputation. It has thus been somewhat difficult for a nonchurchman to secure a job in the mill.[41] The ministers have found it convenient to have a complete and continuous list of prospective church members, especially when it is composed of persons already strongly predisposed toward the church.

This system worked so well, according to mill executives and ministers alike, that it was continued until 1939. One of the ministers, who has been stationed in the village since 1925, characterizes the system as "the finest thing in the world." Elaborating, he says that it has been fine for the mill, giving it steady, dependable labor; fine for the churches, giving them active, loyal members; and fine for the community, populating it with a high Christian type of citizen. "There is all the difference in the world between the community now and when I came here," he concludes. "When I came, there were whores, bootleggers, and other sorry people aplenty in the village. But the recommendation system has helped to keep out drunkards, whores, whore-mongers, bootleggers, and the like."[42]

40. Firestone superintendent, Interview, Gastonia, December 31, 1938. One minister calculates that about half of the replies he has received have been unfavorable to the applicant—thereby demonstrating the perspicacity of ministerial judgments.

41. One worker complained that a man must pay a tithe to the Loray Baptist Church in order to get a job at the mill, because the recommendation of the long-established Baptist minister is crucial (Textile Worker H. D, Interview, Gastonia, September 11, 1939). This notion certainly represents an exaggeration but illustrates convictions which can arise among workers concerning the system of ministerial recommendations.

42. Interview, Gastonia, August 30, 1939. This minister has forgotten that the system of recommendations did not prevent moral deterioration in the village

The Loray management and ministers joined in other respects in a new program of coöperation. A monthly conference between the mill superintendent and the village pastors was instituted and held regularly for several years in the superintendent's office. At these conferences the superintendent inquired as to the church programs, as to any new ventures or movements under way in the village, and as to general welfare problems.[43] He in turn would share with the ministers some of the problems of the mill and would solicit their assistance. For example, at one time when the mill had been on part-time operation for a considerable period, and pay envelopes had been much thinner than usual, a wave of unrest swept over the workers and many of them began to talk of leaving the village. The mill superintendent asked the ministers to assure the people, on good authority but without using the superintendent's name, that the mill would soon be on full-time operation again and that there was no reason for concern among the workers. The ministers, thus endowed with an authoritative prognosis, spread the word about, and the unrest subsided.[44] The mill was able to resume full-time operations shortly thereafter.

The ministers have not been unappreciative of the confidence vested in them by the mill management. One of the Loray pastors in 1930 expressed publicly his approval of the new policy, saying: "The hearty coöperation between church and Manville-Jenckes officials has made the Loray church a vital factor in the religious life of the community."[45] His gratitude is representative of the other pastors involved. The four pastors stationed in the village in 1939, two of whom had been there since before the strike in 1929, all expressed approval of the "splendid coöperative policy" of the mill management which has been

during the period from 1930 to 1934, when the economic bases of the community were highly disorganized. He also fails here to give credit to the police force maintained in the village since Firestone took charge; as the mill superintendent explained, "the mill has its own police force, which keeps things pretty quiet. When trouble occurs, the policemen handle it."

43. Loray pastor, Interview, Gastonia, August 24, 1938. These conferences have been continued to the present but have been held more infrequently recently as there have been fewer problems to discuss. When the mill operates full-time, as it has most of the time under Firestone management, fewer moral and labor problems arise, according to the superintendent.

44. Firestone superintendent, Interview, Gastonia, December 31, 1938.

45. *Gastonia Gazette*, p. 7-B (September 30, 1930).

continued under Firestone ownership.[46] None of them, apparently, suspected that they might be instruments used for ulterior purposes—nor did the superintendent of the mill recognize any such implication. The cultural context in which executives and ministers alike live and work bluntly decrees that making good tire fabrics and good Christians are correlative processes, and the directors of each process have learned that coöperation is profitable for them all.

The mill management, in turn, has continued to demonstrate its appreciation in numerous ways. For a long time the superintendent used to give each of the four ministers a five-dollar bill at the end of the monthly conference. In 1939 parsonages were furnished to three of the pastors by the mill, with water and lights supplied without charge. The mill had a fixed policy of paying all expense of upkeep on church property, kept open an offer to pay half of the expenses incurred by any village church for permanent improvements, and was generally willing to make an extra contribution when some crisis arose in the affairs of a church or minister in the village. It was even willing to help worthy religious influences outside the village, provided their influence touched some of the mill's employees; one interdenominational evangelist in Gastonia, whose popularity with mill workers is an item of community pride, was overheard begging an executive of the mill for a contribution, citing as a precedent the recollection that a former superintendent of the mill had contributed $25 a month from the mill and $15 a month personally toward the support of his Christian endeavors.[47]

Two additional projects sponsored by Gastonia ministers and churches, and wider in scope than the confines of the Loray village, merit attention. Both were directed specifically against vestiges of Communism in the county. The Gastonia Chamber

46. More recently one of the Loray pastors has become troubled by the personal indifference of the mill executives to the church. The superintendent of the mill tells the young people of the village that they should go to church on Sunday night, but the young people, on the way to church, see him in his house playing cards. The young people say that he ought at least to pull down the shades. The minister says that he ought at least to come to church occasionally, to convince the people of his interest.

47. The Loray ministers disapprove of this evangelist and his methods; they insist that he is insincere, being an evangelist simply for "the money that's in it." They admit, however, that he gets the money.

of Commerce set up a special committee to eradicate Communist teachings from the vicinity, and selected the long-time pastor of the First Presbyterian Church as chairman. Under the auspices of this committee a former mill pastor who had wielded large influence among the mill workers of the county was persuaded to return and direct an anti-Communist program. The ministerial director of the program chose to work through a fraternal order, the Patriotic Order of the Sons of America, rather than directly through the churches, "because the sole purpose of the P.O.S. of A. is to teach patriotic American principles."[48] He thought that through teaching patriotic principles and Americanism to fathers in the mill villages, who would in turn pass them on to their sons, he would be using the most direct and frontal method of attack on the un-American principles of Communism. Knowing "that there would be plenty of money available," he organized a chapter of the P.O.S. of A. in almost every industrial village and section of the county, had numerous lodge halls built, and carried on an extensive advertising campaign in their behalf.[49] The slogan of the order was: "GOD—OUR COUNTRY—OUR ORDER." One local lodge professed: "We believe in and practice PATRIOTISM, RELIGION, LOYALTY AND FELLOWSHIP."[50] Many chapters of the order still survive in the county. The director of the program believes that his efforts were completely successful, and except for the small Communist cell of which Gastonia is unaware there is no evidence to the contrary.

This program was continued from the late summer of 1929 until toward the end of 1930. It occasionally embraced direct use of the churches, as in a special full-page advertisement which appeared in the *Gastonia Gazette* just before Easter, 1930, urging attendance "At the Church of Your Choice on Easter Sunday and Every Sunday." The advertisement was sponsored by the civic clubs, American Legion, Chamber of Commerce, and Merchants' Association. An article in the same issue, written by the director of the anti-Communist campaign, declared that this manifestation by civic groups of interest in

48. The minister brought back to direct the program, Interview, Gastonia, August 30, 1939.
49. See, for example, the full page of P.O.S. of A. advertisements in the *Gastonia Gazette*, p. 5-B (September 30, 1930).
50. *Ibid.*

the churches proved false the assertion of radicals that Gastonians were only so-called Christians, and indifferent to the welfare of their people.[51]

The other program definitely designed to offset Communist influences was sponsored directly by a denomination. In 1930 the Department of Missions of the Baptist State Convention of North Carolina reported that $2,100 had been appropriated to employ two young women to work in Gaston and contiguous counties, "to offset the incoming tides of materialism, unbelief, and anti-Americanism . . . flowing in ever-increasing volume into these fast-growing industrial centers."[52] One of the young women spent all her time in Gaston County for two years, working with children, young people, and women in an effort "to offset Communism," for which purpose she was definitely brought into the county, according to one of the ministers with whom she worked.[53] Her technique was that of organizing church groups for women and young people in Baptist churches throughout the county, and stimulating existing groups. Ministers in whose churches she worked, among them the pastor of the Loray Baptist Church, report that she achieved excellent results, enlisting the interest of many mill workers' families. The Department of Missions of the State Convention reported that the work of the two young women "fully justified our fondest expectations. . . ."[54]

Otherwise, no evidence survives of attacks by the churches on the influences left by the Communists in 1929. References to the strike and to the bad publicity it brought to the community still occur occasionally in sermons, and atheism appears to be more favored as a foil for pulpit oratory in Gaston County than elsewhere. Normally the ministers seldom speak of the part played by the churches in the cultural crisis through which the community passed; when the story of their activities is recalled to them, they express pride in their role, in the secure place their institutions occupy in the scheme of things, and in the security the churches in turn guarantee to the community.

51. *Gastonia Gazette,* April 18, 1930.
52. *Annual of the Baptist State Convention of North Carolina, 1930,* pp. 58–59.
53. Interview, Gastonia, August 30, 1939.
54. *Annual of the Baptist State Convention of North Carolina, 1930,* pp. 58–59.

CONCLUSIONS AS TO REACTION OF MINISTERS AND CHURCHES
IN THE CULTURAL CRISIS

The overwhelming weight of evidence indicates that the conduct of the ministers in Gaston County afforded a powerful sanction to the prestrike economic structure, from the beginning of the Communist challenge to that structure. Such action as it has been possible to discover was of a type calculated to rid the community of the strike leaders and to bring a restoration of prestrike conditions. The religious institutions were not themselves under attack to the same degree as economic institutions; the Communists had refrained for the most part from attack on religion, and had even countenanced religious observances by the strikers. In fighting the Communists the ministers were primarily defending economic institutions, and only indirectly their own. The fact that their strategy was pitched chiefly on the religious level is a matter of method and does not modify the relation of the religious forces to the economic crisis.

Ministers were at the same time, of course, defending their own economic interests, as they conceived them. Their position within the general social structure supported by the cotton mills and their cultural conditioning thereby were probably the factors most determinative of their reactions to the strike, rather than direct coercion by mill owners. Relatively favored within existing conditions, they had no desire for social upheaval. No ministers "of recognized standing" in the community engaged in any action that might support the strikers or encourage modification of the former ways. They did not condemn, however, such departures from customary procedure as were calculated to rid the community of its disturbers. Their silence after the acts of mob violence was especially significant when contrasted with their efforts to keep the strikers from "doing anything rash."

The notion that "the ministers simply stood outside the whole business" is untenable. They did not evade the issues posed by the strike, even in intent. They could not have evaded them so far as having some effect on their resolution was concerned, even if they had tried. Communists count the ministers and churches as having been among their worst enemies in the Loray strike,[55] and their estimate is supported by many facts, rather than resting simply on their own doctrinaire antipathy to religion.

Silence of the Gastonia ministers and churches over the introduction of religion into the ensuing judicial process further indicates that they were willing, without protest, to lend the sanction of religion to the punishment of disturbers of economic and cultural life. Certainly the role of religion in the trial was neither indifferent nor irrelevant to economic institutions, and the failure of ministers and religious institutions in Gaston County to protest in any way indicates their tacit acquiescence. A similar conclusion can be drawn from their silence concerning the use by employers, early in the strike, of appeals to religious belief as a method of discrediting and condemning the Communists in the eyes of the community.

The actions of ministers and churches in the county after the Communist leaders had been expelled are especially revealing. There was no attempt to secure modification of economic practices foundational to the strike, such as increased social regulation of the power of employers, higher wages, shorter hours, better living conditions, or the like.[56] Rather, the approach was negative, so far as economic affairs were concerned; namely, that of ridding the community of the last vestiges left by the troublemakers. From the standpoint of the religious institutions, the postexpulsion program of ministers and churches was positive, consisting of efforts so to extend the influence and power of the churches that "outside agitators" might not again

55. Bennett Stevens, *The Church and the Workers* (pamphlet, 3d ed., New York, 1932), p. 12; Myra Page, *Southern Cotton Mills and Labor* (New York, 1929), pp. 48–51; *New Masses*, Vol. 5, No. 6, p. 13 (November, 1929).

56. As noted previously (see Part II), larger bodies of ministers and churches were moved by the strikes of 1929 to call for positive changes in the textile industry. All the major denominations in North Carolina, except the Presbyterians and Lutherans, adopted pertinent resolutions at their state meetings in the latter part of that year. Ministers and churchmen from Gaston County were present in these meetings and did not protest the adoption of the resolutions. National religious bodies, including the Commission of the Church and Social Service of the Federal Council of Churches, also issued statements dealing with the textile disorders in the South (see especially the issue of *Information Service*, published by the Federal Council of Churches, for December 28, 1929). Within their own county, however, the religious leaders of Gaston County made no effort to propagate or translate into practice the principles enunciated in such resolutions and statements.

be able to get a foothold in the county. The decline of the churches in the Loray village had been a symptom of conditions that made the strike possible; after the strike, employers and ministers alike resolved that mills and churches must work together more closely. The new employment system instituted at the Loray mill made it difficult for a nonchurchman to get a job there. On their side, ministers and churches carried out programs specifically designed to eradicate seeds of future trouble through extending the power of religious and semireligious institutions.

To sum up, for emphasis, in statements too sharply put: in the cultural crisis of 1929 Gastonia ministers revealed that their economic ethicways were products of the economic system in which they lived, with no serious modification by any transcendent economic or religious standard. They were willing to allow the power of religious institutions to be used against those who challenged this economic system, and themselves assisted in such use. At no important point did they stand in opposition to the prevailing economic arrangements or to drastic methods employed for their preservation. In no significant respect was their role productive of change in economic life. By and large, they contributed unqualified and effective sanction to their economic culture, insofar as their words and deeds make it possible to judge.

POSTSCRIPT

IN relation to events which have transpired in Gaston County since 1880, the economic interpretation of history, if offered as a sufficient interpretation, results in a gross oversimplification of complex patterns. As a hypothesis to be tested in successive situations, it is often illuminating and of considerable heuristic value; as an article of faith to be demonstrated, it vitiates objective and accurate research and distorts the picture of actual events. Economic factors are invariably conditioned by non-economic factors, unless by perverse definition they are made to include all social phenomena.

Similar strictures must be made against the theory, seriously held in many ecclesiastical circles and in a few sociological treatises, that religious factors are basically determinative of all social patterns. It may be that they are ultimately determinative, or that they ought to be determinative; such affirmations are not subject to nice verification through examination of observable social relations. Religious influences, insofar as demonstrable, have not provided either the center or the circumference of culture in the context under observation here. If a normative judgment may be intruded, there is serious doubt whether the churches ought to occupy either of these roles in relation to culture unless they themselves are drastically changed.

At nearly all points the relation between religious and economic institutions has been symbiotic, or reciprocal, in character, whether in processes of institutional growth, social control, or cultural defense. It has not been parasitic or completely unidirectional in any of these processes; the pattern of interaction has been composed of mutual interrelationships at each point. This does not mean that each sphere has been equal in influence at each successive moment of social development or throughout the entire period under observation. Religious institutions in Gaston County sixty years ago were considerably more active in helping to shape economic affairs than they are at present. Cotton mills exercised less influence over the churches at the outset than now. During the period as a whole,

economic factors have more nearly shaped religious institutions
than been shaped by them. Even so, the churches have been of
tangible significance in the life of the mills, both in giving early
impetus and in according subsequent support. At various times
and in diverse ways they have been both source and product of
economic developments. Both indifference and irrelevance to
economic affairs have been notable characteristics of their strategy. They have provided powerful sanctions for prevailing
economic arrangements. Slight traces of antagonism to those
arrangements have likewise appeared at times, though the
churches have been less active in this mode of relationship than
in any other. In short, all six of the possible types of interrelationship between religious and social institutions have been exemplified at one time or another.

None of the general, comprehensive theories of social scientists and philosophers is adequate, taken alone, for interpretation of the developments in this particular laboratory. Religious forces have not been the crucial dynamic factor in culture; neither have they been simply an opiate of the people or
an unmitigated sanction of the status quo. Sweeping assertions
of this sort are too uncritical and undiscriminating to represent
accurately the diverse ways in which religious agencies function. Several of the general theories illumine particular sectors
of interrelationship but are false when applied to other areas;
each fails adequately to allow for the multiplicity and reciprocity of relationships. Perhaps Henri Bergson's theories, which
represent a reconciliation of certain elements from Max Weber
and Marx, are most nearly adequate for interpretation of the
total development. The churches have tended to pass from a dynamic force for social change to a static sanction of the change
effected.

Partially a source of industrial transformation sixty years
ago, the religious institutions have become increasingly a product of that transformation and a guarantor of prevailing economic arrangements. In the contemporary scene the churches
seldom define or implement new social values in the county. The
economic sphere is now the fundamental source of social inno-
vations. There is nothing automatic, however, in the adaptation
of the churches to economic variations; they retain a measure

of separateness, and religious changes are always shaped in part by traditional religious configurations.

The churches may come again to a creative and definitive role in the culture of the county, though this possibility depends on several imponderables. Changes in economic institutions, deriving partly from industrial conditions and partly from federal and state legislation, may create a social flux in which religious institutions can help create a new economic pattern, as they did at the beginning of the industrial revolution. The further expansion of the textile industry in this area is highly uncertain, and diversification of industry has begun, as in the industrial revolutions in England and New England. As industry is diversified, greater conflict of interest may occur between economic institutions themselves, weakening the high degree of control over culture by the managers of a single type of economic enterprise. The disintegration of the mill village system and the growing possibility that trade-union organization will be effected in the county also indicate that the traditional pattern of economic control is on the verge of extensive changes. By the march of economic developments, therefore, the churches may come to a more independent status, though in so doing they may likewise suffer loss of control over the population, as they have in some other regions.

Discussion of the social role most appropriate for the churches poses questions beyond the range of this volume.[1] Their lack of knowledge concerning economic and social affairs renders very pertinent the question whether ministers can criticize or help to mold economic and social life effectively. Ministers and churches in Gaston County presume, nevertheless, to be a force working for social change. If this presumption is to be implemented efficiently, the churches and ministers will need

1. The subjectivism and moralism involved in any effort at formulation of a positive program of action have made it seem wise to discuss elsewhere the strategies which may be most appropriate for the churches of Gaston County, and for other churches in similar situations. Readers interested in types of practical action which might lead toward greater independence of the churches and toward regulation and change in economic relations are referred to a list of about fifty concrete proposals by the writer to be found in the issue of the magazine *Social Action* for September 15, 1941. Copies may be secured from the Council for Social Action of the Congregational and Christian Churches, 289 Fourth Avenue, New York City.

to be more realistic in their analysis of the economic situation in the county. Thus far religious and economic leaders alike have failed to be hard in social analysis and cold in appraisal of the results attained. They have viewed both economic practices and religious professions under the guise of paternalism, thereby equating current economic patterns and religious ideals.

The churches can become effective implements of economic regulation only if they achieve larger structural independence and cultural transcendence of the economic institutions in the county. They may be able to achieve greater structural independence by recognition of their subservient status at present, and by willingness to sacrifice status in favor of autonomy. Though individual action may sometimes pave the way, modification of institutional interrelationships, whether in the direction of independence of the churches or restriction of the power of the mills, depends on direct institutional action. There is no evidence that reliance upon changed individuals will be decisive either for the emancipation of the churches or for the transformation of economic practices.

At the same time, religious institutions can be a source of culture transformation only as they transcend the immediate culture in which they function. Their insistence that they already have a transcendence of this sort is largely unwarranted so far as economic and social standards are concerned. Unless they find economic standards, as such, other than those of the economic culture from which they draw immediate substance, they will not be able to stand in effective judgment or criticism. If they find such standards, the danger will be that of irrelevance to the immediate situation—a hazard escapable only by intimate knowledge of economic relativities, issuing in skill in social engineering. Transcendence will be of no significance in the first place, of course, unless it produces institutional antagonism at many points to economic life as organized at present, thereby impelling to criticism of existing conditions and positive steps toward social change.

BIBLIOGRAPHY

BIBLIOGRAPHY[1]

I. UNPUBLISHED MANUSCRIPTS AND DOCUMENTS

General:

Application of Fred E. Beal for a pardon: brief in support of petitions. Submitted June 8, 1939, to his Excellency, the Governor of North Carolina. Typewritten, pp. ii, 107. On file in office of Edwin Gill, Parole Commissioner, State of North Carolina, Raleigh, N.C.

Articles of Agreement Made and Entered into this 27th day of April 1816 between Michael Shenk & Absolom Warlick of the County of Lincoln & State of North Carolina of the one part, and Michael Beam of the County and State aforesaid of the other part. Typewritten, 1 p. Archives of North Carolina Historical Commission, Raleigh, N.C.

ATKINS, JAMES W. Crimson tide in Dixie: being a true story of the first invasion of the cotton textile manufacturing section of the Piedmont by a Communist labor union, resulting in floggings, murder and a long list of lawless deeds. Unpublished manuscript in possession of its author, Gastonia. Typewritten, 174 pp. A novel of the Loray strike in 1929. Names are fictionized; otherwise, it follows actual happenings very closely. Interpretations are largely those of the uptown community of Gastonia.

BARNWELL, MILDRED GWIN. The worm has turned. In possession of its author, Gastonia. A brief paper on developments in the Southern textile industry, by the executive secretary of the Southern Combed Yarn Spinners Association.

Gastonia and Gaston County, North Carolina. Prepared for Gastonia Industrial Commission, L. H. Duncan, consultant. March 31, 1932. c. 150 pp. On file at Gastonia Chamber of Commerce. A fairly comprehensive economic survey.

Gastonia Ministers' Association. Minutes, 1932–39. In possession of the secretary, Gastonia.

Minutes of Gastonia District Conference, Methodist Episcopal Church, South, 1925–39. Manuscript. In possession of the district superintendent, Gastonia.

1. The large number of fugitive sources used in preparation of this volume makes it impossible to present a complete bibliography without exceeding all reasonable bounds of space, and without listing many items hardly worthy of inclusion. The bibliography that follows includes only the major sources that have been used and those minor ones which will continue to be accessible to investigators.

Myers, James. Confidential field notes on trip to Charlotte, North Carolina, and Marion, North Carolina. 1929. Typewritten, 80 pp. On file in office of Department of Social Relations, Federal Council of the Churches of Christ in America, New York City.

—— Field notes on textile strikes in the South. 1929. Mimeographed, 18 pp. On file in office of Department of Social Relations, Federal Council of the Churches of Christ in America, New York City.

Report of subcommittee on mill villages, December 28, 1933, to Hon. Hugh S. Johnson. Typewritten, 3 pp. and 2 pp. At Cotton-Textile Institute, New York City.

Southern Golden Rule Association, Inc. Statement of principles. 1937. Typewritten, 3 pp. In writer's possession. Constitution of a company union in a Gaston county mill.

State *vs.* Fred Beal, *et alii.* Brief No. 456, Fourteenth District, presented to Supreme Court of North Carolina, spring term, 1930. Mimeographed, 419 pp. Official transcript of the second Gastonia trial in 1929, mimeographed for presentation to the Supreme Court of North Carolina.

In Montreat Historical Foundation, Montreat, N.C.:

Arrowood, Stella. History of Long Creek Presbyterian Church, Gaston County. 1936. Typewritten, 6 pp. MS. No. 45416.

Book of minutes of Home Missions Committee of Kings Mountain Presbytery. 1922–23. Manuscript, 17–37 pp.

Currie, Rev. William. History of the Belmont Presbyterian Church. Typewritten, 3 pp. MS. No. 42844.

Hall, Rev. J. K. History of Goshen Church. Manuscript, 9 pp. MS. No. 26373.

History of the Mt. Holly Presbyterian Church. 1938. Typewritten, 5 pp. MS. No. 49971.

History of West Avenue Presbyterian Church. April 8, 1938. Typewritten, 3 pp. MS. No. 49972.

Robinson, S. A., Kennedy, J. H., Henderlite, J. H. (committee). History of the First Presbyterian Church of Gastonia. Typewritten, 6 pp. MS. No. 42844.

Sparrow, Mrs. G. A., with supplement by Baker, Rev. W. L. The history of Union Presbyterian Church. 1936. Typewritten, 11 pp. MS. No. 45416.

Walkup, J. W., compiler. History of Hephzibah Presbyterian Church. *c.* 1938. MS. No. 48458.

Wolfe, W. D. Historical sketch of New Hope Presbyterian Church, Gastonia, N.C. 1936. MS. No. 44433.

BIBLIOGRAPHY

In Library of Wake Forest College:

A brief historical sketch of the First Baptist Church, Gastonia, North Carolina, 1876–1930. *c.* 1903. Typewritten, 2 pp.

ALLEN, H. H., and BEACH, Rev. J. J. Cherryville Baptist Church. 1930. Typewritten, 2 pp.

CAMP, W. G., and STROUPE, D. R. Shady Grove Baptist Church. 1930. Printed, 1 p.

CAMPBELL, I. E., and BAUCOM, Rev. F. W. History of Bethel Baptist Church. *c.* 1930. Typewritten, 2 pp.

CLINE, A. L. History of Flint–Grove Baptist Church. *c.* 1930. Typewritten, 2 pp.

Dallas Baptist Church. 1930. Typewritten, 1 p.

East Baptist Church. *c.* 1930. Typewritten, 4 pp.

GUICE, J. A. History of the Tuckaseegee Baptist Church. *c.* 1930. Typewritten, 2 pp.

HAWKINS, LUTHER. History of South Marietta Street Baptist Church. 1929. Printed, 3 pp.

History of the Harden Baptist Church. *c.* 1930. Typewritten, 1 p.

History of Loray Baptist Church. *c.* 1930. Typewritten, 6 pp.

History of the McAdenville Baptist Church. *c.* 1930. Typewritten, 3 pp.

History of Riverside Baptist Church of Spencer Mountain, Lowell, N.C. *c.* 1930. 1 p.

History of the Temple Baptist Church. *c.* 1930. Typewritten, 2 pp.

HUDSON, Rev. E. V. A brief sketch of the history of Cramerton Baptist Church, Gaston Association. 1930. Typewritten, 4 pp.

MARLEY, W. A. History of Calvary Baptist Church. 1930. Typewritten, 2 pp.

Sandy Plains Baptist Church. *c.* 1930. Typewritten, 2 pp.

Spencer Mountain Baptist Church. *c.* 1930. Typewritten, 1 p.

II. UNPUBLISHED GRADUATE THESES

BOUCHARD, ANGELINE. An analysis of the southern combed sales yarn industry, 1928–1938. M.A. thesis, Columbia University, 1938. iii, 114 pp. A study based on field work in Gaston County in 1938.

GOEBEL, W. B. A history of manufactures in North Carolina before 1860. A.M. thesis, Duke University, 1926. 160 pp.

HAMILTON, CHARLES EVERETTE, JR. A comparison of the intelligence of three social classes in North Carolina. A.M. thesis, Duke University, 1930. vi, 63 pp. Results of the application of Otis tests to children of uptown, mill, and Negro classes in Gastonia.

HARDIN, ELLIOTT WANNAMAKER. The attitude of the Methodist Episcopal Church, South, in North Carolina toward the textile industry in North Carolina. B.D. thesis, Duke University, 1938. iv, 117 pp. A study based on ecclesiastical minutes and journals.

HARRIS, H. L. Slave membership in the churches of the South Atlantic region. A.M. thesis, Duke University, 1929. 228 pp.

HARTZ, EDWIN R. Social problems in a North Carolina parish. A.M. thesis, Duke University, 1938. iii, 149 pp. A case study of a small cotton mill village in North Carolina, by a student who had been Methodist minister there for three years. Written with some insight, and close observation.

HIPP, BERTHA CARL. A Gaston County cotton mill and its community. M.A. thesis, University of North Carolina, 1930. 101 pp. A competent but unimaginative community survey.

HOOD, ROBIN. The Loray mill strike. M.A. thesis, University of North Carolina, 1932. 184 pp. A balanced, excellent study of the 1929 Loray strike, without knowledge of role of churches.

KISER, OSCAR LEE. The growth and development of education in Gaston County. M.A. thesis, University of North Carolina, 1928. 78 pp.

LACY, DAN MABRY. The beginnings of industrialism in North Carolina, 1865–1900. M.A. thesis, University of North Carolina, 1935. iv, 169 pp. Detailed treatment of three industries: cotton goods, tobacco, and furniture. Based entirely on literary sources.

LEDBETTER, MARGARET M. The village church in North Carolina. A.M. thesis, Duke University, 1931. 126 pp. A statistical study of all villages of less than 2,500 population.

LOOPER, T. L. The causes of elimination of pupils in the elementary schools of Gastonia, N.C. M.A. thesis, University of North Carolina, 1929. xiv, 44 pp. Based on firsthand analysis.

NEWBY, G. E., JR. The cotton manufacturing industry: New England and the South. M.A. thesis, University of North Carolina, 1925. 251 pp. An able summary of manufacturing differentials.

RANKIN, EDGAR RALPH. A social study of one hundred families at cotton mills in Gastonia, North Carolina. M.A. thesis, University of North Carolina, 1914. 32 pp. An early study based on interviews.

RHYNE, J. J. The place of the social studies in mill village schools. M.A. thesis, University of North Carolina, 1925. 257 pp. Analysis in Gaston County, by a native.

SINIAVSKY, B. M. The Cotton-Textile Institute, Inc., a stabilizing agency in the cotton textile industry. M.S. thesis, University of North Carolina, 1931. 157 pp.

SMITH, BENJAMIN HARPER. The social significance of the Southern cotton mill community. M.A. thesis, Emory University, 1925. 43 pp. Based on 471 family records of mill workers in Georgia, South Carolina, and North Carolina.

BIBLIOGRAPHY 341

SPEARS, R. W. The attitude of the Southern Methodists of South Carolina in regard to the textile industry in South Carolina. B.D. thesis, Duke University, 1936. iv, 183 pp. Main sources were minutes of the annual conferences, and the *Southern Christian Advocate,* all of which were thoroughly covered.

III. MINUTES OF ECCLESIASTICAL BODIES

Journal of the annual convention of the diocese of Western North Carolina, 1931, 1937, 1939.

Journal of the missionary district of Asheville, Protestant Episcopal Church, 1905, 1910, 1912, 1920.

Minutes, annual convention of the United Evangelical Lutheran Synod of North Carolina, 1921, 1931, 1937, 1938, 1939.

Minutes, North Carolina conference of the Wesleyan Methodist Connection (or Church) of America, 1910, 1920, 1930, 1938, 1939.

Minutes of the assembly of the Church of God, 1937.

Minutes (or annual) of the Baptist state convention of North Carolina, 1880, 1899, 1900, 1913–39.

Minutes of the Blue Ridge conference of the Methodist Episcopal Church, 1881, 1890, 1900, 1910.

Minutes of the Ebenezer Baptist Association [Negro], 1934, 1938.

Minutes of the eighth biennial convention of the United Lutheran Church in America, 1932.

Minutes of the Gaston County Baptist Association, 1927, 1935, 1938.

Minutes of the general assembly of the Presbyterian Church in the Confederate States of America, 1863, 1864.

Minutes of the general assembly of the Presbyterian Church in the United States, 1865, 1875, 1880, 1885, 1890, 1895, 1900, 1905, 1910, 1920, 1930, 1938, 1939.

Minutes of the general synod of the Associate Reformed Presbyterian Church, 1880, 1890, 1900, 1910, 1920, 1930, 1939.

Minutes of the Kings (or King's) Mountain Baptist Association, 1880, 1882, 1883, 1890, 1897, 1900, 1910.

Minutes of the Kings Mountain Presbytery, 1929–39.

Minutes of the North Carolina annual conference, Methodist Episcopal Church, South, 1880.

Minutes of the North Carolina annual conference of the Methodist Episcopal Church, 1880, 1892, 1900, 1910, 1919, 1929, 1938.

Minutes of the North Carolina conference of the Methodist Episcopal Church (colored), 1910, 1920, 1930.

Minutes of the South Fork Baptist Association, 1880, 1882, 1890, 1897, 1900–03, 1910.

Minutes of the Western North Carolina annual conference, Methodist

Episcopal Church, South, 1890, 1900, 1910, 1911, 1919, 1920, 1927–39.

Minutes of the Western North Carolina conference of the Pentecostal Holiness Church, 1930, 1937, 1939.

Minutes of the York Baptist Association, 1882.

Official journal of the Blue Ridge–Atlantic conference of the Methodist Episcopal Church, 1920, 1930, 1936.

Proceedings, annual convention of the Evangelical Lutheran Tennessee Synod, 1863, 1880, 1889, 1891, 1900, 1910.

Proceedings of the Beaver Creek Free-Will Baptist Association, 1938.

IV. PAMPHLETS

ALDERMAN, E. A. The growing South. New York, 1908. 24 pp.

American Civil Liberties Union. Justice—North Carolina style: the record of the year's struggle for unions in Gastonia and Marion, April, 1929 to April, 1930. New York, 1930. 14 pp.

ATKINSON, EDWARD. Report to the Boston Board of Trade on the cotton manufacture of 1862. Boston, 1863. 21 pp.

Bessemer City Mining and Manufacturing Co. Prospectus. Richmond, 1891. 12 pp.

BLACK, C. J. A history of Loray Baptist Church. Gastonia, 1923. 71 pp.

BLANSHARD, PAUL. Labor in Southern cotton mills. New York, 1927. 88 pp.

BUCK, PEARL H. The poor whites of the ante-bellum South. New York, 1925. Reprint from *American Historical Review*.

Building a union of textile workers: report of two years progress to the convention of the United Textile Workers of America and the Textile Workers Organizing Committee, affiliated with the Congress of Industrial Organizations. Philadelphia, 1939. 79 pp.

Carlton Yarn Mills, Inc. Anniversary edition, 1922–38. A pictorial pamphlet describing conditions in a "model mill village" in Gaston County.

COCHRAN, Rev. J. B. Historical sketch of New Hope Church, Lowell, Gaston County, N.C., 1906. Montreat Historical Foundation. 24 pp.

DEXTER, ROBERT C. Report on conditions in the Southern textile industry to the board of directors of the American Unitarian Association. Boston, 1930. 21 pp.

—— Study of the New England cotton textile industry made for the American Unitarian Association. Boston, 1931. 38 pp.

Duke Power Co. Piedmont Carolinas, where wealth awaits you. Charlotte, N.C., c. 1930. 48 pp.

DUNNE, WILLIAM F. Gastonia: citadel of the class struggle in the new South. New York, 1929. 59 pp. Communist interpretation.

EDMONDS, RICHARD HATHAWAY. Facts about the South. Baltimore, 1894.

—— Sunrise in the South. Baltimore, 1909.

—— The South's redemption. Baltimore, 1890. 63 pp.

Gastonia Gospel Tabernacle. Descriptive booklet. In writer's possession.

Gastonia, North Carolina, the South's city of spindles. Three radio talks made over station WBT, Charlotte, N.C., May 14, 1930. Available from Gastonia Chamber of Commerce.

HERRING, HARRIET L. Worker and public in the Southern textile problem. Greensboro, N.C., 1930. 21 pp.

High Shoals, Gaston County, N.C. Charlotte, N.C., 1908. Published and copyright by the Observer Printing House, Inc.

History and souvenir of Presbyterian Church, Gastonia, N.C., 1899. Gastonia, 1899. c. 50 pp. At Montreat Historical Foundation.

HOOD, ROBIN. Industrial social security in the South. Chapel Hill, 1936. 22 pp.

JOHNSON, TOM. The Reds in Dixie. Rev. ed. New York, 1936. 47 pp. Communist pamphlet.

JOHNSTON, Rev. R. Z. Historical sketch of Goshen Presbyterian Church, Gaston County, N.C. Shelby, 1899. At Montreat Historical Foundation.

LLOYD, JESSIE. Gastonia: a graphic chapter in Southern organization. New York, 1930. 31 pp. Pamphlet published by National Executive Committee of the Conference for Progressive Labor Action.

Long Creek Gold Mining Co., Gaston County, N.C. Boston, c. 1880. 7 pp. Report of a mining engineer.

McELROY, I. S. Some pioneer Presbyterian preachers of the Piedmont North Carolina. Gastonia, 1928. 50 pp. At Montreat Historical Foundation.

Manual of the Kings Mountain Presbytery. 20 pp. Adopted at stated meeting, October 29, 1924.

MEIKLEJOHN, KENNETH and NEHEMKIS, PETER. Southern labor in revolt. New York, 1930. 24 pp. Pamphlet written by two Swarthmore College students, illustrating widespread interest aroused in Southern strikes.

National Emergency Council. Report to the President on the economic conditions of the South. Washington, 1938. 64 pp. A report to the President of the United States, depicting the South as "the Nation's No. 1 economic problem."

PAGE, MYRA. Southern cotton mills and labor. New York, 1929. 96 pp. Communist viewpoint.

PIPKIN, CHARLES W. Social legislation in the South. Chapel Hill, 1936. 42 pp.

Rehn, Henry Joseph. Scientific management and the cotton textile industry. Chicago, 1934. A field study of eleven small Texas mills and one South Carolina mill.

Sparrow, Rev. George A. History of the Presbyterian Church of Olney, Gaston County, North Carolina. 1902. 46 pp. At Montreat Historical Foundation.

Statement of the Southern States Industrial Council in the matter of the minimum wage recommendation and report of Industry Committee No. 1 (textiles). 30 pp. Presented at the hearing before Administrator Elmer F. Andrews, Atlanta, Ga., July 5, 1939.

Stevens, Bennett. The church and the workers. 3d ed. New York, 1935. 31 pp. Communist pamphlet.

Vance, R. B. The South's place in the nation. Washington, 1936. 32 pp.

Winter, F. Report on the High Shoals property in Gaston County, North Carolina. 1873. 15 pp. A mining prospectus.

V. BOOKS PERTAINING ESPECIALLY TO GASTON COUNTY

Barnwell, Mildred Gwin. Faces we see. Gastonia, 1939. Published by a textile manufacturers' association.

Beal, Fred E. Proletarian journey: New England, Gastonia, Moscow. New York, 1937.

Black, Rev. C. J. A short history of Sandy Plains Baptist Church. Gastonia, 1923.

Foote, Rev. William Henry. Sketches of North Carolina, historical and biographical, illustrative of the principles of a portion of her early settlers. New York, 1846. Chapter xxviii depicts early Presbyterian churches in Gaston County.

Graham, Maj. W. A. The history of the South Fork Baptist Association, or, the Baptists for one hundred years in Lincoln, Catawba and Gaston Counties, North Carolina. Lincolnton, N.C., 1901.

Griffin, Clarence W. The history of Old Tryon and Rutherford Counties, 1730–1936. Asheville, 1937. A history of counties in which Gaston was formerly included.

Hobbs, S. H., Jr. Gaston County: economic and social. Raleigh, 1920. A laboratory study in the University of North Carolina, department of rural economics and sociology.

Hoffman, Laban Miles. Our kin: being a history of the Hoffman, Rhyne, Costner, Rudisill, Best, Hovis, Hoyle, Wills, Shetley, Jenkins, Holland, Hambright, Gaston, Withers, Cansler, Clemmer and Lineberger families. Charlotte, 1915. A compendium of names and dates of early Gaston County families.

Logan, Deacon John R. Sketches, historical and biographical, of the

Broad River and King's Mountain Baptist Associations, from 1800 to 1882. Shelby, N.C., 1887.

PUETT, MINNIE STOWE. History of Gaston County. Charlotte, 1939. Deals chiefly with the period of the Revolutionary War.

RHYNE, JENNINGS JEFFERSON. Some Southern cotton mill workers and their villages. Chapel Hill, 1930. A statistical study of five hundred mill families in Gaston County, based on interviews.

SEPARK, JOSEPH H. Gastonia and Gaston County, North Carolina, past, present, future. Gastonia, 1936. Contains much useful information, carefully assembled.

—— ed. Illustrated handbook of Gastonia. Gastonia, 1906.

SETZER, PEARL. Visions old and new: a historical pageant of Gaston County. Gastonia, 1924.

SHERRILL, WILLIAM L. Annals of Lincoln County, N.C., 1749–1937. Charlotte, 1937. History of a county from which Gaston County was formed in 1846.

VI. NOVELS ON THE GASTONIA STRIKE

BURKE, FIELDING. A stone came rolling. New York, 1935.

—— Call home the heart. London and New York, 1932.

LUMPKIN, GRACE. To make my bread. New York, 1932.

—— A sign for Cain. New York, 1935.

PAGE, MYRA. Gathering storm: a story of the Black Belt. New York, 1932.

ROLLINS, WILLIAM, JR. The shadow before. New York, 1934.

VORSE, MARY H. Strike! New York, 1930.

VII. GENERAL BOOKS

ALLEN, R. H., et alii. Part-time farming in the Southeast. Washington, 1937. A monograph prepared by the Works Progress Administration.

—— S. M. Fibrilia: a history of cotton culture and manufacture. Boston, 1861.

Associate Reformed Presbyterian Synod. The centennial history of the Associate Reformed Presbyterian Church, 1803–1903. Charleston, 1905.

BADER, LOUIS. World developments in the cotton industry. New York, 1925.

BAINES, EDWARD. History of cotton manufacture in Great Britain: with a notice of its early history in the East, and in all the quarters of the globe. London, c. 1835.

BERGLUND, A., STARNES, G. T., DE VYVER, F. T. Labor in the industrial South. University, Va., 1930.

BERNHEIM, G. D. German settlements and the Lutheran Church in North Carolina and South Carolina. Philadelphia, 1872.

BRUNNER, EDMUND DE S. Industrial village churches. New York, 1930.

CASH, W. J. The mind of the South. New York, 1941.

CLARK, ELMER T. The small sects in America. Nashville, 1937.

—— V. S. History of manufactures in the United States, 1609–1860. 1929 ed. New York, 1929. 3 vols.

COOK, J. H. A study of the mill schools of North Carolina. New York, 1925.

COPELAND, M. T. The cotton manufacturing industry of the United States. Cambridge, 1912.

COUCH, W. T., ed. Culture in the South. Chapel Hill, 1934.

CRAIG, Rev. D. I. A history of the development of the Presbyterian Church in North Carolina, and of synodical home missions, together with evangelistic addresses by James I. Vance, D.D., and others. Richmond, 1907.

CURTIS, WILLIAM RANDOLPH. Some labor problems in the cotton textile industry. Urbana, Ill., 1936.

DAVIDSON, ELIZABETH H. Child labor legislation in the Southern textile states. Chapel Hill, 1939.

DAVIS, H. S., TAYLOR, G. W., BALDERSTON, C. C., BEZANSON, ANNE. Vertical integration in the textile industries. Philadelphia, 1938.

DUNN, ROBERT W. and HARDY, JACK. Labor and textiles: a study of cotton and wool manufacturing. New York, 1931.

EATON, CLEMENT. Freedom of thought in the Old South. Durham, 1940.

GEE, WILSON. Research barriers in the South. New York, 1932.

GRADY, HENRY W. The new South. New York, 1890.

GRAY, LEWIS CECIL. History of agriculture in the Southern United States to 1860. Washington, 1933. 2 vols.

HEER, CLARENCE. Income and wages in the South. Chapel Hill, 1930.

HENKLE, SOCRATES. History of the Evangelical Lutheran Tennessee Synod. New Market, 1890.

HERRING, HARRIET L. Southern industry and regional development. Chapel Hill, 1941.

—— Welfare work in mill villages: the story of extra-mill activities in North Carolina. Chapel Hill, 1929.

HUNTER, C. L. Sketches of Western North Carolina, historical and biographical, illustrating principally the Revolutionary period. Raleigh, 1877.

INGLE, EDWARD. Southern sidelights, a picture of social and economic life in the South a generation before the war. New York, 1896.

JACOBS, W. P. The pioneer. Clinton, S.C., 1935.

JOHNSON, CHARLES S. Statistical atlas of Southern counties. Chapel Hill, 1941.

——, GERALD W. The Wasted Land. Chapel Hill, 1938.

KENDRICK, B. B. and ARNETT, A. M. The South looks at its past. Chapel Hill, 1935.

KENNEDY, S. J. Profits and losses in textiles. New York, 1936.

KOHN, AUGUST. The cotton mills of South Carolina. Charleston, 1907.

LEFLER, H. T., ed. North Carolina history, told by contemporaries. Chapel Hill, 1934. A collection of documents from various periods of North Carolina history.

LEMERT, B. F. The cotton textile industry of the Southern Appalachian Piedmont. Chapel Hill, 1933.

LYON, R. M. The basis for constructing curricular materials in adult education for Carolina cotton mill workers. New York, 1937.

MACDONALD, LOIS. Southern mill hills, a study of social and economic forces in certain textile mill villages. New York, 1928.

MCLEISTER, I. F. History of the Wesleyan Methodist Church of America. Syracuse, 1934.

MIMS, EDWIN. The advancing South. Garden City, 1926.

MITCHELL, BROADUS. The rise of cotton mills in the South. Baltimore, 1921.

—— William Gregg: factory master of the Old South. Chapel Hill, 1928.

—— and MITCHELL, GEORGE S. The industrial revolution in the South. Baltimore, 1930.

—— GEORGE SINCLAIR. Textile unionism and the South. Chapel Hill, 1931.

MURCHISON, C. T. King Cotton is sick. Chapel Hill, 1930.

MURPHY, EDGAR GARDNER. Problems of the present South, a discussion of certain of the educational, industrial, and political issues in the Southern states. New York, 1904.

MYERS, JAMES. Religion lends a hand. New York, 1929.

NICHOLSON, ROY S. History of Wesleyan Methodism in the South. Syracuse, 1933.

NIEBUHR, H. RICHARD. The social sources of denominationalism. New York, 1929.

ODUM, HOWARD W. Southern regions of the United States. Chapel Hill, 1936.

ORMOND, J. M. The country church in North Carolina. Durham, 1931.

PAGE, WALTER HINES. The rebuilding of old commonwealths, being essays toward the training of the forgotten man in the Southern states. New York, 1902.

PASCHAL, GEORGE W. History of North Carolina Baptists. Raleigh, 1930. Vol. I, 1663–1805.

PHILLIPS, U. B. Life and labor in the Old South. Boston, 1929.

POTWIN, MARJORIE. Cotton mill people of the Piedmont; a study in social change. New York, 1927.

RANKIN, ROBERT S. When civil law fails. Durham, 1939.

RAPER, ARTHUR and REID, IRA DE A. Sharecroppers all. Chapel Hill, 1941.

SCHWENNING, G. T., ed. Management problems, with special reference to the textile industry. Chapel Hill, 1930.

SIMMONS, E. L. History of the Church of God. Cleveland, Tenn., 1938.

SMITH, ELLIOTT DUNLAP, in collaboration with RICHMOND CARTER NYMAN. Technology and labor: a study of the human problems of labor saving. New Haven, 1939.

SPERO, STERLING D. and HARRIS, ABRAM L. The black worker: the Negro and the labor movement. New York, 1931.

THOMPSON, HOLLAND. From the cotton field to the cotton mill: a study of the industrial transition in North Carolina. New York, 1906.

—— The new South: a chronicle of social and industrial revolution. Johnson, Allen, ed. Chronicles of America, Vol. XLII. New Haven, 1919.

TIPPETT, THOMAS. When Southern labor stirs. New York, 1931.

TROELTSCH, ERNST. The social teaching of the Christian churches. Wyon, Olive, tr. New York, 1931. 2 vols.

Twelve Southerners. I'll take my stand: the South and the agrarian tradition. New York, 1930.

VANCE, R. B. Human geography of the South. Chapel Hill, 1932.

WARE, C. F. The early New England cotton manufacture. New York, 1931.

WHEELER, JOHN HILL. Historical sketches of North Carolina, from 1584 to 1851. Compiled from original records, official documents, and traditional statements. Philadelphia, 1851. 2 vols.

WHITE, G. S. Memoir of Samuel Slater. 2d ed. Philadelphia, 1836.

WINSTON, GEORGE T. A builder of the new South: being the story of the life work of Daniel Augustus Tompkins. Garden City, 1920.

WOOD, CHARLES G. Reds and lost wages. New York and London, 1930.

YELLEN, SAMUEL. American labor struggles. New York, 1936.

VIII. NEWSPAPERS AND PERIODICALS

American Federationist, 1929. Monthly: official magazine of the American Federation of Labor.

Baltimore Evening Sun, 1929.

Gastonia Gazette (title varies), 1880–1940. Published daily after 1921.
Gastonia Gospel Tabernacle. Tabernacle Telescope, 1938–39. Published irregularly.
Greensboro Daily News, 1929, 1939.
Information Service, 1928–40. Published weekly by the Federal Council of the Churches of Christ in America.
International Press Correspondence, 1929. Communist international news service.
Labor Defender. Monthly; official publication of the International Labor Defense.
Manufacturer's Record, 1893—. A weekly devoted to the industrial interests of the South.
Mechanical Engineering, 1926, 1929. A monthly of the American Society of Mechanical Engineers.
New Masses, 1929–30. Communist monthly.
North Carolina Christian Advocate, 1894–1940. Official Methodist paper.
North Carolina Labor and Industry, 1939. Issued monthly by the North Carolina Department of Labor.
Raleigh Christian Advocate, 1880, 1890, 1904. Official Methodist paper.
Raleigh News and Observer, 1927, 1929.
Southern Textile Bulletin, 1911–40. Published at Charlotte, N.C.
Textile Labor, 1939. Official monthly publication of the Textile Workers Union of America, C.I.O.
Textile World, 1925–29, 1938–40. The most important magazine for the textile industry. Published monthly in New York City.
The Charlotte Observer, 1924–40.
The Christian Century, 1929.
The Church of God Evangel. Published weekly at Cleveland, Tenn.
The Communist, 1929–30. A monthly.
The Daily Worker, 1929. Communist newspaper.
The Free-Will Baptist Herald. Official organ of the Cape Fear and Wilmington conferences of the Free-Will Baptist Church. Published monthly at Clinton, N.C.
The Industrial Leader, 1939–40. A labor paper published weekly at Winston-Salem, N.C.
The Literary Digest, 1929.
The Nation, 1929.
The New Republic, 1929.
The New York Times, 1929.
The T.W.O.C. Parade, September 11, 1937. Published at Atlanta, Ga., by the Textile Workers Organizing Committee.

IX. SPECIAL ARTICLES

ALEXANDER, FRANK D. Religion in a rural community of the South. *American Sociological Review,* VI, 241–251, 1941.

ASHE, S. A. George Alexander Gray. Ashe, S. A., Weeks, S. B., and Van Noppen, C. L. Biographical history of North Carolina. From colonial times to the present. VII, 122–129.

BAILEY, FORREST. Gastonia goes to trial. *The New Republic,* LIX, 332–334, 1929.

BEAL, FRED E. I was a Communist martyr. *The American Mercury,* XLII, 32–47, 1937.

BIGGS, J. CRAWFORD. Religious belief as qualification of a witness. *North Carolina Law Review,* December, 1929.

BLANSHARD, PAUL. Communism in Southern cotton mills. *The Nation,* CXVIII, 500–501, 1929.

—— Industrial problems of the New South: the Southern mill village. National Conference of Social Work, *Proceedings,* 1928.

BOISEN, A. T. Religion and hard times. *Social Action,* Vol. V, No. 3, March 15, 1939.

BONNER, MARION. Behind the Southern textile strikes. *The Nation,* CXXIX, 351–352, 1929.

BRIGGS, CYRIL. The Negro question in the Southern textile strikes. *The Communist,* Vol. VIII, No. 6, 324–328, 1929.

BROWN, C. K. Industrial development in North Carolina. *The Annals of the American Academy of Political and Social Science,* CLIII, 133–140, 1931.

BYNUM, JEFFERSON. Piedmont North Carolina and textile production. *Economic Geography,* IV, 222–240, 1929.

CLARK, DAVID. Fifty years of cotton manufacturing in North Carolina. *Proceedings of the 50th Anniversary Session of the North Carolina Press Association,* 1922, pp. 55–59.

—— ELMER T. The psychology of the small sects and its significance for evangelism. The twelfth biennial meeting of the American Association of Theological Schools, *Bulletin* (No. 14), July, 1940, pp. 83–99.

CONNOR, R. D. W. The rehabilitation of a rural commonwealth. *The American Historical Review,* XXXVI, 44–62, 1930.

COPE, ROBERT F. History of early cotton mills in Gaston County. *Gastonia Gazette,* November 20, 1934.

CRAWFORD, BRUCE. Whose prosperity? *The Virginia Quarterly Review,* V, 325–335, 1929.

DANIELS, JONATHAN. A native at large. *The Nation,* December 14, 1940, p. 608.

DAVENPORT, WALTER. All work and no pay. *Collier's Magazine,* November 13, 1937.

DE VYVER, F. T. Southern textile mills revisited. *The Southern Economic Journal,* IV, 466–473, 1938.

—— The present status of labor unions in the South. *The Southern Economic Journal,* V, 485–498, 1939.

DIETRICH, ETHEL B. The present status of the cotton textile industry. *International Labour Review,* XXII, 423–444, 1930.

DUNNE, BILL. Gastonia: a beginning. *New Masses,* Vol. V, No. 2, pp. 3–5, 1929.

EBERLING, ERNEST JACOB. The strikes among textile workers in the Southern states. *Current History,* XXX, 450–453, 1929.

ELLIS, L. B. A new class of labor in the South. *Forum,* May, 1901, pp. 306–310.

FORD, ELLA. We are mill people. *New Masses,* Vol. V, No. 3, pp. 3–5.

Gastonia Strikers' case. *Harvard Law Review,* XLIV, 1118–1124, 1931.

HERRING, HARRIET L. Cycles of cotton mill criticism. *The South Atlantic Quarterly,* XXVIII, 113–125, 1929.

—— Selling mill houses to employees. *Textile World,* May and June, 1940.

—— Toward preliminary social analysis: I. The Southern mill system faces a new issue. *Social Forces,* VIII, 350–359, 1930.

HOLT, JOHN B. Holiness religion: cultural shock and social reorganization. *American Sociological Review,* V, 740–747, 1940.

JOHNSON, GERALD W. Service in the cotton mills. *The American Mercury,* V, 219–223, 1925.

—— The cotton strike. *The Survey,* XLVI, 646–647, 1921.

JONES, WEIMAR. Southern labor and the law. *The Nation,* CXXXI, 14–16, 1930.

JORDAN, G. R. Churchmen and jurymen. *The Christian Century,* XLVI, 1186–1187, 1929.

KENDALL, HENRY P. Cooperation or coercion? *Textile World,* February 1, 1930.

—— The textile industry can control its own conditions. *Textile World,* April 12, 1930.

KNIGHT, EDGAR W. The lesson of Gastonia. *The Outlook and Independent,* CLIII, 45–49, 76, 1929.

LANDIS, J. M. Freedom of speech and of the press. *Encyclopaedia of the Social Sciences,* VI, 457–459.

LARKIN, MARGARET. Ella May's songs. *The Nation,* CXXIX, 382–383, 1929.

—— The story of Ella May. *New Masses,* Vol. V, No. 6, pp. 3–4, 1920.

—— Tragedy in North Carolina. *The North American Review,* CCVIII, 686–690, 1929.

LEACH, DEFOREST. The old churches in the New South. *The Christian Century*, XLVI, 1277–1279, 1929.

LEWIS, JOHN L. Labor looks South. *The Virginia Quarterly Review*, XV, 526–534, 1939.

—— NELL BATTLE. Anarchy *vs.* Communism in Gastonia. *The Nation*, CXXIX, 321–322, 1929.

—— Tar heel justice. *The Nation*, CXXIX, 272–273, 1929.

LEYBOURNE, GRACE G. Urban adjustments of migrants from the Southern Appalachian plateaus. *Social Forces*, December, 1937.

LIBAIRE, GEORGE. Gastonia: outpost of recovery? *The New Republic*, LXXVI, 233–235, 1933.

LIEBER, O. M. A fragmentary contribution to the vein geology of the Southern states. *Mining Magazine*, February, 1858, pp. 108–112.

MACDONALD, LOIS. Normalcy in the Carolinas. *The New Republic*, LXI, 268–269, 1930.

MAIN, CHARLES T. and GUNBY, FRANK M. The cotton textile industry. *Mechanical Engineering*, XLVIII, 999–1004, 1926.

MATTHEWS, T. S. Gastonia in court. *The New Republic*, LX, 119–121, 1929.

MILLER, CLARENCE. From a Gastonia defendant. *The New Republic*, LX, 377, 1929.

MILTON, GEORGE FORT. The South fights the unions. *The New Republic*, LIX, 202–203, 1929.

MITCHELL, BROADUS. George A. Gray. *Dictionary of American Biography*, VI, 516–517.

—— Southern spindles. *The Yale Review*, XIV, 506–508, 1924–25.

—— Why cheap labor down South? *The Virginia Quarterly Review*, V, 481–491, 1929.

MOORE, HARVEY W. Education and community welfare. *Textile Bulletin*, L, 46–47, 1936.

NELSON, FREDERIC. North Carolina Justice. *The New Republic*, LX, 314–316, 1929.

O'CONNOR, HARVEY. Carolina mill slaves. *New Masses*, Vol. IV, No. 12, p. 7, 1929.

OLAND, ARNOLD M. The mill village: should we sell it? If so, to whom? *Cotton*, CIII, 55–58, 1939.

PORTER, PAUL. Justice and chivalry in Carolina. *The Nation*, CXXIX, 214–216, 1929.

POTWIN, MARJORIE A. Cotton mills, professors and preachers. *Southern Textile Bulletin*, XXXIII, 1, 2, 1928.

RATCHFORD, BENJAMIN ULYSSES. Toward preliminary social analysis: II. Economic aspects of the Gastonia situation. *Social Forces*, VIII, 359–367, 1930.

SCHWENNING, G. T. Prospects of Southern textile unionism. *The Journal of Political Economy*, XXXIX, 783–810, 1931.

SHAFFER, E. T. H. Southern mill people. *The Yale Review*, Vol. II, No. 19, pp. 325–340, 1929.

SHAPLEN, JOSEPH. Strikers, mills and murder. *The Survey Midmonthly*, LXII, 595–596, 1929.

SHEPHERD, W. G. Humanity, common, goes up. *Collier's Magazine*, XCII, 7–9, 1933.

SPAHR, C. B. The new factory towns of the South. *The Outlook*, March 4, 1899, pp. 510–517.

SPOFFORD, WILLIAM B. Marion, North Carolina. *The Christian Century*, LXVI, 1502–1503, 1929.

—— The church in textile towns. *The Churchman*, CXL, 16–17, 1929.

STARK, LOUIE The meaning of the textile strike. *The New Republic*, LVIII, 323–325, 1929.

STEWART, ETHELBERT. Present situation in textiles. *American Federationist*, XXXVI, 689, 1929.

TAYLOR, ALVA W. The South pays for its new mills. *The Christian Century*, XLVI, 774–776, 1929.

TROUT, JOHN M. The churches in a community crisis. *The Christian Century*, XLVI, 864–866, 1929.

VORSE, MARY HEATON. Elizabethton sits on a powder keg. *New Masses*, Vol. V, No. 2, p. 6, 1929.

—— Gastonia. *Harper's Magazine*, CLIX, 700–710, 1929.

WEISBORD, ALBERT. Passaic–New Bedford–North Carolina. *The Communist*, VIII, 319–323, 1929.

WHARTON, DON. Gastonia: another Harper's Ferry. *The New Republic*, LIX, 299–300, 1929.

—— Poor-white capitalists. *The Outlook and Independent*, CLIII, 252–253, 1929.

WINTON, GEORGE B. Is the South permanently conservative? *The Christian Century*, XLVI, 422–425, 1929.

WOOLF, DOUGLAS G. South continues to expand and diversify despite depression of 1924. *Textile World*, February 7, 1925, p. 180.

—— Southern bishops uninformed, even if sincere. *Textile World*, LXXI, 2493–2494, 1927.

X. STUDIES AND DOCUMENTS OF FEDERAL AND STATE AGENCIES

Committee of Cabinet Members Appointed by the President of the United States. Survey of cotton textile industry problems. New York, 1935.

Journals of the Senate and House of Commons of the General Assembly of the State of North Carolina, 1846–1847.

KEITH, ARTHUR and STERRETT, D. B. Tin resources of the King's Mountain District, North Carolina and South Carolina. U. S. Geological Survey Bulletin, 660 D. Washington, 1917.

MAGNUSSON, LEIFUR. Housing by employers in the United States, October, 1920. Washington, Bureau of Labor Statistics, 1920. No. 263, miscellaneous series.

North Carolina Department of Agriculture. North Carolina and its resources. Raleigh, 1896.

North Carolina Department of Conservation and Development. A North Carolina directory and reference book, with information on 2,632 manufacturing establishments, ratings of public utilities, and statistical summary of each county. Raleigh, 1938.

North Carolina Department of Conservation and Development. North Carolina: today and tomorrow. Raleigh, 1936.

North Carolina Department of Labor and Printing. Annual reports, 1887–1916; Biennial reports, 1916–38.

North Carolina Department of Labor. Biennial report of children employed in North Carolina, 1932–34.

North Carolina Department of Labor. Labor laws of North Carolina, 1939. Raleigh, 1939.

North Carolina Geological and Economic Survey. Timber resources of Gaston County. Press Bulletin No. 84, July 3, 1912.

North Carolina Reports, Vol. 199. Cases argued and determined in the Supreme Court of North Carolina. Spring Term, 1930. Raleigh, 1931.

Public Laws of North Carolina, 1846–47, 1899, 1903.

U. S. Board of Inquiry for the Cotton Textile Industry. Report to the President. Washington, 1935.

U. S. Congress (71st, 3d Session): Extract from House Report 2290. Investigation of Communist propaganda [Report of the "Fish Committee," pursuant to H. Res. 220]. Submitted January 17, 1931.

U. S. Department of Agriculture: W. E. Hearn, et alii. Soil survey of Gaston County, North Carolina. Washington, 1911.

U. S. Department of Commerce: Bureau of the Census. Biennial census of manufactures: North Carolina, 1933, 1935, 1937.

U. S. Department of Commerce: Bureau of the Census. North Carolina: final 1933 census results for service establishments, places of amusement and hotels. No. 8050. October 1, 1934.

U. S. Department of Commerce: Bureau of the Census. North Carolina—final retail census: 1933. Special release, September 29, 1934.

U. S. Department of Commerce: Bureau of the Census. Retail trade in Gastonia, N.C. (preliminary report). March 23, 1931.

U. S. Department of Commerce: Bureau of the Census. Tenth census
of the United States: 1880 (and each subsequent census through the
sixteenth, 1940).

United States Department of Commerce. Religious bodies: 1926.

U. S. Department of Labor: Bureau of Labor Statistics. Average
hourly earnings in cotton-goods industry, 1937. Washington, 1938.
Serial No. R. 747.

U. S. Department of Labor: Bureau of Labor Statistics. Consumption
habits of the American people. Washington, 1938. Serial No. R. 722.
Includes studies in Gastonia.

U. S. Department of Labor: Bureau of Labor Statistics. Boris Stern.
Effects of mechanical changes in the cotton-textile industry, 1910 to
1936. Washington, 1937. Serial No. R. 612.

U. S. Department of Labor: Bureau of Labor Statistics. Personnel
policies in the cotton-textile industry. Washington, 1936. Serial No.
R. 398.

U. S. Department of Labor: Bureau of Labor Statistics. Regional differences in cotton-textile wages, 1928 to 1937. Washington, 1938.
Serial No. R. 689.

U. S. Federal Trade Commission. Report on combed cotton yarns, April
14, 1921. Washington, 1921. Covers years 1914–20.

U. S. National Recovery Administration. Code of fair competition for
the cotton textile industry (as amended to November 8, 1933).
Washington, 1933.

U. S. Senate, Seventy-first Congress, Committee on Manufactures, Report No. 28. Report on S. Res. 49, working conditions in the textile
industry in North Carolina, South Carolina, and Tennessee. Washington, 1929.

U. S. Senate, Seventy-first Congress, First Session. Hearings before
the Committee on Manufactures on S. Res. 49, a resolution authorizing Committee on Manufactures . . . to investigate immediately the
working conditions of employees in the textile industries of the states
of North Carolina, South Carolina, and Tennessee. Washington,
1929.

WILLIAMS, C. B., et alii. Report on Gaston County soils and agriculture.
North Carolina Department of Agriculture Bulletin, Vol. XXXVIII,
No. 6 (June, 1917).

XI. PROCEEDINGS, COMPILATIONS, ETC.

American Federation of Labor. Report of the proceedings of the forty-
ninth annual convention. XLIX, Washington, 1929.

National Association of Cotton Manufacturers. Transactions, No. 127
(October, 1929), No. 131 (October, 1931).

Public papers and letters of Oliver Max Gardner, Governor of North

Carolina, 1929–1933. Gill, Edwin, compiler, and Corbitt, David Leroy, ed. Raleigh, 1937.

Southern Combed Yarn Spinners Association. Annual report, 1938–39. Gastonia, 1939.

Textile Workers Union of America. Proceedings. Philadelphia, 1939.

The coming of industry to the South. *The Annals of the American Academy of Political and Social Science.* CLIII, 1931.

XII. REFERENCE BOOKS, DIRECTORIES, ETC.

American Federation of Labor. Industrial survey of Southern textile area. Washington, 1930.

BRANSON, Rev. L., ed. North Carolina business directory. Raleigh, 1872.

—— Branson's North Carolina agricultural almanac, 1890. Raleigh, 1890.

Clark's directory of Southern textile mills. January 1, 1938, ed.

Davison's textile "blue book," 1902–03, 1930.

Manufacturers Record Publishing Company. Blue book of Southern progress, 1939. Baltimore, 1939.

Moody's manual of investments: industrial securities (title varies slightly). 1920, 1922, 1924, 1926, 1930, 1931, 1933.

National Association of Cotton Manufacturers. Year book, 1930.

National Industrial Conference Board. A picture of world economic conditions in the summer of 1929. New York, 1929.

Official American Textile Directory (title varies slightly). 1900, 1910, 1920, 1922, 1924, 1930, 1938. Available in office of *Textile World,* New York.

POLK, L. L. Hand Book of North Carolina, embracing historical and physiographical sketches of the state, with statistical and other information relating to its industries, resources and political condition. Raleigh, 1879.

Textile manufacturers' directory of the United States and Canada, 1891. New York, 1891.

WEBER, H. C., ed. Yearbook of American churches. Elmhurst, 1939.

XIII. BIBLIOGRAPHIES

DAY, EMILY LOUISE, compiler. Economic development of the cotton-textile industry in the United States, 1910–1935—a selected bibliography. Washington, 1935.

U. S. Bureau of Foreign and Domestic Commerce. Government publications relating to textiles. 3d ed. Washington, 1931.

WOODBURY, C. J. H. Bibliography of the cotton manufacture. Waltham, Mass., 1909.

XIV. MISCELLANEOUS

Brief submitted by Southern Combed Yarn Spinners Association before the Committee on Reciprocity Information, relating to the consideration of tariff reductions on combed yarns in the prospective trade agreement with the Government of the United Kingdom and with that Government on behalf of Newfoundland and the British Colonial Empire. February, 1938. 15 mimeographed pp.

Letters of Lucy Randolph Mason to Southern editors, 1937–40. Occasional letters from the public relations representative of the Textile Workers Union of America. On file in T.W.U.A. office in Atlanta, Ga.

Original and supplementary briefs of the National Association of Cotton Manufacturers, Boston, Mass., before the Committee for Reciprocity Information in regard to the proposed trade agreement with the United Kingdom. 11 mimeographed pp. Sent out to members March 22, 1938.

POPE, LISTON. Mill village churches. *Social Action,* September 15, 1941. Pamphlet containing proposals for social change.

Southern States Industrial Council. Statement in the matter of the minimum wage recommendation and report of Industry Committee No. 1 (textiles). Atlanta, 1939. 30 pp.

Statement submitted by the Cotton-Textile Institute, Inc. to the Committee on Reciprocity Information relating to trade agreement negotiation with the Government of the United Kingdom. February 18, 1938. 31 pp. plus exhibits. Mimeographed.

Textiles—Inc. Condensed statements, September 17, 1936, February 23, 1937, August 15, 1938. Financial statements of a corporation operating fifteen mills in Gaston County. In the writer's possession.

INDEX

INDEX

YALE STUDIES IN RELIGIOUS EDUCATION

I. A History of Religious Education in Connecticut to the Middle of the Nineteenth Century by George Stewart, Jr.

II. A History of Religious Education in the Episcopal Church to 1835 by Clifton Hartwell Brewer.

III. Horace Mann and Religion in the Massachusetts Public Schools by Raymond B. Culver.

IV. Presbyterian Parochial Schools, 1846–1870, by Lewis Joseph Sherrill.

V. Community Organization in Religious Education by Hugh Hartshorne and J. Quinter Miller.

VI. Case Studies of Present-Day Religious Teaching by Hugh Hartshorne and Elsa Lotz.

VII. Church Schools of Today by Hugh Hartshorne and Earle V. Ehrhart.

VIII. Children and Puritanism by Sandford Fleming.

IX. Standards and Trends in Religious Education by Hugh Hartshorne, Helen R. Stearns and Willard E. Uphaus.

X. The Church Follows Its Students by Clarence Prouty Shedd.

XI. From School to College. A Study of the Transition Experience, conducted by Lincoln B. Hale, D. W. Bailey, G. H. Menke, D. DeK. Rugh and G. E. Schlesser. Hugh Hartshorne, Editor.

XII. The Presbyterian Doctrine of Children in the Covenant by Lewis Bevens Schenck.

XIII. Tennant's Philosophical Theology by Delton Lewis Scudder.

XIV. The Rise of the Social Gospel in American Protestantism, 1865–1915 by Charles Howard Hopkins.

XV. Millhands and Preachers by Liston Pope.